CITY LIGHTS

A STREET LIFE

&

STREETS AHEAD

LIFE AFTER CITY LIGHTS

———————

MEMOIRS OF

KEITH WATERHOUSE

THE BRITISH LIBRARY

This edition first published in 2013 by
The British Library
96 Euston Road
London NWI 2DB

Text © the Keith Waterhouse Estate 2013
City Lights first published 1994
Streets Ahead first published 1995

British Library Cataloguing-in-Publication Data
A catalogue record for this book is available from The British Library

ISBN 978-0-7123-0964-6

Cover designed by Lucy Morton at illuminati, Grosmont
Printed in Great Britain by TJ International

CONTENTS

FOREWORD

BY ROBERT WATERHOUSE

Shortly after his eightieth birthday, my father was interviewed by *Saga* magazine, to which he was a regular contributor, and recalled a story about a writer who goes to heaven. The angel shows the writer around and the two come to the celestial library, where the writer sees a row of books that stretches into infinity. 'What are all those books?' asks the writer. 'Those,' says the angel, 'are the books you never wrote.'

My father loved libraries, his ideal one being a marble-floored sanctuary of card catalogues and reading tables, its silence broken only by the echoing ricochets of the librarian's rubber stamp. He would therefore be greatly proud to learn that the British Library is reprinting his two books of memoirs, *City Lights* (1994) and *Streets Ahead* (1995), in a single volume. (This edition is a companion volume to *How to Live to Be* 22, which is being published by the British Library for the first time. It was written by my father in 1951, when, having realized his ambition to become a reporter, he decided he wanted to be a writer of books as well. The British Library came across this hitherto unpublished manuscript after kindly agreeing to house my father's papers.)

City Lights and *Streets Ahead* are united by the twin obsessions that drove my father all his life: writing and fun, or, more particularly, the ability to be entertained by what he called 'life's passing show'. The first took the form of the Depression-era industriousness, learned in poverty and inherited from his mother, with which he hammered at his typewriter every morning, for all the world as though writing were a form of manual labour and long after computers had rendered typewriters obsolete; the second was distinguished by his lifelong love of cities, a category that might be further subdivided into trams, markets, town halls, libraries, railway stations, newspapers, mooching without purpose, 'tickling cats under the chin', lunching with friends, and, of course, theatres, though in truth he simply regarded cities as theatres in themselves.

City Lights he regarded as the best book he ever wrote, and it is for me the most beautiful. It allowed my father to return to a fascination with urban childhood that informed such early works as his first novel, *There is a Happy Land* (1957), and the screenplay he and Willis Hall wrote for *Whistle Down the Wind* in 1961, for the book provides a magical account of growing up in Leeds in the 1930s and 1940s. *City Lights* thus recalls my father's boyhood explorations of the sooty byways of the city, his adventures as a curious truant, and the slightly bewildered stoicism of his mother (who was to be the subject of his last but uncompleted memoir, *Mother's Day*), who encouraged her 'weird child' with second-hand books and toy theatres and from whom he wisely concealed such hair-raising escapades as a narrow escape from a paedophile or his own explorations of Murder Wood. The book's final chapters, in which he recalls such adolescent adventures as attempting to seduce a girl in a phone box while her father passes by on his way home from the pub, are as funny as the earlier ones are beautiful, and the book as a whole is rich in minute, comic detail.

In *Streets Ahead* the cityscape shifts to London and the streets of New York, Hollywood, Moscow, and Australia, as my father recalls such collaborators and colleagues, friends and rogues, as Willis Hall, Alfred Hitchcock, Julie Christie, Paul Newman, Billy Whitelaw, Peter O'Toole, Jeffrey Bernard, Ned Sherrin, and 'Cap'n Bob' Maxwell, from whose clutches he extracted himself just as Maxwell was warming to his infamous pension scheme. These exploits are at times distinguished by my father's reputation for hollow legs, as he was famously capable of stretching lunch with friends into the evening and stretching an evening into the early hours, but the atmosphere that dominates the recollections of *Streets Ahead* is one of celebration: of success, of friendship, of life itself.

Both books also pay homage to the authors who influenced my father as a writer, such as Edgar Wallace, P.G. Wodehouse, and Arnold Bennett. My father especially identified with the hero of the latter's book, *The Card*, who was 'dedicated to the great cause of cheering us all up'. I like to think that my father's angel, having tactlessly brought up the books he never wrote, gestures in a feathery, conspiratorial sort of way to those he did. 'But these,' the angel might say, in a sublime undertone, 'are the ones that cheered me up.' *City Lights* and *Streets Ahead* will remain foremost on the angel's list.

CITY LIGHTS

A STREET LIFE

Keith as a child (*front*)
with his sister and older brothers

ONE

There is a Happy Land

'You had to crawl through a big drain pipe at the edge of the park, it was an old sewer I think, and where it brought you out was in a long road with houses that had been there for ages, made out of stone. You were clean out of the estate then. You just had to walk up this road and there was a coal mine with a lot of slag heaps, and railway lines that went right over the street, so that lorries bumped when they went over them. The houses were all in long rows and made of black stone, and all the streets were just rough cobbles with sooty grass growing through them. Not like our blinking street.'

– THERE IS A HAPPY LAND, 1957

1 In the stifling August of 1936 the black American athlete
Jesse Owens arrived in Berlin to claim four gold medals at
Hitler's Olympic Games; the King took Mrs Wallis
Simpson on an Adriatic cruise; the *Queen Mary* regained the Blue
Riband for Britain with an Atlantic crossing of three days, twenty-
three hours, fifty-seven minutes from the Ambrose Light, New
York, to the Bishop Rock, Scilly Isles; and I, aged seven and a half,
set off on an expedition to a faraway country, clutching a borrowed
cardboard suitcase.

I was reassured in some measure, as we assembled for our journey
into the unknown at the departure point outside the offices of the
Leeds Poor Children's Holiday Camp Association, by the discovery
that our mode of transport was to be one of Saml Ledgard's navy
blue charabancs. For Sammy Ledgard, as he was familiarly known
to all his passengers, could be trusted. And while he was unlikely to
be driving his coach personally, he had at least signed it.

Just about everything of any significance in Leeds at that time, it
seemed, bore a signature that was at once frighteningly authoritarian
yet comforting, like the word of God. The trams were signed, and in
gold leaf at that, by W. Vane Morland, General Manager, Leeds
Corporation Transport Dept; so that when you read the notice "No
Spitting, By Order", you were left in no doubt by whom the order
had been given. Council rent books and notices prohibiting ball
games and the hanging out of bed linen were signed by the Housing
Director, with his impressive array of initials front and back –
R.A.H. Livett, ARIBA. The dense acreage of park bye-laws was
signed by a municipal celebrity, none other than Thos Thornton,
Town Clerk & Clerk to the Council. Anything to do with hospitals or
clinics was signed, as I would have cause to remember, by J.
Johnstone Jervis, Medical Officer of Health.

But the most famous signature of all was that of Geo Guest,

3

Director of Education, whose Christian name I thought to rhyme with Leo (the name my father had wanted to bestow on me, until dissuaded by my mother), just as I thought the Saml who had signed my charabanc rhymed with enamel. Geo Guest's signature, rubber-stamped in heliotrope, sent quivers of fear through generations of Leeds schoolchildren, to whom it was as familiar in its ubiquitous facsimile – on reports, on playground notices, on circulars to parents, even on school dinner menus – as that of Elizabeth I or Guy Fawkes after torture. I was amazed to read in the usually memory-perfect Richard Hoggart's autobiography, where he recalls actually being summoned personally before this awesome figure as a student, that "I think his name was George Guest." It was as if someone granted an audience by the Italian dictator of the time had written, "I think his name was Mussolini."

It was Geo Guest's signature stamped on a cyclostyled chit from Middleton Council School that had delivered me up to serve fourteen days in the Poor Children's Holiday Camp at Silverdale in Lancashire, a grassy promontory inhabited only by gulls and temporary orphans, overlooking Morecambe Bay. I was terrified.

I took what solace I could from the spiritual presence, via his waiting charabanc, of Saml Ledgard, whose name was almost as familiar to me as Geo Guest's. A publican who had diversified into steam wagons to service the beer tents of the north-eastern racecourses, he had gradually built up a bus and coach fleet to rival the de luxe operation of Wallace Arnold – another Leeds enterprise – and was a local legend, like Mr Scarr of Scarr's Stores who had come to the city with only one clog to his feet, or Harry Ramsden, the self-crowned King of Fish and Chips, or Tommy Wass who was famous for running a famous pub which was famous for being known as Tommy Wass's, to which folk came from far and wide simply to have been there.

These were swaggering days when every city had its larger than life figures, not only its Tommy Liptons and Jesse Boots but hosts of lesser luminaries who had started with one greengrocery stall and now ran twelve, or who had evolved from bicycle repairs to a chain of filling stations, and who smoked cigars and wore straw boaters and gave racy interviews to the evening papers on matters of the day; and it was to this grade that our Sammy Ledgard belonged. And now here was his dark blue charabanc, signed, outside the Leeds Poor Children's Holiday Camp Association offices which were housed

4

where they are still housed (though in these euphemistic days the adjective "poor" has long been quietly dropped), in the upper rooms of a humble converted shop quite out of keeping with its grand surroundings – the spanking new Portland stone Civic Hall, the domain of Thos Thornton, Town Clerk & Clerk to the Council; the equally pristine and ultra-modern Brotherton Wing of Leeds Infirmary, in the charge of J. Johnstone Jervis; and, so close across the square that it threw a looming shadow over the pavement where our huddle of pinched-faced refugees blinked and squinted in the morning sunlight, the brooding, soot-black headquarters of Leeds Education Department with the words SCHOOL BOARD etched in the uncompromising stone above a row of tall upper windows from the most imposing of which – the one with the curtains – Geo Guest was doubtless inspecting his ragamuffin charges. All was safe – for those not venturing beyond the city boundaries.

My mother, of course, had escorted me thither, on one of the new streamlined trams that didn't make you sick, known as Lance-corporals because of the chevron adorning their fronts. It was my second tram-car expedition of the week, the other having been on one of the old open-fronted bone-rattlers, plastered with enamelled advertisements for Melbourne Ales and Tizer, that positively did make you sick and whose conductor kept a bag of sawdust under the stairs against that contingency. I had been brought into Town – the city centre was always known as Town, with a vocalised capital T – to acquire the new shoes that now chafed my ankle bones and bruised my toes, even though they were a size too big to allow for my growing into them. We had gone to the Public Benefit Shoe Co. which, despite its imposing fascia and superior location in a popular shopping street (it was just a few doors from the Murder Shop, so-called because "We don't cut prices, we murder 'em"), I imagined, by virtue of its name and the fact that my mother paid for my shoes with a Board of Guardians voucher, to be a charity affair – probably an offshoot of the Boots for the Bairns Fund.

To tell the truth I did not have a great deal of time for the Boots for the Bairns Fund, for all that it was organised by the *Yorkshire Evening Post*, the paper that twelve years later was to employ me, and to which its readers adhered with fierce brand loyalty (the only time its rival, the *Yorkshire Evening News*, came into our house was when it was wrapped round the fish and chips). Earlier in the year, while playing choo-choo trains in the school playground, I had been hauled out of the game by a teacher and in front of all my classmates reprimanded as an ingrate for abusing what she assumed, because it was charity grey in colour, to be a Boots for the Bairns Fund jersey. I was too tongue-tied to explain that we were not Boots for the Bairns clientele, being a family of shoe-wearers. (In the pecking order of our community, shoes were favoured by those who "kept themselves to themselves" and did not frequent the pawnshop. Boots were worn by the rougher element, then came clogs, with plimsolls at the bottom of the social heap. The ragged throng now shuffling on to Sammy Ledgard's charabanc were predominantly plimsoll-wearers.) When I recounted the experience to my mother she was indignant and all for going down to the school. I persuaded her to drop it — she would only have compounded my embarrassment, which was what I had endured rather than humiliation. I do not think humiliation figured much in our lives — it would have been a daily occurrence had we allowed it. Certainly when my best friend Jackie Allerdyce had a birthday party and everyone in our class but me was invited to it, his excuse for my exclusion, namely that his mother had said I was too dirty, seemed to me an altogether reasonable explanation, my only cavil being that there were at least two guests who were dirtier.

Neither did any humiliation attach to assembling outside the Poor Children's Holiday Camp Association with the next-door neighbours' suitcase containing my brother's pyjamas (mine were too patched). It was, anyway, one up on its rival good cause, the Leeds Never Seen The Sea Fund, which boasted that it had despatched "2,000 poor bairns and many tired mothers" to Scarborough. To be accompanied by a tired mother would have been the last straw. It was bad enough being kissed goodbye by one — a rare and fleeting gesture, for we were not a demonstrative family.

This token display of affection signalled the end of one huge adventure — two trips into Town in the same week, two glimpses of the Black Prince on his granite plinth in City Square, surrounded by an improbable coterie of naked bronze nymphs; two glimpses of one of the wonders of the world, the rotating news scanner atop the Majestic Cinema which flashed out the headlines in electric light bulbs: HALFPENNY ON FOUR POUND LOAF — and the beginning of another, for which I had no stomach. No one had consulted me as to where I wished to take my holiday. Had they done so, I would never have opted for fresh air — I should have gone for the fetid air of Leeds, rising in a sulphurous haze over the cloth mills. I had yet to make the acquaintanceship of Wordsworth, but Earth had not anything to show more fair than the view from Leeds Bridge of a swirling palette of factory dye drifting down the River Aire. A daily tram ride into Town, even on one of the rocking street galleons that made you sick, would have been holiday enough for me.

But now we were off, leaving the waving mothers to disperse themselves among the arcades and department stores and pork shops and markets of the busy city. Lucky mothers. We bowled along a western-bound trunk road past civic buildings, suites of Victorian office chambers with gold lettering on their frosted windows, chapels and tabernacles, factories, rows of shops, pubs, terrace-ends, and then there were municipal pebbledash housing estates dispiritingly like my own, and municipal grass.

Even before the Silverdale experience I already had a strong aversion to grass, especially where it had been grown deliberately, as in the pointless verges and roundabouts, big enough to stage the Olympic Games, which were such a feature of the council estates where I was to grow up. It would be a long time before I knew anything about the work of Ebenezer Howard, the garden city pioneer with his vision of "the marriage of town and country" in the ratio of twelve houses to the acre; but what I did know was that so far as I was concerned the experiment didn't work. I was only two years old when we were decanted from the southern fringe of the city, so I could no longer remember having lived anywhere else; but I must have retained an Ur-memory of those sardine-packed mean streets, for so long as I lived in Leeds I was always drawn to them, and my heart always quickened at the sight of a row of red-brick terraces with donkey-stoned steps, and sank at the sight of pebbledash and grass.

The grass was getting serious now. We had left the tramlines behind – I had always understood that you could go all the way from Leeds to Manchester and beyond by tram, with only a fifty-yard walk between the various termini; but perhaps we were going a different route – and we were climbing. This would be the moorland I had heard about, somewhat like the rolling field that led down to the railway lines back home, but more of it. Craning your neck and gazing over the drystone walls you had a tantalising view of crowded rooftops and tall mill chimneys far below – the curlew's-eye image caught by Priestley in the opening pages of *The Good Companions*, the big thick library book I had already had a stab at reading: "The

7

roof of the Midland Railway Station glitters in the sun, and not very far away is another glitter from the glass roof of the Bruddersford Market Hall . . ." There were stifled sniffles as the younger of us thought of our mothers tucking into boiled ham sandwiches and hot sweet tea at the oilcloth-covered tables of Birkbeck's café in the covered Market.

To keep our peckers up as we tilted over the Pennines, one of our accompanying adults, a Rover Scout if ever I saw one, began goading us into singing campfire ditties — "Ten Green Bottles", "They'll be Coming Round the Mountain", and "A Tisket A Tasket" which fizzled out because it was a popular wireless hit so none of the plimsoll-wearers knew the words (no wireless set). Then, from the back of the charabanc, two or three bullet-headed urchins who were evidently old Silverdale hands began to pipe up what I was to learn was our unofficial camp song:

> There is a happy land, far, far away,
> Where they have jam and bread three times a day,
> Eggs and bacon they don't see,
> They get no sugar in their tea,
> Miles from the familee, far, far away.

I found this so unbearably poignant that my eyes pricked with tears. But I was not homesick, I was Town sick, city sick, street sick. (And twenty years on, I did get the title of my first novel out of that moment.)

The landscape was full of sheep and I longed for bricks and mortar. I was grateful even for a stray cluster of farm buildings; then came a straggle of stone cottages, and then bungalows and semis with bay windows — what we council house dwellers called "bought houses". These heralded our proximity to one of the Lancashire mill towns, and my spirits lifted to see, presently, gasometers, fish and chip saloons, cobbled streets with the trams back where they belonged although in an unfamiliar livery, gabled blank walls painted with advertisements for Bile Beans; but it was only a small town and soon my heart sank again. More grass.

But it was not as desolate as the endless, curlew-circling moors. This was fair-to-decent scrubland, enlivened by gravel pits and cinder heaps and allotments with their attendant shanty towns of lean-to shacks cobbled together out of old doors, railway sleepers, corrugated iron and tarpaulin. It was semi-urban, and after a few miles I began cautiously to warm to it as even now I warm to a car dump in some interminable tract of natural beauty.

Not for long. Soon we were among potato fields, getting on for real countryside, and then forlorn acres of reeds, relieved only by the friendly pylons, and then by a cheerful settlement of caravans; and then there was the sea, as grey as zinc. It was not the sea as I understood it. I had seen the proper sea — I had been taken by my Uncle Edward and Auntie Orrie in their little Singer four-seater with the celluloid windows to Bridlington, where the proper sea, pea-green, had been alive with pleasure boats and there had been donkeys and ice-cream carts on the beach, and the shore had been lined with amusement arcades and funfairs and Crazy Golf. Not here. This was Silverdale.

Had I possessed any knowledge of prisoner-of-war camps — all I knew on the subject was that my father had spent most of the Great War in one, where he had been fed on black bread, which from my mother's hushed tones when she recounted this oft-told tale I took to be a vicious Hun punishment diet — I should have made the comparison with Silverdale. A collection, at that time, of connecting wooden huts — dormitories, refectory, ablutions and recreation hall (wet weather only) — with colonial-looking verandahs, it had the air of being surrounded by barbed wire, although that may be a detail I have invented. Certainly it would have been a difficult establishment to break out of. Ahead, across the ubiquitous grass, was a sheer drop down to the sands on the scale, to a seven-year-old, of Beachy Head. Behind was the hut settlement, patrolled by a sergeant-majorly Warden. On either side were boggy-looking fields containing animals — sheep, goats and horses. The Association's publicity material has always played up the enchantment in store for back-street waifs setting eyes on cattle for the first time; all I can say on behalf of our intake is that we steered well clear of all these four-footed enemies, apart from feeding lumps of coke to the goats.

I must not be hard on Silverdale, which is remembered with affection by generations, and is still looked forward to by children who would otherwise never get a holiday. But it was no place for misfits, loners or urban agoraphobics, and I fell into all three categories.

The Warden saw it as his mission to send his whey-faced, rickets-riddled charges home as brown as nuts and filled with as many cubic

9

feet of fresh air as their little lungs could accommodate. Skulking indoors was therefore discouraged. One day, tiptoeing into the deserted recreation hall with its school gymnasium smell of lavender Mansion polish and a linoleum floor you could ice-skate on, I discovered a locked, glass-fronted bookcase, crammed with thick, embossed editions of *The Fifth Form at St Dominic's*, *The Last of the Mohicans* and the like. The Warden arriving to flush me out into the open air, I made so bold as to ask if I might borrow a book. He was genuinely baffled. It wasn't raining, he explained, as to an idiot. Books were for bad weather.

There was no bad weather. The sun beat down remorselessly for the full fourteen days, and I thought longingly of tar bubbles, the Stop-me-and-buy-one man, and the echoing, white-tiled corporation swimming baths. The camp being full of boys − I imagine the girls took up occupation on alternate fortnights − the days were spent in boyish pursuits such as cricket, rounders, birds' nesting and splashing about in the sea; but so long as you were getting your quota of fresh air and sunshine, nobody seemed to mind if you involved yourself in these activities or not. I took to spending most of my time mooning around on the cliff edge, gazing across the bay to where distant Morecambe shimmered like a mirage in the summer haze. I could see the promenade, the pier, tall white wedding-cake buildings, a helter-skelter − an edifice previously sighted only in the pages of the *Film Fun* comic − and buses like Dinky toys.

Or so I now imagine. Maybe I could see very little at all, and this elusive Mecca on the far horizon was what I fervently wished to see. What I do remember is that late one night when I got up to spend a penny I crept out on to the verandah and behold, the sky across the bay was ablaze with a dancing aurora borealis of red neon, and in the forefront was a wide arc of fairy lights twinkling like an illuminated necklace. I stared at this vision, mesmerised, until I began to shiver in the chill night air, when I went to bed and dreamed of the enchanting prospect of my once and future city, so accessible yet so tantalisingly out of reach.

That became a recurrent dream, and I have been experiencing it regularly ever since, for over fifty years, but with a difference. I am still there on the Silverdale clifftop but that is no longer Morecambe across the bay. I have outgrown Morecambe. My Mecca on the opposite side of Morecambe Bay has become an amalgamation, an accumulation, of all the cities I have come to know and love.

Shimmering there in the heat haze are the Chrysler Building from New York, the Sears Tower from Chicago, the Sydney Opera House, the Galleria Vittorio Emanuele II from Milan, the Boulevard du Montparnasse, the Piazza san Marco, the Tivoli Gardens, the Savoy . . . a jostling architectural cornucopia linked to my side of the bay by the Golden Gate Bridge.

But the bridge is too high up: from my perch on the clifftop its near view looks like the towering underside of the Brooklyn Bridge. I can't reach it, can't get up to the Golden Gate Bridge to cross to my golden city.

2   This was by no means the first time I had stayed away from
    home. There had been the Bridlington jaunt with Uncle
    Edward and Auntie Orrie, when I had been brought along
as company for my contemporary, Cousin Jeffrey — and also, I dare
say, because like whichever acolyte of Geo Guest had entered my
name for Silverdale, my Auntie Orrie — Oriel, my mother's sister —
had divined that with my peaky face and skeletal limbs I could do
with a holiday. We stayed in a rented caravan at Flamborough Head,
hard by the lighthouse, where any prospective resemblance to the
Silverdale clifftop was relieved by the wafting stench of fish and
chips and mushy peas from the stall across the cinder track, the
reassuring, richocheting rat-a-tat of a tin-roofed pintable arcade,
and the proximity of the lights of Bridlington, only twenty petrol-
fumed minutes away in the Singer saloon with the celluloid windows.

And then there had been St James's Hospital.

When I was about three a great craze for circumcision swept our
neighbourhood, probably instigated by Dr Sugare, our exotic,
faintly mysterious half-Indian panel doctor who, practising from the
front room of a privet-hedged council house next to the Thrift
Stores, brought a whiff of the Orient to our humdrum estate. Acting
upon advice from Dr Sugare, although I did not at the time see the
connection, my mother one day told me that she was taking me into
Town to see Mickey Mouse.

I was already well acquainted with Mickey Mouse, having been
taken by my sister to a fleapit cinema nestling among my beloved
terraces, called the Rex, to see a Walt Disney Silly Symphony,
and later to a so-called "bug-hutch", the Pavilion in the same
neighbourhood (our own super-cinema, the Tivoli — pronounced to
rhyme with Jolly — was, with its ancillary Chocolate Cabin, still
being built) where Mickey Mouse was also appearing, together with
Laurel and Hardy and a cowboy, probably Tom Mix.

13

I had cracked the miracle of cinematography to my satisfaction by much the same logic as I had used, at the age of two and a half, to work out the principles of aviation. In August 1931 the German airship *Graf Zeppelin*, looking like a great discoloured cucumber, caused a sensation by flying over Leeds. Even more sensationally, it floated over our house in Middleton Park Grove where I was in the back garden, digging a hole to Australia. Somewhere around that time, too, there was an air display of sorts on the big clearing in the middle of the Murder Woods, as Middleton Park Woods had been known ever since the dismembered body of a young woman, distributed in sacks, had been found among the bluebells. As I watched a bright yellow Tiger Moth take off and loop the loop, I was interested to observe that the higher it went up, the smaller it got. The same principle applied to the *Graf Zeppelin*. It did not take me long to work out the explanation. There was, I reasoned, something in the atmosphere, a gas or mysterious impulse like gravity, that caused aircraft to diminish in size, together with their passengers, once they were off the ground. This Tom Thumb process helped these hitherto top-heavy machines and their personnel to stay up in the air. As they descended, they passed out of this sphere of influence and reverted to their normal size.

Cinematography was altogether a simpler and much less phenomenal process. The screen consisted of a giant magnifying glass in front of which these characters, Laurel and Hardy, Tom Mix and Mickey Mouse – a man in costume – would perform. When they were in close-up they were in fact very close up to the magnifying screen, and kneeling down. Tom Mix's horse was on a conveyer belt, with the scenery behind them on a roller (little did I realise that I had invented back projection). As to how the whole pack of them came to be appearing at five cinemas simultaneously, it was obvious that they flitted from one venue to another just as, so my mother had told me, Nellie Wallace and the old music-hall comics used to do. I could see a cinema manager raising his bowler hat to Mr Laurel and Mr Hardy as he tapped on the door of their dressing room at the Rex. "Excuse me, gentlemen, but since you're in the district, I wonder if you'd care to oblige my colleagues at the Pavilion, the Gem, the Crescent, and the People's Picture Palace? There will be something in it for you, of course."

Only one aspect of this latest cinematic expedition gave me cause for concern, and that was the possibility of the MGM lion escaping from the travelling cage in which he was transported from cinema to cinema, or worse still bursting through the screen and eating my mother. Otherwise it was with a jaunty step that I set off for the tram stop, trustingly clutching my mother's hand.

I was enthralled. The journey involved not one tram ride but two – the No. 12 Lance-corporal from Middleton up past the Black Prince and his attendant nymphs plus the magic Majestic news scanner, then the No. 11 bone-rattler from the glass-roofed tram shelters opposite the Corn Exchange, above which, over a brightly lit oyster bar, gleamed an enormous sign for Bovril, its letters picked out in white electric light bulbs that flickered on and off. I had no theories about this phenomenon other than that there must be a man sitting in a little room behind the sign, flicking the light switch on and off all day long.

Mickey Mouse was a long time coming but even as we reached the gates of St James's Hospital I did not realise that I was the victim of a hoax, for all that I had visited St James's before, and in distressing circumstances. Only a few months earlier my father had died there, probably from residual war wounds, aged forty-nine. I keenly recalled the event of his death. Leaving me in the care of my Auntie Lizzie, my mother and sister had gone to see him, perhaps in response to one of the hospital bulletins which in those telephoneless days appeared daily in the evening papers – "Dangerously ill 361; Poorly but making satisfactory progress 393 196 412" etc. My sister came running down the street with the tearful news, "Me dad's dead, me dad's dead!" It was the first time I had ever seen my sister cry and so, in my childish incomprehension of the situation, I pointed a triumphant finger at her and chortled, in the local vernacular of the time, "Hoo-hoo, our lass is roaring!", whereupon my Auntie Lizzie, who was my father's sister, fetched me a resounding clip over the ear. Aunties were supposed to be kindly souls who gave you sweets and money; they were certainly not entitled to strike you and I was filled with burning resentment. I went out into the back garden and continued digging to Australia.

That I remembered, and also my mother coming home with my father's brown suit, from the pockets of which she unearthed a halfpenny, his total estate, which passed to me; but I did not remember the hospital.

St James's, now St James's University Hospital and known to television audiences as Jimmy's, was then a grim-looking edifice, formerly the Union Workhouse, and it is difficult to see with hindsight how even at that tender age I could possibly have mistaken it for a cinema. All I can say in mitigation is that the fifty-odd picture palaces of Leeds came in all shapes and sizes, from tin shacks and former miners' institutes which accepted jam jars as payment, to the de luxe super-cinemas with their Wurlitzer organs. There was a cinema, St Patrick's, in a converted church; another, the Gem, under the railway arches. Why should not the gaunt yet imposing frontage of St James's house a cinema too, bigger even than the Paramount?

Even I cannot have mistaken the children's ward for an auditorium but I do recall being assured by the nurse to whom I was delivered up that I was indeed going to the theatre – a wicked play on words, for of course she meant the operating theatre. I am happy to say that upon waking up later back in the ward, the deed done, I promptly wet the bed, when I was bundled off into a freezing bath. Upon my complaining about the icy cold water the same nurse retorted smugly, "That's what you get for wetting your bed." Had she been more of a psychologist she might have troubled to explain that the only reason the water was cold, as I did not realise for years, was that at that hour all the hot water had been run off the boilers.

All in all the St James's episode should have been a deeply traumatic experience, yet while in later childhood I did develop, for a while, a mild fear that our house and everyone in it would disappear off the face of the Earth while I was at infants' school, I do not believe any lasting harm was done. Indeed, once the operation was over and done with, my stay in hospital was hugely enjoyable. We had dorm feasts like the ones I was to read about in public school stories when I was old enough to join the library, and every day the paper seller would come round with the latest comics. Although I was not myself in funds I did manage to borrow from an extraordinarily kind and apparently wealthy older boy – the organiser of the midnight tuck-ins who spoke with what I took to be an upper-class accent, which is probably to say that he pronounced the occasional aitch – all the exciting twopenny coloured comics like *Rainbow*, *Bubbles* and *Tiger Tim's Weekly* that had always been outside our household's price range.

But the real pleasure of St James's was that we were snugly cocooned in what no one had yet learned to call the inner city. All day I could hear the clanging of the trams and at night the shunting of trains from the nearby marshalling yards, and in the small hours the parish church clock chiming, and in the morning the clatter of horses' hooves, the rumble of wagons and lorries, the distant street cries from the Market, the droning trams again, the factory hooters, the clanking of brewers' drays delivering their crates and barrels, the small thunder of cattle on their way to the slaughterhouse, the revving-up of buses, the shouts of the newsvendors, the voices of workmates exchanging banter, the bolting back of doors, the whistling of porters and errand boys, the rat-a-tat of postmen, the far-off tinkling of the arcade carillons, and all the instruments of the city, brass, strings, timpani and woodwind that gradually orchestrated themselves into the concerto of the day-long hubbub.

3 And even from the earliest age I was no stranger to the city. One of the only two memories I have of my father is of being scooped out of bed in the middle of the night (it would have been about five in the morning, adult time), swaddled in a potato-sack and jogged through the sweating cobbled streets to the wholesale Market on the back of his horse and cart. (The other is of him standing magisterially astride the fireplace, like God in a brown suit, while my sister badgered him for her Saturday penny. He dug deep into his pocket and flung a handful of coins across the room – an upturned cornucopia of pennies, threepenny bits, sixpences, shillings, florins, even a half-crown or two. As we scrambled for the treasure I thought what a wonderfully mad, larger-than-life gesture; but I saw that my mother was not impressed, and she impounded the lot as housekeeping money. It was not until I reached the maturity of six or seven that I guessed, from guarded remarks, that he must have drunk a lot.)

My father, Ernest by name, was a costermonger, selling fruit, veg and unskinned rabbits from a horse and cart all over south Leeds. His interest in the trade must have come from his mother Sarah, who despite being unable to read or write had run a greengrocer's shop among the back-to-backs of Hunslet. His father Henry and grandfather Job were cloth fullers – that is, engaged in the thickening of raw cloth as it was pulled through rollers lubricated by troughs of stale urine (their own) – probably at Armley Mills, then the world's largest woollen mill and now a prestigious industrial museum.

Neither Job nor his wife could read or write either (although Job's cross on the marriage certificate is altogether more dashing than bride Elizabeth's). Illiteracy, indeed, seems to have run on both sides of the family. My maternal grandfather, a colliery labourer living all his life in Bolsover near Chesterfield, reached the age of ninety-five without being able even to sign his name. After the death of my grandmother, my mother kept in touch with him by sending him, each week, a self-addressed stamped envelope which he would promptly post back to her. When one week he neglected to return the envelope — he had stuck a gardening fork in his foot and developed gangrene — she put on her coat, took the train down to Chesterfield, and buried him.

From the tales told about him, my father, born 1884, had led something of an adventurous life. He joined the King's Own Yorkshire Light Infantry as a boy soldier and saw service in India before being bought out by his mother. He seems to have called himself an engineer at one point — he is so described on the marriage certificate — but that probably means only that he was a machine hand for one of the many Leeds engineering companies. With the outbreak of the 1914 — 18 war he was recalled to the colours, wounded and taken prisoner at Mons, and escaped twice from German POW camps, on the second attempt nearly reaching the Belgian border before he was recaptured. After his death I used often to look at his Mons Star, a campaign medal which I believed was an award for valour only a little below the Victoria Cross. We had some bound volumes of the *Vivid War Weekly* and I would pore over them looking for a picture of my father among the gruesome battle scenes, and reading over and over again the legend of the Angel of Mons and how the filthy Huns were supposed to have tied nuns by the heels to the bellropes of the cathedral and used them as human clappers.

But just now Father in his brown suit and his shock of iron-grey hair, too unruly to accommodate the cloth cap of his calling, was still very much with us and here we were bowling into Town on a cart painted like a fairground carousel by the dawn's early light.

Father gave employment to at least three horses in his time, or "Gallawas" as he apparently always called them, from a tradition that the best Yorkshire and Lancashire pack horses were bred in Galloway, south-west Scotland: a bomb-happy ex-army nag which would shy and bolt at any loud noise; Peter, who would not budge from the kerb until fed with two of mother's home-made buns, but who when bored with waiting would find his own way home from the most distant pub; and Tommy, stabled in the field that ran down to the railway lines where it was my brothers' pre-breakfast task to catch him, who took life at the trot. This must have been Tommy for it was at a spanking pace that we approached Kirkgate Market, as the covered Market, retail and wholesale, is properly named, although it has always been universally known simply as "t'Market".

"Aladdin's Cave" is now an expression usually applied to the clearing-house of burglars, but at that time it still had its fairytale connotations as exemplified by the lavish scenery and glittering props of the Leeds Grand Theatre pantomime; and while I had yet to see a panto I did know Aladdin's Cave when I saw it and this, as we rode into its depths under a high wide iron arch, was out of the story books. All was light and dazzle and noise and the Christmas smell of oranges. In those disorganised days the wholesale and retail markets were all of a cheek-by-jowl jumble so that around the corner from the potato merchants' stockpile of King Edwards, as high as slag heaps it seemed, was Game Row with its multi-tiered racks of poultry, and across from the wholesalers' pyramids of apples was Pets' Row where budgerigars tweeted and canaries sang sweetly, and there were rabbits to feed with cabbage leaves rescued from underfoot. Granelli's sarsaparilla stall must have been somewhere near at hand but for me it was a beaker of milky cocoa and a doorstep of bread and dripping from the wooden-sided workmen's café, pushed into my hands by a gentle giant in a stained white overall and a straw boater.

I was to roam the Market times without number in my childhood and youth and have never subsequently visited Leeds without making the pilgrimage to these domed and turreted halls of plenty with their glazed brick walls, ornate balconies embellished with cast-iron dragons, and Corinthian columns adorned with the city's coat of arms (what appears to be a dead sheep, although it is in reality a fleece, between a pair of owls), supporting a glittering glass roof. Yet whenever I think of Kirkgate Market I see in my mind's eye what was indelibly stamped on it by that first confused and dreamlike impression – a shimmering crazy-mirror montage of burnished scales, brass weights, marble slabs, naptha lamps, mountains of pomegranates, horses' breath, billy-cans, iron-clad wheels, squashed blood oranges, and big men with pencil stubs behind their ears shouting the price of carrots. My father's cart piled high with replenished produce, I rode home on top of a sack of Brussels sprouts still nibbling my wedge of bread and dripping and feeling, as we passed out into the awakening streets, that I had been in a grotto, the personal guest of a wizard.

It was that dawn outing to the Market, I would guess, when I was

21

less than the height of a cart wheel, that awoke in me my lifelong love affair with cities. It was theatre, it was the circus come to town, it was promise, it was enfolding warmth, it was light brighter than the Bovril sign, it was life. I was home where I belonged.

4 I was an only child, the youngest of five.

My brother Kenneth was the eldest, my senior by ten years. Then, over a seven-year span, came Stella, Dennis and Stanley. I was an afterthought, or perhaps an accident, three years later. Accordingly I was the lone one of the family, the odd boy out. Because of the age gap I did not get to play much with my brothers who understandably did not want a snivelling moppet (I had a head of ash-blond Fauntleroy curls) traipsing after them on their secret expeditions to relieve the Clerk of Works' compound of a handful of nails and staples, or to chomp the rhubarb growing in forbidden fields (Leeds was, and is, the rhubarb capital of the universe).

Besides, from my perspective they were adults. At twelve or thirteen Kenneth seemed a grown man. Indeed, at the age of fourteen upon leaving school, a grown man he perforce became: we had fallen on hard times by then and Kenneth, working for the tailoring firm of Sumpter & Barge, was the sole breadwinner. To mark his first day at work my mother determined to give him a proper workman's tea. The only funds in the house consisted of a three-halfpenny stamp, so the rest of the family were despatched to the post office to sell it back. We bought a tin of sardines with the proceeds and clustered round the scullery table to watch our grown-up brother make short work of it.

I was born at No. 17 Low Road next to the receiving office for Beeston Laundry and two doors from the Hunslet Baptist Tabernacle. Low Road, now largely urban desert, was one of the tram-rattling arteries running from the city centre, all of them lively thoroughfares lined with ironmongers' shops, newsagents and tobacconists, small grocers, family butchers, fish and chip shops, pawnshops, public houses without number, breweries, foundries, obscure little factories and workshops, and countless sooty red-brick

23

terraces which stemmed off the main road on either side like herring bones.

Because of Low Road's position between the Aire and Calder Navigation and the railway lines, and its generally insalubrious reputation, I grew into adolescence imagining that I must have been born in one of the city's notorious back-to-backs (mean little terraces backing on to a common spinal wall to save the cost of bricks and the space consumed by an alley), and that it was as victims of the slum clearance scheme that we had been deported to Middleton "housing scheme" as council estates used to be called. Seemingly not. The family's older hands recall that 17 Low Road had been the residence of a doctor. It was a double-fronted house backing on to the Nelson pub cricket ground, with rooms to spare in which my mother had gas meters installed with a view to taking in lodgers. There was even a playroom − the former surgery − and a large walled garden where for some unfathomable reason my father chose to keep a donkey. It had evidently been a seaside donkey since it would give us rides to the bottom of the garden, but not back again.

It would have been pleasant to have grown up at No. 17 but the property stood in the way of a road-widening scheme − Leeds in the early thirties was a veritable beehive of civic works − and so to Middleton we went. There we lived until I was nine. I do not know what the council thought it was about, since it had only lately launched a vigorous programme against overcrowding, for No. 41 Middleton Park Grove was far too small for us and I had to sleep three in a bed with my brothers Dennis and Stanley, sandwiched between them.

Although we always called No. 41 a house, and it boasted front and back gardens and a privet hedge, it was in fact a ground floor flat, one of a block of four built to a pattern then popular with our multi-initialled Housing Director R.A.H. Livett ARIBA, in cunning imitation of a pair of semi-detached houses. The respectability lent by the style of architecture was largely negated by the type of tenant, many of whom came from the bona fide slums of Hunslet and Holbeck. They included a drunken ex-miner whose enraged post-pub cries of "Who's in bed with his boots on?" and "Which of you's put rabbit bones under t' pillow?" were widely imitated; and a slummocking family of plimsoll-wearers who put us to shame by necessitating our evacuation from the block while it was "stoved" − fumigated − for bed-bugs. Another family was evicted for non-

24

payment of rent and lived for a while on the pavement, in a tent made from a clothes-horse draped with blankets.

Upstairs from us was an enormous family of tuberculosis sufferers who, one by one, were carried off to the sanitorium with the regularity of Brontës. "Galloping consumption", as it was known, was common in the neighbourhood, as was rickets (I nursed a secret desire to have my leg clamped in iron callipers, which to me at least had the glamour of a sling or eye patch). These were, after all, the Hungry Thirties. If the inhabitants of No. 41 were not yet hungry, it was because my father brought home the rabbits and pomegranates he could not sell.

Our turn was to come. Shortly before his death my father, a man of somewhat grandiose dreams by all accounts, much given to saying "When my ship comes in . . .", borrowed some money either with the idea of expanding his business from one horse and cart to two horses and carts, or − another theory − of setting himself up as the Cucumber King of Kirkgate Market. Neither enterprise materialised and no one knows what happened to the money, except that he did like a drink and his interest in horses extended beyond those which pulled fruit and veg carts for a living. At any rate, after he died penniless − his last words, according to my mother, being "My ship's come in" − the bailiffs arrived and took away all the furniture except the mattresses and a stool for my mother to sit on. There was no war pension. He had forfeited it by omitting to wear a surgical belt at an army medical for the war-wounded. We were in the hands of the Board of Guardians.

I vaguely, though by no means vividly, remember there being nowhere to sit down except on the bare floorboards. My mother nevertheless always seemed to be receiving visitors − welfare agents of one kind or another, who came into the house without knocking, examining the rent book and other documents that were kept with Father's Mons Star in a biscuit tin, and shining torches into the bed linen. One of them was the Means Test man who ordered my mother to sell her few remaining possessions, including a pair of electro-plated fairground vases, known proudly as "the ornaments", which I always imagined to be silver. Instead of selling them − she would have died rather than go into the pawnshop − she hid them under the coal. This I thought quite a lark.

Another survivor was a handsome harp zither which my father had bought on the instalment plan from a man at the door. Although I loved to play with it, and could pick out tunes from the time I was three, the harp zither was barred to me in case the Means Test man returned, and hidden away in the airing cupboard. There being little else in the denuded household to detain a small boy, I turned to outdoor pursuits: the digging of my hole to Australia in the back garden, and expeditions, a fixation with me ever since I had been strong enough to work the iron catch of the garden gate.

The simple object of these expeditions was to see how far I could get before the search party caught up with me. I had no idea where I was going, for the very good reason that I had no idea where I was: Middleton might have been at the North Pole for all I knew. Yet although I could have set off in any of a dozen directions I was always magnetically drawn to but two alternative areas of exploration – the Murder Woods or the park.

The Murder Woods route was a straightforward matter of following the tram track which cut through them – just as all roads lead to Rome I knew that all tramlines led to Town, to the Black Prince, the Majestic Cinema electric news scanner, and the Bovril sign. As for the park, that did not in itself much interest me, apart from the boating lake where in the snowy winter I tried to launch myself on a floating piece of ice and all but drowned. But at the far side of the park, at the end of a creepy-looking lane through the rhododendron bushes, was a storm drain through which a four-year-old of slight build could easily wander. It led out into a new housing development, at which point I was usually rounded up by my breathless pursuers.

Since one council housing estate looks much like another, I had no particular interest in this neighbourhood beyond the storm drain and could not explain to my exasperated mother why I was so inexplicably drawn to it, like Alice going down the rabbit hole. It was not until I was old enough to wander off by myself with parental approval or anyway lack of active disapproval, and I had formed the Middleton Hiking Club (membership: one) that I realised, as the circumference of my explorations got wider and wider, where I had invariably been heading.

Like a cat finding its way back to its old home across miles of unfamiliar countryside, I was making unerringly for a long straight thoroughfare called Balm Road which led across the railway to Hunslet, the terraces, and No. 17 Low Road.

5 Had they survived, the proceedings of the Middleton Hiking Club, meticulously entered in a penny notebook, would have shown that while the club's membership remained static, the sphere of its activities expanded. The club's aims were to see what was around the next corner or beyond the near horizon, a mission that led me farther and farther afield.

The club would meet either on Saturday morning or immediately after Sunday midday dinner, when I would roam until driven home by hunger. Thirst was never a problem: under a far-ranging unwritten constitution governing the care and protection of Leeds minors, every child was entitled to knock on any door and request a cup of water. If you were lucky, you might get a glass of Tizer ("the Appetiser") instead.

As with my unauthorised earlier ramblings, these journeys usually began either at the park or the Murder Woods – or, presently, both: for one serendipity-touched Sunday in the search for a new route out of the park after finding my storm drain about a foot deep in rainwater, and descending a grassy valley I had never known was there, I stumbled across the pit wheels and waste tips of Middleton Colliery on the northern fringe of the park. I had never been so close to a coal mine before, although I knew that seams ran under the whole of Middleton, and the earliest sound of the day, before even the blackbird, was the clomping of miners' clogs. I drank in the sight of the old brick sheds, the chimneys, the winding gear, the washing-line of overhead tip-up tubs like a fairground ride, the cartloads of pit props, the cogs and cranks of ancient machinery, all but the steam pumps idle on a Sunday, and marvelled that below my feet when the pit cage rattled down again tomorrow morning, neighbours of ours would be burrowing beneath the rhododendron bushes and rolling lawns of Middleton Park.

I was almost as fascinated by the railway lines that carried the old

Puffing Billy steam engine that pulled the trucks that carried the coal. I knew enough of our local history – everybody did: it was passed on by your parents, long before you got the official version at school – to be aware that this was probably, after its fashion, the first steam traction railway system in the country if not in the world, certainly the first to be established by Act of Parliament. It was the Industrial Revolution I was looking at here, and while Middleton Colliery and its coal railroad were still and silent on this butterfly-fluttering Sunday afternoon, and while I knew little about the Industrial Revolution beyond the story of James Watt and his steaming kettle, it was in my bones and I could smell the cindery excitement of it.

I decided to follow the railway lines and see where they took me. Where they went, I was to discover, was through the Murder Woods, emerging in a donkey-grazing scrubland area of Hunslet known as Parkside, home of the greyhound stadium and the Hunslet Rugby League ground; then over an acre or so of flattened cinders known as Hunslet Moor, where a great fair – Hunslet Feast – was held every August Bank Holiday; and via a succession of viaducts, cuttings and tunnels above and below and beneath the high mill walls, to the coal barges on the River Aire and the Leeds and Liverpool Canal.

I half recognised the district from my occasional tram rides into Town – the tramlines and the railway lines crossed at Parkside, and now I remembered the coal train waiting for our tram to pass, steam evidently giving way to electric – and from the annual family visit, a keenly anticipated compulsory ritual, to Hunslet Feast.

I could confirm at once my previous fleeting impression that here was a neighbourhood of great liveliness. Even on a Sunday afternoon when just about everything was closed, there were still people abroad, chatting at street corners or in doorways, looking in shop windows, waiting at tram stops or drifting towards Hunslet Moor for a constitutional around the cinders. The dingy streets were made even livelier by their richness in what conservationists now call street furniture – public clocks; shop signs suspended from wrought-iron brackets; glass pavement canopies; white blinds painted with the names of grocers, chemists and drapers; barbers' poles; iron bollards; newspaper placards and lurid cinema posters, and enamelled advertisements for Mazawattee Tea and Bisto, and the names of Turog and Hovis picked out in golden letters over the bakers' shops, and every blank wall plastered with fly-posters or

28

painted with huge slogans – "Uncle Joe's Mint Balls. They Keep You All Aglow"; and a medley of overhanging lamps and pub signs, horse troughs, statues of benefactors, public lavatories resembling family tombs, and, surpassing all, a great ornamental drinking fountain to rival the Albert Memorial.

Whenever I glance at those Then and Now photographs comparing the way a particular locality looks now with the way it looked thirty or forty or fifty years ago, the modern picture always looks sadly barren, stripped as it almost invariably is of all the features that gave the streets their colour, all the details that have been tidied up and planned out of existence. And denuded, too, of people: it did not take much precocious perception on the part of the sole member of the Middleton Hiking Club to divine that it was the environmentally busy air of Hunslet that gave the place its vitality, and that drew the people into the streets.

Not that we lacked for street life in Middleton Park Grove. While separated from the soot and grime of industrial Leeds by a *cordon sanitaire* of trees and greenery, we were townies by nature, children of the terraces from which we sprang. Accordingly, although there were fields in plenty a mere two minutes' walk away, nobody ever played in them. Cricket was a street game, with the lamppost as wicket. Football was played down the middle of the road with heaps of pullovers for goalposts, just as it had been in the cobbled past. Hide and seek – "hiddy" – and Relieve-oh were played not in the nearby woods where there was ample scope for concealment, but through a trampled series of back gardens, which were regarded, at any rate by us, as the public domain. Our territory for street activities extended between one so-called "opening" – a street turning – and another, beyond which it was not done to venture. Was it by coincidence that this stretch was the length of the average Hunslet terrace?

Nor was our street life by any means all our own creation. Lacking corner shops (although one enterprising woman did illicitly sell small grocery items from her sideboard drawer, this venture being known as "the house shop") we probably had more pedlars and itinerant traders than Hunslet and Holbeck where no one was more than a hundred yards away from the shops.

Not a day went by without a handbell, a street cry or a knock on the door announcing the presence of, say, the fried fish man, the pea and pie man, the firewood man, the bread man, the pop man who dispensed lemonade (and for some reason slabs of pork dripping) on Sunday mornings, the gypsies hawking clothes pegs and lavender, the scissors grinder, the chair mender, the Indian herbal medicine man, the legitimate ice-cream man (Walls's stop-me-and-buy-one) and the non-legitimate ice-cream man (a cupful of ice-cream, a villainous yellow in hue, for a halfpenny, manufactured in a corrugated iron shack in the vendor's back yard), the roundabout man who gave rides on a mobile carousel in exchange for jam jars, the tingle-airy man with his barrel organ and attendant monkey; and even a muffin man, or more accurately a pikelet man, who true to tradition carried his basket on his head.

The most venerable of all our street hawkers was the Tea Man, a walking bazaar, a one-man Woolworth's, who would stand patiently on the doorstep, a heavy tray slung from his shoulders by thick canvas straps, while his customers browsed among his display of pins and needles, razor blades, press studs, bobbins of cotton, bootlaces, hair slides, tapes and ribbons. Whatever he didn't have he would fetch the next week, committing effortlessly to memory a hundred tiny orders for combs and collar studs, cards of elastic and gramophone needles. The one thing the Tea Man did not dispense was tea – this was delivered each Saturday by the firm of Rington's in a shiny green brougham drawn by a smart black horse with plumes, a ritual on a ceremonial par for us with the Changing of the Guard.

Yet despite all these comings and goings the street never felt properly alive. This was to no small degree down to the dead hand of the council estate architect who in common with most of his brethren had not only placed an obsessional stress on aimless breathing space but, with a view to relieving the dullness of his own design, had garnished the development with an entirely pointless and ultimately dreary series of curves and crescents following no known contours. A simple grid would have done it. But mainly, the problem was that there was little to do in Middleton except live there.

It would be years before Jane Jacobs wrote *The Death and Life of Great American Cities* but while I could not have articulated her principles I had already, from my meanderings around Hunslet, an instinctive understanding of what she would be driving at – that what gives a neighbourhood the vibrancy that my council housing estate almost completely lacked was what planners disparagingly call "mixed use". Hunslet had mixed use in abundance. "Housing", to use another planning expression, was but one ingredient, if a major one, of a rich mixture which, with its accompanying mishmash of street ornamentation, included small factories and great foundries, shops, warehouses, offices, schools, swimming baths and wash houses, public libraries, churches, chapels and mission halls, pubs, recreation grounds, coke dumps, scrap yards, coal staithes, police stations, fire stations, cinemas, billiard halls, cemeteries, railway shunting yards, dog racing tracks, football grounds, breweries, workmen's cafés, savings banks, temperance hotels, garages, stables, hairdressing salons, gasworks, Territorial Army barracks, tailoring establishments, steam laundries, allotments and even a smallholding or two with pigs and hens, all within the same crowded square mile.

While delighted to have discovered Hunslet, I was puzzled as to how it was possible to set off in precisely opposite directions − the storm drain at the edge of the park, and the railway line through the Murder Woods − and arrive at the same place. Putting the solution down to the curvature of the Earth, I set about exploring the parish where I was born, originally with the intention of locating No. 17 Low Road. That proving elusive from this particular end of Hunslet, and it never occurring to me to acquire or at least consult a map, I abandoned my mission after one or two tries and took to rambling about the district more or less aimlessly, always relying on the tramlines to guide me home again.

Curiously for one who from infancy was determined never to work in one, come what may (despite the assertion of Jackie Allerdyce's mother, I had an aversion to getting dirty), I discovered that I had an affinity with factories, of which there was a profusion in Hunslet and its environs, ranging from the Yorkshire Relish works at one end of my perambulations to the Hunslet Printing Sheds at the other. Leeds at that time was known, or claimed to be known, as the City of a Thousand Trades, and most of them seemed to be represented in Hunslet. Many of them were nook-and-cranny businesses crammed into small yards or down narrow alleys or "ginnels": organ builders, oyster merchants, penholder manufacturers, shroud makers, coffin makers, Welsh slate merchants, skin factors, horse harness dealers, blacksmiths, lard refiners, lamp dealers, a Berlin Wool depository, in what was itself a depository of now long-lost trades.

In contrast to these back-street enterprises were the great set-piece mills and factories, sturdy and substantial and standing out like steel engravings against the sulphurous yellow sky: Thwaite Mills; the chemical works; the sweet-smelling coffee works; the fireclay and brick works; Hudswell Clarke's Railway Foundry, shipping locomotives to the Argentine and every dominion in the Empire; a nail mill; a soap factory; Alf Cooke's mighty Printing Works where I would often linger, already savouring and unaccountably excited by the smell of printer's ink; and Marshall's Mill, an exact replica of one of the temples of the Nile, on whose grass-covered roof sheep were supposed to graze, although I never saw them doing so nor solved the mystery of how they got up there in the first place.

Probably from my search for overhead sheep, I learned early Gropius's dictum that one must always gaze up to a building's roof level; and it was there above their frowning porticos that I would find the names of these great industrial dynasties chiselled in the stone, as if they expected to be there for ever.

The same air of permanence attached to the shops, whose monograms or colophons would be picked out in polished granite mosaic in their recessed doorways, and whose elaborate fascias — tiled representations of farmyard scenes for the butcher's and the dairy, sober varnish and deeply etched lettering in gold for the chemist's — were integral to the fabric rather than a glued-on afterthought. The tram-cars droned by and it all looked as if everything would still be the same in a hundred years' time. The motorway cuts through Hunslet now.

I gradually got to know these streets of the Leeds 10 postal district well, and to me their names were as romantic as that of the Silk Road to Samarkand (which I was to travel less than twenty years later). Meadow Lane, South Accommodation Road, Pepper Road, Sweet Street, Balm Road, Beza Street, Joseph Street . . . and at last I stumbled upon Low Road, only to find No. 17 and its neighbours demolished. The Hunslet Baptist Tabernacle, miraculously, was still standing, and I put this down to a mysterious rubric on the wall, "Ancient Lights", which I imagined protected it from the wrecker's ball. (Even more miraculously, the Tabernacle stands to this day, although by now, surrounded by fresh air, it has all the Ancient Lights it could possibly desire.)

I discovered that Low Road, as it pursued the No. 25 tram route into Town, became Hunslet Road; and Hunslet Road, a lively two-mile strip of small shops, took me past Joshua Tetley's Brewery with its magnificent shire dray horses (another survival) to Leeds Bridge, where Town began.

Now that I had located it, I rarely ventured beyond this point. The city bustle was different from the Hunslet bustle: it was a cash-register-ringing, mercenary, metropolitan kind of hubbub. Instinctively I must have known that at not yet eight years old, poorly clad and penniless, I was not yet ready for these lush pastures. Instead, I would content myself with a wistful look up Briggate, the long and busy shopping thoroughfare that runs from one side to the other of the city centre; and I would linger just long enough to take in the golden time ball atop Dyson's the jeweller's, which glided up and down to mark off the hours for all that there was a perfectly good clock beneath it, and a famous one at that, surmounted by a model of Father Time and the motto *Tempus Fugit*, a Leeds landmark and the meeting place for courting couples going back to the 1870s. And then the Middleton Hiking Club would turn back.

I did, none the less, achieve the odd jaunt into Town, in company with my mother. Often these would be but tantalising cross-city journeys, when we would descend from the No. 12 tram only to board the Sammy Ledgard bus that would transport us to Sunday tea with Auntie Orrie, in what is now a Leeds suburb but which then seemed a remote country village, Horsforth, in my eyes saved from the stigma of Silverdale only in that Auntie lived in a terrace house and the main street was known as Town Street. Or, but this was only once a year, we would change to the No. 3 from Briggate to the many acred, lake-endowed and, so we believed, world-famous Roundhay Park for the annual Children's Day, a Germanic orgy of athletics and gymnastics. I was never a competitor and the sports bored me, but oddly for one who had roamed a good part of the city by now, I took care to stay close to my mother for fear of ending up in the Lost Children's tent.

Luckily for me my mother was herself to some degree under the magnetic influence of Town, to which she was drawn compulsively every Friday morning, returning always with two ounces of mint imperials, a quarter of polony and half a pound of tomato sausages from Redman's pork shop, lights for the cat (which would always meet her at the tram stop), a bag of broken biscuits and sometimes a bargain remnant from the back of the Market such as a bit of oilcloth or a piece of chipped crockery. And on school holidays, as a prudent alternative to leaving me at home to "mind the house" when in the absence of my sister and brothers I was apt to occupy myself in such pastimes as sticking the poker in the fire until it became red hot and then burning holes in pieces of wood, she would occasionally take me with her. Or, on the odd occasion, a promised trip to Town would be an inducement to lure me to the school dentist, presumably because I was no longer of an age to be taken in by the Mickey Mouse ploy. I went willingly: the dental clinic was deep in the heart of my beloved Hunslet, and I would have had all my blackened teeth extracted one by one for one more visit to those blackened terraces.

I must have been a tiresome companion for my mother, since our ideas of what constituted the attractions of Town differed. Hers veered towards the cheap clothing stores and cut-price shops; mine, reasoning that one could get all that sort of thing in Hunslet, towards the municipal grandeur of City Square, the Majestic news scanner, the Bovril sign and suchlike wonders of the world. I would allow myself to be dragged away from the Majestic's electric headlines – BALDWIN RESIGNS: CHAMBERLAIN NEW PREMIER – only on condition that she took me to one of the splendid Edwardian arcades which were, and are, a feature of Leeds – either Thornton's and its celebrated animated clock with Robin Hood, Friar Tuck, Richard Coeur de Lion and Gurth the swineherd from Sir Walter Scott's *Ivanhoe*, striking the quarter hours with their fists; or, preferably, the Grand Arcade where, above an inscription from *Macbeth*, "Come what may, time and the hour runs through the roughest day", two knights with battleaxes would bash out the hour, whereupon the doors of a Windsor Castle straight out of the Theatre Royal panto would creak open, and out would whirr a saluting guardsman followed by the bowing figures of a kilted Scotsman, an Irishman with his shillelagh, a Canadian trapper, and an obsequious Indian, the tableau being completed by a cockerel which flapped its wings and crowed like the one in the Pathé newsreel.

My mother had seen all this a hundred times and would grow impatient if we had to hang around the Arcade for more than ten minutes to see the action begin. But our tastes did converge in our next port of call – a leisurely wander around Kirkgate Market, with which I believe she felt almost as close an affinity as I. Then to Woolworth's where she came by her mint imperials. Only if pestered would she take me up Briggate to Lewis's, the big and still spankingly newish department store – there was nothing in there my mother could afford and she most likely felt it was all a bit too grand for her. It was certainly not too grand for me – it was like being aboard the *Queen Mary* – and I resolved, as I rode its moving staircase (the first in the north of England, so we proudly learned), to return in my own time and on my own terms.

By a combination of sheer good luck, initiative and brass nerve I was able to do this far sooner than I anticipated, and with gratifying frequency.

6 One of my regular calls was down through the rhubarb fields to watch the *Flying Scotsman* go by. A stone wall overlooking the railway gave me a grandstand seat. A survival from when Middleton was farmland, it was one of the traditional drystone walls that you can still see all over the Yorkshire Dales, although less so now that the farmers have taken to selling the stone by the truckload to building contractors. The drystone method, so we learned at school, goes back to pre-cement and indeed pre-Roman days and relies on a simple dovetailing formula to hold the heavy slabs of undressed stone together. Properly constructed, a drystone wall can last for centuries.

This one can't have been properly constructed. As the *Flying Scotsman* thundered by leaving a rocket trail of steam and sparks and cinders, and my friend the fireman waved to me as he always did, the wall collapsed beneath me, no doubt weakened by the vibrations of one too many express trains. To my surprise, lying there among the debris, I seemed to be unhurt, although had the stones landed on me instead of the other way round, I should unquestionably have been seriously injured or even killed. As it turned out, I sustained only minor grazes and a dislocated rib.

My mother took me to Dr Sugare, who painted my wounds with iodine and referred me to Leeds Infirmary for an X-ray. Another trip to Town. The outcome was that although medical science could do nothing for my bent second left rib, the doctors wanted to keep an eye on it as I grew up, and to this end my mother was given a white printed card requiring me to report to the X-ray department every six months. Signed J. Johnstone Jervis, Medical Officer of Health.

The white card was lodged among a mélange of picture postcards, public library tickets, Co-op vouchers and soap coupons behind the mantelpiece clock, where I discovered it during the course of one of the routine ransackings of the house on which I embarked every time

37

my mother was out, in the hope of turning up something interesting such as my father's death certificate or − a rare find, this − a photograph of my late-Victorian mother wearing trousers, when she was working at the Barnbow munitions factory during what we then called the Great War.

I was intrigued to note that the frequency of my Infirmary appointments was not specified − the card simply directed my mother to a particular reception room where, upon its presentation, I would be processed for examination. I at once impounded it, perceiving immediately that here was my passport to freedom. Whenever I fancied a few hours off school − I must not, of course, overdo it − all it required was to show the teacher my official white card and then it would be heigh-ho for the No. 12 tram and the bright white lights of the Bovril sign.

That I could get away with it I had not the slightest doubt. A cunning and devious child, I had a low opinion of the teaching staff's intelligence, not to mention that of my schoolfellows, and frequently put my assessment to the test. On one occasion I had chalked the legend KW IS A FOOL under the headmaster's window and then loitered by my graffito until he came by, solely so that when accused of defacing the wall I could point out with a sigh that I was unlikely to incriminate myself by chalking up my own initials, let alone accuse myself of being a fool. Baffled by this warped logic the headmaster went on his way, whereupon I turned back to my handiwork and underlined it for good measure, judging correctly that he would not remember whether it was underlined or not.

Then there was the affair of the cruet. This was in my first year at school, or rather in my pre-year, for, already able to read and write, I had been admitted to the infants' department at aged four. On the first day of the winter term our teacher, Miss Pease, turned up in class with a ceramic salt, pepper and mustard set in the form of a donkey and fruit-cart. I have no idea how she came by it or what possessed her to offer a cruet as a suitable prize for children barely weaned off rusks; but offer it she did. It was to go to the boy or girl judged by Miss Pease to have been the best behaved during the term. I craved that donkey-and-cart cruet and determined to have it.

So did most of the other children in the class, so perhaps it was not such a bizarre idea after all. But I was smarter than they were. I reasoned that being of such tender years they would quickly forget why they were behaving so nauseatingly well, and would lapse into their old disruptive ways. I, however, would remember. Instead of wasting my energies being indistinguishably well behaved along with everybody else, I would continue being routinely naughty until the last couple of weeks of term, by which time all my classmates would have fallen by the wayside. I would then bring myself to Miss Pease's attention with a sustained spurt of angelic behaviour, and so win the prize. The ploy worked, as never for a second did I doubt it would. I bore the donkey-and-cart cruet home with smug pride and it stood on my mother's mantelpiece, between the coal-dented ornaments, for the rest of her life.

So there was no doubt in my mind that with the aid of my trusty white card I could fool all of my teachers all of the time. Or as much of the time as was prudent. Once a month, I reckoned, would be about right, this arrangement to incorporate the non-fictional six-monthly visit with my mother, which could not be avoided (and when she looked for the white card behind the mantelpiece clock I would deny all knowledge of it. What would I want with an Infirmary appointment card?). I would make them afternoon expeditions, so that my regular absences would not show up on the school attendance register, which was marked up only in the mornings. That would prevent my name from coming to the attention of Geo Guest, Director of Education.

The only lessons I really hated were woodwork and metalwork, and so I would always choose a woodwork or metalwork period from which to embark on my city excursions. The drawback was that I had to set off for afternoon school wearing my woodwork apron rolled up under my jacket – an obvious giveaway to any eagle-eyed truant officer, or Board Man as he was known. The apron being too bulky to stuff into my pocket I had to find a hiding place for it. The hole I was digging to Australia was too risky in case my mother caught me red-handed, and so I chose the depths of a privet hedge near the tram shelter. If it went missing I could always claim to have left it in the school cloakroom, from whence it had disappeared. But my luck was always in.

The Board Man, a dreaded figure dressed all in black like an undertaker, loomed large in my calculations from the start. It was universally understood that persistent truants were sent to the reformatory, a stark-looking institution standing high on a hill in the sinister-sounding suburb of Shadwell on the other side of Roundhay Park, without hope of reprieve or remission. The inmates were said to be beaten daily as part of their punishment; I was not sure I believed this but I did put Shadwell on the Middleton Hiking Club's agenda, when I went and stared through the railings. There were some shaven-headed boys in grey jerseys, grey shorts and grey stockings being marched from one building to another. While not looking abject they did not seem too happy and I resolved to keep out of the reformatory if I could.

Not so much from paranoia as from prudence, I took the view from my first white card outing onwards that I was being followed by Geo Guest's representative the Board Man. Getting off school had been all too easy: the teacher had barely glanced at the appointment card and had only half listened to my explanation of having to go for an X-ray. But this could be a trap – he could be in collusion with the Board Man, who was frequently to be seen hanging around the school premises. Accordingly, after getting off the tram at the Swinegate terminus near the Yorkshire Relish factory, pausing only to glance at the Majestic news scanner – EUROPEAN POWERS SIGN MUNICH PACT – and making but the slightest detour to go and gaze at my treasured Bovril sign opposite the Corn Exchange, I headed firmly for the Infirmary in case I was being tailed by the Board Man.

I was only too well aware, as I crossed the expanse of civic grass on the approach to the Brotherton Wing of the Infirmary, that I was in dangerous territory. To my left were the offices of Geo Guest himself, Director of Education. To my right, guarded by two seven-foot gold-leafed owls, was the Civic Hall, housing the no doubt palatial chambers of Thos Thornton, Town Clerk & Clerk to the Council. Behind me was the ramshackle HQ of the Leeds Poor Children's Holiday Camp, whose manager's filing cabinet almost certainly contained a classified report on my failure to inhale the proper quota of fresh Silverdale air. And ahead of me was the Brotherton Wing itself, named after one of the city's host of local benefactors, and the dominion not only of J. Johnstone Jervis, Medical Officer of Health, but of a mysterious and powerful-sounding figure known as the Lady Almoner, whose title I had seen on a polished door on my first and only visit, printed in gold. And these mighty personages were here and now in their various inner sanctums, surrounding me. All this and the Board Man too. Putting on a limp to convince any of them who might be watching that I was a bona fide invalid, and brandishing my white card, I entered the

Infirmary's reception hall with as much boldness as I could muster.

Once inside, my trepidation eased. The place was milling with people, including several children of around my own age, and it was easy to mingle myself into invisibility. I liked the Infirmary, or anyway that portion of it I had visited with my mother, which reminded me, with its brilliantly white exterior and railed, rounded balconies, of a Mediterranean cruise liner I had seen a picture of somewhere. It smelled more like a public library than a hospital; and as my mother and I had discovered, it had its very own milk bar, next to the Lady Almoner's office. Here, on this and subsequent visits, among the old biddies wobbling in on their bad feet to nurse thick mugs of tea and boast that the finest specialist in the country had been unable to do anything for them, or that they had refused to be put on a port wine diet, I was able to buy a glass of milk and an individual custard pie for twopence – no doubt it was subsidised. This deliciously illicit snack consumed – illicit because I knew perfectly well that the little cafeteria was for genuine patients and their friends only, and the Lady Almoner might come out of her office at any moment and, having examined my spurious credentials, denounce me to J. Johnstone Jervis – I would strike out confidently along the corridors until the lavender polish smell gave way to disinfectant and the streamlined decor of the Brotherton Wing's emulsion paint, parquet and concealed lighting handed over to age-crazed buff and green tiles and I knew I was in the original part of the Infirmary, a Gothic, collegiate-looking pile to the immediate west of the Town Hall. Having thus shaken the Board Man off, I was free to commence my wanderings.

My first exploration was of the Town Hall itself. This noble municipal pile, in whose otherwise completely unfunctional tower curlews were reputed to nest, had commended itself to my attention when my mother had brought me into Town on the first leg of my exile to the Poor Children's Holiday Camp a few months earlier; and on our recent visit to the Infirmary I had heard organ music wafting out of the Town Hall as we went by. The only serious organ music I had so far ever heard being of an ecclesiastical nature (as distinct from the frivolous I-do-like-to-be-beside-the-seaside stuff we got on the wireless), I had therefore concluded that the Town Hall, as well as being where the Lord Mayor had his parlour – I already knew that from school civics lessons – must also double as a church or perhaps, given its size and architectural stature, a cathedral even.

My mother put me right on that, then told me enough about what went on in the Town Hall to leave me burning with curiosity to see its interior.

Mounting the back steps, then – the front steps, leading up from Victoria Square, were altogether too exposed, and the Board Man might be lurking behind one of the stone lions flanking them – I already knew that as well as housing a mighty concert chamber, Victoria Hall, the Town Hall was also (at that time) an Assize Court where wife-poisoners and other murderers were tried by a judge in scarlet robes and wig, and twelve good men and true.

It was into Victoria Hall that I ventured first, simply because the great doors happened to be open. I was suitably impressed by its opulence, the richly decorated semicircular ceiling, the coloured window glass, the giant pillars surmounted by yet more civic owls, and particularly by the fifty-foot-high organ, which made the organ of the Holy Cross Church, Middleton, look like a set of Pan pipes out of a lucky bag. Then there were the various improving mottoes around the frieze – "Good Will Towards Men", "Forward", "Weave Truth With Trust", "Honesty is the Best Policy" and, oddly, "Trial by Jury". Or perhaps not so oddly, for this legend was a reminder that the Town Hall played Nemesis to all the wife-poisoners in the West Riding; and fascinated though I was to find the grandiloquent source of the organ music I had heard, I was even more fascinated by wife-poisoners.

Murder was a popular preoccupation of the time, part of the theatre of city life. George Orwell got it right in his celebrated essay, "Decline of the English Murder". Many was the raw evening I was sent pelting out in my stockinged feet at the cry of "Special! Special!" from the paper boy racing down the street with the late, late extra of the Buff Final, as the last edition of the *Yorkshire Evening Post* was known. It was nearly always a murder – it would have been a swindle had it been anything less, such as Hitler annexing Austria; with any luck it would be human remains found wrapped in brown paper parcels at a left-luggage office, or perhaps even another dismembered corpse in our very own Murder Woods. As to editorial content, these "Specials" somewhat short-changed the reader: all you got for your penny was a duplicate of the same paper you had had pushed through your letter-box a few hours earlier, plus an inch or two of cable-ese in the Stop Press column. No matter: it would all be fleshed out in the *News of the World* on Sunday.

All human death was there and we feasted upon it, the mass communication age equivalents of the crowds at Tyburn. We would have made a good audience for the *Police Gazette* had it still existed. Buck Ruxton was the most recent murderer to seize the popular imagination, and the subject of a school playground song: "Red stains on the carpet, red stains on your knife, Oh Dr Buck Ruxton, you murdered your wife. The nursemaid she saw you, and threatened to tell, Oh Dr Buck Ruxton, you killed her as well." But Dr Crippen, hanged 1910, was still alive in our minds. So was the Thompson-Bywaters case, seven years before I was born. Charles Peace, known affectionately and anarchistically as Charlie Peace, tried at these very Leeds Assizes and hanged at Armley Jail fifty years before my birth, was still a local legend because of his audacious escapes from the police when he was supposed to have dressed up as a woman to elude arrest. (Armley Jail, quite near Hunslet and built to resemble a mediaeval castle, was almost as much an object of my morbid fascination as Shadwell Reformatory, and the Middleton Hiking Club was to lay on a special expedition to go and stare at it.)

While it had been easy enough to get into the Town Hall – I had feared a major-domo asking name and business – I was not so unrealistic as to suppose that at my tender age I would be allowed into the Assize Courts to watch the trial of a trunk murderer or two. I loitered for a while outside the tall wooden doors of No. 1 Court, guarded by sentinels who from their uniform and general demeanour could have been park rangers, in the vain hope of catching a glimpse of the prisoner at the bar. I did see one or two beefy-faced men in wigs and black gowns – judges, they would be, I expected – stalking the high tiled corridors, but no trunk murderers being frogmarched into court between two policemen.

Of policemen, however, there was no shortage. The Town Hall, I now noticed to my alarm, was milling with them. Clearly, if any one of them paused to question me, it was going to be a Shadwell Reformatory job. Like some juvenile bit-player in a Pinter film adaptation of Kafka, I scurried along the outer corridor as fast as I dared, keeping close to the wall and looking for an exit. The corridor proved to be circular and I was back where I began. Under the eyes of what by now seemed to be the ranks of the entire Leeds City constabulary, I sauntered out, with as much sangfroid as a wanted truant could muster in the very shadow of the courts of justice, the way I had come. I was not to enter the Town Hall again until I was sixteen, when I learned that you could get a bargain Woolton Pie in the basement British Restaurant.

7 The two main thoroughfares of central Leeds, Briggate and the Headrow, form a St George's cross. Once the visitor has established this, as I quickly did, it is easy to fit their adjacent cross-streets, lanes, arcades and passages into position. Thus I never once got lost.

The Town Hall lies at the top of the Headrow, up Park Row, the banking quarter (where I was impressed to notice the Bank of England) from City Square. Next to it is the Central Library which I placed off limits on account of its uncomfortable proximity to Geo Guest's Department of Education – they then actually backed on to one another, and for all I knew there was a secret pass door between the two. Then comes the Art Gallery, equally out of bounds in case I bumped into a school party being taken to look at the pictures. I was not, in any case, at the time all that taken with art, which from what I had seen of it in old magazine illustrations consisted entirely of rural scenes featuring village ponds and haywains. Had I ever heard of Atkinson Grimshaw whose Leeds cityscapes adorn its walls, I should have been up the Art Gallery steps two at a time and taken the risk.

For the present, however, I was far more interested in the next building in line, the modernistic head office of the Leeds Permanent Building Society. I had learned from an answers to correspondents paragraph in the *Leeds Mercury*, the popular morning paper for those who found the *Yorkshire Post* too indigestible, the explanation of that curious word "permanent". The original building societies had always automatically wound themselves up after the last subscriber had been paid out. The Leeds had been the first society to establish itself on a perpetuating, permanent basis. For some reason I found this information deeply fascinating and relayed it to anyone who would listen. The new red brick and Portland stone fabric of the Leeds Permanent Building Society was therefore favoured with a

45

prolonged, scrutinising stare before I passed on.

The only other attraction in the Headrow, apart from the Scout Shop whose window display featured far too much camping and outdoor equipment for my taste, was Lewis's department store at the junction of the Headrow and Briggate, as fleetingly visited in the reluctant company of my mother. But Lewis's could wait, as could Briggate with its arcades and their striking clocks; for if I kept on going down the Headrow I would reach Vicar Lane and the northernmost entrance to Kirkgate Market, in other words the one in closest proximity to the wholesale Market.

It was the first time I had ever ventured into the Market alone and I felt immediately at home. Far from any fear of being recognised and reported to the Board Man by traders who could have known my father – they might, after all, spot the family resemblance even if they did not remember my sole visit in his company when I was half the size I was now – I actively wanted to be recognised, wanted to be hailed and hugged and to have a bread and dripping doorstep and a mug of cocoa pushed gruffly into my hands, wanted to be welcomed into that masonic temple of pomegranates and blood oranges.

I had already worked out that the Market was laid out in the form of streets, like a miniature indoor Hunslet consisting entirely of brilliantly lit shops and stalls, where the terraces were paved with sawdust. Each row, while not necessarily as slavishly devoted to a particular branch of produce as Game Row, Butchers' Row or the fish market, had its speciality.

On one row I could find the crumbly Cheshire – though my own preference was for processed cheese triangles – that my mother always bought (invariably, like everyone else to this day, from the specific stall of her choice, although to my untutored eye at least there would be the same crumbly Cheshire at the same price on five different stalls, and with shorter queues); and Red Leicester, Wensleydale, Derby Sage, and another kind of crumbly in three versions labelled Mild, Medium and Tasty; and blue-veined Stilton that was said to have maggots running through it; and cartwheels of Double Gloucester, and slabs of butter the size of the granite speakers' podium in Middleton Park where fanatics in salt-and-pepper suits frothed and fulminated; and mountains of brown eggs, and basins of green duck eggs nestling in straw.

On another would be hams swinging from brass rails and stuck with cloves like mapping pins; and below them white enamel trays piled high with chitterlings, polonies, Yorkshire ducks, stand pies, Aintree pies, whist pies, pork sausages, beef sausages, tomato sausages, Cumberland sausages, black pudding, white pudding, boiled ham, tongue, corned beef, sliced roast beef, salt beef, brawn, pigs' trotters – the same robust fare, in short, as could be found in any of the dozens of pork shops dotted around the city, which then as now could rival any Soho delicatessen or even Harrods Food Hall itself.

The top row, being dedicated to such preoccupations of the ladies as felt hats, Liberty bodices, surgical stockings and skeins of wool, held little to detain me, save only the glassed-in Invisible Mender's with an animated model of a seamstress sewing away in the window and, I was half ready to believe, the invisible mender himself (it would have to be a he, like H.G. Wells's *Invisible Man* at the Tivoli cinema) lurking somewhere on the premises. But below this comparatively tranquil corridor of haberdashery and ribbons and bows were the cakes and fancies and sweets and confectionery rows, where as well as a tabernacle Whitsun treat of barm cake, Long John cobs, Dunster spiced loaf, iced buns, cream horseshoes, parkin, currant teacakes, gingerbread men, Sally Lunns and twelve kinds of slab cake; and humbugs, treacle toffee, licorice allsorts, Pontefract cakes, cough candy and buttered Brazils, there was one stall selling nothing but broken biscuits and yesterday's buns at a penny a bag, and another awash with broken chocolate, broken nougat, broken bars of fudge and broken coconut ice. This was sold by the pound; I cannot recall the price but it was way beyond my empty pocket. I would press my nose waif-like against the glass ledge that prevented this toothsome merchandise from spilling out on to the flagstones, in the hope that the lady would take pity and give me a chocolate misshape. She never did.

And just below the broken chocolate stall, and across the way from Birkbeck's café where I could have murdered a boiled ham sandwich in a Yorkshire teacake, was Stringer's bookstall, trading in second-hand magazines and comics, as well as American comic books and Canadian Sunday newspaper supplements imported to these shores as ballast. These literary curiosities I would browse among until requested by the management to move on. I was also intrigued by back numbers of a peculiar-looking magazine called *Punch*, the cover of which, depicting Mr Punch himself and an advertisement for Fry's Pure Concentrated Cocoa, was exactly the same week after week. I thought this decidedly odd.

This first solo visit to the Market then took me down through the pungently smelling fish hall in search of the corporation slaughterhouse, another morbid preoccupation. Although I didn't want to see any animals actually being put to death I did want to give the slaughterhouse a good long stare. With any luck, too, I might be witness to one of the occasional stampedes of veal calves that sometimes occurred as they were being herded over from the railway marshalling yards across the way, whence they had travelled from the flat wastes of the East Riding. I had heard stories of terrified passengers being marooned on their tram-cars while fear-maddened cattle rampaged all around them.

The slaughterhouse was right at the end of the Market opposite the parish church with its graveyard full of victims of the Black Death, a plague which it was popularly believed would break out anew if the graves were ever dug up – the parish church too was on my visiting list. But somehow, having been deflected from my mission by a flower market I had never known existed, and in which I could see no commercial purpose since no one in Leeds ever bought flowers except at the gates of cemeteries, I found myself in the Tatters Market – "t' back o' t' Market" as it was known to all who patronised it – an open-air shambles of tarpaulin-sheltered stalls that functioned every Tuesday and Saturday. So my first white card afternoon must have been a Tuesday.

The blue-jowled hawkers in their sharp pinstriped suits and cocky hats seemed a different breed from the solid straw-boatered and white-aproned traders in the indoor Market; they called their wares in different accents too – had I yet travelled to any of these places I should have recognised the voices of Nottingham, Liverpool, Newcastle, Sheffield, London even. They were travelling men with a fairground aura about them, employing the same mock auction patter to sell their dinner services and rolls of linoleum that always so mesmerised me on my annual outings to Hunslet Feast.

Some, in a haze of menthol, eucalyptus, glycerine and wintergreen, were noisily peddling elixirs and potions and cures for barber's rash. Others were demonstrating patent varnishes and quick-drying enamel paints: I have an image, whether from this first visit or no I could not begin to remember, of a hawker so engrossed in painting a kettle bright blue that he quite forgot his spiel, yet he continued to attract an audience who watched him with the encouraging attention they would have given to a rather good pavement artist.

Then, on the periphery of this peripheral open market, there was a shanty town of tattooists' and fortune tellers' booths, pea and pie stalls, and tumbledown little lock-up shops housing barbers, cobblers, knife-grinders, dubious-looking chemists and "family planning" establishments, whatever they might have been, all clustered around this teeming northern souk like pedlars' tents around the walls of a mediaeval town. I liked it here. It had an unsettlingly transient air that made me itch to join this gaudy, gimcrack caravan and see where its rag-tag-and-bobtail band of itinerants led me.

But with my time strictly limited — allowing myself the customary half hour or so of dawdling after school, I had better be no later than five o'clock in getting home if my mother were not to wonder where I'd been — I had to be moving on before they did.

My Bovril sign was only just around the corner from the Markets and so there I repaired for the second time that truant afternoon, to stand on the steps of the Corn Exchange opposite, quite transfixed by the glowing battery of white electric light bulbs winking on and off as they responded to the man in his little room behind the sign manipulating what I had come to suppose, for so large a consumption of power, would be a big lever rather than a conventional light switch like the ones at home.

Hitherto I had regarded our Victorian Corn Exchange as little more than a tram stop. I had no idea, and little curiosity about, what went on in this great elliptical domed structure (popularly believed to be round) except that when I was about five it had staged the world's biggest mouse show, but neither my mother nor my sister would take me, on the incredible grounds that they did not like mice. Now, temporarily sated with my Bovril sign and perhaps emboldened by my successful sortie into the Town Hall, I decided to explore the place.

To my surprise and delight there was a corn market going on. Stone steps led to an iron-railed balcony under the partly glassed dome, where coal merchants and estate agents had their offices. Creeping up them I had a bird's-eye view of about a hundred gaitered or tweeded farmers and corn chandlers clustered around black wooden stands that somewhat resembled kitchen dressers, with their names printed on them in gold (all the names in Leeds seemed to be printed in gold), holding hushed and important conversations with flour merchants and manufacturers of cattle cake as they trickled maize, oats and Yorkshire barley judiciously through their fingers. A ray of sunlight illuminated a big clock framed in golden sheaves of corn. Serendipity.

The Corn Exchange at once went on my list of regular ports of call on my white card excursions. But the next time I crept in I was disappointed to find the huge oval hall eerily deserted – I hadn't realised that the Corn Market, like the Tatters Market, functioned only on market days. It did give me chance, though, to peruse the Bye-laws (I was an avid reader of all kinds of bye-laws, which I studied to make my own flesh creep like an introspective Fat Boy from Pickwick): "A person shall not bring a dog into the Market Place . . . A person shall not smoke tobacco or any like substance in the Market Place . . ." Signed, Joseph Hepworth (of Hepworth's the clothiers, I rightly surmised), April 1907. The Bye-laws are still in position; and the Corn Exchange, while now prettily restored and given over to candle boutiques and cafés, is a corn market still, although the kitchen dresser stands are by now reduced to a bare dozen.

From the Corn Exchange I struck out up Briggate, resisting the temptation to get there through Woolworth's. Although Woolworth's was a powerful draw – they had a counter of lead model sheep, cattle and milkmaids going for a penny each, good to suck meditatively or lick the paint off when you were playing at farmyards – it was notoriously a hotbed of young shoplifters, and I should most assuredly be taken for one and delivered up to Shadwell Reformatory by the private detectives who were known to patrol the store.

Instead I had a quick look around Marks and Spencer's, a store I had yet to enter in my mother's company without her recounting the story of how Mr Marks had started his great enterprise with a penny bazaar in Kirkgate Market. It was a saga I never tired of hearing, better than any fairy tale. But Marks and Spencer's soft furnishings, hardware and ladies' clothing failed to fascinate, and I quickly resumed my walk up Briggate, heading now for one of the arcades – not Thornton's or the Grand but the County Arcade, which, while lacking little men striking the hour, was (and remains, although now tarted up into "the Victoria Quarter") a multi-domed riot of Sienna marble, wrought iron, gold-capitalled columns and allegorical mosaics.

The attraction for me, however, was Banks's Music Arcade, the big double-fronted store that stood on the corner of the County Arcade and the smaller Cross Arcade that was the approach to the Mecca Locarno opposite. Banks's windows featured grand pianos and clarinets and accordions and, the centrepiece, a big gleaming xylophone which I craved, as played by Teddy Brown, a wireless performer of enormous girth whose picture I had seen in the *Radio Times* and who had once honoured Leeds by appearing in person at the Empire.

But even more than I wanted to play the xylophone, I wanted to write music. Along with the piano scores of Haydn, Mendelssohn and other unpronounceables which adorned the foot of Banks's windows, there were always a few folios of blank manuscript paper which I longed to fill with clefs, quavers, crotchets and other pleasing squiggles. The very moment I set eyes on these enticing virgin staves I resolved to teach myself how to compose music. It never occurring to me for a second that there would be textbooks on the subject in the reference library — for a bright child I could be extraordinarily stupid at times — I set about painstakingly compiling my own dictionary of musical terms and symbols, copying them from the sheaves of old sheet music freely available in the horsehair-covered piano stools of Middleton Park Grove; whenever I came across an interesting expression such as *allegro* or *andante*, I would search out a translation and jot it down.

Meanwhile I had begun to compose simple tunes on the harp zither my father had bought at the door. While I have never been able to play a musical instrument properly I found that I had a musical ear and to this day can pick out any tune with one finger, although only in the key of C. Having taught myself the rudiments of musical notation I began writing my compositions down, first on blank paper which I ruled out into staves myself, and then on proper manuscript paper, for as a treat my mother one Friday brought me back from Town a whole twenty-four-page Banks's manuscript book. An expensive buy, but the family circumstances had improved a little by now. Helped either by the Board of Guardians or relatives or both, she had scraped enough together to buy a few sticks of furniture on the hire purchase, the first of these purchases being a stool, "the buffet" as it was always called, which the entire family went down to collect from a cut-price shop at the bottom of Middleton Ring Road, four of us bearing it home like a trophy, one to each leg. Although my mother would frequently sit on the buffet by the fireside with her lips moving as she juggled the family finances in a little notebook, our fortunes, with the prospect of four out of five of us reaching the working age of fourteen, were gradually if modestly on the mend.

My first compositions were variations (a word I had picked up from the *Radio Times*) on the little tunes I had made up. I then embarked on a full-scale opera, scored not only for piano but for brass and two kinds of strings, on the theme of Robin Hood. This fragment, for of course this ambitious work was quickly abandoned, was never played, and indeed for all I know was unplayable, for I was more concerned with the busy appearance of the symbols on the page than with the practical harmonics. I also found myself more interested in the libretto than in the music, which I blamed for the vicious cuts and calluses on my thumb sustained by plucking out the melody on the harp zither with a home-made plectrum fashioned out of a strip cut out of a cocoa tin with my mother's scissors, the original having been lost. Before long my career as a composer languished and I went back to my first love, writing stories.

From the County Arcade there was time now only for a quick look around Lewis's and a ride up and down the escalators. Lewis's, completed only three or four years earlier, was in my estimation the most modern building on the face of the Earth. Everything about it dazzled with streamlined up-to-dateness, from the reflecting chrome of its purring escalators to the shining bronze of its silent lifts, from the pristine tiles of its American soda fountain to the burnished glass of its Ladies' and Gentlemen's Hairdressing Establishments.

But the reason Lewis's was a must on all my white card outings was that it was a rare week when there was not something going on in this go-ahead store, where novelties like American soft ice-cream were being introduced, and where girls with Roundhay High School accents in white smocks would demonstrate egg whisks patented in Kalamazoo or the latest thing in potato peelers. Lewis's had recently surpassed itself by exhibiting on its ground floor -- how they had got it through the doors I puzzled over at length – the Bluebird, the racing car with which Sir Malcolm Campbell had established the new land speed record of 301.7 mph. I could not hope for another Bluebird on this occasion but at least there was sure to be something new in the kitchen gadget line and indeed there was, although I cannot now remember what it was. I remember only tearing myself with reluctance from the basement demonstration, taking one more ride on the escalators and then making for the tram stop.

At home my mother asked me how I had got so dirty — in those pre-Clean Air Act days, if the wind in Town were blowing in the wrong direction, it snowed flakes of soot from the cluster of factory chimneys across the river — and, plainly suspecting that I had been playing truant, what I had learned at school that afternoon. I said that we had first done dovetail joints (I had recovered my woodwork apron safely from its privet hedge depository) and after that we had learned all about the Corn Exchange and did she know there was still a corn market held there? My mother gave me one of the old-fashioned looks that meant she wasn't sure whether to believe me or not, but did not pursue the matter.

8 Architecture was a word I had yet to encounter, and so I had no idea that I had an interest in the subject. What I did know was that buildings, their shape and proportions and fabric and style of adornment or lack of it, fascinated me. Although I suppose my love of the cobbled terraces and the dark satanic mills made me a traditionalist, I had great enthusiasm for the modern, Lewis's being a gleaming example.

It did not require any great knowledge of the passing show to be able to grasp from the contrast between the white Portland stone frontage of the Civic Hall and the soot-blackened Yorkshire stone of the Town Hall, or between the streamlined Middleton trams and the old bone-rattlers clanging along Hunslet Road like land-locked tramp steamers, that Leeds – and, insofar as I knew anything about it, the rest of the country all around – was in a state of transition.

Leeds was in many respects at that time of the mid-to-late Thirties a schizophrenic city, half of it with its clogs firmly planted in the Edwardian and Victorian past, the other half determinedly modernistic. We still had a lamplighter and a knocker-up in our street and there were still horsedrawn funerals (my father was the first in Middleton Park Grove to be seen off by motor – ironic, since he was the only one in the neighbourhood to own a horse); but the Tivoli Cinema with its rounded brick frontage and the tram shelter at the top of the street were, although neither I nor anyone else in Middleton had ever heard the expression, pure Bauhaus.

The roadway out of City Station alongside the new Queen's Hotel overlooking City Square was constructed of rubberised briquettes so that slumbering guests would not be disturbed by the sound of Silver Line taxis gliding in and out of the station; yet in Hunslet and Holbeck, when somebody was lying ill, the cobbles were still spread with stable straw to deaden the rumble of cart wheels.

55

Behind the lace curtains of our up-to-the-minute council residences, with their every modern convenience such as gas pokers and an indoor coal shed, you could find what looked like waxworks tableaux of Victorian domestic life, with old grandmothers dressed from head to toe in black presiding over stuffy parlours crammed with rocking chairs, horsehair chaise-longues, wax fruit in glass domes, copies of the Stag at Bay covering the rising damp, and the family Bible open at the Book of Psalms.

Bakelite wireless sets driven by accumulators — among my routine tasks was to take ours to be recharged at Morrison's Garage on the shopping parade, taking care not to let the acid splash my bare legs — blared out slick American-style comedy patter to an audience which in large part still spoke in a dialect that would have been barely comprehensible to anyone in the next postal district, let alone the next county. The *News of the World* each week printed half a page of sheet music for a populace still thumping away on its cottage pianos every Sunday afternoon; but the songs were no longer tasteful ballads but wireless and gramophone hits like "It's a Sin to Tell a Lie", "Nice Work If You Can Get It" and "Horsey, Horsey". While over her washtub and scrubbing board my mother was still singing her favourites from the old music-hall, "On Mother Kelly's Doorstep" and "The Little Shirt My Mother Made For Me", my sister subscribed to McGlennon's sixpenny song book which gave the words to all the latest tunes as recorded by the popular dance bands such as Jack Payne, Ambrose, and Carroll Gibbons and the Savoy Orpheans.

Even in the small world of childhood there was change in the air. There was high excitement when a new chocolate bar called Aero came on the market, consisting mainly of bubbles. Mars bars were another sensation. We all ran to the top of the street to see the first double-decker bus go by. Our old-fashioned penny comics like the *Joker*, the *Jester*, *Illustrated Chips* and *Funny Wonder*, printed on flimsy blue, green or pink paper, were giving way to the new coloured D.C. Thomson titles, the *Dandy* and the *Beano*, and later the *Magic*, with "Free inside — sugar bullets for you to eat". *Mickey Mouse Weekly*, the first photogravure paper for children, had a swop value of three conventional comics.

We could speak the local dialect effortlessly — "Sither" for "See thou", "Weer's ta bahn?" for "Where are you bound?" and so on, but we did so in a parodying way, aware that it was a different language from a different time; and while we had access to a rich anthology of street songs and snatches as later identified by the Opies in their *Lore and Language of Schoolchildren*, and would still repeat the saws and sayings used by our elders and betters, many of them quite baffling – "Not a pot washed and the house full of Chinamen" was one I could not fathom: another music-hall relic, probably – our repertoire was beginning to silt up with wireless and cinema catchphrases and jingles – "I thang yew", "You dirty rat!", "It's Monday night at seven, Oh can't you hear the chimes" etc. In the *Yorkshire Evening Post* wireless columns I read of the public surveillance potential of an invention called television which could see around corners, and pondered on the dire consequences of such a device falling into the hands of the Board Man.

So I was very conscious of living in a melting-pot, and every time I took out the white card from its hiding place between the pages of a book called *Fifty Years of Progress: the Story of Hemingway's Brewery*, which Uncle Herbert, who worked there, had introduced into the house upon hearing from his sister my mother that I was a big reader, I knew that my trip into Town was bound to yield some further example of the old giving way to the new.

One day, for example, I ventured into the newly completed booking hall of the City Station adjoining the Queen's Hotel and its rubber roadway, to find a breathtakingly spacious chamber straight out of Hollywood, its high, pastel-painted concrete arches hung with what I did not yet know were art deco lanterns, its walls lined with what I did not yet know was glazed terracotta, its floor carpeted with what I did not yet know were faience tiles, its back-lit advertising displays for permanent waves and the new Black Magic chocolates framed in bronze in the manner, and I did not yet know this either, of the display cabinets in the lobbies of New York skyscrapers. (Monstrously, and unforgivably, it is now a British Rail car park.) But beyond the trellis gates of this elegant thirties hall were chuffing, cinder-scattering steam trains; and below it were the Dark Arches, the Dickensian labyrinth of brick catacombs on which the station was built, and under whose viaduct spans gushes the converging waters of the River Aire, the Leeds and Liverpool Canal and the Aire and Calder Navigation.

There was Leeds modern and Leeds ancient; and when, the booking hall having been admired and inspected, I retraced my steps past the passengers' private carpeted corridor into the Queen's

Hotel, and the adjoining flower shop and Parfumerie Continental and the News Theatre on the corner, it was to Leeds ancient I returned as I found myself back in the brooding presence of the Black and blackened Prince, his attendant nymphs and, now that I had the leisure to inspect them, the statues of Joseph Priestley, discoverer of oxygen but also, more importantly, a minister of Mill Hill Chapel across the street; Dr Hook, Vicar of Leeds 1837 – 59; John Harrison who founded the Grammar School; and James Watt of steam-kettle fame, who like the Black Prince seemed from his inscription to have no local connection. Back to the past. But the Majestic news scanner's electric-light headlines – GERMAN TROOPS MARCH INTO SUDETENLAND – spelled out the uneasy future to those who understood what they meant.

There was no statue in City Square to the Rev Charles Jenkinson, Vicar of Holbeck and a councillor, but there might well have been had he not been still alive and active, for while he was known to his political enemies as "Red Ruin", his ambitious slum clearance programme had made him a local hero (though not necessarily with the slum dwellers themselves). My interest in him was that he was the instigator of Quarry Hill Flats, another wonder of the world. Leeds modern again: the biggest housing development in Europe, made of ferro-concrete and as up to date as Lewis's. Architect: R.A.H. Livett ARIBA.

Quarry Hill, not yet finished, was always in the columns of the *Yorkshire Evening Post* for one reason or another – its revolutionary rubbish chutes would do away with dustbins; it would have its own laundry and ironing rooms; the Great Curve of Karl Marx House, with a frontage of half a mile, was now completed – and I wanted to see it all. Which I did, proceeding through Kirkgate Market to what was still officially called Leeds Central Omnibus Station, newly built together with a reinforced concrete air-raid shelter, and subjecting the Great Curve opposite to a good long stare. Then I wandered across the road into the development through one of its whalebone-arched gateways, and had a self-conducted grand tour. I approved of Quarry Hill and wanted to live there. How jolly to live two minutes' walk from the Market, five minutes from Lewis's and the Paramount Cinema, ten minutes from City Square! Despite its huge size – twenty-three acres – the Great Curve somehow gave the estate a human scale. Nor did it feel in the least remote, possibly because of its proximity to Town and the clanging trams; also, to my satisfaction, it had a homely gas works in the middle.

I had no way of knowing that I was gazing at one of the few mass housing developments that could have worked, but for some quite stupid structural flaws. Quarry Hill has long been pulled down after years of going to seed. It seems incredible now that there was a time when what after all was no more than a block of council flats would be proudly pointed out to relatives visiting from out of town; along with Lewis's, City Station and the Civic Hall, Quarry Hill was a Leeds landmark to be shown off — and if your aged aunt would not come to view these modern marvels in person you could send her tinted picture postcards of them.

As for my own unguided city tours: from the start my informal architectural field studies always embraced a few pleasing shopfronts. Many was the detour I took to gaze at the frontages of Boots, Cash Dispensing Chemists, Montague Burton the Tailor of Taste, or W.H. Smith & Son, Booksellers, Librarians, Newsagents, Stationers, simply because it gave me an inner glow to look at them. I had no idea what it was that pleased me about them — that Smith's with its fumed oak, pictorial tiles, chaste fascia lettering and newsboy hanging sign, was designed on Arts and Crafts principles, or that Boots and Burton's were classic examples of the use of decorated clerestory glazing: it was to be many years before I rationalised from books what as a boy I simply sensed.

The presence of some other shops on my itinerary was down less to good taste than to gusto. The Horse Meat Shop in the stew of tumbledown premises at the side of the Market was always a draw, principally because it took very little imagination to visualise the unappetising purplish joints and lumps of yellow fat in the window as horse, and partly because its frontage was painted in a vivid red, like blood; I liked to hear my mother tell me, as she often did, that it had to be painted this colour by law, to distinguish it from ordinary butchers' shops.

The herbalist's shop in Vicar Lane, with row upon row of little saucers containing powdered ginger, bee salve, prune and senna mixture, licorice root, cinnamon, dragon's blood (was it real dragon's blood?), was also good for a stare. So was the Murder Shop whose window display of scissors and kitchen knives I imagined in my confused way to be murder weapons. There was a secondhand bookshop at the bottom of Kirkgate where I could actually finger the old books in the nothing-over-sixpence trough outside, but it was to be some years before I would dare venture inside. Back to the modern: the Polyfoto studio on Boar Lane was a much talked about recent arrival to Leeds: the latest high-speed camera snapped twenty-four pictures of you and you selected those you wanted enlarged to the postcard or cabinet size from a specimen sheet. Examples of these multi-snap sheets were in the window and I would pause to count up in how many wasted exposures the subject was blinking.

The pork shops were always an attraction, and I would feast my eyes on their marble slabs of pies and pasties and polonies, not out of hunger but simply because these gastronomic displays were visually pleasing — particularly the bisected veal, ham and egg pies in Redman's in the County Arcade, which always left me puzzling how they got a whole hard-boiled egg into the middle of a meat pie. It was while I was figuring this out one day — they would cook an ordinary oblong pie, I reasoned, then scoop out an egg-shaped quantity of meat, then wedge the egg into the aperture, then seal the pie up again with some kind of edible glue — that I thought I spotted the Board Man keeping an eye on me from across the Arcade. It was not him at all, I saw at once, just someone waiting for his wife to come out of the corset shop; but it did set me wondering how I should explain things had the Board Man been following me and seen that while I had given barely a glance to the toy shop up the Arcade with its Meccano suspension bridge in the window, here I was staring at pork pies and previous to that at the Horse Meat Shop and the Murder Shop, and then Montague Burton the Tailor of Taste (not only did I admire Burton's decorated clerestory glazing but I was beginning to hanker after a Burton's suit).

It was, as I could readily acknowledge in moments of insight, weird behaviour for a boy of eight or nine. I suppose I was a weird child all round.

9 The wonder is that I never came to any harm in the course of my wanderings. It never swam into my head that I might. Streetwise I may have become to some extent, but I was still as sexually naïve as most children of my age. Child molesters were as remote a threat as Bluebeard. Occasionally in school assembly the headmaster would utter an obscure warning against strangers who might offer us sweets, but beyond thinking that chance would be a fine thing we never gave this improbable prospect any further contemplation, or if we did it stopped short at the sweet-offering stranger carrying us off in a sack — what his motive could be we had none of us the faintest idea. My mother, too, would sometimes, and to her own embarrassment, feel obliged to advise me to keep out of public lavatories but to go behind the bushes instead. I thought she was talking about hygiene.

No doubt somewhere in the length and breadth of Leeds sex reared its ugly head but not to my knowledge, and the subject was kept out of the papers, or anyway dressed in euphemisms that took it way above my head (this was when a body found cut up into small pieces could be described as "not interfered with"). Homosexuality was unknown — not only to a sexually witless child such as myself but, I would conjecture, to most of the adult population, at any rate of Middleton: certain men were known to be good to their mothers, and that was as far as it went.

There were some peculiar characters about, true — Silly Alan, as he was known, who went about in a school cap and was said to have been shell-shocked in the Great War; and Barmy Ginger who wore a yellow raincoat at all times of year and rode about on a bicycle making quacking noises: such as they were harmlessly at loose in the community long before the concept of being returned to the community was thought of, but beyond warning us euphemistically never to "go anywhere" with them or their like, our parents were

61

unconcerned. More serious cases were carted off to what was still called the lunatic asylum, at a place out on the edge of the moors called Menston. I always thought Menston merited a stare, but I had no idea where it was and could not persuade any of my elders to tell me − not because they thought my curiosity about the care of the insane in any way bizarre, but because adults simply did not answer questions put to them by children: if I asked my mother who was the man she was just talking to at the door, she would reply cryptically, "Him on the Quaker Oat box."

Some odd characters were to be found in Town also; but these were "characters" in inverted commas, well-known local personalities, part of the passing show − every town had its company of street eccentrics at that time. Our star "character" was Woodbine Lizzie, a grimy-faced lady tramp who wore a tram conductor's cap, hobnailed boots and three or four overcoats including an army greatcoat, who used to stand outside a public house called the Whip, aggressively demanding Woodbines from all who passed by. Of course there were stories that Woodbine Lizzie was high-born, the illegitimate daughter of a duke and so on; in fact she had been a mother with six children living out in Pudsey, where the crows fly backwards (to keep the soot out of their eyes); something had snapped and she had become what would nowadays be called a bag lady. Her bedroom was a park bench on Woodhouse Moor, the cinder-paved inner north Leeds equivalent of Hunslet Moor. Having heard of Woodbine Lizzie almost since birth − she was more famous even than the royal personage, a gibbering lunatic, who local legend had it was locked in a garret in Harewood House, just outside Leeds − I judged her worth a stare. Catching me at it, she streamed tobacco juice in my direction.

Our supporting, second-billing "character" was the deformed shoe black who was always to be seen outside Trinity Church in Boar Lane. His useless legs were tucked away behind his back, giving the impression of a man with no legs at all, and he propelled himself about on a small bogie, a rough cart on pram wheels, clutching well-worn wooden blocks to push himself along. Naturally he had his own mythology too: it was widely believed that when he got home to Hunslet each evening he would straighten up, put the bogie under his arm and walk into his house like any normal person. Seeking clues to this supposed imposture I gave him one of my longest stares until he told me to go away.

Other than the tram conductor, and the odd Market stallholder if I had any money to buy anything, the Trinity Church shoe black was the only person in Town who had so far spoken to me. These were completely solitary explorations of mine and I never sought company. I had no need to: I was an immensely self-contained child, and such conversational nourishment as I needed to sustain me took place inside my head. But I must have been noticed: a pale-faced, staring, wandering boy must have stood out among this teeming Township of adults and their infants. Yet no one ever asked me what I was about, not even those who were recognisably – and reassuringly, so long as they kept their distance – official personages such as tramways inspectors, commissionaires, railway porters and the like, not to mention policemen.

I did once become aware that a stranger was taking an interest in me. This was in City Square, where there were then public lavatories. Down in the Gents' I noticed that a man in a belted mackintosh and soft-brimmed hat, which made him look altogether too much like a detective for my peace of mind, had his eye on me as he slowly lit a cigarette while loitering under the "No Loitering" sign. I climbed the steps up into the Square as casually as I could and went to stare at one of the nymphs. There was a legend that at midnight the torch-bearing young hussies came down off their plinths and danced, and while it was still broad daylight and I did not expect any hint of terpsichorean activity, I was always on the lookout for some sign that the nymphs had changed their posture since my last visit. Convinced that Eve, the particular bronze lady I had under scrutiny, had switched her weight from one foot to the other, I was giving her a good long stare when I saw that the stranger had followed me up out of the lavatories and was having a good long stare at me. As he began to saunter towards me I felt a frisson of panic; but then, noticing, I think, that the City Square newsvendor was giving him a good long stare in turn, he changed his mind and walked quickly away. Not a detective after all. For the benefit of the newsvendor, who could himself have been a detective and master of disguise, I looked earnestly at my white card as if checking an address and marched decisively off in the opposite direction.

The Dark Arches, not two minutes from City Square, were genuinely dangerous – there had been more than one murder down there, and muggings, to use a then non-existent term, without number. So naturally I wanted to go and have a look at them. What I did not know at the time was that the Dark Arches were notoriously the haunt of sex deviants of every kind.

Even today, when the area has been gentrified into the north's answer to Camden Lock, the vaulted tunnels still have a sinister air. Then, when they were practically pitch dark, the only light seeping in from the culverts below my feet through which coursed the seething waters, they were positively frightening. Was there anybody lurking in the shadows? I couldn't be sure, but halfway through the dank vaults I did hear echoing footsteps other than my own – unless they were my own re-echoing. By starting to count up to eighteen million – the number of bricks used in the Dark Arches' construction, so I had heard or read – I managed to keep at bay the certain knowledge that there were black rats scuffling and sniffling around my ankles. I got through somehow, and somehow got through unscathed, and never went there again.

The river which flowed under the Dark Arches, on the other hand, unwisely became one of my haunts. I had lately become acquainted with the stories of W.W. Jacobs – adult books, but I had been allowed to commandeer all the family's library tickets in consideration of an undertaking to bring back my brother Kenneth a Crime Club novel and my sister Stella a romance ("Not an *I* book," she would stipulate, which ruled out *Jane Eyre*) whenever I changed my books, and so I had the run of the grown-up library. One evening, selecting a third-person novel by Naomi Jacob to whose work my sister had taken a fancy, I espied a row of books by W.W. Jacobs and out of curiosity took one out. Most of my reading was inspired by this kind of serendipity: I discovered Evelyn Waugh's row of works by looking among the W's to see if there was yet any writer called Waterhouse.

Jacobs's village tales I didn't much care for, being too countrified by half for me; *The Monkey's Paw* and suchlike macabre stories I enjoyed; but most of all I relished the night watchman's yarns of the rogues and vagabonds aboard the bobbing tramp steamers and barges around the East India Docks. This dockland sounded right up my street and I resolved to go there one day.

But then I was delighted to discover, upon venturing off Leeds Bridge and along the river walk one afternoon, that we had a dockland of our own in Leeds. I spent many hours absorbing it, either on my white card voyages or as representative of the Middleton Hiking Club. There was a constant traffic of boats and barges in and out of the timber yards, coal wharves and olive oil and wool sheds below Warehouse Hill; the sun glittered on a thousand warehouse windows and once I heard funeral hymns being sung in the tiny riverside mission church. I found it all incredibly romantic, as any boy would. I wandered then through dark alleys and found the quieter waters of the Aire and Calder Navigation and pottered about around the locks and canal basins. Here it could be very quiet, and when the sun went in I could feel a sudden chill, but having no previous experience of premonition I did not know I was scenting danger. But, as in the Dark Arches, my guardian angel was watching over me and I came to no harm.

My one real moment of peril, when it did come, was in the very centre of Town, and not even in one of the twisting gas-lit alleys behind the city streets, but in busy Briggate itself, outside Lewis's. I had just emerged from the store and was wondering what to do next, whether to go down and look at the Horse Meat Shop or at another interesting shop I had found which sold false limbs, when a very kind gentleman, small of stature and wearing a grubby raincoat – that is all I can remember about his appearance – came up to me and explained that since it was his birthday he would like to give me a shilling.

I thanked him very much: I had been warned against taking sweets from strangers but no one had said anything about shillings, and it was an enormous sum. With a shilling I could buy a milkshake at the White Rose milk bar across the street and still have eightpence over, perhaps for a soft ice-cream and a chocolate eclair at Lewis's soda fountain. I had always wanted a chocolate eclair of my own.

But the kind gentleman had other plans. He would furthermore like, this being his birthday, to take me to the pictures. I didn't particularly want to go to the pictures – with all this money in my possession there were picture houses around Middleton I could go to, and in my own free time rather than in precious white card time – but having accepted his shilling it seemed churlish to refuse. Clutching the coin in one hand and placing the other trustingly in his, I allowed myself to be led over not to the Paramount super-cinema opposite, whose Wurlitzer organ I wouldn't have minded seeing rise out of the floorboards, but to the rather fly-blown Tower Picture House a little way up Briggate, noted for its cheap prices.

Of the performance I can remember nothing save that the main film was Gary Cooper in *The Adventures of Marco Polo*, that the cinema was nearly empty at this early hour, and that the kind gentleman for reasons of his own wanted to rest his hand lightly on my knee, which I found slightly embarrassing. But he had not offered me sweets; I was rather surprised that no sweets were forthcoming, since it was his birthday and he was pushing the boat out.

When we came out of the cinema I thought it was high time I was making tracks for home, but I didn't quite know how to detach myself from the kind gentleman's company. Confessing an interest in old buildings and firmly gripping my left hand while I with my right hand firmly gripped my shilling, he led me across Briggate to the church of St John the Evangelist opposite.

I still had no sense of danger: my only concern was that the kind gentleman didn't seem to know when he had outstayed his welcome and would be difficult to shake off. He pushed open the wooden gates of the churchyard. Although it would still be some months before war was declared, public shelters and static water tanks were appearing all over Leeds, and there was a brick shelter among the gravestones of St John's.

The kind gentleman seemed as interested in air raid shelters as he was in old buildings – more so, indeed. He said he had always wondered what they were like inside and asked if I had ever been in one. Although I wasn't going to let on, I had, as a matter of fact, once made it my business to inspect one of the shelters down at Quarry Hill Flats. It was dark and smelled of cat pee. The kind gentleman's grip had transferred itself from my hand to my wrist and had tightened; as he reiterated that he would like to see inside the air raid shelter I realised at last that he was not such a kind gentleman after all and that he was prepared to drag me into the shelter if necessary.

Although we were but feet from the teeming pavement of Briggate, the entrance to the blank-walled air raid shelter was round the back, out of sight of passers-by. Alarm bells rang inside my head and with a mighty effort I tugged myself free of the not so kind gentleman's grasp and tore out of the churchyard and across Briggate, narrowly missing being sliced in two by an approaching tram. I ran all the way down the Lower Headrow and threw myself headlong through the swinging doors of the Vicar Lane end of the Market. Here I felt among friends. I dodged through the length of the Market, zigzagging around the stalls in case I was being followed, and came out at the far end near the Corn Exchange, where, barely giving my Bovril sign a glance, I hurried to the sanctity of the No. 12 tram stop.

All this time I was clutching my shilling, which I now felt to be contaminated money. Although at the very last second I had managed to extricate myself from some unimaginable fate, I regarded myself, in an obscure way, as tainted, and was anxious to wipe my predatory benefactor and his gift from my mind. I considered giving it to my mother with the explanation that I had found it in the street; but then I thought it would taint her too. The church collection box was rejected for the same reason. I debated whether to present the money to Woodbine Lizzie on my next trip to Town but decided that the gesture would draw too much attention to myself. In the end the shilling went into the funds of the Middleton Hiking Club and was frittered away on sweets and lemonade within the week. I had no more alarming adventures. I was now streetwise.

10 All these excursions had to be paid for, naturally, and it was not every day that strangers were handing out shillings on the street.

One source of revenue was the handleless teacup in the chocolate-brown cupboard by the hearth, half filled with worn Victorian pennies for the gas meter. (There was a theory, based on what scientific evidence I have no idea, that the thinner the penny the more gas you got for your money, the belief being that thick coins caused the dials to go round faster.) Provided the Plimsoll line of pennies was not too low, and being ever careful not to carry the pitcher to the well too often, I could rely on perhaps twopence or threepence a fortnight from the gas money, enough for a return tram ride into Town plus light refreshments at Granelli's sarsaparilla stall at the entrance to Kirkgate Market, or for a sustaining bag of chips on the Middleton Hiking Club's continuing explorations into the interior of Hunslet.

Another source was my income, legitimate and otherwise, from my first ever employment, as a choirboy with the Church of the Holy Cross, aka the Holy Hoss (Horse). Having learned, at the age of eight, that the Holy Hoss choir paid the astounding rate of ninepence a quarter to its juvenile members, I auditioned with a rendering, in my bell-clear treble, of "There is a green hill far away, without a city wall", a rendering so well received that I was later emboldened to offer it as my contribution to the 23rd SE Leeds Wolf Cubs' Christmas concert, when I was mortified to be told it was not suitable.

My ninepence a quarter was augmented by the tithe I regularly extracted, with the aid of the bread knife, from the church funds collection box that was issued to all choir members to rattle in the faces of their relatives and acquaintances. Given that the box was in the shape of the Holy Cross itself and that its predominant colour was an awesomely ecclesiastical purple, I was keenly aware as I prised out my illicit share of the takings that I was committing a mortal sin. Consequently each act of theft was always accompanied by a prayer, when I would set out to convince God that He must regard these twopences and threepences as a loan, and that He would be getting His money back with interest one of these fine days. My failure to donate the kind gentleman's shilling to the church probably scotched that particular piece of special pleading. But even had it been put to me that in helping to finance my trips into Town in this way I was paving my path to Hell, I should have settled for the Bovril sign and the Arcade tableaux vivant and the Majestic news scanner and the trams squashing spilled blood oranges to pulp as they rocked past the back of the Market, and let my chance of any future, further heaven go.

Another and far more audacious criminal activity, which would have led me straight through the gates of Shadwell Reformatory had it gone wrong, was the lucrative Yorkshire Penny Bank Forgery (twenty-odd years later to be turned to even greater profit as the basis of a short story).

The Yorkshire Penny Bank — now the Yorkshire Bank and no longer even Yorkshire-owned — was the people's bank, with reassuringly Corinthian-columned branches in even the poorest suburbs. Several times I had jumped up and down outside the tall windows of its headquarters building in Town, just to catch a glimpse of its mahogany-lined, commissionaire-protected interior. I felt I had a personal interest in the institution, for it was known to every child as our very own school bank, its management having hatched out a scheme whereby every Monday morning all the teachers in all the schools in Leeds turned themselves into unpaid bank clerks for half an hour while they collected our threepences and sixpences and entered them in the blue, linen-covered miniature paying-in books issued by the Bank. While no one ever said it was compulsory to have a Yorkshire Penny Bank account from the age of about eight onwards, no one ever said it wasn't, and some faint social stigma attached to those who did not come to school on Monday mornings clutching a threepenny or sixpenny bit wrapped in a scrap of newspaper.

Having seen a good deal of Leeds by now I was developing a hankering to have a look at Bradford. Bradford was regarded as pretty well our twin city, certainly our rival city. Plum-coloured

Bradford Corporation buses went from City Square, and Bradford LNER trains from the misnamed Central Station well out of the city centre. It was also well known that you could travel to Bradford all the way by tram, changing at a distant Leeds terminus and crossing a no-man's-land of cinders to the Bradford border.

Bradford was accessible. I had not costed such an ambitious excursion but I reckoned that it would be realistic to capitalise the venture at a shilling. My weekly contribution to the Yorkshire Penny Bank was threepence. I could be in Bradford within a month.

The money would have tobe repaid some time, somehow, of course. While my mother was not in the habit of inspecting my bank book week by week, she was bound to check it sooner or later, upon which − I had my story already worked out − I should explain that the teacher had been too busy to mark it up lately, but that every penny was accounted for in his register whenever she wished to draw our savings out. This she would undoubtedly wish to do at once. There would be a shilling to find.

This was an impossibly large sum to conjure out of thin air, and short of out-and-out theft, for which I had had little appetite ever since the gates of Shadwell had clanged upon an ashen-faced classmate after he had been found stealing from the teachers' common room, my only hope was that the day of reckoning would coincide with the three-monthly payout from the Holy Cross choir, which I could augment with coppers saved by forgetting to pay in my school milk money, or, when despatched to the fish and chip shop for five twopenny pieces and sixpennorth, buying only fourpennorth of chips in the hope that no one would notice (they always did). The sensible thing would have been to wait until I had the Holy Cross stipend in my hand before embarking on the Bradford adventure; but I was too impatient to cross that cinder-patch frontier.

In the event I was never to get to Bradford, or at least not at that stage in my exploring career. On the first Monday morning upon having hatched my plan I duly withheld the Yorkshire Penny Bank's threepence, telling the teacher without a blink that my mother could not afford it this week − a common excuse for every kind of non-payment, and one which was always accepted without comment except, semi-sotto voce, from the snickering plimsolled have-nots in the back row. My explanation was rendered more convincing by the circumstance that my account was currently empty, my life savings of half a crown or so having been withdrawn the previous week to pay for some household necessity or other. Thus I should have raised a quarter of my required capital. Alas, the threepenny bit did not survive the week; like the kind gentleman's shilling it was squandered on aniseed balls and licorice allsorts. Despite my assurances to myself that this was a one-off indulgence and that next Monday the savings programme would begin in earnest, the following week's threepence went the same way – and the next week's, and the next.

By now, the Bradford adventure indefinitely shelved, I had begun to regard the Yorkshire Penny Bank contributions as part of my income. I had unleashed a voracious appetite for sweetmeats that had to be fed. One week I invested in a foot-long bar of everlasting toffee that so much lived up to its name that I could not finish it even by dawdling the long way home from school. I was obliged to bury it in the hole I was digging to Australia. Much later, when my brothers requisitioned the hole as part of the foundations for the Anderson air-raid shelter that we and every other family were by now erecting, I felt as Christie must have done when the police came to dig up the floorboards of No. 10 Rillington Place. But the remains of my bar of everlasting toffee were never unearthed; or if they were, nobody disclosed the fact.

By the time the inevitable day came round when my mother took it into her head to examine my bank book, it was all of one and sixpence in the red. The expected scene took place – what a way to run a school bank etc. I had all my answers ready, even for the contingency that my mother might decide to go down to the school in person and sort the matter out (teacher off ill). Happily this nightmare scenario did not arise, but as expected I was ordered to close down my Yorkshire Penny Bank account instantly. I had until Monday to find one and six.

But how? My Holy Cross quarterly ninepence, always erratic, had yet to materialise. The gas money was low. I had but one possible source of quick revenue, and that was the 23rd SE Leeds Wolf Cub pack's impending trip to Belle Vue Zoo, Manchester, for which intended participants had been paying in threepence a week for some weeks past. There was two shillings in the kitty so far – one and six plus sixpence over.

An interview with Baloo was called for – a matter for some apprehension. Baloo, a lady so heavily moustached that she was almost a Kipling lookalike, was the assistant cub mistress who attended to administrative matters such as this. She was believed to be in love with Akela, a remote figure approachable only by those of the rank of sixer and above. Whatever Baloo's feelings for Akela, there was certainly no love lost between Baloo and me. Baloo it had been who had scotched my notion of singing "There is a green hill far away" at the Christmas concert. Then, when I had concocted a little magazine called the *Wolf Cub Weekly* and painstakingly made six copies of it with their pages neatly stitched together with needle and thread, she had confiscated the entire issue on the grounds that my illustrated article on knot-tying might be – not was, might be – misleading. I hated Baloo and I believe she hated me for the odd creature I was, but she had to be faced.

On cub night, Friday, therefore, I approached Baloo and put it to her that after all I would not be going on the Belle Vue trip, since it clashed with a projected family outing to Bridlington, so please could I have my money back. Baloo, knowing full well that we did not possess the means to get collectively past the end of the street, was deeply suspicious, and asked, cunningly it seemed to me, if I would like her to go and see my mother and talk it over. Equally cunning, I intimated that it was not my mother but my Uncle Edward she ought to be talking to, since it was in his car that we would be going to Bridlington, and in his caravan that we would be spending the weekend. This supplementary piece of misinformation seemed to convince Baloo and after Taps she handed over a florin in a clean white envelope.

A forged withdrawal from the Yorkshire Penny Bank would require red ink. Luckily there was for some reason a supply in the house, otherwise I should have had to sink my surplus sixpence in the purchase of a bottle. As it was, it went into a quarter-pound of Dairy Box chocolates, then new on the market, which I had seen in the window of the Tivoli Chocolate Cabin and coveted. They took even longer to eat than everlasting toffee, and I couldn't finish them. Sooner than bury them in my hole to Australia I took the remaining two or three caramel cups and nut clusters home with me and told my mother that our teacher had come to school with an enormous box of chocolates and handed them round. She was even more suspicious than Baloo had been, but I was able to mollify her with the production of one and sixpence in cash and a Yorkshire Penny Bank book in which, during her absence at the shops over the weekend, I had forged, with a fair imitation of my teacher's scrawled initials, the blue ink entry of six sums of threepence paid over in successive

73

weeks, and the red ink entry of one shilling and sixpence withdrawn, the transaction being neatly ruled off with a double red line. Should my mother wish to re-open the Yorkshire Penny Bank account at some future date — I doubted that she would, and she never did — then I would tear the bank book into shreds and declare it lost.

I was not out of the wood yet, although it was some consolation that the wood was more garlanded with confectionery than the one frequented by Hansel and Gretel. I thought it prudent not to mention to my mother that I had opted out of the Belle Vue Zoo venture and so threepences continued to be provided towards the trip over the next four weeks, when the fund was supposed to be maximised at three shillings. These threepences, needless to say, went on sweets. I was by now sated on slab toffee and all-day suckers — this was a time when threepence would buy you thirty chocolate caramels or six sherbet dabs — and I almost longed for the day when the endless supply of threepenny bits would dry up.

When it did, I had a problem. I had not thought too deeply about what I proposed to do about that fateful Saturday when the 23rd SE Leeds pack would be roaming around Belle Vue — secretly I hoped that the outing would be rained off, or that three shillings would fall out of the sky and I should be able to go on it after all. I now bitterly regretted having frittered all that money away — I didn't particularly want to see the zoo, but I did want to see Manchester.

The black letter day dawned. I had thought of feigning illness but rejected the idea in case my mother demanded her money back. There was nothing for it but to go through the motions. Accordingly I rose at six and was in my uniform, neckerchief straight and green garter tabs in position, by half past, and with a packed lunch and a packed tea inside my rolled-up mackintosh. My last fear was that my mother would insist on accompanying me to the Holy Cross scout hut from which the coach — a Sammy Ledgard one, of course — was to depart. But she didn't. She gave me twopence to spend on myself, counselled me to go to the lavatory before embarking on the return journey, and waved me on my way.

With twopence I could get to Town and back and have a penny for a glass of sarsaparilla in the Market. But in my uniform I felt too conspicuous: I would be a marked boy. For the same reason I rejected the streets of Hunslet. I headed, instead, for the park. If questioned, I would explain that the rest of the pack were roaming about in the rhododendrons playing hide and seek. The park was not

74

even open at that hour and I had a considerable amount of trudging up and down to do before a uniformed ranger finally appeared and unlocked the gates. I filled in some of the time wandering down to the old parish church of St Mary's where my father was buried, and staring at his grave for a while.

It was the longest day. I walked several times around the boating lake, skimmed stones across it until my arm ached, played on the swings until the melancholy creak of their chains induced tears of self-pity, traipsed aimlessly through the Murder Woods, set off to crawl through my storm drain but found it silted with mud, went and looked at the colliery and the coal railway, and then ate my lunch of potted meat sandwiches and seed cake. It could not yet have been nine o'clock. I resumed my meanderings, spent my twopence on chocolate macaroons in the park café, visited the drinking fountain for the tenth time, carved my initials in the old men's shelter with a piece of broken bottle, ate my packed tea, trudged back into the Murder Woods and had a lie down.

When I woke up it was pitch dark. There was a lot of rustling going on among the ferns and I was quite frightened. I hurried out of the park, fearful that the gates would be locked, but they were still open. I had no idea what time it was – the only nearby clock was on the tower of St Mary's but it would be far too dark to see it. So far as I knew it got dark at this time of year around nine o'clock – I could not say for certain for I had developed a minor neurosis which compelled me to close my eyes at seven p.m. promptly and not open them again until morning, otherwise I should sleep in and be late for school. I kept to this regime so rigidly that I would not open my eyes even to get up and go to the lavatory, and one day when my brother Dennis went on a school trip to Filey and came home late at night with a souvenir cardboard telescope, I refused to open my eyes to look at it but sat up in bed and felt it like a blind man, and put it to a blind eye like Nelson.

My mother was in the scullery when I got home, washing clothes and straining her eyes in the gloom to save electricity. It meant that she did not notice the filthy state I was in. She gave me a slice of bread and dripping and a mug of cocoa and allowed me to prattle on about the animals I claimed to have seen. I had mugged them up in Arthur Mee's *Children's Encyclopedia* at school so my account of the chimps' tea party and the elephants squirting water over one another was pretty convincing, or so I thought. My mother showed no signs of disbelief and my only worry was that it was long past my curfew and I should be late for church in the morning.

The next day the conversation in the Holy Cross vestry was exlusively and excitedly about Saturday's total eclipse of the sun, which had plunged our little world into darkness at around lunchtime. It could not possibly have been later than one in the afternoon when I got home from my fictitious journey across the Pennines. Yet my mother never asked me, then or ever, how I could have got to Manchester and back in so short a time, nor did she ever question my colourful account of a day at the zoo.

I have often wondered how much my mother secretly knew about my bizarre goings-on — the white card truancies, the wanderings around Hunslet, the petty thefts from the gas money, the childish figures in my bank book. She regarded me, I know, as a strange, mutant child — she was at the same time proud of me but, I believe, a little frightened of me. She seemed to have blind faith in my ability to do whatever I set out to do — she bought me that manuscript paper from Banks's music arcade when I was set upon becoming a composer, notebook and pencils when I decided I wanted to be a writer, a battered old volume of the plays of J.M. Barrie, which I still have, when I showed an interest in the theatre. Once, because she had heard me mention the magazine *Punch*, she bought me a bundle of back numbers, circa 1920, from Stringer's bookstall in Kirkgate Market — a periodical that would have been as comprehensible to her as *Pravda*. Another time, having heard me trying to speak French from some phrases in a public school story I was reading, she came home with a secondhand copy of Daudet's *Lettres de mon Moulin*. When, a few years on, my own stories and articles began to get published, she never showed the slightest surprise nor made any comment, although when I got to Fleet Street I did hear that she had remarked to someone that it was a pity my father wasn't alive, as he would have liked to have seen how her cuckoo in the nest had risen in the world.

The Yorkshire Penny Bank forgery marked the end of my criminal career, for shortly afterwards I gained a regular income of two shillings a week as a paper boy, contrary to the provisions of the Children and Young Persons Act of 1933 which required me to be two years older before I could legitimately hoist the *Yorkshire Evening Post*'s hessian satchel across my shoulder. My first round was the evening one, when I lived in hopes of being summoned to run

76

through the streets shouting "Special! Murder! Special!" The call never came; but in due course I was awarded a second round, and then a morning round. In the fullness of time I had five newspaper rounds: two morning, two evening and one Sunday. In addition, I was assigned the task of collecting the paper money in my spare time. By now, I was earning twelve and sixpence a week.

A perk of my newspaper rounds was that I got to read my fill of comics and magazines. I had noticed that while most of the weekly papers came out on Tuesday or Wednesday, their publication date was always given as the Saturday. I therefore saw no harm in delaying delivery by a day or two until I had read them; my own house being on one of my rounds I made it a habit to drop in with a pile of literature which I would squat under a sofa cushion to read at my leisure. Thus I had access to the expensive twopenny comics like *Tiger Tim's Weekly* and *Playbox*, as well as to the D.C. Thomson "Big Five" – the *Hotspur*, the *Wizard*, the *Rover*, *Adventure* and the *Skipper*; and popular magazines such as *Answers*, *Titbits* and *John Bull* (for which, twenty years later, I was to write a moonlighting weekly column under a pseudonym). To my regret there was no call on our estate for the *Strand* magazine, price one shilling, which I had seen on W.H. Smith's railway bookstall and which was currently running the Eggs, Beans and Crumpets stories by P.G. Wodehouse; but we did have one customer for the twopenny journal *John O' London's Weekly* which I read avidly before passing it on to its rightful owner, a lonesome-looking, owlish figure who was said to be very good to his mother. That a literary weekly crammed with articles on the likes of Hardy, Victor Hugo, Shaw, Wells, Arnold Bennett, could be successfully targeted at the working classes, or anyway at a night school audience of aspiring clerks and office boys, now seems incredible. My illicit reading of *John O'London's* taught me a good deal about books and their authors; and in due course I subscribed to it myself.

But I was still at an age when my favourite reading was the comics, and of all the papers at my disposal – the *Butterfly*, *Chips*, *Comic Cuts*, *Crackers*, *Funny Wonder*, the *Jester*, the *Joker*, *Jingles*, *Larks*, the *Sparkler*, *Tip-Top*, the *Dandy*, the *Beano* – my favourite was the black-and-white *Film Fun*, with Laurel and Hardy on the front and back covers. Just as I had accepted that the priceless pair, as they were billed, came regularly to Leeds to act behind the magnifying-glass screens of the Tivoli, the Crescent and the Rex, running or catching the tram from one cinema engagement to the next, so did I entirely accept the *Film Fun* artists' proposition that they and all the rest of the paper's characters – Old Mother Riley, George Formby, Harold Lloyd, Wheeler and Woolsey – lived in the equivalent of Hunslet terraces, ever threatened by top-hatted rapacious landlords, their only access to wealth being the occasional feed at the Hotel de Posh as a reward for catching a striped-jerseyed burglar, or a charabanc visit to Shrimpton-on-Sea. I think I was ten before I gave up hopes of bumping into Laurel and Hardy or Frank Randle outside the Joseph Street baths.

My newspaper rounds not only provided me with a considerable income, even after I had donated three-fifths of it to the hard-pressed family coffers, but they gave me a taste for earning money. It was a lark.

On Saturday mornings, equipped with a soapbox on pram wheels which my brothers had knocked up for me, I would station myself outside the Thrift Stores and volunteer to transport old ladies' groceries home for them (this was when a stone of flour was still a regular part of the grocery order), for which my reward was usually twopence, or, in the case of the Little Sisters of the Poor who were most generous, threepence. Another Saturday morning activity was to hop on an errand boy's bike and cycle down to the Walls factory to restock the fridge for the newsagent who employed me as a paper boy; this would add another sixpence to my earnings. Then on Saturday afternoons I would often go golf-caddying for a shilling, a back-breaking chore in the days before golf carts. In due course I secured a regular Saturday afternoon job, in tandem with my friend Eric Bright – a three-and-sixpence-a-week contract to clean out a cobbler's shop, which involved clambering around the innards of a leather-grinding machine, from which I would emerge covered from head to foot in leather dust and stinking of hide like a cobbler's water baby. Eric went to work for the shop full time after leaving school, and subsequently inherited the business which he runs to this day. He is welcome to it.

Cleaning windows was another sideline – ground floor flats only, since I had no ladder -- as was my firewood round: a bucket of raw wood chips for twopence, ransacked from council building sites and chopped with the lethal family hatchet over a brick. All in all, I was earning almost as much as I was to make in my first job after leaving school a few years later. While these activities did limit the outings of the Middleton Hiking Club except in the holidays, my expeditions into Town were carried off in some style, and I was no stranger to the soda fountain at Lewis's.

11 At some very early point in my life, possibly on the occasion of his death in 1932, although I would have been only three years old, I saw a picture of Edgar Wallace in the paper which was to have the most profound influence on my future.

It was of Wallace wearing the peaked cap of a Reuter's war correspondent when covering the Boer War. Shortly afterwards, on what must have been one of my first journeys into Town with my mother, I observed that the two newsvendors standing under the Bovril sign opposite the Corn Exchange also wore peaked caps, one emblazoned with the legend Y.E. POST, the other Y.E. NEWS. These, I reasoned, would be newspaper reporters like Edgar Wallace. Wearing their peaked caps and carrying their spiral notebooks, they would set off in the morning to find out all the news that was going. This they would write up, and the papers would print what they had written. The reporters would then don their hessian satchels and set off with quires of newspapers fresh off the presses, which they would sell opposite the Corn Exchange and other strategic points. This seemed to me an altogether agreeable way of earning a living, and from that day forward I never seriously contemplated spending my working life in any other fashion.

My resolve to follow Edgar Wallace's footsteps was considerably strengthened at the age of nine when Margaret Lane published her colourful biography of Wallace. Having learned about this from the pages of *John O' London's*, I promptly borrowed the book from the public library on one of my brothers' tickets and devoured it at a single sitting, crouching over the fire with my knees mottling bright red. I have re-read it once a year or so ever since. Wallace's romantic career – from street urchin to soldier poet, war correspondent, prolific journalist and novelist, dramatist, racehorse owner, Hollywood scriptwriter – was so crammed with adventure that the idea of pursuing any other course, even though he died with

81

liabilities of £140,000, seemed unthinkable.

The other great influence on me was the theatre, but despite the example of Edgar Wallace who had six West End plays on in two years, this did not immediately strike me with the same thunderclap enthusiasm as my passion for journalism.

Like every other child in the north I was taken annually to the pantomime, although not usually until around April when the seats were cheaper (it was not unknown for the Leeds pantos to run on into the summer), and always to the Theatre Royal where the cut-price seats were cheaper than the Grand. We would perch up in the balcony, which raked so steeply that I went through the evening clutching my wooden arm-rests for fear of being pitched down into the stalls. I did not become a pantomime addict. While I enjoyed the transformation scenes and Kirby's Sensational Flying Ballet, I found the straight scenes leaden and the knockabout stuff involving bailiffs and dames inferior to what I could get from Old Mother Riley and Co. at the pictures. The audience participation spots ("He's behind you!") were a good excuse for indulging in juvenile hysteria, but in truth I was more impressed by the occasion than the event − being taken into Town in the evening when the trams and the streets were all lit up, queuing under a lamp-twinkling frosted glass canopy before the doors were open, the real live "augmented" orchestra playing the National Anthem before the performance instead of after it like the cinemas, the pungent stench of oranges that gradually permeated the whole theatre, the safety curtain − "For thine especial safety" − in the interval, and the lantern slide advertisements for Melbourne Ales, Sparkling Phosferrade and the King Charles First restaurant ("opposite circle entrance").

The panto apart, my first visit to the theatre was to the Leeds Moss Empire, when out of the proceeds of an afternoon's golf-caddying I treated my mother to a seat in the gods to watch the *Billy Cotton Band Show*, a favourite of hers on the wireless. I cannot remember who else was on the bill but they would have been mainly radio personalities of the order of Stainless Stephen whose gimmick, indeed his entire act, was to speak the punctuation marks in his patter; or Nosmo King who took his name from the No Smoking sign in a railway carriage and specialised in maudlin monologues; or Revnell and West who dressed up as schoolgirls; or any of a dozen comedians and comediennes whose faces I had hitherto seen only in the pages of the *Radio Fun* comic. It was interesting to identify them in the flesh, but while it was a red-letter evening I cannot claim to have yet been hooked on the theatre, which I regarded as very much an occasional divertissement like Belle Vue Zoo or Hunslet Feast, and not something that would become a part of the fabric of my life.

My conversion came about in a convoluted way. A fondness for the Red Circle school stories in borrowed copies of the *Hotspur* (Billy Bunter, Greyfriars and the *Magnet* were unheard of on our side of Leeds) had led me to start taking public school yarns out of the public library – among them, selected only because it was a big thick book, *Mike* by P.G. Wodehouse, which I recognised as being far superior to any of the stuff in that genre I had so far come across. *Mike* of course introduces Psmith, the very first of Wodehouse's gallery of comic characters. Browsing in the adult library, I subsequently came across, with my usual serendipity, a couple more Psmith stories – *Psmith in the City* and *Psmith Journalist*. These were enough to start me on a course of reading everything Wodehouse had published, and before long I was his disciple, able to quote long passages of his work years before I knew how to pronounce his name properly, and writing stories in what I believed to be an exact imitation of the Master's style.

One Saturday I read in the "Stage and Screen" notes in the *Yorkshire Evening Post* that a play adapted by my hero from the Hungarian of Ferenc Molnar, and starring Clive Brook, would be coming to the Grand Theatre the forthcoming week. It was *The Play's The Thing*, a touring revival, I imagine. I had never heard of Molnar nor of Clive Brook either but I would have walked to Bradford to see P.G. Wodehouse's name on a theatre programme, such was the extent of my fan-worship. Accordingly, the following Saturday I played truant from my stint at the cobbler's shop and took myself off to the matinee performance of *The Play's The Thing*. This was on my own: although my mother enjoyed the occasional play on the radio, I did not think Wodehouse's adaptation of a writer from a far-off country of which we knew little would be quite her cup of tea.

While I found the Grand an intimidating institution, a gilded palace in comparison with the rather down-at-heel Theatre Royal, and bristling with strange varnished signboards indicating *loges* and *fauteuils*, it was a great adventure; but on this occasion, as the afternoon wore on, even the thrill of being at the theatre by myself could not deflect from the excitement of what was going on down there on the stage. The play was indeed the thing. I was grabbed.

I cannot at this distance recall a single thing about the plot, the cast or the set. What I do remember, vividly, is the Act II curtain, which was an eye-opener. The characters start to argue about how they would end the act if life were a play. One of them delivers his idea of a curtain line and the curtain begins to come down – only for it to be halted by another, who has a far better ending. As the argument continues, so the curtain yo-yos up and down until, to roars of applause and laughter, they find an ending to Act II to suit all tastes. I found the device more theatrically breathtaking even than the transformation scene in *Cinderella* (and indeed was so impressed by its audacity that fifty years later I stole it for the ending of my play *Bookends* starring Michael Hordern and Dinsdale Landen). In those few anarchistic moments I had learned that the dramatist has manipulative powers equal to those of any wizard, and from then on the theatre had me in thrall. I went as often as the string of odd jobs that provided me with the means for theatregoing permitted. The Theatre Royal was the home of a thriving weekly rep company, Francis Laidler's Court Players, where a seat cost all of fourpence, so that as well as the post- or pre-West End touring productions at the Grand I saw a fair selection of the standard Thirties repertoire together with a certain amount of junk theatre in the way of bad detective plays and sub-Rattigan light comedies. I lapped it all up uncritically.

But life was not all the bright lights of the theatre and the Bovril sign. While I would sneak off to Town or into the bowels of Hunslet at every opportunity, like every boy of my age I spent the greater part of my spare time either at home or in the near vicinity, especially in winter when the nights were dark. Although I played my quota of street games I preferred to be indoors, where I could indulge my twin obsessions with journalism and the theatre.

Almost from the moment I learned to read and write I was making up little magazines, hand-printed on any scrap of paper I could find or on cheap scribbling blocks foraged from the Market by my mother, in purple ink which I manufactured by extracting the lead from indelible pencils and grinding it up into powder.

Most of these publications, like the *Wolf Cub Weekly* banned by Baloo, ran for only one issue – and at least one, the *Middleton Evening Argus*, not even that, since I could not find any news to put in it; but where readership surveys indicated a favourable response (the readership usually consisted solely of my mother), then some of my efforts might flourish for six or seven numbers. One such was *Ronnie Rabbit's Weekly*, intended as a direct rival to *Mickey Mouse Weekly* and featuring the adventures of Ronnie Rabbit, Percy Pig, Freddy Frog and any other alliterative creatures I found easy to draw and colour in with crayons. Another long-runner was the *Flag*, a monthly short story magazine in imitation of the *Strand*. Most of my publications were derivative: *Scotland Yard Weekly* (one issue) was a slavish copy of my brother Kenneth's favourite *Detective Weekly* starring Sexton Blake (mine starred one Inspector Steele); the *Film Fan* owed much to *Film Fun* — so much, indeed, that its contents consisted entirely of glued-up pictures snipped out of that paper.

But my most ambitious journalistic venture was the *Daily Treasure*, published six days a week for the enlightenment and entertainment of my friend Eric Bright, and put through his letter-box each morning along with his father's *Daily Herald*. The *Daily Treasure* consisted of pages torn out of an exercise book and folded across to make usually eight pages — ten on Friday, six on Saturday, twelve for the Bumper Xmas Number. It contained a serial story, a strip cartoon, a puzzle page, a jokes page (courtesy of the Merry and Bright column in the *Joker*), and several other features including a readers' letters corner which I had to make up myself in the absence of any contribution from my only reader. As if this were not enough, the back page of the first Saturday's edition, for no other reason than that I had run out of editorial copy and my newspaper round beckoned, rashly promised the launching of the *Sunday Treasure*. Resisting the temptation to add an *Evening Treasure* to the stable, I managed to keep up this prodigal feat of journalism for a good month before the *Daily Treasure* languished into a mere four pages filled with easy-to-compile maze puzzles, finally suspending publication with the announcement: "GREAT NEWS. From tomorrow the *Daily Treasure* amalgamates with the *Sunday Treasure* — bigger and better than ever! Order your copy now!" The *Sunday Treasure* lasted another two issues before following its former companion into oblivion.

At this time my favourite possessions were a toy Simplex typewriter on which I picked out short stories (very short stories, since the tiny little machine's keys were activated by a dial system, like a telephone, and it took about half an hour to compose a sentence); a John Bull printing set from whose rubber type I made up the billheads of the Middleton Printing Works (props: the *Daily Treasure*, *Ronnie Rabbit's Weekly*, the *Flag* &c. &c.); and a length of draught excluder attached to a Tate and Lyle sugar carton which was my wireless station, Radio Middleton, broadcasting comb and tissue paper and mouth organ recitals, occasional harp zither concerts, news bulletins culled from the *Yorkshire Evening Post*, and variety performances in silly voices (script again courtesy of the *Joker*'s Merry and Bright column). But one morning while eating my breakfast of Dalton's corn flakes — a local brand which we favoured as being cheaper than Kellogg's — I saw on the side of the packet a coloured illustration of a magical model theatre, free to anyone sending in eight packet tops plus a few stamps for postage and packing. I had to have it.

I already had a model theatre of sorts, which I had constructed myself out of an orange box. Part of my required reading at the time was a book which I kept out on more or less permanent loan from the public library, called *Let's Do A Play*. Fascinating and useful though this volume was in its advice, it did rather call for a double drawing room divided by folding doors behind which one could set up one's stage, besides presuming the existence of a dressing-up chest and a large repertory company of cousins and friends. Lacking all these components I tried to organise alfresco productions in the local Clerk of Works' sapling plantation, somewhat on the lines of the Regent's Park Open Air Theatre, with a grass hillock for a stage. Unfortunately I had difficulty in recruiting acting talent for the little plays I wrote and was soon reduced to using home-made hand-puppets with papier-mâché heads and rag costumes, after the manner of Punch and Judy. I gave performances out on the pavement, charging buttons for admission (buttons, abstracted from parental workboxes or in desperation ripped from one's own clothing, were the accepted currency for all street activities demanding payment, a humble trouser button being worth one unit, a mother-of-pearl hexagonal from a lady's coat representing six). Attendances were low.

But now came the Dalton's Corn Flakes Theatre. Eight packets to collect: not only were their torn-off tops to be saved up but, it seemed, the packets themselves would be required for the framework of the theatre — four boxes nestling horizontally for the stage, twin towers of two vertical boxes atop one another for either side of the proscenium. Eight boxes in all. It was a lot of corn flakes. Eating double my fill of them every morning, and sometimes for tea as well, did not make them go fast enough. Impatiently I took to filling my pockets with corn flakes each morning, scattering them behind me on my way to school or flinging them by the handful into privet hedges. Once I tipped half a packet into the hole I was digging to Australia.

At length the eight packets were accumulated and the packet tops sent off with the requisite stamps. After a nerve-racking wait of days that seemed like weeks, a large flat package eventually arrived by parcel post. Unlike most "sensational offers" then as now, my free gift was not a disappointment. In fact it was an enchantment. Fashioned on the lines of a Pollock's toy theatre, it consisted of a highly coloured pasteboard proscenium arch and orchestra pit; two sets of pasteboard gilt and red plush boxes or *loges* as I knew they were called; a deep blue pasteboard curtain with realistic wrinkles; a stage covering and three sets of wings; two pasteboard backcloths, one a castle interior, the other a castle exterior, together with some bits of cut-out scenery; and several cut-out characters. All this had to be constructed, with the aid of glue and much pushing of tab A through slot B, around the assembly of cornflakes boxes. The result was impressive. It was good and solid and it really did look like a proper theatre. I christened it the Grand and got down at once to preparing posters for my opening production with the aid of my John Bull printing set.

My wonderful theatre, I soon found, was capable of improvement. The accompanying scripts, which to my disgust were in rhyming couplets, were for *Cinderella* and *Aladdin and his Wonderful Lamp*. They made no provision for the low comedians and novelty acts I had seen fleshing out the Theatre Royal pantos, and after a couple of performances, one in front of my mother and the other in the presence of the cat, I proceeded to remedy this deficiency by cutting figures out of Donald McGill comic postcards and mounting them on strips of cardboard so that, like Cinderella and her cronies, they could be pushed on and off the stage. I then set about rewriting the scripts, interpolating comic dialogue which as usual owed much to the *Joker*'s Merry and Bright column. I then turned my attention to the scenery which was too skimpy for my satisfaction; I proceeded to augment it with scenes of my own construction, including three-dimensional furniture made out of matchboxes, plus some special effects such as a trap-door cut into the stage through which a demon king might emerge when required, and a Christmas tree fairy who could fly across the stage invisibly suspended on cotton in fair simulation of Kirby's Sensational Flying Ballet. Finally, I got my brothers to help me set up proper footlights – a string of torch bulbs concealed behind a strip of cocoa tin, and connected to a bicycle lamp battery.

While the Middleton Grand Theatre was to remain my most cherished toy until I put childish things behind me, the pantomime as an art form quickly palled and I began to mount more or less original productions of my own devising, including a melodrama based on some penny dreadful yarn I had read in one of the comics, which featured not only a realistic snow effect but, anticipating *Miss Saigon* by half a century, a cardboard autogiro which landed on the stage after circling the flies. I also, pandering to a street audience of reluctant button-payers who were not overly impressed by the legitimate theatre, introduced a season of variety shows after the fashion of the *Billy Cotton Band Show* and featuring Donald McGill characters whom I pedantically insisted on endowing with proper names such as McDonald & Fraser ("Scots Wae Hae!") and Bobby Lupin ("Here to Amuse You") so that they would look the more authentic in the John Bull-printed programme. These performances, needless to say, were favourably reviewed in whatever publication I happened to be editing at the time.

So a supposedly deprived childhood drifted blissfully by. Looking back I can see that a good deal of it – the white card trips to Town, the urban rambles of the Middleton Hiking Club, the hours spent making up little magazines or playing with my toy theatre – was pure escapism. But it was an escape into realism, not away from it: I wanted to be in this real world of smokestacks and department stores and printing works and newspapers and theatres and wireless stations. All along, I was rehearsing for what I was determined would be the shape of my adulthood.

TWO

Billy Liar

'I did nothing but walk around town for an hour and a half, watching Saturday evening begin to happen and the slow queues forming outside the Odeon and the Gaumont. The people walked about as though they were really going somewhere. I stood for a quarter of an hour at a time, watching them get off the buses and disperse themselves about the streets. I was amazed and intrigued that they should all be content to be nobody but themselves.'

— BILLY LIAR, 1959

1 When I was ten and a half my mother, after first asking if I
would like to see where we might soon be going to live, took
me so far into the outskirts of the city that the suspicion
arose in my mind, as the landscape grew more remote and grass-
dominated, that this was another Mickey Mouse ruse and I was
about to be delivered up to Shadwell Reformatory.

It was a dual tram ride: the familiar No. 12 Lance-corporal into
Town and then the unfamiliar, foreign-looking No. 20 – for each
area had its own style or class of tram, models readily identified by
tramway buffs as the Chamberlain, the Beeston Air-Brake, the
Brush-bodied Horsfield and so on – whose roller indicator
pronounced that it was going to a place I had never heard of, Halton.

Setting out from Kirkgate Market we trundled past Quarry Hill
Flats, beyond Beckett Street and St James's Hospital, and so up the
York Road, which seemed interminable. Fortunately the tram,
whatever make it might have been, was not one of the old sick-
making bone-rattlers. Rows of terraces, so much cleaner on this side
of the city that their brickwork might have been scrubbed like the
donkey-stoned steps, gave way to modern, single-storey clothing
factories – single-storey because land was cheaper out here, and it
was more efficient to have all the work processes on one level – and
pockets of "bought houses" interspersed with mock-Tudor
shopping parades and the odd luxury cinema; then an alarming vista
of fields and what I suspected could be even meadows before we
passed under a railway bridge and alighted at a modern pub, almost
a roadhouse had I known anything about such things, called the
Wykebeck Arms.

This was strange territory indeed. Ahead of us was a dismal
scrubland, through which had been cut a long, straight, unmade
road. A good half mile ahead of us, shimmering in the summer haze,
was a brand-new housing estate, Halton Moor. Shadwell, I reflected,

as we plodded along the caked mud path towards it, would have been an improvement. We were at the end of the Earth.

The estate was so new that it smelled of raw wood, paint and putty. Not yet of tarmac: there was no tarmac. The earth road and dust pavements, and the wooden-framed rooftops of houses waiting to be tiled, reminded me of a Wild West town as seen at the Tivoli — or perhaps I was romanticising, from a wish that I was in Main Street, Dead Man's Gulch, rather than Cartmell Drive, Halton Moor estate. (All the streets and crescents and the drives wide enough to herd cattle down were named after Lake District beauty spots — Kendal Drive, Ingleton Drive, Ullswater Crescent, Windermere Crescent — with the aim, no doubt, of persuading us that we were somewhere else.) As my mother led me up the dried mud path of No. 105 and let us in through the violently red front door — its redness reminded me of a surfeit of raspberry lollipops I had endured during my period of Yorkshire Penny Bank affluence — I tried to come to terms with my new address, putting it in as favourable a light as possible.

It was, to begin with, a proper house and not a flat masquerading as a house. The architectural style was R.A.H. Livett ARIBA in his Dutch period — white pebbledash with overhanging red-tiled eaves, so that the bedroom windows peeped out of the roof. I rather approved of that. There were more of these bedrooms, furthermore, than at Middleton — practically one each (we were being moved because of overcrowding). I wasn't sure I approved of that — being squashed three in a bed with two of my brothers, while it had led to many a midnight demarcation dispute, had been a cosy arrangement. Stairs were a novelty and I looked forward to sliding down the banister like Just William. The back garden boasted a brick air-raid shelter and that, once we had got some bits of furniture and a storm lamp in, could double as the clubhouse of the Halton Moor (late Middleton) Hiking Club and the offices and factory of the Halton Moor Printing Works.

But the house, as even my mother had to concede — and she was quite taken with such mod cons as the galvanised stove that didn't need blackleading and the indoor coal shed — was "at the back of beyond". If the planners had got Middleton wrong they had got Halton Moor even more wrong. It was half a mile to anywhere anyone wanted to go: half a mile to the tram stop, half a mile to the shops, half a mile to school which was in fact on an older,

Middleton-vintage estate across the wasteland. The fish and chip shop was so far away that the five pieces and sixpennorth were cold before we got them home. There was no public library, no church, no scout hut, no park, no cinema. How would I get to Hunslet? How would I get to Town?

We moved in – "flitted", as the vernacular had it. With three wage-packets coming in our circumstances had much improved by now and I was awarded my own bed. In place of the oven-hot house brick wrapped in an old woollie that had been my bed-warmer, I now had a proper hot-water bottle. I missed my brick. To my surprise, I even missed Middleton, and took to wandering around the neighbouring estate, Osmondthorpe, because of its resemblance to what was already beginning to seem, in retrospect and in contrast to the harsh open space of Halton Moor, a mellow, human-scale estate. But most of all I missed Hunslet, particularly since I had no idea how to get there from here.

The Halton Moor Hiking Club drew a blank. Exploring what was left of the original Halton Moor – the tract of pointless grass that our little settlement of Dutch houses overlooked – I found that a wandering stream – the Wyke Beck, after which the Wykebeck Arms was named – ran through it. It was an unappetising beck, scummy with waste from the TB hospital a couple of miles upstream and sometimes bobbing with hideous, misshapen bladders which youths who knew the facts of life swore were human foetuses but which I believe were the bloated carcases of stillborn water rats. But it was fast-flowing and, at about four feet wide, quite navigable for anyone with a small craft. Almost certainly, I reasoned, with hazy recollection of something I had read about waters and their tributaries, it must lead either down into the canal or the river. I had lately been reading *Tom Sawyer*: my immediate resolve was to build a raft and sail it into Town, mooring at Leeds Bridge.

That evening, on a scrounged sheet of greaseproof paper, I drew up an elaborate blueprint. It was an ambitious raft: it would have a mast and a sail, a rudder, a cosy shelter aft with a roof, and a handsome supplies box with rope handles and my initials burned into it in pokerwork which would serve also as a seat. The craft would be called the *Spirit of Loidis* (I had also been reading about the exploits of Lindbergh: and we had learned at school that Loidis was the olden-days name for Leeds).

First I had to get my materials together. Of prime importance was the raft itself, which ideally should have been constructed of logs trussed together with rope. Although there were more than enough trees about I had no access to a proper saw, and the voice of reality told me that the task of chopping them down was beyond me. The next best thing would have to be a ready-made substitute. The Halton Moor estate at the time was one great building site and there was wood about in plenty, most of it unguarded (very handy for anyone with a new firewood round to build up). I knew where there was a supply of unpainted front doors, stacked under a tarpaulin like Middleton Park deckchairs. They were on the side of the unmade road very near to a convenient loop in the beck, and it was with no great difficulty that I managed to dislodge one and drag it down through the scrub to a stretch of cracked mud below the bank of the beck which I intended to serve as my boatyard.

While I appreciated that I had yet to find my mast and sail and all the other accoutrements necessary for the *Spirit of Loidis*'s maiden voyage, I saw no harm in launching my council house front door at once and taking her for an experimental sail. Accordingly I pushed it into the beck, climbed gingerly aboard, and with the aid of an overhanging branch cast off. My front door raft at once took on water through the keyhole and promptly sank, leaving me standing up to my knees in the middle of the Wyke Beck as a dead rat floated gently by.

I was puzzled and disappointed. If I knew anything about elementary physics it was that wood does not sink; yet sunk my raft was and sunk it remained, in the fullness of time silting over with mud until it was all but invisible on the bed of the murky beck. Thus ended the first and last voyage of the *Spirit of Loidis*. It was as well. Subsequently I learned that had I managed to negotiate the weir a little way downstream, the Wyke Beck did indeed flow into the Aire and Calder Navigation – but only after it had become, for a spell, the main effluent channel of the Skelton Grange sewage works.

My bacon was saved by the declaration of war, which came soon after the move to Halton Moor. The morning of 3 September 1939 found me sitting on the garden gate with no particular place to go. Mr Chamberlain's tired voice floated out from a dozen open windows: ". . . No such undertaking has been received . . ." The implications were blindingly clear: I should have access to my brother Kenneth's bicycle.

Kenneth was (and remains) a cycling freak. He had accumulated three machines over the years: his lightweight racing model with the cane-spoke wheels, which he kept in his bedroom and greased with Vaseline; his touring bike on which he was (and is) in the habit of going to Wales and back, which was kept either in the hallway or leaning up against the sideboard; and his everyday working bike, which was usually left out by the back door or, if wet, in the scullery. The word conscription had been in my vocabulary for some time: Kenneth's call-up, I knew, was imminent (the other two brothers would follow him into active service in due course). There was no point in asking his permission to ride either his racing bike or his touring bike, both of which in any case would be smothered in Vaseline and immobilised for the duration. But he would not mind my borrowing his workaday machine. At least I assumed he wouldn't. He had gone for a soldier before I ever had the chance to ask.

The immediate consequence of the outbreak of war, then, was the disbandment of the Halton Moor Hiking Club and the formation of the Halton Moor Cycling Club. I immediately pedalled forth in search of Hunslet. A pall of sulphurous smoke − smog, as it came to be known − hovering in the far distance beyond a cluster of cooling towers told me that that was as likely a direction as any. (I had yet to acquire a map of Leeds. Probably it never crossed my otherwise enquiring mind that there was such a thing. Maps were what you found in school atlases, and they were of oceans, deserts and mountain ranges rather than of Sweet Street, Meadow Lane and Pepper Road.)

The Halton Moor Cycling Club's inaugural spin began unpromisingly, taking me off the by now tarmacadamed boring streets of the estate to bumpy tracks leading first to the sewage works, where I should have ended up on the *Spirit of Loidis* had the voyage down the Wyke Beck ever got underway; and then even more dismayingly to a farmyard complete with animals. Doubling back on my tracks, however, and keeping the cloud of smog firmly in view, I eventually established that I had taken a simple wrong turning. By wheeling right at the end of Cartmell Drive instead of pushing straight on through the self-evidently rural lanes I found myself bowling along a good firm lane of crushed cinders known as Black Road, which led, through a gate proclaiming PRIVATE ROAD, into a good firm lane of packed red sand known equally appropriately as Red Road. And this in turn, via a couple of twists and turns, led me to a familiar-sounding thoroughfare called Easy Road, which either

Ur-memory or the change in the texture of the surrounding buildings from smallholding stone to factory brick persuaded me that I was in the proximity of Hunslet.

So it proved. Easy Road, to my delight, led me into South Accommodation Road, which took me across the river Aire and into Hunslet Road to the right and Low Road to the left. I was home.

2   As for the war itself, apart from some initial frissons at the possibility of the Germans invading Leeds and using the Little Sisters of the Poor as human clappers for the parish church bells, it was for a ten-year-old a huge adventure.

The expeditions into Town offered fresh excitements, starting with the tram ride. All the tram windows were covered with thick protective netting against bomb blast or shrapnel, with little diamond-shaped apertures so the passengers could see where they were. If I was lucky I might board a tram stripped of its advertisements and painted khaki, as if about to join a great invasion armada of trams that would sail across the Channel and rock from Ostend to Berlin. The fact was that there was a national paint shortage and the corporation had run out of its livery blue.

Town on a war footing had to be re-explored to the full. The entrances to Kirkgate Market were reduced to narrow slits in a barricade of sandbags, while the glass roof was painted black in accordance with the Air Raid Precautions regulations, as were the roofs and domes of all the arcades. No paint shortage there. The windows of all the shops were draped in netting like the trams, except for one or two go-ahead establishments such as Lewis's and Montague Burton the Tailor of Taste, whose windows were protected by a patent contraption of cross-diagonal taut wires that would prevent their shattering – a principle I did not entirely trust. To enter a shop you had to claw your way through swathes of blackout material, and the effect, if you were stepping out of the dusk into a brightly lit Woolworth's or Marks and Spencer, was of entering an Aladdin's cave.

Air raid shelters like the one in the churchyard of St John the Evangelist had dotted the city for some time. They were now augmented by huge static water tanks, like free-standing swimming pools, which were erected in the middle of the Headrow and the other main thoroughfares for the benefit of firefighters with their stirrup pumps. Hastily built brick air raid wardens' posts and first-aid stations appeared in all the public squares, there were fire boats on the river painted grey like submarines, and concrete pillboxes with machine-gun slits guarding such strategic points as Leeds Bridge, the marshalling yards and, more importantly to my mind, the back of Kirkgate Market. It was comforting to think that if the enemy wanted to take Game Row he would have to go round to the front entrance.

My Bovril sign was extinguished for the duration, as were all the other lights in Town. It was the first time I had ever seen it unlit and I gave its naked light bulbs a long and melancholy stare. Although I had never yet set foot in a theatre by daylight, when the sun streaming through the open exit doors shows up the tattiness of the moth-eaten red plush and the peeling caryatids, that was the effect: the Bovril sign was reduced to a structure of girders and nuts and bolts and a tangle of wires, like a signal gantry over the railway lines.

Hunslet, too, had to be rediscovered. With my gas-mask case bobbing against my hip I prowled the area noting that the incidence of sandbags and static water tanks was much higher even than in Town. The reason of course was the high concentration of factories and mills in Hunslet, most of which had gone over to war work. Factory walls were now topped with coiled barbed wire, and the tall gates of some of them were guarded, to my great satisfaction, by rifle-bearing soldiers in sentry boxes. The Halton Moor Cycling Club, noting these developments, militarised itself into the 1st Mobile Cadet Corps and regularly patrolled Hunslet in search of spies and unexploded bombs.

In fact, much to my disappointment, not a single enemy bomber had yet come anywhere near Leeds, although I listened hopefully each night for their ominous drone, and searchlights sweeping the sky picked out the barrage balloon that protected the Skelton Grange cooling towers like a stationary *Graf Zeppelin*. The searchlight unit was on Hunslet Moor and the 1st Mobile Cadet Corps had been along and given it a good stare.

At home, there was the novelty of ration books, blackout blinds on the windows, the bucket of water at the ready to put out incendiary bombs, Churchill and Lord Haw-Haw on the wireless, and officious neighbours in the regalia of air raid wardens patrolling the streets shouting, "Put that light out!"

My comic papers were doing their bit, or some of them were: all the characters in *Film Fun*, with the understandable exception of Old Mother Riley, enlisted as privates in the British army the moment war was declared – even Abbott and Costello, Harold Lloyd and Joe E. Brown who were American citizens. From the nature of their lowly duties, Laurel and Hardy appeared to be in the Pioneer Corps, which squared with the humble working-class dwellings behind the gasworks from which they had been mobilised. The inhabitants of *Radio Fun*, on the other hand, excepting only Jack Warner who was a soldier already by virtue of appearing in the wireless show *Garrison Theatre*, remained non-combatants to a man, the Western Brothers even flouting wartime austerity by continuing to wear top hats and tails.

Needless to say, the publications of the Halton Moor Printing Works were fervently patriotic. The *Flag* magazine was resuscitated, its front cover featuring, in full crayon colour, the flags of all the Allies. For the first time the *Flag* carried advertising, in the shape of government exhortations to lend to defend the right to be free and not to be a squanderbug, which I clipped out of the newspapers. Until now I had always resisted printing advertising matter: although it would have made my magazines look more authentic and reduced the number of editorial pages that had to be slogged out, I resented the idea of giving free space to the likes of De Reske Minors cigarettes and Chilprufe Vests.

My mother sanguinely saw three of her sons off to war and informed me, in a rare sentimental moment, that I was the man of the house now – a post that seemed entirely honorary, since in common with all northern mothers she took even the heaviest household chores upon herself, accepted personal responsibility for locking up and winding the clock, and slept with her handbag under her pillow. Her own war effort was to enlist as the street National Savings collector. When my various preoccupations permitted, I would accompany her on her rounds, and when I was twelve I was to write a short humorous account of some of the odd customers we encountered. This I copied out in the neat purple lettering I employed in my magazines and sent it off to the *National Savings News*. They published it – my first-ever professional appearance in print – but without fee.

The subject of evacuation came up. I was ambivalent about the scheme. On the one hand it was a lark. You were billeted on complete strangers who by all accounts were benevolent auntie and uncle figures who gave you their sweet ration and other treats. On the other, you would be living in the country. Several boys of my acquaintance were evacuated to a tolerably large Dales village called Pateley Bridge. Their mothers, after visiting them at weekends, reported that they were as brown as nuts. I did not like the sound of this at all. I had been as brown as a nut myself once, and that was during my sojourn at Silverdale Poor Children's Holiday Camp. It was when I heard that Silverdale itself was to become an evacuee reception centre that I firmly vetoed the whole idea. My mother seemed relieved. She liked having me about the house, even though she sometimes complained about the interminable squeaky voices on Radio Halton Moor, which was now on a war footing and broadcasting nightly.

The most significant event of the "phoney war", as this uneasy period of nothing very much happening was known, was yet to come. This was the momentous announcement by the headmaster in assembly one Friday morning that the school would be closed until further notice.

I could not believe my luck. I had not yet dared try on the white card trick at my new school – the card was by now grubby and dog-eared, and I very much doubted that it would deceive my teachers who seemed altogether smarter than the Middleton bunch. The school closure, which was occasioned by the need to find training camp space for battalions of conscripts, meant that for the foreseeable future I could roam around Town as I pleased without fear of the Board Man's heavy hand on my shoulder as I sipped my glass of sarsaparilla while watching the passing show in Kirkgate Market.

I quickly developed a routine. Each morning after delivering my newspapers and perhaps cleaning a few windows or selling a bucket or two of firewood, I would go and stare through the railings at the squads of soldiers drilling in the playground and digging trenches in the playing fields. Since I had always been hopeless at games this sight afforded me a great deal of quiet satisfaction. I would then either set off into Town or on one of the excursions of the Halton Moor Cycling Club.

I did not invariably cycle over to Hunslet, in fact I set about thoroughly investigating the east side of Leeds where our new estate was situated. My most notable discovery, in the course of trying to

100

locate the Barnbow munitions factory where my mother had worked in the First World War and subjecting it to one of my stares, was that of a splendid custom-built public library, the Percival Leigh branch, in a residential district of "bought houses" known as Crossgates. I was so taken by it that I quite lost interest in the nearby munitions plant. Middleton library, while I had been greatly attached to it, I could now see was a poor affair by comparison – it was in fact the school assembly hall converted into a public library in the evenings by sliding back the series of panels which concealed the shelves of books. Osmondthorpe library, such as it was, was also housed in the school. There had apparently been plans to build a proper library on the Halton Moor estate, but these had been scotched by the war. But the Percival Leigh branch – whoever he may have been – was all a library should be. It was an airy, elegant, single-storey Thirties structure of red brick, with many windows, and cork-tiled floors. Its wide steps were used as a gathering place by girls in green blazers from a nearby private school, giving it to my mind the air of the college campus in the Andy Hardy movies. The girls were a sight more clean and wholesome than any I had so far encountered in my life and I fell in love indiscriminately if platonically with all of them.

But I was even more in love with the Percival Leigh branch itself. Besides a well-stocked adult library and an entirely separate children's library where, had one still considered oneself a child, one could sit at modern light wood tables and browse, it had a reference library containing the *Encyclopedia Britannica* – a work I had often read about but never set eyes on. To my delight and astonishment there was also a big reading room with rack upon rack of all the latest publications, most of which I had never heard of – not only *Punch* and *John O' London's Weekly* but the *Times Literary Supplement*, the *Quiver*, *Sea Breezes*, the *Wheatsheaf* (journal of the Co-operative Wholesale Society), *Britannia and Eve*, the *Illustrated London News*, the *New Statesman & Nation*, all of which became regular required reading. I was to spend very many happy hours in that reading room.

I also decided to patronise the lending library proper in future, since it was so much more superior to the one housed in Osmondthorpe Council School. Reasoning – wrongly, as it happened – that I should not be able to use my Osmondthorpe branch tickets in Crossgates, I set about applying for two sets of tickets for this wonderful library – one for the children's section, the other for the adult. Again wrongly, I was of the impression that one could only belong to a particular branch library if one lived in that particular district: accordingly, I deemed it prudent to give a false address — 82 Templemeads Way, Crossgates. In the belief — this one probably well founded — that they kept a central membership record, I thought I had better use a false name too, and so I registered myself on the application form as one Trevor Austin. That was for the juvenile tickets. For the adult ones I raised my father from the dead and rechristened him Ernest Arthur Austin, trade or profession bank clerk (a touch of snobbery creeping in here, I fear, under the influence of the girls in green blazers. At least I did not make him a bank manager). With E.A. Austin's signature adorning both forms, in my case as parent or guardian, I had no trouble at all in acquiring my tickets. The pleasures of the Percival Leigh branch were mine for the taking.

This harmless deception was, however, to have an unfortunate sequel. When I was around fifteen, I began to "go out", as the expression was, with an attractive assistant at the Percival Leigh branch, a former green blazer-wearer named Doreen. By fast-forwarding my age to sixteen I was by now a member of the adult library in my own right, if not under my own name. Doreen, stamping my books while we engaged in the tongue-tied conversational rituals of teenage courtship, naturally took the view that my name was Trevor Austin. There was nothing I could do to disabuse her of this idea even if I had wanted to, which I did not particularly — Trevor Austin I considered a dashing, Crossgates sort of name, and in any case to confess all would mean also confessing that I lived on a council estate (more snobbery — Doreen was the first girl I had ever taken out who lived in a "bought house").

All went swimmingly until one evening when we were travelling by tram to the Shaftesbury Cinema halfway between Crossgates and Town, the film at the local Regal being not to our taste. As we stood on the platform waiting to alight when the tram drew up at our stop, the conductor asked if we had paid our fares. We had not. This was not criminal intent but standard practice: you parted with your tram fare only if directly asked for it. When challenged as we were now, it was usual to come clean. Doreen, however, for some reason took it into her head to claim recklessly that we had indeed paid — since we were going Dutch she probably had plans for the copper or two she hoped to save by this deception.

The conductor said in that case he would trouble us for our tickets. By way of lending Doreen immoral support I said we had thrown them away. The conductor said in that case he would trouble us for our names and addresses. Doreen said her name was Janet Smith and that she lived at some fictitious address in a densely populated area known as Burmantofts. I said my name was Trevor Austin of 82 Templemeads Way, Crossgates. The conductor said we would hear more of the matter and we got off the tram.

Doreen was alarmingly upset. How could I be so stupid as to volunteer my real name and address? The police would now trace her through me and she would get into awful trouble, not only for evading her fare but for giving a false name and address. The case would bring shame upon her parents and even if she wasn't put away – I tried to reassure her that Shadwell Reformatory didn't admit girls but she would not be comforted – she would certainly get the sack. Doreen then began to weep copiously and there was nothing for it but to put her on the next tram home, counselling her to be careful to pay her fare. Not wishing to waste the evening, I went to the pictures alone.

It seemed time to bury Trevor Austin. It would be embarrassing to go on meeting Doreen, and since by now I had access to the Central Lending Library in Town, under the name of Michael Fox, 79 Karl Marx House, Quarry Hill Flats, it seemed prudent to bid a fond farewell to the Percival Leigh branch library. It remains the repository of some of the pleasantest and most fruitful memories of my late childhood and early youth. When I last revisited it the reading room was a branch of the social services and the reference library had become a police post.

The no-school idyll ended as abruptly as it had begun. The soldiers marched away and a proclamation by Geo Guest was hung on the school gates, rather in the manner of the pronouncements that from time to time appeared on the gates of Armley Jail after an execution (I once went and stared at one), to the effect that our interrupted education was to be resumed. We had been left to roam the streets for three months or so. For me, this period was an education in itself. I had read much of the *Encyclopedia Britannica*, become acquainted with a fascinating fat volume called *Bartlett's Book of Popular Quotations* (and begun to compile my own – *Waterhouse's Dictionary of Everyday Quotations*), and become a regular reader of the *Lady, Horse and Hound*, the *Methodist*

Times and the *Stage*, among other journals.

The return to school marked the end of the phoney war. I had begun to despair of Leeds ever being bombed but eventually the air raid sirens wailed at last, and not in vain. As exclusively reported in the Special (and only) Edition of the *Halton Moor Gazette* (more orthodox newspapers were subject to censorship restrictions), incendiary bombs followed by high-explosive bombs rained down on the city one unexpected moonlit evening, causing satisfactory conflagrations along a far spectrum of the horizon ranging, so it was to be confirmed by eye-witnesses to the damage, from Quarry Hill Flats and Marsh Lane goods yard to Low Road, Holbeck, my spiritual home. By standing out in the front gardens instead of repairing to the shelters as recommended, Halton Moor had a grandstand view of the fires, the flares, the enemy bombers caught in the criss-crossing searchlights, and the noisy pyrotechnics of the anti-aircraft guns.

At the earliest opportunity over the weekend I rode out to Hunslet in my capacity as war correspondent (alas, I had no peaked cap) of the *Halton Moor Gazette*. Many of the familiar terraces of Holbeck and Hunslet had "copped it" as the saying went, and the hosepipes of the auxiliary fire tenders snaked all over the cobbled roads around the great engineering works. The impressive Holbeck railway viaduct, a favourite artifact, to my relief mingled with regret for the histrionic potential of such a tragedy, had not come down in a spectacular heap like a toppled pile of building bricks, but the factories all around had had their roofs blasted off. It needed a solid two or three hours' staring to do justice to the damage. Later I journeyed into Town and inspected the shattered glass roof of Kirkgate Market, the shrapnel wounds to the stone lions guarding the Town Hall, the fire-bombed umbrella shop in Schofield's Arcade and other points of interest. The City Museum, with its dinosaur skeleton and mangy Bengal tiger, had sustained a direct high-explosive hit, and on the pavement outside I picked up a splinter of what might or might not have been bone that might or might not have belonged to the dinosaur. This I added to the fragments of shrapnel I had been collecting during the course of my observations. In the absence of my brother Dennis at the front I had converted his bedroom into a Halton Moor War Museum, and my finds went to flesh out the display of army greatcoat buttons, cap badges, sleeve flashes, German propaganda leaflet and my father's Mons Star which formed the basis of the collection.

There were about half a dozen more raids on Leeds but nothing again so spectacular, and deprived of a proper Blitz and nights spent in a deep shelter singing "Run, Rabbit, Run", my interest in the war began to pall. Austerity and the blackout became a bore. I began to pine for the city lights, for the flag-bedecked illuminated trams which had plied Briggate and City Square on special occasions such as the Silver Jubilee and the Coronation; for the electric news scanner over the Majestic Cinema; for the red neon; for sunbeams streaming in through the glass roof of the Market and bouncing off the prismatic surfaces of pyramids of pineapples (what were pineapples?); and above all for my brightly twinkling Bovril sign.

3 It was always taken as read, not least by me, that I was the brightest boy in the school. It therefore came as a considerable shock when I failed the entrance examination for Cockburn High School, south Leeds's answer to the grammar school on the other side of the tracks.

It has to be said I was in good company. Richard Hoggart has recorded that he too failed the Cockburn exam; but in his case his headmaster canvassed the great Geo Guest who wisely interceded and had a place found for him. My friend Willis Hall failed too, but poor as his parents were they managed to scrape together the money to send him on a fee-paying basis. In fact between us we know so many successful Leeds men who muffed that exam that we once toyed with the idea of having a Failed Cockburn tie made. As for me, my own headmaster would not appear to have been on interventionist terms with Geo Guest, and any idea of my mother paying the fees was out of the question.

Doubtless the fact of having been deprived by the exigencies of war of three months or so of formal schooling had an effect on my performance; nevertheless I was mortified. It had never crossed my mind for a second that I should not pass with flying colours, and I had set my heart on wearing a school cap and carrying a leather satchel containing a Latin primer and an apple. Besides, Cockburn was on the very edge of Hunslet, just past the Pavilion picture house and across from Hunslet Moor. Had I not flunked that exam I should have taken a tram every day for the rest of my schooldays to Kirkgate Market and then changed to the No. 25 bone-rattler into the heart of Hunslet and crunched across the Moor, satchel swinging. What more, short of my mother moving her temporarily depleted family into a terrace house off Low Road, could I possibly ask of life?

I had taken Cockburn to my heart at first sight when I had gone there to sit the entrance exam, somewhere around my eleventh birthday. It was an Edwardian building four or five storeys high, set in half an acre of uncompromising tarmac surrounded by walled railings, and not a blade of grass in sight. Inside, there were clattering stone steps, high grime-stained windows, bottle green and livid orange tiles, dark wood, downward-sloping desks with lids to hide behind such as you saw in the illustrations by H.M. Brock in public school stories; all this and the heady smell of cabbage wafting up from the basement. It was all that a school should be and in marked contrast to Middleton and Osmondthorpe, replicas of one another, which were single-storey modern buildings with too many French windows for their own good, grouped around playing fields big enough to land Spitfires on. Too airy by half.

There was nothing for it but to make the best of a bad job. Leaving school at fourteen would, after all, be more in the Edgar Wallace mould than indulging myself in a secondary education. And it wasn't as if I were not enjoying my elementary schooldays.

I liked everything about school except, at the top of the list, physical training which I abhorred and in due course managed to be excused by waving my white card about and pointing out my displaced rib; cricket which I was also excused after sustaining a permanently damaged tendon caused by a muffed catch; football, where I was so hopeless that I was quickly reduced to linesman; and woodwork and metalwork, in the course of each period of which I usually drew blood, at the end of term producing hideous malformations of dovetailed pine and bevelled copper purporting to be bookends, ashtrays or serviette rings. Swimming I was able to endure only because, while we were at Middleton, the nearest baths were a noisy tram ride away in Hunslet. While the shivering experience of undressing and dressing on wet, slimy duckboards was not to my taste, I liked the echoing white-tiled institutional feel of the place, and the post-swim option of either a cup of steaming Ovaltine or Bovril. (While frankly I preferred the taste of Ovaltine, I stayed loyal to Bovril.) At Osmondthorpe, there were no swimming baths near at hand and so we did not swim.

For the rest, while I would never have volunteered for elementary science, technical drawing, nature study or arithmetic, I could tolerate them as school subjects and was reasonably proficient at all of them. Where I came into my own, however, was in English, geography, history and scripture – all interlinked subjects to my mind, since they each required the writing of an essay or "composition" in tests or exams. If I had not been top in all these subjects at the end of term, I should have wanted to know the reason why.

But my favourite period by far was the last hour of Friday afternoon, when the whole school was allowed to read quietly while the teachers marked up their registers. You were allowed to bring reading matter of your choice from home, barring only comics, comic annuals and, following a test case, bound volumes of the *Vivid War Weekly*. This set me something of a poser, since apart from the *Vivid War Weekly*, Daudet's *Lettres de mon Moulin* in the original French, the plays of J.M. Barrie and *Fifty Years of Progress: the Story of Hemingway's Brewery*, the only remaining books in the house were a big fat volume of household hints that had been given away by the *Daily Herald* and a book of *True Tales of Horror* which I had read many times, particularly the account of a man-eating orchid in South America. Fortunately, there was a brisk swopping service in operation on these literary Fridays, and my book of horror stories was much in demand. Thus I had the bartering power to keep me ploughing contentedly through volumes of *Chums*, the *Scout Annual*, *Boy's Own Annual*, *Fifty Famous Murders* and suchlike improving reading.

Lessons aside, while both Middleton and Osmondthorpe were roughish schools where the teachers took care to arm themselves with unauthorised weapons such as T-squares, chair legs and cricket stumps, the atmosphere was congenial enough. But I was not much of a one for joining in. On the whole, with my dislike of team spirit and organised activities of any kind, my policy was one of studied non-co-operation; in consequence I was never made a prefect or even a milk monitor.

On only one occasion did I display any qualities of leadership. I had always enjoyed morning and afternoon breaks, when the playground was a seething forum of news and rumour, such as that the newly established Richard Shops were giving away pairs of silk stockings for every 100 – or was it 500? – tram tickets with their advertisement printed on the back (sisters would pay good money for them); or that the paradoxical miracle of white chocolate had been invented; or that so-and-so, hitherto believed to be in the TB sanitorium, was in reality in Shadwell Reformatory. But the playground was also the stronghold of shaven-headed, clog-flaunting school bullies, whose idea of fun was to stamp on the feet of lesser privileged plimsoll-wearers. It was I who dealt with this unpleasant situation.

In my last term at Middleton I had been reading a school story by, I think, one Michael Poole, in which the denizens of Study Ten form a secret society called the Cranks, the main object of which is that if any member of the society finds himself being bullied by the cads of the Remove, all he has to do is shout "Crank! Crank! Crank!" and hundreds of boys will come running to his rescue. Without much faith in my own ability to evoke anything like such a response, I started my own Cranks society, more as a lark than anything. The thing captured the imagination of my classmates and soon caught on like wildfire. Only a few days after its formation, as I was walking home from school, I saw a small boy in tears at having his arm twisted by one of the bullet-headed clog-wearers. There were a few schoolmates near at hand. I cried "Crank! Crank! Crank!" and to my astonishment not only they but just about every boy in the school came tearing to the scene from all directions, like the urchins in the Ealing comedy *Hue and Cry*. As the bully took to his heels, pursued by the whooping, terrifying mob, I stood amazed, flattered and awe-stricken at the Pandora's box of mass hysteria I had unlocked. The organisation was proscribed by the headmaster the very next day.

My teachers were a mixed bunch, so far as I was concerned. Those in charge of sport or handicrafts despised me as a milksop. Others thought I was too clever by half. One or two, who were not themselves all that bright, were wary of me. Two teachers, both at Osmondthorpe, went out of their way to help me.

The first, whose name I have shamefully forgotten, encouraged me to draw cartoons, a modest peripheral talent I had brought to the art class from the pages of the *Daily Treasure* and *Ronnie Rabbit's Weekly*. He went to the trouble of putting my efforts together in a book and placing it in the school library, where for all I know it remains to this day.

The other, Clifford Exley, taught me English. That he did this spectacularly well (another, later, pupil of his was the writer Jack Higgins) could have been in some degree due to his not being a regular English teacher. His subject was science, but since most of the staff had been called up for national service, those who remained because they were medically unfit had to become educational jacks-of-all-trades. Mr Exley approached English as he approached science – as an adventure, a voyage of discovery. He had a talent for enthusing even the dullest of the dullards amongst us. None of us appreciated, as pupils never do, that he was a superb teacher – to be frank, most of us thought he was a soft touch. For instance, when he was supposed to be teaching us elementary algebra he spent most of the lesson reading us that classic essay of Stephen Leacock's, where A, B and C are always laying wagers that one can fill a cistern faster than the others – but B has a leaky bucket and C's cistern has a hole in it. In the end C dies of exhaustion and A and B have to bury him. A can dig twice as fast as B who has a broken spade . . . Not only did we find all this hilarious, but with many a nudge and snigger we congratulated ourselves on having got out of a whole boring lesson. Little did we realise that we had been learning algebra. In addition, I had been acquiring a taste for Stephen Leacock – one of the many writers to whom Mr Exley introduced me, including Conan Doyle, Jack London, Kipling, Arnold Bennett . . . His usual ploy was to toss a book on my desk with the throwaway remark, "You might find this worth a glance some time."

Because of his grey hair, shapeless tweedy jackets and flannel bags, and his faintly eccentric disposition – I was once quite shocked to come across him eating a pork pie in the street – for many years I looked back on Mr Exley as an elderly, Mr Chips figure. It was only quite recently that I learned he must have been in his mid-thirties when he was teaching me. But he had the wisdom of a Mr Chips. It was entirely down to him, as I also subsequently learned, that one day in 1941, when I was thirteen, I found myself in an Osmondthorpe Council School classroom in a mildly bemused state of mind as I sat an unusually stiff series of test papers on English, elementary maths and geography. While exams seemed to come round fortnightly at Osmondthorpe, it was quite out of the ordinary to face this minor ordeal, as it was to some but never to me who welcomed the chance to shine, with a motley crew of boys from other forms. I conjectured that the idea was perhaps to settle which stream we should all be moving into next term (this was when school classes were still categorised – or stigmatised – A, B or C according to academic performance). I thought no more about it and got on with my work, taking no particular pains over it but in due course learning that I had won a special place award at Leeds College of Commerce.

The trick was in the casualness of it all. Had I been told in advance that I was to take the College of Commerce scholarship exam, or if I had had to report at a quarter to nine on an execution-grey morning to the College itself, and to sit at a strange desk in a strange classroom with a strangely clanking radiator, as I had had to do for the Cockburn High School fiasco two years earlier, I should undoubtedly have failed that examination too. With what consequences, I have no idea. School-leavers of fourteen went into the clothing factories or foundries. But then Alan Sillitoe went from elementary school into the Raleigh bicycle factory and a few years later he had written *Saturday Night and Sunday Morning*.

My cup ran over. The College of Commerce was in the middle of Town. Daily, after all, I would be taking that tram as far as Kirkgate Market, thence to meander along Vicar Lane, or through the Market itself if I so pleased, to school. The world, or anyway Town which to me came to the same thing, was now my oyster.

There was more. I received a letter personally from Geo Guest himself. "I have pleasure in informing you that you have been successful in gaining a Special Place at the College of Commerce, Woodhouse Lane, Leeds. The Scholarship is awarded for two years, and the award will cover the whole of the tuition fees and carry an allowance of £7/10/0d. The Education Committee reserve the right to revise the value of the award at the end of the school year, having regard to your family circumstances at that time. I am, Yours faithfully, Geo Guest, Director of Education."

Then there was a letter to my mother from Dr Austin, Principal, Leeds College of Commerce, on crested notepaper with the College's Latin motto, *Fortiter, Fideliter, Feliciter*. A real academic doctor, like Dr Arnold in *Tom Brown's Schooldays*! ". . . I congratulate you on your son's success. I am enclosing a permit for the School Cap, which may be obtained at Messrs Rawcliffe, Duncan Street, Leeds."

I knew Rawcliffe's, the school outfitters, with its display of college and high school uniforms. I had given its windows a stare many a time. I knew that the College of Commerce cap was segmented navy blue and maroon, like a jockey's, and that the blazer was all maroon, like a Butlin redcoat's. I knew too that I would never get the blazer — my seven pounds ten a year allowance was barely enough to pay for my keep when I should have been about to start earning a wage packet, never mind blazers. I didn't care. I would swagger off to the tram stop each morning with my satchel bouncing against my bum and the School Cap on my head and the clog-wearers' cries of

"College cad!" ringing in my ears, and every day I should be in
Town.

While I had never played my white card at Osmondthorpe I had
suffered from Town withdrawal symptoms after the unexpected
freedom of three months off school, and I had taken to playing
truant regularly with the explanation that I had to have an X-ray at
the General Infirmary for my dislodged rib. Many years later at some
school reunion I asked one of the staff, an old friend of Mr Exley's,
whether my old mentor had ever suspected that I was playing
hookey. He laughed. "Suspected? He knew all along − you were
seen going into the Central Library!" Then why did he never say
anything? "He didn't want to cramp your style."

4 The College of Commerce, Woodhouse Lane, Leeds, proved not to be in Woodhouse Lane at all, the premises having been requisitioned by the wartime Ministry of Food. Instead the College was relocated at what had formerly been Darley Street Elementary School. Why the Ministry of Food couldn't have been housed in Darley Street was never explained. Nor did I ever learn what became of the school's former pupils. Perhaps they were given an indefinite holiday, like Osmondthorpe when the army moved in.

I found the arrangement perfectly agreeable. The school was an Edwardian or late-Victorian pile of the same model as Cockburn High School — all tiles and tarmac. The street itself was a cul-de-sac off North Street, an extension of Briggate and only three or four minutes' walk from Lewis's. This I found most convenient. It was a run-down neighbourhood of shabby terrrace houses, seedy corner shops, small clothing workshops where hunchbacked tailors sat cross-legged in the windows to get the available light, and a dusty little patch of grass and shrubbery known uneuphemistically, indeed officially, as the Jews' Park.

Far more interestingly, it proved to be a red light district. We were apprised of this fact in our first assembly by Dr Austin's deputy, who in a speech of consummate and cryptic delicacy warned newcomers to the school against having any truck with persons loitering in the street, however amiably disposed they might seem. It had to be explained to me by more worldly boys what he was driving at. I had never consciously set eyes on a prostitute, although it was by now part of my secret general knowledge that such creatures as "woars" as they were known in the Leeds vernacular did exist and were recognisable by the bangles around their ankles. From now on, when out and about in the murky environs of the College of Commerce, I would keep a sharp lookout for ladies sporting ankle bangles or other manifestations of their trade such as a fur stole or an over-abundance of lipstick, and treat suspects to a good long speculative stare. In reality most of them were probably pocket hands and trouser machinists from the clothing factories, waiting to meet their boyfriends.

Nor was this the only manifestation of my newly awakened interest in the opposite sex. I knew, because obviously I had hurried along to stare at the place the moment I heard about my scholarship, that Leeds College of Commerce was co-educational, and I had been keenly looking forward to sizing up the maroon-blazered equivalents of the pretty girls in their green blazers loitering on the steps of the Percival Leigh branch library. What I had not been prepared for was that girls would account for a good half of the College of Commerce's new intake, most of them quite fetching, and that we would sit in mixed classes.

The pairing-off process began at once. Three or four of the boys in my form were blond young Adonises who carried steel mirrors and pocket combs and had creases in their flannels, and they quickly commandeered, or were commandeered by, the three or four most comely girls. This was the signal for the rest of us similarly to seize partners. Only the boldest spirits made a direct approach: the convention at the callow age of thirteen was to despatch an emissary to test the water. Should he report back that the girl nominated for attention was prepared to entertain overtures, then if in funds you would invite her to the pictures, or if not then for a walk round the Jews' Park after school. Having prudently kept on my morning and Sunday paper rounds plus my various Saturday chores, I was still reasonably affluent, and the girl of my choice lived on my side of town within walking distance of the Shaftesbury Cinema in York Road, which had those double seats in the back rows known as "love seats". She was a raven-haired beauty called Heather, with full, generous lips and what even I could recognise was a good figure, and I could not believe my luck. We became engaged to be married on her fourteenth birthday during the *Gaumont British News* and were to remain in this state of innocent bliss until pitched out into the cold world at the end of our two-year course.

My emissary (and I his) was a lad I had known slightly at Osmondthorpe called Ray Hill. We were the only two in our year to have made it to the College of Commerce — in fact it emerged that most of our fellow-examinees were being tested for the College of

Technology, where their skills at fashioning bookends and copper ashtrays in woodwork and metalwork classes would be channelled into jobs that would give them a future as engineers and draughtsmen in the great foundries and locomotive and printing works of Hunslet. For our part, we were to be trained as clerks. Ray and I, in our scornful mutual rejection of so dreary a scenario – he was to become a teacher, jazz clarinettist and subsequently a lecturer in drama – were quick to establish ourselves as the best of friends, and have remained so all our lives.

Despite the distraction of Heather at the adjoining desk, I quickly settled into the College of Commerce routine. The lessons were novel and interesting: economic history instead of boring kings and queens, commercial geography instead of rivers and mountain ranges, business economics instead of John having twelve oranges and Mary three, and shorthand and typewriting in place of finger-lacerating handicrafts. I could not have enough of either of these latter activities. We were taught touch typing, a tin shield screening the keys from view so that one had to synchronise one's fingers to a representation of the QWERTY keyboard as displayed in the exercise manual. We typed our exercises rhythmically, accompanied by a selection of military two-steps on a tinny old gramophone, to which show-offs would get up and dance when our typing instructress went out of the room, which she did frequently since the wartime shortage of teachers obliged her to take two classes simultaneously. She also taught us shorthand: this I loved from the start and quickly mastered the intriguing grammalogue repertoire of hooks and whorls and curves, all reminiscent of the extravagant hieroglyphics with which I had covered the staves of my Banks's Music Arcade manuscript paper so long ago now. Billets-doux in near-impeccable Pitman were soon passing to and fro between Heather and me.

The atmosphere of the place was delightfully informal after the constraints of a council school. At break-time you were not turned out of doors regardless of the weather but could loaf around in form room or assembly hall chattering or catching up on homework. At lunchtime, after you had eaten your sandwiches (exotic ration-stretching concoctions of dried currants and raisins, grated carrot and cocoa powder, inspired by the government's Food Facts hints in the newspapers) in the basement refectory – there were no school dinners available – you were expected to remain on the premises and certainly not to go into Town, perhaps because of the good Dr Austin's fears about the ankle-bangled street-corner influences we had been warned against (it did cross our minds to wonder, the subject of the North Street "woars" being a recurring topic of conversation, why the College had agreed to move into a red light district in the first place); but the rule was widely ignored.

Ray Hill and I therefore regularly gulped down our sandwiches or even ate them on the hoof in our hurry to get into Lewis's or over to the Market; or, increasingly, to such intriguing venues as the rubber goods shop on Leeds Bridge with its baffling but provocative display of faded booklets with titles like *What Every Single Man Should Know* and *Talks to the About-to-be-Wed*; and to the City Varieties, a theatre then of low repute, where we would feast our eyes on the display case of star-spangled photo-stills of scantily dressed showgirls appearing in such daring revues as *Strip, Strip Hooray* and *Nudes of the World*. This distinct widening of my Leeds horizons was under Ray's influence. While I suppose my age of innocence would have been drawing to a close anyway, he was certainly instrumental in hurrying it along.

More innocently, if no less foolhardily had we been spotted by anyone in authority, we became habitués of the city's only amusement arcade in a dingy street near the Corn Exchange, where we would try to win cigarettes — then in chronic short supply like practically everything else — from the penny-in-the-slot mechanical crane. Like most boys in Leeds I had been smoking whenever the opportunity arose from the age of about eight, usually the odd cadged Woodbine or dog-ends picked up at tram stops. Now that I was in long trousers I regarded smoking, along with going about with Heather, reading much-passed-around copies of a racy magazine called *Razzle*, and staying out till what my mother indulgently called "all hours", as part of my emancipation. With my new-found freedom, the allure of Town was stronger than ever: it now promised illicit joys of which I had so far had only a glimmer, and I wanted to be on hand when the time for sampling them came around.

While I had left Hunslet and the Halton Moor Cycling Club somewhat in the lurch by now, I would still continue my explorations of Town whenever the opportunity presented itself, now often with Ray who shared my insatiable curiosity about facets of Leeds not previously encountered. Ray was something of an artist and so we would sometimes amble around the Art Gallery, giving any portrayals of naked or near-naked females a particularly attentive stare; we were also to be first in the queue when a travelling exhibition of Picasso and Matisse came to Lewis's, loftily distancing ourselves from the ribald comments of those – the majority, it seemed – who had come to scoff. Ray was interested in poster work and would happily travel great distances across the city to study the latest handiwork of some admired commercial artist. I was equally happy to accompany him, and through him learned to recognise individual styles. One lunchtime, having discovered in the course of my travels that Hemingway's Brewery, of *Fifty Years of Progress* fame, had a spanking new advertisement hoarding of quite impressive design, I insisted on taking Ray by tram to stare at it, and to the bemusement of passers-by blindfolding him with my handkerchief as we neared the spot so that the head-on impact of this splendid work of art should not be spoiled for him. The consequence of this aesthetic pilgrimage was that we were fifteen minutes late back for the afternoon typing class. We were sent to Dr Austin's deputy who questioned us keenly if obliquely, plainly not believing the account we gave of our movements and probably suspecting that we had been lured into a house of ill-fame. No such luck. Though solemnly warned that we must not venture beyond the school gates without permission in future, after a decent interval we cautiously resumed our lunchtime rambles, but taking care to steer clear of such pits of iniquity as the City Varieties, the rubber goods shop, the amusement arcade, and – a recent acquisition – what passed at the time for a smutty bookshop, stocking pin-up magazines, Hank Janson paperbacks, *Razzle*, and a saucy local publication entitled *A Basinful of Fun*. But siren-like, they were beckoning.

It does need to be said about the *Basinful of Fun* that my interest in its mildly risqué contents was not exclusively lascivious but also vocational. As a published, if not paid, contributor to the *National Savings News*, I had for some months been looking fruitlessly for another market undemanding enough to take my standard of work of the time. *A Basinful of Fun*, a compilation of feeble short-short stories and feebler jokes, seemed right up my street: I had a whole cupboard drawerful of feeble material at home. Furthermore, the editorial announcement in each issue of the *BOF* could not have been more encouraging: "The Editor invites contributions of Jokes, Bright and Breezy Articles, or Sketches. All material accepted is paid for at the Highest Rates on Publication. Address your contribution to: Editorial Department, A Basinful of Fun, Stafford Street, Leeds 10.''

Having raided the pages of the *Flag* and other Halton Moor Printing Works titles, I assembled a batch of my work at once. Realising from the postal address that the *BOF* must be in Hunslet, I then set off to hand in my submissions and at the same time have a good long stare at the editorial offices. With any luck, I might catch a glimpse of the editor himself, sitting with his waistcoat unbuttoned at a roll-top desk and chuckling over the galley proofs of his next issue – perhaps, with even more luck, including one or more of my own effusions, although I was bound to concede that since I was still clutching them in my hand this was more than unlikely. After asking directions I was happy to discover – an encouraging portent – that Stafford Street was but a short step from Low Road. I looked around for the Editorial Department of *A Basinful of Fun*, which in my mind's eye I had occupying a building of the size and grandeur of Alf Cooke's Printing Works. There were no commercial premises of any kind in the street, which was an ordinary cobbled terrace hung with lines of washing. The offices of the *Basinful of Fun* were undistinguished by so much as a brass plate or even a bakelite one. The editorial sanctum could only have been either a net-curtained front room or the spare bedroom. Putting disappointment behind me – after all, had not Edgar Wallace produced a racing sheet from a garret over a barber's shop in an alley off Fleet Street? – I emboldened myself to rattle the letter-box. There was no reply, and so I posted my contributions through it, never to set eyes on them again.

My two years at the College of Commerce ticked pleasantly by. Academically the competition was tougher than at my elementary schools, while the laxity of discipline provided more opportunities for fooling around, a combination which at the end of my second term was to result in my coming a humiliating fourteenth out of twenty-seven in English. This was after I had skimped an essay and comprehension test in my eagerness to complete a surreptitiously hand-printed samizdat magazine entitled, in Gothic lettering inspired by the masthead of the *Yorkshire Evening Post*, the *Prostitute*, a supposedly satirical review of the activities of the ladies of North Street and their imagined connection with thinly disguised members of the staff and some of my fellow-students, both male and female (though not, of course, including Heather). This disgraceful

120

production, for which I should surely have been expelled had it fallen into the hands of Dr Austin, was to be the last in a line of hitherto wholesome publications that had stretched all the way from *Ronnie Rabbit's Weekly* via the *Flag* to the *Daily Treasure*. It was a lamentable end to the Halton Moor Printing Works.

In one subject, however, I consistently excelled, and that was commerce itself, which might have been tailor-made for me. Since the business of the College was to turn out succeeding waves of the city's office fodder, doubtless in the hope that we should all imperceptibly rise over the decades to become bank managers and chief accountants (as indeed most of us did), it had evidently been decided that we might as well know something about the trade and commerce of Leeds itself. To this end, rather than dealing in concepts so remote that they were near-abstract, such as the volume of New Zealand's wool exports, we were talking about the actual arrival of actual bales of wool on actual barges on the River Aire and the Leeds and Liverpool Canal, and their progress through the named mills of Leeds such as the Perseverance or the Albion to the named clothing factories of Leeds like John Barran's who invented the ready-made tailoring industry or Montague Burton the Tailor of Taste, to known retail outlets like Marks and Spencer who had got their start in Kirkgate Market, or the Mutual Clothing Club. It was like a non-alcoholic version of *Fifty Years of Progress: the Story of Hemingway's Brewery*; and while our commerce teacher was no Mr Exley, commercial Leeds came vividly to life for me in these lessons.

We also did commercial history, and this embraced the expansion of Victorian Leeds when it was throwing up public buildings with such vigour and confidence – Cuthbert Broderick was only twenty-nine when he designed the Town Hall, and only a few years older when he built the Corn Exchange – that I rather pined to have been a part of it all, to have attended improving classes at the Leeds Mechanics' Institute and public meetings at the Coliseum and *conversaziones* at the Leeds Philosophical and Literary Society, to have risen in the world to rub shoulders with the clothing barons and philanthropists at the Leeds Club and the Leeds Stock Exchange, to have had my account at Beckett's Bank and bought my cravats and linen at the Pygmalion, to have bathed at the Oriental Baths and worshipped at the Ebenezer Chapel and to have read my *Leeds Mercury* in the newsroom of the Leeds Church Institute and borrowed three-decker novels from the Leeds Library and taken my luncheon at the Great Northern Station Hotel. They must have been heady days and the effect of hearing about them was to make one itch to get out and take one's place in the commercial life of Leeds. Perhaps that was the idea.

5 Another favourite period in my College of Commerce days was sports afternoon, Friday. This was because, after putting in one or two tentative appearances when my services were never called upon, I ceased to attend it. Nobody seemed to notice, let alone mind. In the admirable absence of playing fields of our own, games – cricket or rugger for the boys, hockey or basketball for the girls, according to season – were held in Beckett Park, near the Headingley Cricket Ground. You were supposed to make your way there under your own steam, but the convention seemed to be that if you hadn't actually been picked for a game – and after the initial trial scrums, I never was – you were not obliged to turn up unless you wanted to watch or take part in a scratch kickabout. I for one had other fish to fry.

There was at that time a small chain of weekly newspapers in Leeds which rather grandiosely called itself the Leeds Guardian Series, comprising the *Armley and Wortley News* covering south Leeds, the *North Leeds News* covering north of the river, and the *Leeds Guardian* itself covering the central area in between. They were dull little papers, the equivalent of today's free sheets, devoting their editorial columns largely, indeed almost exclusively, to blurred group photographs and long lists of the names of those present at various functions ranging from weddings and funerals to whist drives and sales of work. I had been bile-green with envy to learn that a boy in another form at the College of Commerce, who went by the exotic-sounding name of Connor Walsh, had a Saturday job working as a part-time reporter for the Guardian Series. Covering bring-and-buy sales and Women's Institute bunfights might not have been exciting but it was a much better way of spending a Saturday than scraping out the innards of a leather-grinding machine, and so I sought out Walsh's company.

Alas, the Guardian's Saturday shift was over-subscribed, being abundantly supplied by a seething Fagin's mob of schoolboys hurtling about the city on their bicycles, feverishly picking up news snippets from parish halls and other centres of local intelligence, for which they were paid at the rate of about half a crown a column. However, I was granted an interview with the editor himself, the first editor I had ever met, a Mr Glover I think his name was. I was a little put out to find him wearing a leather apron — it seemed that as well as being the editor, Mr Glover was also the compositor, advertisement manager and chief reporter. The aproned editor was encouraging. While he could not offer me any work he was willing to consider for publication any items that I might bring in off my own bat. He gave me some valuable advice. "Remember," counselled Mr Glover, "that names make news." He meant that names sell local newspapers.

Enlisting the support of the Halton Moor Cycling Club, and armed with a list of contacts culled from church hall notice-boards, I began at once to devote my College of Commerce sports afternoons to pedalling furiously from vicar to vicar and social secretary to social secretary, filling my notebook with the names of marrow show prizewinners, dancing class medallists, best iced cake awards, and the like. Thus, as often as not, I was able to scoop the Guardian's authorised representative who came plodding behind me on the Saturday. It didn't matter to Mr Glover. He would give me half a crown and set my sheaf of news-making names in closely packed type.

In my last term at Darley Street, our commerce teacher transmogrified himself into our careers teacher and began to talk about jobs. It was assumed that most of the boys would go into banks and insurance companies or the council rates department, while the girls would become junior secretaries in the building societies and solicitors' offices. I had different ideas. My shorthand was verbatim, I was by now, after the initial shock, consistently top in English, and I had had some reporting experience. I went to Mr Glover and asked if he could see his way to taking me on full time. I was gratified to be offered a job there and then. I took this to be in recognition of my initiative in getting my Friday afternoon scoops, but he would probably have given the post to a horse had it accepted the terms. These were ten shillings a week.

I knew before even broaching it with my mother that it was out of the question. With the war droning on and three breadwinners at the front, she had been looking forward to my bringing home a proper wage packet. An extra thirty shillings a week coming in, the going rate for a fifteen-year-old clerk with shorthand and typing certificates, would make a great deal of difference. Even with the selfishness of youth, I could see her point. Her clothes were shabby – so were mine, come to that – the cheap oilcloth under the clip rugs was threadbare, and she was tired of counting the pennies. The clip rugs themselves had seen better days. I could remember, as a child, sitting by the fireside clipping strips from a carrier bag of old cloth remnants, which my mother would fashion into a rug by pricking them through a hessian backing. Now, in the modernistic Forties, she had been developing an insane desire for a proper factory-made half-moon hearthrug as seen in the Littlewood's catalogue. A proper rug demanded a proper job.

I ruled out Lloyd's Bank in Park Row, where Ray Hill and a few other classmates had taken themselves. I similarly resisted the temptation to follow Heather into the Leeds Permanent Building Society. In both these institutions you toiled in large open-plan offices under the beaky gaze of stoop-shouldered senior clerks. I knew precisely what I wanted: a small family establishment where the office was divided by frosted-glass partitions, preferably in one of the Victorian rabbit-warren chambers with which Leeds was then well endowed, where I should have access to a typewriter, and where I should be left in charge of the office during my employers' lunch hour. If I could not be a reporter then I would be a freelance journalist, writing articles and short stories under cover of the day ledger and typing them up on the firm's trusty Remington.

Consulting the list of available vacancies at the College of Commerce, I found what promised to be the ideal situation, although our careers teacher thought it an eccentric first choice. This was with the firm of J.T. Buckton & Sons, the Leeds Funeral Furnishers, whose motto was "We Never Sleep" (to which the sniggering rejoinder from everyone who heard it was "Maybe not, but the customers do"). Why an undertaker felt obliged to offer a twenty-four-hour service (all it meant was that the telephone was switched through to one of the partners' homes at night, so that the bereaved could ring up at three in the morning if they so wished) I never properly understood. The small office was in a converted shop at No. 18 New Station Street, a turning off Boar Lane between a Finlay's tobacco kiosk where I should ingratiate myself with the

125

motherly type who ran it and thus be favoured with under-the-counter cigarettes, and a famous pen shop where I had had many a stare at the intricate fans of nibs in the window and whose advertising placard I knew by heart: "They come as a boon and a blessing to men, the Pickwick, the Owl and the Waverley Pen." It was so near City Station that the windows rattled as the trains pulled out – the perfect address from my point of view.

The office was divided, as required, into cubicles and cubby-holes, and in one of the cubby-holes reposed the required trusty Remington. I was interviewed, or rather auditioned, by one of the two partners, Mr Palmer, a tall, schoolmasterly individual, reedy of voice and reedy in appearance, with a stiff collar a size too big for him to accommodate a prominent Adam's apple, who dictated a not too difficult letter which I took down in shorthand, and then directed me to transcribe it on to the typewriter. The subject-matter of the letter, concerning the sale of a suburban bungalow, seemed a curious choice for an undertaker, unless J.T. Buckton & Sons had a sideline in selling off the estates of the deceased. All became clear when I rolled a sheet of the firm's headed paper into the machine. As well as being funeral furnishers and incidentally a car hire service, which made sense when they had a fleet of limousines to maintain, they were also in business as auctioneers, surveyors and valuers, and estate agents. The explanation for all this diversity was that Mr Palmer, the estate agent, had married into the family of Mr Buckton, the undertaker – or perhaps Mr Buckton had married into his. At any rate they found it convenient to pool their resources and share an office. From my point of view it meant that my duties, however onerous, would at least be invigorated by the spice of variety.

In fact my duties – for my shorthand and typing having passed muster, I was appointed without further ado – proved remarkably light and extremely congenial. My first task of the day was to take down the heavy window shutters, which, in the first flush of working for a living, made me feel romantically like Kipps. Then I had to go across the street to the Craven Dairies cake shop and café with a filing tray of mugs for our early morning coffee. There were eight of these, the office being absurdly overstaffed. Besides Mr Palmer and Mr Buckton there was Mr Stead the cashier, Mr Pepper the rent collector, and four clerks including myself. Mr Palmer was out and about a good deal doing his surveying and valuing, while Mr Buckton – a dapper rubicund, bustling figure who was known as Mr

126

Percy to distinguish him from his extremely aged uncle Mr Willie who sometimes pottered into the office – was for ever hurrying off like the White Rabbit with the words "Get me next at the Infirmary" or "Get me next at the Old People's Home", where it was assumed he hustled for business for the undertaking side. Mr Pepper, a saturnine-looking fellow much given to singing snatches of obscure low music-hall ditties such as "My old woman Marie Anne, scraped out me ears with a corned beef can", would gulp down his morning coffee, seize his rent register and disappear for the day, not returning until around five o'clock to cash up. This would leave the office in the possession of the four clerks and Mr Stead, an amiable soul who sat over his ledgers smoking his pipe and when the chattering got out of hand would look over his glasses and say, "You all remind me of that phrase 'generally speaking'."

I was put in charge of the postage book. This suited me perfectly, for much of Buckton's correspondence was with other firms in Town, and it was the partners' policy that any letters within the Leeds 1 postal district had to be delivered by hand to save postage. From the start, then, I enjoyed a carefree forty-five minutes or so each morning wandering around Town. My daily post round, furthermore, got me into buildings I had only dared stare at before – a rare chance to gape into the magnificent interiors of the Gothic banks and assurance companies with their mosaic floors and marble pillars and brass grilles and mahogany fittings and Venetian windows, not so very long before they were all brought tumbling down by the developers; and at the domed university library, as splendid as the British Museum Reading Room, and which I got a peep at while delivering a letter to an improbably appointed Professor of Leather with whom Mr Palmer had some business; and, by contrast, the stunningly modernistic lobby of the Queen's Hotel, where I ventured down into the men's lavatory to see what it was like, and was so impressed that I abandoned the smelly City Square Gents' and in future – so long as I was clutching a bundle of letters as my passport – always made use of the Queen's.

There were other regular errands from which there seemed no pressing need to hurry back: collecting inscribed coffin plates from the engraving firm of Ingall, Parsons, Clive and Co. in Basinghall Street, or placing death notices and property column small ads with the *Yorkshire Evening Post* and *Yorkshire Evening News* – I never crossed their thresholds without reminding myself that I was walking into a real live newspaper office; and while of course I never got beyond the advertising counter, there was always an interesting display of news pictures to look at. Then, the car hire wing of Buckton's being in the habit of booking out limousines just when they were needed for funerals, I was quite often required to run along to the cab rank at the side of the Majestic Cinema and requisition a couple of taxis. This, by and by, gave me privileged access to the Quebec Street Taxi Shelter, a ramshackle wooden structure going back to the horse-cab days, built for the cabbies by sympathetic Quakers as a place to have a warm and a cup of tea. It was also used extensively for games of penny brag, which perhaps the Quakers did not have in mind. Losing all my money to the taxi drivers made me feel immensely grown-up. And they never charged me for the tea.

Another source of dalliance was the basement Gambit Café in Park Row, a real find — an Edwardian survival where all the tables were marked out as chessboards and not only rheumy-eyed old men but keen young clerks and middle-aged bookkeepers played out their tournaments over a cup of coffee and a Marie Louise biscuit, and the waitresses went about on tiptoe. Office staff, in the absence of canteens or dispensing machines, were then commonly allowed leave from their desks for a fifteen-minute morning and afternoon break, usually extended to half an hour or so, when they were entitled to relax in the café or teashop of their choice. I imagine the privilege extended to me too, but I was never in the office long enough to exercise it. The Gambit Café, long ago demolished of course, became a regular haunt. Although I did not myself play chess it was a fascinating game to watch, and the players even more so — perhaps I did not yet recognise that many of them were ever so self-consciously "characters". Heavily under the influence of P.G. Wodehouse, I planned a series of tales with a chess club background in emulation of his Oldest Member golf stories. Since I did not know the first thing about the game the project fortunately never got under way.

Back at the office, life went at a leisurely pace. A good deal of Craven Dairies coffee was drunk and such work as there was to do was performed against a background of chit-chat and badinage. My little cubby-hole was tucked away at the end of the still extant shop counter, and there I spent much of my time none too surreptitiously scribbling away at my sub-Wodehouse stories set in Mayfair, wherever that might have been (the notion of using an undertaker's parlour as a setting did not cross my seething mind). Occasionally these endeavours would be interrupted by Mr Palmer who was in the habit of dictating long letters on the subject of property tax and death duties to the *Yorkshire Post* (like me, he never got to see his efforts in print); or by the even more occasional tinkling of the shop bell when I would have to turn away some hopeful looking for a flat to let or assume a suitably sombre expression for someone wishing to arrange a funeral. With so much freedom to come and go during working hours, I rarely went out in my lunch hour but spent the time typing up my stories, invariably sustaining myself with two toasted teacakes from the Craven Dairies. (I subsequently calculated that in my service with Buckton's I consumed some 1,400 toasted teacakes.)

When I had nothing to type up and fresh inspiration flagged I would sometimes potter around in the basement stockroom where I took a morbid interest in the stacked cardboard boxes of shrouds, coffin plates and coffin handles in a range of qualities to suit every pocket. (The actual coffins, or caskets as they were known in the trade, were carpentered in one of the many back-street workshops of Hunslet.)

It was while mooning about in this manner that I discovered something of an incendiarist streak in myself. There was rather unwisely stored among the cotton shrouds and cardboard boxes a can of petrol for the emergency use of the limousines. I had heard that petrol was highly combustible but had never wholly believed it, since I knew what an age it took to set fire to the small quantity of brandy my mother allowed on the Christmas pudding, and what a dismal flicker it finally produced. I decided to put the theory to the test. I poured a few drops of petrol into the stone sink next to the lavatory and tossed in a lighted match. It blazed merrily. During subsequent lunchtimes I developed the experiment further. There was a tin wash-bowl in the sink. I found that by uptipping the bowl, pouring a little petrol beneath it and then throwing in a match, there would be a small explosion and the bowl would most satisfactorily jump a few inches into the air. In easy stages I increased the dose until the wash-bowl was shooting up ceilingwards like a flying saucer, and the sink was a blazing inferno in miniature. Fortunately for me — for if a leaping tongue of flame had ever touched the nearby stack of shroud boxes the whole office would have gone up and I with it — the petrol-can began to feel alarmingly light and I thought I had better desist.

That did not, however, quite put an end to my arsonist tendencies. One day I was sent on some errand to the firm's garages up in the university district, opposite the Leeds Maternity Home. Here there was a petrol pump to service the hearse and limousines. Recently there had been a delivery to the pump and a few feet away from it was a shallow pool of petrol where the tanker driver had allowed a good couple of gallons to escape. I was smoking a cigarette and wondered idly whether I could get as spectacular an effect from this pool of petrol as I had been getting from the more contained basement sink. Without further thought I stupidly threw in my cigarette end and stood well back.

If there were flames I could not see them, for instantly a black, impenetrable cloud began to rise from the ground. It went on rising and expanding at an alarming rate, its acrid billows fanning ever outward. A light breeze carried the black smoke, as thick as any smog, through the open windows of the maternity home, which was instantly evacuated. As bewildered hordes of pregnant women in their nightdresses and nurses clutching armfuls of mewling babies streamed out into the forecourt, two or three of Buckton's drivers, carrying buckets of sand intended to extinguish incendiary bombs, dealt efficiently with the conflagration. One of them asked if I had been smoking. I denied doing anything so half-witted, and blamed a passer-by. Again I had been lucky: had the pool of petrol been connected by the merest trickle to the pump and its underground reservoir of hundreds of gallons, it would have been not a tin basin but a hearse and six limousines that had flown sky-high. That episode concluded my experiments.

After I had been with Buckton's about a year, the senior clerk who had been Mr Pepper's assistant, collecting stray rents from outlying districts two or three afternoons a week, was called up into the army and I was appointed in his place. Mr Pepper took me across to the Craven Dairies for coffee and Kunzle cakes and, so to speak, marked my card. The rent rounds I had been assigned were all a long bus ride away and, he intimated with a wink, you could wait a long time for some of these buses. If by any chance I did happen to get back into Town much before five, there was little point in giving anyone the impression that the job could be done in a couple of hours, now was there? Better while away the time at the News Theatre or take myself off for afternoon tea somewhere – not Jacomelli's, because that was where Mr Percy took his afternoon tea. I got the message, and I would certainly not be the one to let Mr Pepper down. With another wink, this time a lascivious one, he gave me one further piece of advice. When I got to a certain street, I might find a certain tenant quite obviously wearing nothing but a dressing-gown. If I was nice to her and didn't press her for the arrears, she might be nice to me and give me one of her home-made baps. Mr Pepper cackled wickedly. I got that message too.

My rounds were all in isolated mining villages on the outskirts of Leeds, each consisting of no more than a dozen to fifteen calls — mostly the estates of ladies of a certain age who had been left a clump of cottages or even a street or two by their fathers, like Mrs Codelyn in Arnold Bennett's *The Card*. Most of the properties were near-slums and the war-controlled rents, half a crown a week or three and sixpence at most, barely worth collecting. The certain lady in the certain street, on my first day as a rent collector, when I rapped on her door with beating heart and called "Rent please!" in a near-falsetto voice, proved to be a toothless old crone — Mr Pepper had been pulling my leg. Or had he? For the grimy rag on her back was undoubtedly a dressing-gown, and wrinkled skin was visible through the tatters. I took the rent money and fled.

But Mr Pepper was certainly right about one thing. My rents collected, I could comfortably have made it to Town by three o'clock. My predecessor, like the senior rent collector himself, had never got back to the office before five at the earliest. I wondered how Mr Pepper spent his afternoons.

As I stood at the corporation bus stop, tossing up in my mind between the News Theatre and a stroll round Kirkgate Market followed by a visit to the White Rose milk bar, I saw an unfamiliar Yorkshire Woollen District double-decker coming the other way. It was going to Bradford. On impulse, I ran across the road and flagged it down. It had been a long time since my burning desire to go and have a look at Bradford had culminated in the Yorkshire Penny Bank forgery, but I had made it at last.

Thus began a new series of expeditions and explorations to places that had hitherto only been names in the newspapers or on the fronts of buses — Bradford, Dewsbury, Wakefield, Halifax, Heckmondwike . . . each with its covered market (Bradford's was impertinently called Kirkgate; even more impertinently, it has long since been pulled down and replaced by the Kirkgate Shopping Centre), each with its Town Hall and municipal offices and chapels and tabernacles, each with its arcades and accompanying carillons, each with its tram-cars or anyway trolley buses, each with its theatres and cinemas and pork shops and Pen Corners and Montague Burton the Tailor of Taste and department stores, each with its statues of aldermen and benefactors, yet all so different from Leeds.

I liked the smaller mill towns, nestling under the moors so that from the top of the unfamiliar bus before the steep descent you had a bird's-eye view of the whole community from its cradle to the grave − schools, chapels, shops, office buildings, factories, meeting halls, pubs, hospitals, all crammed together in one compact hollow, the crowded mill chimneys poking upwards like the sticks in a saucer of cocktail snacks, and the graveyards edging slowly up the hillsides.

Wakefield, the West Riding's county seat, I cared for less − too clean and orderly by far, and too much like a southern market town − not that I had ever set foot in a southern market town − for my liking. As for Bradford, on the other hand, if at first sight it seemed superficially a replica of Leeds I soon saw otherwise: not only was its Lewis's called Brown Muff's, its Grand Theatre the Alhambra and its *Evening Post* the *Telegraph & Argus*, but the buildings were blacker, their stone stonier and sturdier, the accents broader, the very air tangier from the city's closer proximity to the Pennines; and the people were more confident, cockier even, conscious that if Leeds was the city of a thousand trades then Bradford was the city of one, and that one was wool. Woolopolis.

I took to Bradford and went there often, as happy to be wandering its streets and squares as those of my home city. I was, so I was discovering, cosmopolitanly promiscuous. I belonged anywhere, so long as it was big enough and bustling enough and brash enough, and sported a Bovril sign picked out in electric light bulbs.

6 As to where I went after I had put up Buckton's shutters, my last duty of the day, that would depend. It was rarely straight home to Halton Moor.

If I had a girl in tow we might go to the pictures — nearly always one of the local houses, half the price of the super- and not-so-super-cinemas in Town. The trick was to find a girlfriend who lived on your own side of the city; otherwise, after the prolonged goodnights by the garden gate or, if she lived in one of the back-to-backs, within the communal midden, you would find yourself tramping miles homeward from the catchment area of some God-forsaken Electra or fleapit Picturedrome where the tramlines ended.

There was, happily, no shortage of cinemas on my side of town. As my friend Gerald Kaufman reminds me in the entertaining Leeds chapters of his book *My Life in the Silver Screen*, the best volume of film-going memoirs ever written by a politician, there were then fifty-five cinemas in Leeds, and while there was none within walking distance of Halton Moor — or not the distance anyone would trouble to walk without the incentive of a girl waiting at the other end — there were a good dozen within fairly easy reach, all changing their programmes twice a week, and ranging in quality from the first suburban super-cinema in Leeds, the Regal at Crossgates, to the nearby Ritz as it laughingly called itself, which was little more than a corrugated-iron-roofed brick shack within rattling distance of the railway.

My routine on these occasions was to have a modest high tea in Town and then meet the girl at about half past seven on the steps of the appointed picture house. This was not meanness but economy: with the few shillings my mother allowed me back out of my wages, plus the earnings from my Sunday newspaper rounds which I still had the sense to keep going, plus the odd coppers my creative bookkeeping methods managed to squeeze out of Buckton's petty cash for my rent-collecting expenses (I had found that one ninepenny bus ride only cost sixpence if I got off a couple of stops early and walked an extra third of a mile), I had little more in my pockets now than when I had been a schoolboy entrepreneur; and my expenses were heavier. Besides, it was received wisdom that girls always liked to go home and change before they went out for the evening – and anyway, they were in with a good chance of being treated to a fish and chip supper after the speeded-up, scratchy notes of the National Anthem had emptied all but the patriotic one-and-nines where the patrons still stood to attention. For just about every cinema was ringed by fish and chip saloons, and their siren, batter-and-vinegar tang and the tempting sight of them, even in the blackout – some of them little art deco gems with enamelled sunburst cooking ranges; others, the older ones, with their leaded windows and stained-glass galleons, looking like miniature naval memorial chapels; and all of them with seagoing pubby names, the Argosy, the Neptune, the Golden Hind, the Lighthouse, the Mariner – was irresistible.

And besides again, I was enjoying exploring the cafés and restaurants of Leeds on my own – a novel experience, for of course I had never dared cross the daunting threshold of any of these premises on my white card perambulations or even in my College of Commerce days, although I had often stared at some of their more prepossessing exteriors.

Even though it was wartime it was still possible to eat in some style in Leeds, or in any provincial city. While the days had long gone, to my great regret, when one could dine at the Grand Restaurant in Boar Lane to the strains of the Imperial Viennese Orchestra, or in the onyx and marble splendour of the King Edward in its heyday when it was described as the handsomest grill room in the kingdom and by the then Lord Mayor as the finest building he had ever seen in his life, there was still the Kardomah where I could sit on a leatherette banquette with my back against the oak veneer wainscoting and be served a Welsh rarebit by a properly uniformed waitress. Or I could enjoy cinammon toast – a hitherto unknown delicacy which I knew I had to experience the instant I saw it on the menu – in the elegant surroundings of Betty's Café, an establishment which continues to this day in Harrogate, Ilkley and York but whose Leeds branch closed in the 1970s over Betty's inability to provide sufficient emergency exits to the satisfaction of the city council, for all that the only fire risk was that the toasted afternoon teacakes might be slightly overdone for the blue-rinse ladies of Roundhay and Moortown.

Down in Lower Briggate on the roof of what was now a bicycle shop I had long ago espied, and stared at, the faded, painted sign "Cocoa House", a relic of those Victorian and Edwardian days when the city had more cocoa houses than it now has kebab houses. We were now about two-thirds between that epoch and the fast food era, when the popular café was still all the go, very much in the mould of the Lyons Corner Houses. While we did not have a Lyons Corner House — we had two Lyons teashops, full of muttering old-age pensioners and newsvendors cashing up their takings — we did have Jacomelli's and we did have Powolny's and we did have Hagenbach's, and all the department stores had their "high class" (their expression) cafés, including Marshall and Snelgrove's who, in the after-whiff of the lunchtime haddock special, put on the occasional fashion show — Ray Hill and I took afternoon tea there once in the hope that slim-hipped mannequins would be modelling peach-coloured underwear. They were not.

If, at the time, some of these establishments were too pricey for my purse, I was glad to know that they were there and I did not envy the businessmen who sat down to their five-shilling (the wartime maximum price) dinners in oak-panelled ease. With my *Yorkshire Evening Post* propped up against an electro-plated teapot, and a fishcake (3d) on my plate, I whiled away many a happy hour in Joe Lyons.

And so to my rendezvous: seven thirty at the Regal or the Ritz or the Hillcrest or the Shaftesbury or the Star or the Harehills or the Regent. Like everybody else in Leeds — everybody in the country — I had been an inveterate cinemagoer since I could walk, cutting my milk teeth at the children's "Saturday rush" and graduating to the grand double feature plus full supporting programme (news, cartoon and "interest" — anything from *The March of Time* to a *Pete Smith Speciality*) at around the age of seven. If the big picture had an "A" certificate, requiring children to be accompanied by an adult, you simply hung around the box-office pleading, "Take us in, mister!" until some grown-up patron obliged. Unless you were a real film buff like the young Gerald Kaufman, who, as obsessed with cinemas as I was with cities, would go as far afield as Bradford to track down the latest recommendation of his hero critic Richard Winnington, you would see pretty well anything that was going, so that even with a preference for George Raft you would settle for Sonja Henie if necessary. So my cinemagoing being on the whole indiscriminate and uncritical, it did not matter to me in the least that by seven thirty when the usherette's torch guided us into, with any luck, the back row, the main feature would be half over. In those days programmes were continuous, an endless belt of cellulose nitrate, so anyone with any interest in how the film began would simply wait for it coming round again. What would now seem a bemusing way of seeing a film has never been better described than by Gerald Kaufman:

Then, at very long last, the lights dimmed again. The huge curtains swished open, revealing another curtain, this time satiny and frilled, which always startled by rising instead of parting. The screen, illuminated in colour, was revealed. The censor's certificate appeared. Then the lion roared or the searchlights flashed, or the WB shield challenged or the mountain encircled by stars loomed, or what appeared to be the Statue of Liberty shone her torch, or the World revolved or staccato radio signals sent their message, and the credit titles told me that I was at last to see the first part of what I had come to see.

Right from the beginning I recognised characters starting upon adventures whose outcome I already knew. I nodded with comprehension as some plot element which had puzzled me in its dénouement was made clear by its exposition. This act of deduction was not easy, for every few moments my concentration on the screen was interrupted first by the distracting beam of the usherette's torch and then by newcomers stumbling over my feet and impeding my view as they took their places, to be perplexed in their turn by what they saw . . .

By this system, when in 1944 we were afflicted with a passion for the scat songs of Danny Kaye, Ray Hill and I contrived to see his film *Up In Arms* four times in succession for the price of one at the Paramount on the corner of Briggate and the Headrow – at 12.35, 3.30, 6.15 and 9.15, sustaining ourselves with packed sandwiches during the long afternoon and evening.

But my experience when taking a girl to the pictures was that neither of us was particularly interested in the plot. The object of every youth in the auditorium was to insinuate his arm around the shoulders of his companion by the end of the trailer for next week's "forthcoming attraction"; the second and first features, with perhaps an ice-cream interval, were but the backdrop to his ongoing endeavours to perfect the art of French kissing as it was known, his free hand meanwhile setting off on as thorough an exploration of cleavage or stocking top as would be allowable. Opinion had it that factory girls from Montague Burton the Tailor of Taste were "easier" in this regard than office girls. That was not my experience: I found them equally resistant to whatever charms I supposed myself to have. When the sound of slapped wrists was ricocheting through the cinema to the distraction of Stewart Granger fans wishing to give *Fanny By Gaslight* their undivided attention, mine was not uncommonly the loudest.

Curiously, despite my fondness for the theatre, and the fact that a seat in the gods was a fraction of the price of the cheapest cinema seat, I never once invited a girl to the Theatre Royal or the Grand for as long as I lived in Leeds. Or perhaps not so curiously: I should have wanted to watch the play. There was also the problem of where to take them afterwards. Taking a girl to the pictures endowed one with the right to a minimum half an hour's dalliance in some blacked-out shop doorway or up a dark alley. An evening at the theatre would have culminated in nothing but a tram ride home, by which time it would be the moment for her to announce that she had to "go in", the gloom-inducing indication that the parentally imposed curfew hour had arrived. These curfews were rigidly imposed. When, over a two-year period, I was taking out Heather from the College of Commerce, we always said our goodnights in a telephone box at the top of her street. Nightly her father would pass within inches of us on his way home from the pub. Never did he show the slightest flicker of recognition of his daughter or the remotest concern over the white-faced young sex maniac who, his face twisted with lust fired by an intensity of purpose rather than an intensity of passion, had just hastily released her from his clutches. Heather's father knew that she would be home in precisely nine minutes, the moment her H. Samuel wristlet watch ticked up to the half hour.

There were other, and cheaper, venues than the pictures. There was what was euphemistically called going for a walk, which meant finding a secluded patch of grass and lying down on it. A favourite spot was Kirkstall Abbey on the River Aire, a celebrated beauty spot just down the road from the smoke-belching Kirkstall Forge, where suitors could conceal themselves among the ruins. Sunday afternoon in Roundhay Park was so popular an institution that come teatime, French-kiss-sated couples brushing leaves from their backs as they re-approached the magnificent gilt-tipped gates would find a whole fleet of a dozen or fifteen trams waiting to convey them back to Briggate.

My own preference for alfresco enjoyment of this sort was the corporation cemetery. One of my duties at Buckton's was to attend funerals and post myself in the church porch with a shorthand notebook in which to record, for the benefit of the deceased's loved ones, the names of all the mourners and which organisations they might be representing. This task I was only too happy to perform, since I could sell the list to the Leeds Guardian Series; it was also good for my ego to be mistaken for a proper reporter by the funeral party. Thus it was that I was acquainted with most of the cemeteries in Leeds, and their potential. It would not have been seemly to steer a girl towards the nearest cemetery on a Sunday afternoon, of course, for the paths between the headstones were busy with relatives changing the cut flowers; but on a dark evening, provided it was fine or anyway not actually raining, there was no better courting territory than among the polished granite vaults and marble broken columns and alabaster angels. Most girls thought it rather a lark, especially if the place was locked and we had to squeeze in through the railings (where these were mounted on a low wall they had mostly been taken away for scrap to help the war effort, and it was even easier to get in). At the convergence of the two wide boulevards that was the standard cemetery layout there would usually be a comfortable wooden shelter in the lee of the chapel of rest. It was a rare evening when it was already occupied, when it would become necessary to find a spot among the gravestones.

On balance I made considerably more progress in the cemetery than in the cinema, perhaps because my fumblings were not subject to the distraction of Alan Ladd.

Despite some modest successes in this area, what I was up against was that it was then extraordinarily difficult to lose one's virginity. The only contraceptive available was the half-crown packet of three bought from such furtive outlets as the rubber goods shop on Leeds Bridge; half a crown was a lot of money and most lads – with the exception of a few incurable optimists who carried a packet of Durex about with them for so long that their wallets became embossed with the circular ridge of its contents – did not care to make the investment until they were persuaded that they were going to get an adequate return. Consequently girls went in terror of becoming pregnant – as did boys of impregnating them, for there could only be one way to go upon learning that, in the misery-drenched words of Ingrid in Stan Barstow's *A Kind Of Loving*, "something that should have happened hasn't happened," and that was up the church aisle. Besides, convention very strongly laid down that respectable girls didn't do it until they were married, or at any rate properly engaged. I did contrive to become informally engaged on several occasions, but to no effect, possibly because no twelve-guinea ring from Dyson's of Time Ball Buildings ever changed hands.

The other route was to deliver oneself into the hands of the professionals. It was said that the minimum rate for the ladies of North Street was ten shillings, but that was for standing up against a greasy wall down a back alley, otherwise it was a pound. I demurred, and not only because I didn't know how to do it standing up (I didn't know how to do it lying down, come to that). We had all read by this time – a copy had circulated surreptitiously throughout the College of Commerce – a manual called *The Red Light*, with a picture of the stop-caution-go traffic lights on the cover, obtainable, by anyone with the unflagging nerve to go in and ask for it, from the rubber goods shop. As well as dealing with birth control, impotence, premature ejaculation, the periodic indisposition of women and so forth, it had a grisly section on venereal disease. While it was fairly specific, for its time, about the symptoms and possible effects, it was evasive on the subject of the cure; thus the wild stories circulating among the youth of the town about what they did to you in VD clinics with red-hot needles went unchecked. If that were not enough, the government – concerned more with its wartime manpower supplies than with the nation's health at large, I suspect – had mounted a fearsome campaign against VD that made today's AIDS onslaught look like a warning against tooth plaque. I particularly remember a poster of a couple of soldiers being enticed into the company of a streetwalker with the line, "Looking for a good time, boys?" or some such. The lady of the night was provocatively dressed and contoured, differing from the pin-ups in *Razzle* magazine only in the detail that instead of a pouting face she had a grinning skull. The assumption, or rather the presumption, was that gonorrhoea and syphilis were diseases passed on to men by women. While this was not one hundred per cent accepted — a strong school of thought had it that VD was introduced into the country by GIs, as the Great Plague was brought in by rats — nobody in my age group ever questioned that it was transmitted pretty well exclusively by prostitutes, or by women of loose morals if only one could find one, and that in the fullness of time it would make your nose drop off.

Like most of the population of Leeds I eventually lost my virginity on Ilkley Moor — in my case to a girl so well spoken that I thought there must be some mistake (I equated good diction with niceness, and it was well known that nice girls didn't do it — it took considerable persuasion to convince me that they sometimes did). Ilkley Moor was reached by a Sammy Ledgard bus and was distant enough from Leeds to persuade prospective lovers that they were practically abroad, where inhibitions are notoriously relaxed. Also the fare was so expensive — a shilling each way — that there was unspoken acceptance that the girl knew what she was letting herself in for. After the deed was done we trekked across the moor to a famous pub called Dick Hudson's — a familiar and almost compulsory pilgrimage for every visitor from Leeds — where, without my age being called into question, I bought us both a shandy. I had never tasted alcohol before, even in this diluted form, and I felt quite grown up. Two firsts in one day.

7   If there was no current girlfriend and Ray Hill was
     similarly unencumbered, we would as often as not meet up
     after work with a view to remedying the deficiency.
Usually we would assemble at the White Rose milk bar on Boar
Lane, in the hope of making the acquaintance of a couple of office
girls. Drawing a blank there, we would then try the Moo-cow milk
bar in Briggate. Failing any luck here either, we would roam the
Town centre in a search for talent, starting with the queues outside
the Paramount, Tower and Assembly Rooms cinemas just along
Briggate. Should we spot any likely candidates, we might insinuate
ourselves into the queue and engage them in conversation. This did
not happen often. We might then go and hang around outside the
College of Art where there were some quite attractive students who
might wish to paint us. This never happened at all.

Should we be feeling particularly desperate for female company,
we might even take ourselves out to Crossgates to see if there were
any recent additions among the green blazers on the steps of the
Percival Leigh branch library. One evening we encountered a set of
quite acceptable identical twins, Susan and Pearl, and persuaded
them to accompany us to the Regal across the road. In terms of
limited sexual progress, the outing could be counted a success. When
next we met this accommodating pair, by arrangement outside the
park gates, it was fairly obvious from their occasional fits of giggles
that Susan had elected to become Pearl and Pearl Susan. We didn't
mind the deception in the least – it added piquancy to the
relationship. This delightful comedy of errors continued throughout
most of one summer.

One evening at the White Rose milk bar Ray and I bumped into
our old College of Commerce colleague Walsh (he was one of those
individuals who are invariably addressed only by their surname, for
no known reason). Although Walsh was destined to become a

141

successful Fleet Street journalist, like me he had regretfully been obliged to turn down the *Leeds Guardian*'s offer of ten shillings a week and was working his way through a bewilderingly rapid series of office jobs, the thinking behind this apparent restlessness being that if you gave the management notice within your first fortnight, they would pay you off and let you go at once sooner than continue to train you for work you would not be doing, thus you would be getting a paid bonus of free time.

Once again I had cause to be envious of Walsh: on the excuse of having to stay up late playing the piano in a jazz group, he had managed to persuade his family to allow him to take his very own flat in Town. That this flat turned out to be the outside coal cellar of a crumbling old villa in the university area in no way diminished its desirability in my eyes. Snugly fitted out with a truckle bed, a primus stove, an old basket chair that Walsh had rescued from a compost heap, and stacked orange boxes to serve as bookshelves, it had all the bachelor cosiness, to me and no doubt to its occupant, of No. 18B Baker Street.

Walsh, with his glasses repaired with sticking plaster and a long yellow raincoat which he never ever removed, even while playing boogie-woogie on some battered old piano when it draped from his shoulders like the wings of a fruit bat, resembled a youthful Ukridge and was well on his way to becoming a bohemian. He had some interesting eccentrics among his friends. One was a formidably intelligent lad called Henry who could play chess blindfold, committing the moves to memory as they were transmitted to him. Unfortunately, Henry was to turn his unusual brain to cheque forgery and he finished up in Armley Jail. (There, remembering the Yorkshire Penny Bank forgery, but for the grace of God . . .) Another was Roy, a boy of restless but undirected intellect who was famous among his cronies for having stood up at a meeting of the Leeds Film Society and earnestly enquired of the visiting lecturer from London whether he would not agree that films made of celluloid were superior to those manufactured out of baked clay, owing to the greater flexibility of the former. Roy, possibly in the course of some teenage experiment, subsequently gassed himself. The jazz band to which he, Walsh and by now Ray Hill belonged played "When the Saints Go Marching In" over his grave, when I, who had had to get leave from an undertaker's to attend a funeral, was more moved than I cared to admit. But not so moved that I did not sell the story to the *Leeds Guardian*.

A third friend of Walsh's was Rick, now a highly respected Leeds solicitor, who while studying for his examinations was living a few doors from the coveted coal cellar in what I understood by the expression "rooms" – another enviable apartment. Rick had the first proper privately owned library I had ever set eyes on, one of his three rooms being devoted entirely to books in their hundred upon hundred, shelved on planks supported by house bricks, arranged not only around the walls but in four or five rows across the room like a public library. Rick was an intensely political animal, and his literary taste was almost exclusively political. He would lend out books by the armful; thus it was that I was introduced to the orange limp-cloth volumes of the Left Book Club, to Jack London's *The Iron Heel*, to Karl Marx, to H.G. Wells other than as the author of *Kipps* and *The Invisible Man*, to Shaw, to a writer known as George Orwell who had written *Down and Out in Paris and London* and *The Road to Wigan Pier* . . .

Then there was Will, older than any of us, a keen Esperantist and world peace fanatic and a great influence on Walsh who in his turn was a great influence on me. Chain-smoking OPs – that category, rather than brand, of cigarettes known as Other People's – and with his patched-up spectacles steamed up with enthusiasm, Walsh would harangue me, in Esperanto, about world peace by the hour. I drank deeply of this company.

On that chance encounter at the White Rose milk bar, however, our first interest in Walsh was that he was on his way to take part in a mixed doubles table tennis tournament at a church youth club in Hunslet. Mixed meant girls. With nothing else to do that evening, Ray Hill and I decided to accompany our friend and lend him our support.

We had never thought of youth clubs. Youth meant male, an impression dispiritingly confirmed by a single fleeting visit to the YMCA hut in Osmondthorpe, where the membership was uncompromisingly of our own sex only. But now we were about to be pitched into a world of mixed table tennis and mixed who knew what else? To Hunslet, then – where it had to be said that first impressions were disappointing, there being only two girls among a company of twelve, and both of them seemingly spoken for. But we acknowledged that Walsh had opened doors for us. And not only did we meet his beguiling friends Henry and Roy but Walsh introduced us to an equally interesting character named Willis Hall, a wiry, intense-looking youth of our own age who like Walsh and me had served his time selling columns of names — in his case, I learned, a sprinkling of them fictitious to eke out the space — to the *Leeds Guardian*. It had never crossed my mind to make names up and I was duly impressed. While this enterprising but taciturn fellow did not straight away admit to so flamboyant an ambition himself, I had it from Walsh that he had set his heart on becoming a writer or journalist or both, and had already made approaches to the *Basinful of Fun* and the *Yorkshire Evening News*. The *News*, in due course, was to take him on to its racing pages; meanwhile he was working in the Yorkshire Relish factory where by way of indoctrination the girls had smothered his private parts not in brown sauce as one might imagine, but in custard powder. We were to meet again, when he would admit to an addiction to vanilla flavouring.

New horizons having opened out for us, Ray Hill and I set about taking sightings of all the youth clubs in Leeds for female content. While there was a fair number of them, they all seemed to be attached to one or other religious denomination, to which members were supposed to owe allegiance and even occasionally to attend church or chapel. Thus, in the course of our researches, we became, in turn and sometimes simultaneously, members of the Baptist, Wesleyan, Congregational and Methodist persuasions, as well as returning to the bosom of the Church of England as and when expediency demanded. Only the doors of the Judean Club were closed to us.

Back in my white card days I had often stared at the Doric porticos and craggy frontages of some of these substantial places of worship and I was glad of the chance now to see the interiors — the youth club was usually down in the crypt — of such temples of non-conformity as the Brunswick Methodist Chapel with its box pews seating thousands, and the Oxford Place Wesleyan Chapel with its steep tiers of plain benches rising from an elegant circular balcony. But it was the attractiveness and availability of the female company rather than the architecture that won the day. Despite its being presided over by a Victorian throwback of a minister who believed modern ballroom dancing to be sinful (that was all right by me, since I couldn't dance), we settled eventually for the Belgrave Primitive Chapel (or if it was not, it certainly seemed it), just a few minutes' walk from Briggate and plentifully supplied with girls in blazers. To both Ray and me throughout the whole of our adolescence, a college blazer and white blouse was the last word in chic.

We settled down to a pleasant routine of Friday evening ping-pong, lantern lectures, mock parliaments and Camp coffee, the reward for which regime of clean living was to walk a selected girl home and see if you could make more progress this week than you had made last week. Sunday chapel was more or less compulsory if you wished to remain a member, and the Victorian throwback's hellfire sermons were interminable; but on these summer evenings there was always the tram ride out to Kirkstall Abbey afterwards with the promise of a white blouse yielding one more button. Admittedly, the promise may have been on the slender side but there was utterly nowhere else to go on Sunday anyway – we were still a good long way off the city referendum that was to permit the cinemas to open on the Sabbath, and all other places of entertainment and non-alcoholic refreshment were as firmly shuttered as if we had been living in Aberdeen.

Then, one golden week, the word began to percolate through the youth clubs and milk bars and office post-rooms of Leeds that an amazing new Sunday night youth club had just opened in the Priestley Hall of the Mill Hill Unitarian Chapel right on City Square, packed to the beams with girls (no doubt girls were hearing that it was packed to the beams with boys). Ray and I instantly became Unitarian converts, and on the following Sunday made haste to the Priestley Hall, named of course after the discoverer of oxygen and Mill Hill preacher whose statue out in City Square I had given many a meaningful stare in my white card era, perhaps unconsciously anticipating that he would be a useful contact one of these days. The place was thronged – not since morning assembly at the College of Commerce had I seen such a gathering of my own age group under one roof. It was only the second Sunday of the club's existence but that night – just in time for Ray and myself – the membership list closed at 250, the maximum allowed into the building. The following week there were hundreds of hopefuls queuing down the street to register their names on the waiting list – a scene that these days would only be replicated outside a commercial disco.

The Sunday Night Youth Club was the brainchild of Mill Hill's minister, the Rev Eric Price, one of the last of that lost breed of pipe-smoking, muscular Oxbridge Christians who used to organise East End lads' clubs back in the hungry Thirties. He had a talent for this sort of exercise such as I have only ever since come across in London club and restaurant entrepreneurs with the flair for magically transforming this or that establishment into the place of the moment. Without his apparently doing very much except puff away at his briar, the Priestley Hall became *the* place to be for the brighter teenagers (as they were yet to be called) of Leeds.

One of his secrets was his recognition that we were all children of the city, as attracted to the centre of things as moths to a candle. Another was his realisation that simply because you were placing a sizeable hall at youth's disposal you did not necessarily have to infest it with lantern slides and ping-pong — you could leave it to itself to become a seething indoor piazza where old friends would meet — Walsh and Willis Hall, I was happy to find, were among the earliest born-again Unitarians signing up with the Sunday Night Youth Club — and new friendships would be made. Besides this main meeting place the Priestley Hall was blessed with a goodly number of side rooms and in these, energetic and enthusiastic coteries quickly established little offspin clubs of their own — a music group, a discussion group, a philately group and so on, plus of course an Esperanto group and a world peace group. We were led to believe that we had started up these enterprises entirely on our own initiative. This was the third of the Rev Eric Price's great talents.

The hall had a proper stage with proper curtains, of the quality I could have done with when I was engrossed in the pages of *Let's Do A Play*. We did not do a play but we did several concert parties, of which I can remember little except that nothing could stop Ray Hill dressing up as a comic vicar and that girls used to come up to me and plead with me not to do my drunk act again. We also did our versions of various popular radio shows, the hit of the season being a spoof *Brains Trust* which Willis Hall and I knocked out together — the first of a series of collaborations which has so far continued, on and off, for close on fifty years.

The Club had not been going long when the Rev Price suggested — he never proposed, only put forward tentative ideas — that we might like to have our own magazine. I at once claimed the right to edit it, with Walsh, Ray and Willis as the editorial team. Fortunately no one seemed inclined to argue over this self-appointment, or I should have been most put out. The enterprising minister, who seemed to know everyone who was anyone in Leeds, went to his friend the general manager of the Yorkshire Conservative Newspaper Company, publishers of the *Yorkshire Post* and *Evening Post*, and persuaded him to print it for us. Having envisaged something run off on a jellygraph, I was most impressed and looked forward keenly to seeing the byline K.S. Waterhouse for only the second time in print (the S was for Spencer, my mother's maiden name: the style, of course, was in emulation of P.G. Wodehouse).

Ray Hill designed the cover. Walsh contributed an article on Esperanto and world peace. I contributed the short-short story that had failed to make the grade with *A Basinful of Fun*. Willis contributed his own *Basinful of Fun* rejections. By the time other members had handed in, or failed to hand in, their notes on various club activities (there was an especially lengthy report from the Esperanto group), there was still a page left over, and so I re-invented Michael Fox − one of my library ticket pseudonyms − who, a long way after the celebrated Cassandra of the *Daily Mirror*, whose waspish column I was one day to inherit, penned an attack on the editorial team for constituting a club within a club: "Whatever K.S. Waterhouse and his cronies may say to the contrary the Club is fast approaching the state where it is being governed by a clique . . ." This was a highly popular feature.

The magazine wasn't half bad as such efforts go, and whatever its deficiencies it did earn one distinction before it ran its course − it was the only youth club magazine I have ever come across to be threatened with a writ for libel.

It was just as I was about to put the Christmas number to bed that Walsh and Ray Hill came to me with the news that the club jazz band, from which they had jointly dropped out in disgust on the purist grounds that it was little more than a dance orchestra peddling Vera Lynn numbers, was demanding a fee of three shillings per performer to play at the Christmas social. While Ray and Walsh no doubt had an axe to grind, this was something for a frustrated journalist to make much of. Accordingly I cleared the Scrooge parody off the middle pages, and in a vitriolic article headed "SCANDAL!" trotted out Michael Fox to do his worst: "Let us expel these members from the club forthwith and make do with a comb and tissue paper . . ."

Unfortunately for me, the father of one of the traduced jazz musicians was a linotype operator on the *Yorkshire Post*, where a copy of the magazine fell into his hands before publication. He consulted the office lawyer who was at once on the telephone to Mill

Hill, warning that an action for libel could lie unless the offending issue was banned. To his great credit the Rev Eric Price did not take upon himself the role of censor as any other youth club leader in this situation would have done – he left it, or anyway gave a very good impression of leaving it, to my editorial discretion. My newly acquired sense of responsibility, naturally, went straight to my head and I agreed to suppress the Christmas number (I couldn't merely excise the offending pages, since in my excitement I had scrapped Ray Hill's standing cover and splashed the word WAR! across the front page in six-inch capitals). Sensing that everything after this would be anticlimax, I shortly afterwards handed over the editorial reins to others.

But Mill Hill remained a special place. Unlike most of the other youth clubs we had sampled, there was no pressure to attend its associated chapel, and I for one never did, for there was always some distraction in the Priestley Hall from early afternoon onwards. But a good number of members did start going to the Unitarian Chapel, out of curiosity or whatever motive – in those long-lost days it might even have been religion – and I was interested recently, upon glancing through a copy of the latest chapel newsletter someone had sent me, to see among the lists of stewards and flower-arrangers and so forth several well-remembered names from those effervescent days. But whether we finished up bona fide Unitarians or not, there cannot be any one of us who has forgotten Mill Hill or the excitement somehow generated by that pipe-puffing parson.

While there were girls in abundance at Mill Hill, the restless search for new talent went on unabated during the remainder of the week. Inspired by one of our fellow-members, a lad of Marxist bent who had given a talk on dialectical materialism, we tapped a new source of companionship – the political parties, beginning with the Young Communists, and progressing, when the only female young communist at the one meeting we tried proved to have a moustache, via the Labour League of Youth where we were similarly disappointed, to the Young Conservatives.

This was more promising. For one thing it gave me access to a handsome building I had often stared at – the Conservative Club on South Parade, next to the Bank of England. The Young Communists had been in a room over a shop and Labour in somebody's front room. For another, not only was there an excess of girls over boys but they were exclusively drawn from the blazer-wearing class. If there was a superfluity of tennis talk, Ray and I were well able to hold our own since we had played the odd game with the Crossgates twins on the municipal courts, using borrowed racquets. We were by now well versed, too, in those softened vowel sounds by which affected northerners try to pass themselves off as southerners, as in "Who's pat batter on the cashion?" The Young Conservatives made us most welcome, and on our very first – and, as it was to turn out, last – evening we were flattered to be invited by the very pretty secretary to attend the Club Flannel Dance the forthcoming Saturday. While we had no idea in what respect a Flannel Dance would differ from the Fifty Shilling Tailors Suit hops we had occasionally attended at Mill Hill, we keenly looked forward to it.

But there was a snag, an insuperable one. The very pretty secretary had no tickets about her very fetching person, and so she proposed to post them to us. And since I had snobbishly, if accurately, sensed that a council house address would not cut much ice with the Young Conservatives, I had resuscitated Trevor Austin of 82 Templemeads Way, Crossgates. Ray was my next door neighbour Nigel Fairfax. Any tickets sent to this completely fictitious thoroughfare would be returned to sender. I could, of course, have asked her to despatch the tickets to my workplace where I could have intercepted Trevor Austin's mail; but J.T. Buckton's the Leeds Undertakers (We Never Sleep) was hardly the most glamorous of office addresses, and in any case I had already told her that I was a reporter on the *Leeds Guardian* – not only to impress her but to corner any Young Conservative news item that might be going. The Flannel Dance would have been good for half a column and it was a shame I had to miss it.

But it did spur Ray and me on to do what we had been meaning to do for some time in our pursuit of the opposite sex, and that was to take dancing lessons.

It was customary at the time for offices to work on Saturday mornings, and a popular pursuit after a lunch of baked beans on toast at Woolworth's or Joe Lyons was to attend one of the several "studios of dance" which then flourished, all of them in upper rooms over shoe shops and dress shops, and all of them with names like the Yvette del Monte or the De Grey Firth School of Dancing. We enrolled at an establishment above the Co-op in Albion Street where, after a fashion, I learned to dance with a cane chair to the strains of Victor Sylvester records. Having grasped the rudiments of

149

the waltz, the quickstep and the foxtrot we graduated to the various dance halls of Leeds which, from their revolving mirrored globes to their fretwork painted plywood music stands, were identical in all respects but one: at one class of dance hall you would be expected to enquire, "Excuse me, may I have this dance?", while at another you would ask, "Are you getting up?"; and the girls for their part would respond, "No thank you, I'm just waiting for my friend" in the former category, or "Go on home, your mother wants your boots for loaf tins" in the latter.

From the Capitol, the Mecca, the Majestic, the Astoria and the 101, we gradually transferred our Saturday evening affections to the Big Top, a draughty marquee on Woodhouse Moor erected by the council as an attraction to persuade the populace to spend its holidays at home in this time of austerity and seaside resorts swathed in barbed wire; and there we danced out the war. The blackout had become the dim-out, and the piles of sandbags round the entrances to the Market and elsewhere were being shifted away at last − rather to my regret, for ever since I had discovered girls it had been as if a friendly local authority had sent a works lorry down Lovers' Lane tipping out mattresses every few yards. Cautiously optimistic advertisements were beginning to appear in the *Yorkshire Evening Post*: "Forward to Victory and normal supplies of Bassett's Original Liquorice Allsorts." Then one day on my way past the Corn Exchange I saw a workman perched on a ladder above the Oyster Bar opposite; he was testing and replacing the electric light bulbs in the Bovril sign. And then I knew we had Hitler on the run.

8 Right from the very beginning of my meanderings I had always been conscious of, if not always intoxicated by, the smells of the city, from the heavy blend of malt and hops and horse manure wafting out from the breweries to the delicate breath of eucalyptus and zinc ointment from the patent medicine shops; from the stench of blood — and was it fear? — that enveloped the corporation abattoir to the scent of Lapsang, Orange Pekoe and Fine Darjeeling drifting in through Buckton's fanlight from Elgie & Co.'s tea warehouse two doors along (where, snug among the tea chests up in the rafters, I was a periodic member of the all-night firewatch against incendiary bombs — a lark, but it would have been a better lark had girls been allowed to firewatch too).

Kirkgate Market was oranges and pineapples and wet fish and spice cake; the glittering arcades were Brasso and Navy Mixture and Thornton's toffee; the pork shops were the Bisto fragrance escaping through the funnel supporting the crust of a meat and potato pie; and Lewis's was the sweet vanilla of the American soda fountain. But perhaps the most pervasive odour was that of stale beer and cigarette smoke from the dozens and dozens of city pubs — especially those tucked away up the alleys, where it had a tendency to be pungently tinged with urine.

As a wandering child, I had found this smell thoroughly obnoxious, and I had not been too keen on it as a wandering College of Commerce student either. Now that I was a little older, while I still found the stink of last night's beer repellent as I mooched about the town delivering Buckton's mail or generally time-wasting, I did notice that as the day wore on these pub smells, except from those of the lowest of low ale-houses, grew less disagreeable and indeed became downright inviting. This was, of course, after the carbolic had done its work and the pubs had opened up again and fresh pints were pulled and fresh plugs of twist lit up, and from behind frosted-glass windows engraved with Prince of Wales feathers and dandified words like LUNCHEON and FINE WINES there was a rising hum of chatter as the first wave of customers compared notes over their racing greens.

I had not until now been particularly intrigued by pubs, not even to stare at. The reverse, in fact: I had regarded them, if I thought of them at all, as places of debauchery, somewhere between the city's illegal but flourishing back-street betting shops which anticipated the Betting and Gaming Act by a good many years, and licensed brothels. This was before the idea of licensed brothels became itself intriguing. I suppose I was influenced by my mother who, probably in reaction to my father's excesses, was a strict teetotaller – apart from the thimbleful of non-igniting brandy over the Christmas pudding, her nearest brush with the demon drink was to be taken by one of my uncles to sit on a bench outside the famous Tommy Wass's with a glass of lemonade, and that only because the original Wass family had run their former farmhouse as a refreshment room serving teas to cricketers and tennis players, so it didn't really count as a pub at all in the drinking-den sense. And then, in my childhood, I had seen enough beer-drunks lurching around the streets of Middleton. I had a vivid recollection of trying, when on my way to the fish shop one Saturday, to help up a drink-sodden miner who was lying flat out on the pavement – I got him into a sitting position but then was forced by his dead weight to let him go, and he snapped back like a hinged box lid, his head crashing against the ground with such a thickening thud that it sent reverberations along the paving stones.

But suddenly I was interested in pubs – though more interested in what went on inside them, I have to say, than in the taste of beer. It was one more layer of city life that I wanted to explore. Fortunately for my sense of curiosity, Ray Hill was simultaneously beginning to awaken to the possibilities of alcohol as an element of social life. We resolved to explore them.

It would be a risky business, for while at sixteen we could probably pass for eighteen, especially since we were both attempting to grow moustaches, the wartime regulations required everyone to carry an identity card and our ages could easily be checked. Furthermore, although we had taken the Conservative Club in our stride we didn't quite know, didn't know at all in fact, how to disport ourselves in a taproom. The secret, we decided, was confidence, and what bred confidence was familiarity. Before, then, entering the pub of our choice, an obscure tavern on the wrong side of Leeds Bridge where no one would know us, we reviewed our studies of the signwriter's art as applied to breweries, recalling phrases useful to the novice pub customer. Our opening line rehearsed, and a toss of the shilling we proposed to spend on beer deciding who would utter it, we marched into the public bar with a fair display of swagger.

I had a confused impression of bevelled mirrors reflecting Victorian green tiles and dark wood and burnished copper, like the interior of a Hansel and Gretel house of marzipan, slab chocolate and glazed gingerbread. The landlord, built like the burly saloon bar-keep in all the westerns we'd seen, detached himself from conversation with the only other customer. Ray cleared his throat. "Could we have two sparkling dinner ales, please?" The customer guffawed. The landlord, with a weary shake of the head, spoke not a word but simply pointed to the door. We shuffled out.

It was not until my initiatory half of shandy at Dick Hudson's on the day I lost my virginity on Ilkley Moor that I was to enter a pub again, and then only peripherally, since Dick Hudson's featured a hatch where hikers with their muddy boots could be served without actually setting foot in the bar parlour. But thereafter, Ray meanwhile having similarly acquitted himself on both counts, we became, if not pub regulars, then fairly constant under-age irregulars.

By trial and error — the error sometimes compounded by an ignominious exit — we learned the grammar of drinking, beginning with the tongue-twister, "Two halves of half and half, please", a half and half being the popular tipple of the day, a mixture of mild and bitter. Then there was one's uncertainty over the multiplicity of socially graded rooms then common. We discovered that if we ventured into the public bar wearing collar and tie, there were strange looks from the overalled regulars — perilous for anyone trying to go unnoticed. If we went into the snug, the domain of gnarled old pensioners and ladies sipping stout, there were stranger ones. Should there be a waiter on duty (as there still was in some saloon bars, where you pressed a bell for service), we could deduce from glares and sniffs that those who bought their own drinks at the bar were not expected to sit down. In some taprooms it was regarded as effeminate to sit down at all, while in the bigger, street-corner tiled pubs peculiar to Leeds it was customary to leave the various

153

comfortably appointed lounges and saloons to the womenfolk and drink out in the mosaic-paved corridor.

The nuances of drinking etiquette fascinated me — it was like being a volunteer in a Mass Observation survey. So, too, did pub architecture, for all that in most of the only licensed premises we dared venture into, usually insignificant little sawdust and spittoon houses well away from the city centre where we were unlikely to be spotted by neighbours out on the town, the decor seemed not so much to have seen better days as given up awaiting their arrival. But having seen pub interiors only in British black and white B movies until now, I was fascinated by their every dust-embedded detail.

But while relishing their cracked eau-de-Nil tiles, scuffed mahogany, blotched etched glass and wobbling cast-iron tables, I was well aware that Leeds could do better, that the city centre boasted gilded gin palaces and gleaming saloon bars to rival anything in the Wild West's roaring Nineties: for instance the historic Whitelock's First City Luncheon Bar, one of the few licensed premises I had ever condescended to stare at, since I had heard that it was frequented by newspaper reporters. While we demurred at crossing the burnished thresholds of these establishments, we did, at my insistence, once try to gain entry to the Wine Lodge (Albert Cowling, Licensee), a vast underground cavern the size and shape of the Albert Hall which featured a Wurlitzer organ among its attractions. But no one had acquainted us with Mr Cowling's personal licensing law, to the effect that no one was allowed down the steps under the age of twenty-one. To this end uniformed bouncers — commissionaires, as he preferred to call them — sporting magnificent plum-coloured uniforms with epaulettes like bath-brushes, stood on duty at the Wine Lodge's three entrances on the corner of City Square and Boar Lane. Turned away by each of these major-domos in turn, it was to be another three or four years before we plucked up the nerve to storm Albert Cowling's citadel again in earnest.

Not, had we been allowed in, that we should have given Mr Cowling a moment's trouble; for it was acceptance into the pub community that we craved, rather than access to alcohol of which, if only out of economic necessity, we drank as sparingly as possible, often making half a pint linger half an hour. That was our rule, but to every rule there is the exception that proves it: our exception was on Christmas Eve 1946 when, the pair of us being flush with a modest annual wages bonus, we elected to make the great leap forward from beer to spirits.

To carry out this daring deed we thought we had better place ourselves, in case of accidents, outside the jurisdiction of the Leeds City Constabulary. On my recommendation, therefore, we took a train to Dewsbury, a town I had by now somewhat familiarised myself with in the course of my Buckton's rent run. We found a homely, back-street inn, crowded enough on this festive evening for two strange young faces to go unremarked. We bought halves and considered our serious drinking policy. Ray favoured whisky: I did not, I didn't like the smell of it. Brandy seemed too medicinal by far. Gin was an old biddy's tipple, as was port, and anyway port wasn't spirits — or was it? While we were dithering, a cheery soul barging past with the sausage-like fingers of both hands clutching two pints and two measures of dark rum called out, "Get a rum down you, lads — it's Christmas!" Now that I did like the smell of — like toffee. We ordered two rums at ninepence apiece.

There must have been a late-night licensing extension in the West Riding that Christmas Eve, for the next thing I could subsequently remember was a distant clock sounding an unearthly hour — two, was it, or three, or four? — as we sat in a deserted, unheated and unlighted train. Had we left Dewsbury yet? Ray was sound asleep. I peered through the grimy window at the forlorn, ill-lit platform, a scene straight out of *Brief Encounter*, a good portion of which I had recently seen in the back row of the Crossgates Ritz in company with a green blazer. The name of the station was spelled out in uncompromising iron lettering on a sturdy board. We were not in Dewsbury. We were not in Leeds. We were in Kingston upon Hull, on Humberside, sixty miles to the east of where we should have been and would have been had we got off the train at the right station.

Under the influence of who knew how many rums chased by who knew how much mild and bitter, we were neither of us in the least concerned. In that era there was still a train service of sorts over Christmas — with any luck, and subject to the availability of a Silver Line cab at Leeds Central Station, we could be back home and in bed before our mothers rose to commence their Christmas Day chores. Meanwhile, in the grey light of dawn, there was a new city to explore.

We stumbled out of the station. There was little of any consequence to see — Hull had been badly bombed during the war and all around us was still rubble and desolation. From the bowels of

155

a boarded-up crater that had once been an office block or a public building came the drunken cries of revellers in an even worse state that we were. We retraced our staggering steps, just in time to catch what I suppose, had there been any milk deliveries on Christmas Day, would have been the milk train – fortunately for us, since the next skeleton service departure was not until around noon.

I got home, still swaying and by now feeling distinctly groggy with the aftertaste of rum welling up in my throat, at about seven in the morning. My teetotal but unperturbable mother, already up and raking out the grate, made no comment beyond a routinely rhetorical "What time do you call this?" Clutching the sideboard, which I was alarmed to find was dipping up and down like a rowing boat, I mumbled something about having fallen asleep in the fish shop. Realising, even in the state I was in, that this made no kind of sense, I felt it imperative to convince my mother that I was sober. For some reason I was persuaded that the way to set about this was to open the sideboard drawer nearest to me and replace therein the chain tie-pin I then affected. Unluckily, I pulled the drawer with such force that it shot clean off its runners and tipped its paraphernalia of rolled-up socks, crêpe bandages, bicycle clips and collar studs all over the floor. Announcing thickly, "Just looking for the Sunday papers," I lurched off to bed.

And there, apart from a brief and half-hearted attempt to participate in the family Christmas dinner, I was to remain for the next two days, rising only from time to time to retch up a thin stream of watery green bile. As with my fictitious trip to Belle Vue Zoo years earlier, my mother made no reference at all to my Christmas adventure, either then or later. Perhaps she didn't need to, for I was never to taste rum again – even today the very smell of it makes me feel ill. Nor have I ever again set foot in Hull, the only city I have ever visited that holds out no enchantment for me at all.

After a suitably subdued interval, Ray Hill and I resumed our drinking activities, within strictly prescribed limits yet growing ever bolder in our choice of venues as our moustaches showed signs of sprouting and we got closer and closer to the time when, excepting only Mr Albert Cowling's Wine Lodge, we might drink legally.

One landmark bar we did finally determine to infiltrate was that of the City Varieties music-hall, less because it was one of the oldest in Leeds than that we had been told it overlooked the dress circle, from which there was an excellent view of the stage on which naked ladies performed their tableaux vivants of Aphrodite Triumphing Over Psyche and the Temptation of Eve. We had this from our friend Walsh, who with his own eyes had seen the revue *We Never Clothed* or some such. He it was who broke the news that the celebrated striptease artiste Miss Phyllis Dixey was about to pay what was tantamount to a state visit to the City Varieties. Not to see Phyllis Dixey playing the City Varieties would have been like not seeing Sir Henry Irving at the old Leeds Hippodrome.

Accordingly, with Walsh as our pathfinder, we slunk up the wet cobbled alley that was then the old variety hall's main entrance, paid our few coppers at the box-office, climbed the scuffed steps, and without let or hindrance from the management entered the circle bar.

I was at once mesmerised, and wondered what on earth had kept me out of the Varieties for so long – my mother's disapproval of the place, I suppose. Reputedly the oldest theatre in the country, it had yet to be refurbished (as it subsequently was, lovingly, by its new owner Harry Joseph, a renovation that was to pave the way for Barney Colehan's long-running TV show, *The Good Old Days*, for which Leeds dressed up in Edwardian finery), and its moth-eaten plush and chipped gilt plasterwork were still agreeably shabby. A surprising feature, considering that its reputation for strip shows went back at least to 1910 when one Miss Pansy Montague was billed as "La Milo, wearing only a smilo", was the royal coat of arms over the proscenium arch. Legend had it, according to the knowledgeable Walsh, that Edward VII, as Prince of Wales, used to pay incognito visits to the theatre after shooting pheasant on the moors, and that he would watch the performance from behind the drawn curtains of what in a more respectable house would have been called the royal box.

The theatre bar was (and to this day remains) all that a theatre bar should be, its ceiling stained milk-chocolate brown with nicotine wafting back to the days of penny cheroots and cigar divans, and every square inch of wall taken up by old playbills and cracked photographs bearing the faded, extravagantly affectionate inscriptions of the likes of Charlie Chaplin (who came to the Varieties in a clog-dancing act called the Eight Lancashire Lads), Lily Langtry, Dan Leno, Marie Lloyd, and so on down to the moderns such as Robb Wilton, Max Miller and Wilson, Keppel and Betty.

Our original intention had been to go out into the circle only for

157

Phyllis Dixey, and spend the rest of the evening propping up the bar in masculine fashion. Walsh, however, was anxious to see a supporting act, the trumpet player Nat Gonella, for whom his uncle had once done some electrical work, a service which Walsh seemed to think brought Mr Gonella into the category of family friend. Thus it was, after the trumpeter had taken his bow and we were about to troop back into the bar, that we happened to catch the entry of the eccentric comedian with the collapsible legs who followed him, and were intrigued enough to linger.

His name was Max Wall; we had barely heard of him but were soon aware that we were in the presence of genius. A comedian who not only didn't tell straightforward jokes himself but mocked the jokes that lesser comedians told was an unusual turn indeed. He had not yet perfected Professor Wallofski but there was a good deal of foolery at the piano, plus the funny walks which, ignorant though we may have been of the ways of the old music-hall, we could recognise as referring back to some of the comics like Little Titch and Chaplin whose sepia likenesses guarded our barely touched halves of bitter back in the bar. Max Wall was so unconventional that we were dismayed when he signalled the end of his act by giving a cue to the orchestra and announcing, in the cloyingly patriotic manner of the times (we were still in the aftermath of war), "And now, ladies and gentlemen, I would ask you all to rise for a tribute to the lads in khaki and in blue." The audience shuffled awkwardly to its feet – and Max, standing to attention, broke into a rendering of "Yes, We Have No Bananas". It could have gone badly wrong and in fact his reception was ragged at best – but in three young would-be sophisticates leaning against the back rail of the dress circle, Max Wall had made slaves for life. Phyllis Dixey's second spot in the show – we had already seen her doing some nifty semaphore work with ostrich feathers in the first half – seemed tame by comparison, consisting as it did of a static series of famous paintings such as Gainborough's *Blue Lady* as they might have appeared if posed for in the nude.

Miss Dixey's total contribution to the evening, indeed, might have proved tamely disappointing but for Walsh's wide theatrical connections. The uncle who had once done some electrical work for Nat Gonella proved also to have done some electrical work for the City Varieties itself, and was thus known to the stage doorkeeper. This gave us – or at any rate the enterprising Walsh, with Ray and I tagging in his wake – the entree to Mr Gonella's dressing room, the first theatre dressing room I had ever entered. Since I was less of a trumpet fan than Walsh or Ray it interested me far more than its occupant, and I gave its yellow-painted brick walls and chipped sink and mirrored dressing-table the keenest of stares.

Nat Gonella remembered, or affected to remember, Walsh, and while completing his change into street clothes was asking after the health of Walsh's uncle in the electrical line when there was a tap on his door and at its threshold appeared a vision I had only a few moments earlier seen totally naked except for the wisp of chiffon she clutched while standing in what looked like a large papier-mâché ashtray to depict Venus rising out of the sea. Miss Phyllis Dixey now wore an excessively sensible candlewick dressing-gown. What her errand was I had no idea: as in a trance I perceived that the obliging Mr Gonella was introducing his guests. ". . . And this is Keith." To which I added, automatically and unnecessarily, "Waterhouse."

The vision spoke. It might have spoken before but I had not been aware of it. "What a funny name," observed Venus.

It was to get worse. I searched for a reply – something witty, brief and sophisticated that would so etch into her mind that she would remember me for ever. "It's better than Nicholas Ridiculous," I heard myself saying, recalling the name of a character in a zany radio show of the time. But while I heard myself saying these words, Miss Dixey did not. My mouth having suddenly gone dry, all that actually came out of it was, "It's better than Nicholas." Miss Phyllis Dixey, I reflected upon reviewing the conversation in the course of a restless night, must have regarded this as the most pointless, goonish, stupid remark ever spoken by any human being since the first ape-man uttered the first grunt. She smiled vaguely and returned to her own dressing room. I did think of writing her a letter explaining that what I had meant to say when she had very kindly joked that I had a funny name was, "It's better than Nicholas Ridiculous," but I never got round to it.

At least I had met Phyllis Dixey as well as Nat Gonella, but I would rather have met Max Wall. (When I did eventually meet him nearly forty years on, it emerged that he was an even greater friend of the distinguished trumpeter than Walsh's electrician uncle, so it could just as easily have been Max Wall rather than Phyllis Dixey who tapped on Mr Gonella's dressing room door that evening. I expect I should have been equally tongue-tied.)

On balance, I believe Willis Hall had the better City Varieties dressing room encounter. Like me, he became a fan of the last master of Grand Guignol, Tod Slaughter, whose touring Victorian melodramas – *Maria Marten, or the Murder in the Red Barn*, and *Sweeney Todd, the Demon Barber of Fleet Street* – were to the Varieties' raucous audience what Donald Wolfitt's company was to the more upmarket Grand (for myself, I would as willingly queue for one as for the other). Willis was a confirmed autograph-hunting haunter of stage doors: he had Billy Cotton, he had Gracie Fields, he had Big Bill Campbell, he had Dante the magician, and one evening under the flickering lamplight of the cobbled alley outside the City Varieties stage door, he secured the sweeping signature of Mr Tod Slaughter.

Over-awed, as I should have been in his place, by the archetypal actor-manager in his spade hat and floor-length overcoat with the obligatory astrakhan collar, it was not until the great thespian had swept into the theatre that Willis realised he was still holding the expensive Waterman pen which Mr Slaughter had chosen to use instead of the proffered stub of pencil. Willis timorously pushed open the stage door, intending to hand the pen in to the stage door-keeper, only to find Tod Slaughter riffling through his mail. He glared at Willis – a tiresome fan who had already been dealt with. Then Willis produced the pen. The bushy eyebrows rose. The thick jowls quivered in surprised gratification. "Honestee," boomed the voice that had packed a thousand twice-nightly performances, "is thee best policee, laddie!" He then beckoned Willis into his dressing room, showed him the bloodstained apron he was about to don as the Demon Barber, plus the prop wooden razor with which he would dispose of his victims; and then, recognising a stage-struck lad when he saw one, presented him with a dozen or so stick-ends of theatrical make-up contained in an old cigar box. Willis's future was sealed.

The circle bar of the Varieties became a regular Saturday evening venue if we were not of a mood for the Hokey-cokey and the Palais Glide at the Big Top marquee. And when we were sated with strippers, comics, jugglers, unicyclists, xylophonists, magicians, bird imitators, funambulists, paper-tearing acts and novelty tap-dancers we would take ourselves off on a pub crawl.

Saturday night in the pubs had an excitement all its own, a special flavour you could almost taste, like the tang of salt and vinegar. There was always something going on. In some pubs, nominated regulars would be persuaded to "get up", i.e. sing, to the accompaniment of an out-of-tune piano. There was always someone doing tricks with coins or matches, always someone selling raffle tickets, always someone collecting for a wreath or for a basket of groceries for a poorly pensioner. Often there would be a darts or dominoes tournament. There were regular, sometimes mysterious, transactions: a bookie's runner would furtively pay out on bets, noses were tapped, winks exchanged, a pint or a few cigarettes would be handed over in consideration of a blue cabbage brought in from somebody's allotment.

The kind of hostelry we allowed ourselves to frequent didn't sell food but hawkers would come in off the street selling hot pies and saveloys. Another vendor would peddle a spoof newspaper called *Billy's Weekly Liar* (a publication that, when I was writing a novel called *Saturday Night at the Roxy* some years later, was to suggest a useful alternative title when one Alan Sillitoe threatened to be coming out ahead of me with the not dissimilar-sounding *Saturday Night and Sunday Morning*). Then there was the Salvation Army lassie selling *War Cry*, and treated with the greatest respect even by the taproom's resident comedian (every pub had one, who kept up a flow of patter on the passing show). There would be one more vendor, peddling bags of custard creams and ginger nuts – an unlikely product, one would have thought, but he knew his market: they were snapped up by husbands anxious to take home a peace offering after having stayed for a pint or two too many.

Finally, as "Last orders" were called, the highlight of the evening: the entry of the paper seller with tomorrow's *Sunday Empire News*, hot off the presses of Withy Grove, Manchester, its black headlines always sending an excited ripple through the pub in reaction to the murders, the society scandals, the soccer sensations, the black market exposures, until the landlord's bell cut stridently through the buzz and his cries of "Time, gentlemen, please!" sent us out into a raw Saturday night that whatever the season always seemed to be tinged with fog.

It beat the Moo-cow milk bar.

THREE

In the Mood

'Nothing there was the same as now. All that happened then, if it happened here, would be strange and fresh. Everything was sharper. Cigarette smoke had a pungency it has since lost. Even stale beer smelled full-bodied and good. Girls' breasts were whiter. Like alabaster, we said, though none of us knew what alabaster was in that long-ago place. The air was as crisp as apples, and all the sad songs were sweeter, then.'

— IN THE MOOD, 1983

1 Yet it was not all play. If the two years since leaving the College of Commerce had seemed to be dissipated in the pursuit of pleasure, it was only because there was a powerful disincentive against settling down to anything like a career. Every able-bodied youth could expect, come his eighteenth birthday, to be conscripted into the armed forces for a couple of years. There was, in consequence, little point in laying down roots – most of us were content to coast along in a dead-end job until our call-up papers arrived. So much for the beneficial effects of national service.

But I wanted so badly to be a journalist that from time to time I would fire off letters to the various newspapers listed between neon sign manufacturers and non-ferrous metal fabricators in the local Kelly's Directory, even though I knew it was an all but pointless exercise. Not the great daily and evening papers, of course: they would obviously have no place in their newsrooms for an office clerk in his teens (I was not aware that the position of copy boy existed, otherwise I should have applied for it). But neither, it transpired, did the *South Leeds Advertiser*, nor the *Keighley News*, nor the *Bramley Advertiser*, nor the *Yorkshire Observer Budget*; nor yet the Leeds office of the *New Catholic Herald*, nor of the *Ironmonger*, out in Shadwell near the Reformatory; nor *Laxton's Builders' Price Book*, nor the *Fish Friers' Review*, nor Kelly's Directories Ltd themselves, for whom I offered to work part-time, incorporating my various rent rounds with knocking on householders' doors and asking who lived there, if that was how one set about compiling a street directory. Still, even had any of these publications shown the smallest interest in retraining an undertaker's clerk to become a journalist, only to lose him to the colours, it was to be doubted whether I could expect any advance on the *Leeds Guardian*'s offer of ten bob a week.

All this time I was trying to write – usually courtesy of J.T. Buckton & Sons, in the course of one of whose working days I could

165

conceive, compose (under cover of the postage book), type up and despatch to a periodical a sketch of some 800 words – the maximum requirement at a time of acute paper shortage. There were longer works in progress – at home I was scribbling away at a novel in the manner of P.G. Wodehouse, and every so often I had a stab at a short story; but it was in the 800-word sketch that I pinned my faith.

Humour, I had long ago decided, rashly or otherwise, was my forte: just as professional comedians are given to confessing that they acted the clown at school to gain the approval of their classmates, so I had found that a school essay written in humorous vein always went down well, if for no other reason than that it made a change. Besides, nearly all my models were humorous writers – and had I not already had my great success with that funny piece for the *National Savings News*? Unknown to myself, I did not yet really understand humour – I equated it with facetiousness – but there were in the mid-Forties a score of magazines that used supposedly humorous material, starting with *Punch* and going down through the pocket magazines such as *Lilliput* and *London Opinion* to obscurer, usually short-lived titles with names like *Stag, Pie* and *Wit & Wisdom* (one issue, as I recall).

My market research was conducted at W.H. Smith's railway bookstall in City Station, where I became, in the course of my Buckton's post round, as regular a daily caller as the *Evening Post* van. I also acquired a secondhand copy, circa 1937, of the *Writers' and Artists' Year Book* which for a while became my standard reading on the rocking tram or propped up against the sugar bowl in Betty's Café. Not only did it most usefully list all the markets and their requirements (*"John O'London's Weekly*: A light, anecdotal treatment is desired where possible and humour is welcome. Contributions are paid for on acceptance; usual rate £3.3s per 1000 words. Articles should be typewritten"), but it was packed with information for the budding writer: the addresses of press-cuttings agencies, a list of firms prepared to consider greetings card verses ("if of high standard"), a table of American and Commonwealth journals, notes on serial rights and proof correcting and publishers' agreements, and BBC Requirements and How to Submit a Film Story, and so on and so on, until one began to feel like a member of the writing fraternity simply by turning the pages. The opportunities seemed boundless: with the proper degree of application it could not be long before the cheques for ten and sixpence, a guinea, two guineas, three guineas, were flowing into the bank (I should have to get a bank first).

I pored rather wistfully over the *Year Book*'s advertisements for correspondence courses and schools of journalism, with their genuine-seeming testimonials: "At a rough estimate I have made over £100 in Journalism as a spare-time hobby since taking up your Course 18 months ago. Your help has been money very well spent." Alas, as I found after sending off for their free booklets, I could not afford the fees that would otherwise have repaid themselves several times over.

One of these schools of journalism, indeed a college of journalism, was actually in Leeds, in Upper Briggate, and I took the earliest opportunity of going along and giving it the kind of transfixed stare I normally reserved for newspaper offices and printing works. The college proved to be so far up Upper Briggate that it was practically in North Street where the red light area began, its premises consisting of a room over a sweetshop and tobacconist's, approached by a steep flight of wooden stairs covered in threadbare linoleum. From the sign in the gloomy doorway I learned that as well as being a college of journalism it was also a typewriting bureau, a secretarial agency, a press cuttings service, and the parcels agent for a shipping line. Since it was nearing office closing time I hung around hoping for a glimpse of the college's staff of distinguished journalists who offered their personal specialised tuition based on years of Fleet Street experience, but the only person to descend the worn stairs, and lock the street door after her, was a dumpy, middle-aged lady carrying, unusually for a woman at that time, a briefcase. I guessed it must have contained manuscripts. Despite appearances, I was impressed.

My own manuscripts continued to be returned to me as fast as I sent them out. I didn't in the least mind, or anyway not much. I had read enough writers' reminiscences to know that in the early days rejected stories regularly and monotonously "came home to roost" or "landed with a dull thud on the doormat"; being of their number was like belonging to a club.

Unlike some of my fellow-aspirants, I did not paper the bedroom walls with my rejection slips, although I was getting an impressive collection of them together. But one I did pin up above my bed. It was from *Punch*, and it bore a scrawled note from the editor, E.V. Knox, whose revered pseudonym Evoe had been familiar to me ever since my mother had brought me home a parcel of *Punch* back numbers from Kirkgate Market all those years ago. It read, "Not quite. EVK." It was as good as an acceptance from any other magazine.

This near-miss was a stylised little piece called "Music Hath Charms" — not a very original title for what I thought was a blazingly original piece of writing. I had hit on the idea, or rather the gimmick, of taking a stretch of dialogue — in this case a conversation in a music store — and transposing it into reported speech, as in "Good morning. We were thinking of taking up some musical instrument. Could they recommend the trombone . . . ?" Spurred on by Evoe's two little words, I freshened up my manuscript by pressing it under a damp towel with my mother's flat iron — a tip garnered from the pages of the *Writer* magazine — and sent it out again, this time to the pocket monthly *London Opinion* ("The Editor will be pleased to consider humorous articles, 1000 words and less. Nothing heavy, morbid or neurotic. Payment: immediately on acceptance, at high rates"). It was accepted. The payment, immediate as promised and at high rates as promised, was two guineas.

This was in November 1944, three months before my sixteenth birthday. The little notebook I kept, as advised by the *Writers' and Artists' Year Book*, recording acceptances and rejections — or in my case, rejections and acceptance — reveals that instead of following my success up, I did no more writing at all for the next six months, not even bothering to re-submit those manuscripts that, as the writers' reminiscences would have put it, had "winged their way back like homing pigeons". The fact was that I was too restless. I was so impatient to see my name in print that, absurdly, I was round at W.H. Smith's and riffling through the pages of the current *London Opinion* on the very day I received my letter of acceptance from its editor — an echo of my surrealistic hopes of finding myself in *A Basinful of Fun* even before my proposed contribution had left my hands.

Monthly magazines, I had observed, generally came out in the last week or so of the previous month. This did not discourage me from keeping a feverish eye open for the December number of *London Opinion* from about 5 November onwards. I developed the habit of making a slight detour via City Square on the way to work each morning, so that the established author could drop in on the station bookstall before bringing himself down to earth by way of taking down the office shutters. When, after what seemed like months, I arrived in City Station one morning just in time to find one of W.H. Smith's waistcoated, brillianted young men cutting the string on a pristine pile of December *London Opinions* hot off the steaming London train, my excitement was as intense as if it had been a Christmas parcel. And when my article proved not to have appeared my disappointment was as great as that of Stephen Leacock's Hoodoo McFiggin when, upon opening his Christmas present in the hope of skates, he found boots.

This was to become a monthly mortification. January ... February ... March ... April was the cruellest month: the magazine was several days late for some reason; I was convinced that this added torment had to mean that when the April *London Opinion* finally did appear, my article would be in it at last. It was not.

While I could not settle down to any actual writing during this incubation period, I did try, in a lackadaisical sort of way, to get some work under way by canvassing for commissions. I wrote to the *Yorkshire Evening News* offering a series about the landmark buildings of Leeds. Rejected. I wrote to the *Yorkshire Evening Post* proposing a humorous column on the lines of Beachcomber. Rejected. I wrote to the *Daily Worker* suggesting an exposure of estate agents, to be called "Your landlord's middleman" (and presumably to be written under a pseudonym). Rejected.

I wrote several times to *Picture Post*, a periodical I very much admired. With its black and white photo essays on the small social foothills that form the real backbone of England − commercial travellers' dinner dances, anglers' outings, amateur dramatic nights, street parties, mystery coach tours, mock parliaments, flower shows, market days, jumble sales, pigeon races, whippet races, brass band contests − it had an editor after my own heart. "Fashionable Birmingham has its lager and sandwich in the snack-bar of the Grand Hotel," ran one caption without a touch of irony. Notwithstanding that I had yet to set foot in the place, I wrote suggesting a feature about Whitelock's First City Luncheon Bar. They regretted that they had already devoted three pages to a similar establishment in Liverpool (the Philharmonic, I imagine). Another picture essay was "A Day in the Life of a Fishmonger". I offered A Day in the Life of Kirkgate Market. This they thought such a good idea that they had already done it, several years earlier. Then how about the Leeds arcades? No, they had done those too.

At least we were on the same wavelength. Encouraged, I flicked through back numbers of the weekly for further inspiration. Only *Picture Post* would have dared run a double spread on "The Drama of Cement". I offered The Drama of Quarry Hill Flats – An Experiment in Living. They had done a major piece on Quarry Hill Flats in one of their first issues. I gave up. But I remained affectionate towards *Picture Post*, with its instinctive understanding of the Englishness of the English, even when, a few months later, I opened the latest issue and found to my disgust a picture feature about Leeds Corn Exchange. The editor, Tom Hopkinson, became a friend years afterwards, and I told him the story. "You should have persisted," he said, and he was right.

"Music Hath Charms" by K.S. Waterhouse at last appeared in the July 1945 number of *London Opinion*. To see my name in print was like seeing my name in lights. As, half prepared for another monthly dose of disappointment, I turned the pages with a sort of hopeful hopelessness or hopeless hopefulness, it seemed to catherine-wheel round and catapult towards me like one of those montages of newspaper headlines in a Warner Brothers gangster movie. By K.S. Waterhouse. The typeface was black and bold but to me it was fluorescent.

One hears of reading the print off a particular piece of text. I came close to doing that almost literally. There and then at the railway bookstall I devoured the piece a good dozen times, being mortified at about the third or fourth reading to find a small misprint which, as I re-read and re-read, seemed to grow in enormity like a carbuncle examined in the mirror, until it made nonsense of the entire article. The eyes of the bookstall manager on me by now, I finally purchased three copies of the magazine, for the not inconsiderable sum of two and threepence. From one I extracted my debut freelance contribution (unless you counted the *National Savings News*, which had long ago disintegrated under too-frequent scrutiny) and pasted it into the cuttings book I had months ago bought for the purpose. The second I gave to my girlfriend of the moment. The third I kept in reserve, to send to editors who might want to see examples of my published work.

I had my moment of glory at J.T. Buckton & Sons, although my fellow-clerks were more interested in the tasteful nudes that were a feature of *London Opinion* than in my article. My mother's comment was that the printers had taken their time about it. After that, anticlimax. The whole world, after all, was not held in thrall by the contents of *London Opinion* and no one stopped to congratulate me in the street. There were no letters from editors. As for the girlfriend, while she was impressed, she was not impressed enough to my liking.

The two-guinea fee, of course, had long ago been spent, but at least it had been spent sensibly. I had started buying secondhand paperbacks to supplement *Lettres de mon Moulin*, *Fifty Years of Progress: the Story of Hemingway's Brewery* and the one or two other volumes that comprised the family library. Old Penguins and Pelicans, I had found, could be bought for coppers at Stringer's bookstall in the Market − I acquired Chesterton's *The Man Who Was Thursday*, *The Thin Man* by Dashiell Hammet, a collection of Saki, *A Passage to India*, *The Diary of a Nobody* and many other treasures, all for less than half a crown, together with unread and unreadable Pelicans like Freud's *Psychopathology* which I bought to impress myself and others.

With my two guineas I added the city's two secondhand bookshops to my daily round, and in the course of my browsings unearthed a four-volume *Don Quixote*, *Lamb's Tales From Shakespeare*, Boswell's *Johnson* and several Everyman titles which I still have on my shelves. I also found a good dozen volumes which to my regret were soon to be no longer on my shelves. In the aftermath of the German broadcast episode, my hero P.G. Wodehouse had yet to recover his popularity and you could buy his books in hardback, with dust-jackets, some of them first editions, for a shilling or two. I took home an armful: *Laughing Gas*, *The Heart of a Goof*, *The Clicking of Cuthbert*, *Ukridge*, a batch of Jeeveses, Mulliners and Psmiths. I then did two stupid things. Wanting my acquisitions to look like a proper library I removed all their dust jackets and destroyed them. And then, having devoured all my Wodehouses and needing cash to finance some outing or other, probably with a girl, I sold them back to the shop for about half what I had paid for them. The last time I looked up the Wodehouse titles in a modern first editions catalogue I calculated that I had cleared my bookshelf − my mother's cupboard top, to be precise − of about £2,000. But I still had my Penguins and Everymans. And I had discovered the joy of secondhand-bookshop serendipity.

My article in print and the two guineas gone it was time to buckle to and edge another inch or so up the slopes of journalism. I was sixteen and a half by now, after all, and time was moving on. I tried a few more pieces in the reported speech style of my *London Opinion* success but − rather to my surprise, since I was convinced that I had found an idiosyncratic writing formula to match Damon Runyon's − they failed to find a home. So did everything else. In fact another seventeen months were to pass by before my next sale. My little record book tells the story over a six-year period: 1944: two guineas; 1945: nothing; 1946: £2.19.6; 1947: £11.15.6; 1948: two guineas; 1949: £19.8.6.

The most significant of these sums was the £2.19.6 for 1946 in my seventeenth year, which was entirely made up of threepence-a-line and half-crown and five-shilling payments from the *Yorkshire Evening Post*, and which I invested in one of the new Biro pens that could write under water. The *Evening Post* had started up a magazine page composed of little feature articles, puzzles, bits of verse, and the kind of piece then usually classified as "a lighthearted look" at this or that topic. The page was usually thrown out after the lunch edition to make way for hard news, but it was right up my street. I submitted three or four "lighthearted looks" without success; then one lunchtime at Buckton's, Mr Stead the cashier, who was smoking a pipe over the early edition of the *Evening Post* which we took in for Mr Palmer to check the property column, suddenly exclaimed, "Hullo! This effusion here by one K.S.W. − that isn't you by any chance, is it, young Waterhouse?" They had printed a piece of unremitting facetiousness about tram queues which I had handed in at their offices only the day before while on my Buckton's mail round. It was out of the paper again long before the Final edition but I didn't care − I had already bought six copies.

Better was to come. A few days later there was a letter for me, ill-typed on rough copy paper, from the editor of the magazine page, one Con Gordon. I was impressed, not to say awed, for Con Gordon was world-famous in Yorkshire. As well as a regular and hugely popular "Courts Day by Day" column about the minutiae of life in the magistrates' courts, he turned out regular signed "specials" and droll "lighthearted looks" which made him a favourite with the readers. Con Gordon, in short, was the *Evening Post*'s star writer, and undoubtedly he could have moved on to Fleet Street had he chosen to do so. But he was content to remain where he had fetched up: a big fish basking in a small pond. Every provincial paper has one, though not necessarily with as much talent.

The letter said, "If ever you have time, come in and have a chat. I would like some more articles from you, if they are up to the standard of the tram article. A good time for me to go out for a coffee is between 10 and 11.30 on Mondays and Thursdays, when I am making up the magazine page. Go through the archway and ask for me at the sales counter."

I was through the archway – the magic, faience-tiled archway that led to the Yorkshire Conservative Newspaper Co.'s editorial offices – at 10.01 that same morning, having disposed of my Buckton's post round at record speed. The sales counter, as I was to find, divided its energies between selling back numbers and photographs and filtering the steady trickle of visitors, unhinged or otherwise, who sought audience with the editor or his staff. I was entranced by the sales counter. A young man in a raincoat passed through on his way upstairs and another young man in a raincoat passed through on his way out. Reporters, clearly (I had long ago realised that they did not wear peaked caps, but I did know that they wore raincoats). It was the nearest I had ever been to an editorial floor. Presently a shambling, balding, grey but still tousle-haired figure in shapeless sports jacket, corduroy trousers, fair isle pullover and sandals appeared, and this was Con Gordon. He was gratifyingly every inch the bohemian. He had the faintest of Irish accents but his was the first properly educated, cultured voice I had heard in Leeds outside the pulpit and the stage.

I had thought the Gambit Café might have been Con Gordon's mark but he led me to the basement Lyons at the bottom of Bond Street down from the office, where he stood me coffee and toast. Not at all fazed by my youth or my job as an undertaker's clerk, he treated me as if I were a professional freelance and spoke sympathetically about the difficulties of getting work into the restricted space then available in newspapers and magazines. He gave me what in my callow way I thought were some pretty obvious tips on his requirements for the magazine page – I had, as suggested by the *Writers' and Artists' Year Book*, already studied the market – and then asked if I had brought anything with me. Of course I had – a whimsical sketch about a chapel concert, based on no observation whatsoever, and a series of pawky Yorkshire aphorisms called "Ahr Edward Sez". To my surprise he bought them on the spot.

Even more to my surprise, considering what slender evidence he had to go on, he said he thought I had it in me to become a newspaperman, and asked what I was doing working for Buckton's. Access to a typewriter, I told him, and the fact that I had to mark time until I had done my national service. He agreed that this was a great nuisance but advised me to keep writing and promised that when I got out of the forces, provided I had enough cuttings to show, he would try to arrange an interview with his editor, Barry Horniblow. Apparently Mr Horniblow was a former Fleet Street livewire who had been brought in to shake the *Evening Post* up a bit. He had already taken on one or two inexperienced young men he had liked the look of, so my chances were far from hopeless. But seventeen, I had to agree, was a bit too young. I could wait. I would have to.

I went back to New Station Street enormously heartened, my head swimming with images of myself swaggering around Leeds with a reporter's notebook protruding from my raincoat pocket, a cigarette on my lips and a press pass stuck in the band of my jaunty fedora. To my utter astonishment, the first of my "Ahr Edward Sez" epigrams – "T' chap who sez what wa' good enough fo' 'is grandfather's good enough fo' 'im, would be in a bit of a fix if 'is grandfather 'ad said t' same thing" – appeared on the magazine page that very day, framed in a little box with a drawing of Edward by the staff cartoonist. I got half a crown for it, or fractionally under a penny a word. Evening paper journalism, I decided, was the life.

Edward continued to be inflicted on the *Post*'s readers over the next two weeks, clocking up half a crown a time for me. Of my concert article, however, there was no sign. Then came a setback. One day the magazine page failed to appear, even in the lunch edition. The next morning's post brought another letter from Con Gordon: "Today the editor tore up my magazine page and ceremonially danced on it, and that went for your concert article too. He said it was an old idea and had often been much better done; which is strictly true but if widely applied would stop every printing press in the country. Anyway, I begin to suspect he doesn't like your stuff quite so much as I do. So you had better administer it in smaller doses until he ceases to be allergic . . ."

Luckily for me, besides the now defunct magazine page Con Gordon also ran the Diary of a Yorkshireman, a miscellany column that paid five shillings a paragraph. Had the paper possessed a features editor he would have been that too, and so was in a position sometimes to more or less smuggle the odd short feature of mine into the early editions. More often, he sent my work back, always with a note: "Don't be discouraged. Times are thin for contributors but the wheel will turn. Write all you can. Even if it doesn't see the light of day it will develop your style."

I wasn't in the least discouraged, truth to tell. However peripherally, I now felt in the journalistic swim. My daily perambulations about the city centre were henceforth enlivened by the search for likely five-shilling Diary paragraphs, and I quickly developed a lively eye for quirky little details of the "not many people know that" variety, usually on points of architecture – the legacy, I suppose, of the many hours spent staring at buildings during my white card period. From time to time, by open invitation, I would have morning coffee at Joe Lyons with Con Gordon. To my slight disappointment, I didn't get to meet any of his fellow-journalists who were said to lunch roisterously off beer and roast beef at Whitelock's each day, for he was something of a hermit and avoided their company, and anyway he was a non-drinker and a vegetarian. But he always seemed pleased, or anyway not displeased, to see me. His nuggets of advice, I now began to see, were not as obvious as I had at first thought – or if they were, they were the wood I had up until now been unable to see for the trees. One piece of wisdom I remember particularly: "Write about the Amalgamated Association of Engineers and all the amalgamated engineers will read your stuff. Write about human emotions and all humanity will read it. Journalism's as simple as that."

I continued to bombard Con Gordon with bits and pieces without let-up for a year, and threepenny line by threepenny line and five-shilling paragraph by five-shilling paragraph my earnings rose. They were blown on a week's holiday in Blackpool with Ray Hill, where for economy's sake we slept head to toe in the double bed of our back-street digs like Laurel and Hardy in *Film Fun* on holiday at Shrimpton-on-Sea.

It was my first seaside holiday on the other side of the Pennines since Silverdale, and I wondered why they couldn't have put a poor children's holiday camp slap in the middle of Blackpool. The resort's razzle-dazzle exuberance was a tonic after the dreary war years. The Tower, visible miles away down the railway line so that you were ready for Blackpool long before Blackpool was ready for you, was a symbol of its energy and enterprise. The Winter Gardens was a people's palace out of a Victorian picture postcard, the Golden Mile a Mecca of Thirties concrete gawdy, the promenade a ramshackle succession of architectural styles so that the long, enjoyable single-decker tram ride along the front was like a geological survey, revealing stratum after stratum of the town's developing prosperity since the Preston and Wyre Railway brought the first trippers. All this and the covered market too – plus the Sensational Severed Living Hands of Patma. Ray and I found ourselves a couple of Welsh girls and went on the town.

When I got back home to Halton Moor my calling-up papers for the Royal Air Force were waiting for me behind the mantelpiece clock.

2   After the usual square-bashing nonsense I was required to
    report to a kind of inland, militarised Silverdale called
    Wombleton on the North Yorkshire moors, miles from
anywhere. The North Yorkshire moors are like Noël Coward's
Norfolk, very flat, and even in the driest of summers give out such an
impression of being marshland that one expects to see Magwitch
staggering across them through the mist.

Even as I humped my kitbag up from the country railway halt I
was already plotting my escape via a more congenial re-posting –
somewhere reasonably near a city or fair-sized town, or at the very
least opposite a bus stop. Such things were possible if you knew
someone in the orderly room and were prepared to take on his duty
chores in return for promised favours.

There was a snag. RAF Station Wombleton was not a proper RAF
station in the sense of having hangars, windsocks, and Spitfires and
Hurricanes on the runway – there was no runway, and in fact to my
bitter disappointment I was never to set eyes on a taxiing aircraft in
the whole of my national service career. It was the transit camp for
the RAF Regiment, the Royal Air Force equivalent of the Marines,
whose task it is to guard airfields, dig slit trenches and garrotte the
enemy – far too like soldiering for my taste. The sprawling camp,
swarming with khaki-clad figures bayoneting sandbags or engaging
one another in unarmed combat, was administered by a small RAF
unit, and it was this unit that I was to join.

Or so I thought. As I was passing a barbed-wire compound where
RAF Regiment recruits were stripping Bren guns and polishing fire
buckets with Duraglit, I was stopped in my tracks by a bellow of
"Idle marching, that man!" from a bulging-eyed, waxed-
moustachioed robot on whose knifecrease-pressed battle blouse
glistened the three blancoed stripes and burnished crown of an RAF
Regiment flight-sergeant. I was marched into the guardroom where

my name was taken and checked against a clipboard list; whereafter, by some piece of legerdemain which I do not understand to this day, I found that I had been kitted out in RAF Regiment khaki and was doubling around a barrack square clutching a rifle above my head. In vain did I try to explain that I was a clerk and not cut out for trench-digging. For the next fortnight I spent my days swinging from ropes, clambering walls, learning how to gouge out eyes, and jumping over, or into, slime-infested ditches. It was only when pay parade came around that they realised they had got the wrong Waterhouse. Or so they claimed. My belief has always been that I had been press-ganged, that whenever an RAF Regiment intake was below strength the flight-sergeant simply positioned himself near the gates and waylaid any stray clerks, cooks or other unsuspecting Air Force types who were on their way to the RAF unit. At any rate I was soon out of khaki and back in blue.

I had opted for the RAF for two reasons − I would get to wear a collar and tie and shoes instead of the tunic, boots and puttees of the army; and as a clerk I should have the use of a typewriter. Given that the war had been over for two years and there was nothing whatever for the RAF to do, I should then be well placed to spend my national service career on light short story writing duties. But it proved that one was not allowed access to a typewriter until one had been on a typewriting course. Keeping quiet about my RSA proficiency certificates in shorthand and typing I immediately applied to be sent on one − wherever it was held it could not be in a more God-forsaken spot than Wombleton. After a few weeks of thumb-twiddling my posting came through − it was to a place called Wythall, such a short bus ride from Birmingham that it was practically in the suburbs. I was well pleased.

On York Station I bumped into Willis Hall, now in the army and stationed at Catterick, who was going home on embarkation leave, having been posted to Malaya. We were not to meet again until twelve years later when Willis's play set in the Malayan jungle, *The Long and the Short and the Tall*, was packing the New Theatre, now the Alberry (with another Hunslet graduate, Peter O'Toole, in a starring role), and he rang me to suggest dramatising my new novel about an undertaker's clerk, *Billy Liar*. No one could say that either of us failed to capitalise on his experiences.

While Wythall seemed small beer compared to Malaya it was a pleasant enough billet, a compact former balloon station with comfortable quarters in marked contrast to the Nissen hut wilderness of North Yorkshire. It had two great advantages. One was the presence of a large quantity of Waafs, the first female company encountered in over six months. The other was the proximity of Birmingham, but a ninepenny bus ride away. I had barely unpacked my kitbag before I was opening negotiations with a pretty Waaf to take her to the pictures in Brum, as I had already learned to call it.

From her point of view the outing cannot have counted among her successes, for I was far more interested in the city than in the girl. Birmingham at that time was a larger replica of Leeds, a seething provincial metropolis of trams, blackened municipal buildings in the Italian Renaissance style, steam-enshrouded railway stations, markets, statues of Queen Victoria, department stores, commercial hotels, grills and butteries, and arcades with striking clocks. The evening was damp but that only served to cast the reflections of shop lights and neon signs and yes, the winking Bovril sign, on the glistening pavement, producing a grotto effect, a quality of excited expectation so intense and electric that if the corporation had been able to feed it through a cable they could have lit street lamps with it. It was the same feeling one still gets in New York and San Francisco. What the city had was the spirit of what Arnold Bennett called "get up and go"; and it was as different from the present-day reconstituted Birmingham as a grainy black and white photograph is from a wishy-washy watercolour. But my Waaf, a country lass, didn't take to Birmingham at all; and when, that weekend, I invited her to come and sample the delights of Wolverhampton, which could also be reached easily by bus from Wythall, she declined with thanks. (I travelled to Wolverhampton alone, and found it grimily, and grimly, entrancing.)

The course I had been sent on was not an exacting one. In the mornings one learned the RAF's clerical and filing procedures, a simple system dressed up as a complex one as a work creation scheme; and in the afternoons shorthand and typing. Since no roll-call was ever taken and I already had shorthand and typing, I saw no point in attending these afternoon sessions – there were about sixty of us on the course and I would not be missed. I developed the habit of sneaking into Birmingham directly after lunch, and very pleasant afternoons they were too, occupied as once I had occupied my white card outings into Leeds, in wandering about, exploring and staring at buildings. I had to keep a sharp eye open for the "Snowdrops", the

RAF police, since I had no white card alibi and was technically – or as it was to prove, not so technically – absent without leave, but so long as I kept away from the railway stations and didn't wander around the city with my tunic buttons unfastened I was on pretty safe ground. And I did come to owe the Snowdrops one favour. Espying a pair of them plodding across Victoria Square one afternoon I sought refuge in the Art Gallery, and discovered the pre-Raphaelites. I was a frequent visitor after that. Until . . .

One evening in the Naafi it came to my notice that, egged on by my example, others had started cutting the shorthand and typing classes – either because, like me, they already surreptitiously had these skills or because they wouldn't much mind failing their proficiency test at the end of the six-week course, when all that would happen was that they would have to stay on and take it again – no great hardship since Wythall was an extremely soft touch as RAF stations went. But how many, I asked, were dodging the classes? A good dozen, I was told – and there would be more absentees tomorrow when the local Regal changed its programmes.

A strong, street-life instinct for survival, developed in the course of my juvenile perambulations around Leeds, warned me that it was time to put in an appearance at the afternoon typing session. I did so. Some twenty airmen and Waafs – about a third of the course – failed to present themselves. The instructor reluctantly took a roll-call. He was a mild-mannered education sergeant who wanted only to be left alone at his trestle table to read his *New Statesman & Nation*, but attendance was so sparse that he had no option. The twenty missing trainee typists were hauled up before the commanding officer the next morning, charged with being AWOL, and given three days "jankers" – confined to barracks and put on potato-peeling chores.

Here I thought I would bring my natural cunning into play. The absentees had been brought to book. An example had been made of them and the skiving-off racket nipped in the bud. The shorthand and typing classes, that afternoon, would have a full turnout and the education sergeant, a naturally lazy man, would have neither need nor inclination to take the roll-call a second time. It would be safer than ever to take myself off to Birmingham. I did so, and went and had a self-satisfied stare at the buttery of the Grand Hotel, "where fashionable Birmingham has its lager and sandwich".

My grasp of human psychology was not yet developed. The officer in charge of the course dropped in to check that the necessary lesson had been learned – no doubt he himself had been torn off a strip, as we erks would have put it – and ordered the sergeant to take the roll-call. One name missing. Five days confined to barracks and a lecture from the CO on my confounded cheek and stupidity. I did not venture into Birmingham again from Wythall. The next time I visited the city they had pulled it down and another city of the same name had been put in its place.

The course finished with a jolly Naafi dance followed by a mass exodus to the surrounding allotments where all who retained their virginity now lost it, and preceded by a day of end-of-term euphoria when we all learned where we were to be posted. I had lived in hopes of being sent abroad like Willis – preferably to the staff of the British air attaché in Washington, or failing that, somewhere in Germany where I could go and stare at Munich or Cologne or even Berlin. Another remote possibility was a posting to the Air Ministry in Kingsway where (so good authority had it) you were allowed to wear civilian dress, were billeted in civilian digs in Bloomsbury and other exotic places, and dined nightly at a Lyons Corner House to the strains of a tango orchestra or gypsy violins. In the event I was sent to the RAF Records Office in Gloucester.

I was content enough. My comfortable billet was right across the street from the Records Office and so close to the city centre that I could stroll to Woolworth's in my lunch hour. While Gloucester wasn't Birmingham or Wolverhampton and wandering among its gabled and half-timbered houses and tea rooms and cloisters was, for my taste, a little too much like going for a walk in a jigsaw puzzle, it was a sight more civilised that some of the remote airfields in far-flung parts of the country to which others had been posted. But I would have had to confess that I was less taken with the splendid cathedral than with the Moreland's Match Manufactory, as it still obstinately called itself, home of *England's Glory* red-tipped matches which, with their jokes and sayings on the back of the highly coloured box, were a great favourite in Leeds pubs. (I wondered briefly if they might consider freelance contributions such as my unused Ahr Edward aphorisms. It was not such a wild thought: years afterwards someone opened negotiations with my agent – abortive, as it turned out – for the right to print paragraphs from my newspaper columns on the back of England's Glory matchboxes.)

Exploring further I found that Cheltenham was but a short bus ride away, in fact there was a stop right outside the Records Office. With its Georgian terraces and tree-lined boulevards Cheltenham was more my kind of town – a bit like Harrogate, where I had once ventured on a staring excursion. Cheltenham turned out to have a thriving rep theatre remorselessly ploughing its way through the kind of fare I was used to from the Theatre Royal Court Players back home. With a companionable Waaf called Patricia who shared my theatrical taste, or lack of it, I became a Saturday evening regular, with *The Shop at Sly Corner* or *George and Margaret* following a high tea of poached egg on toast at the Bon Marché department store café.

Life at Gloucester was congenial. There was a camp magazine and a camp theatre with a busy concert party; to both I contributed material regurgitated from the Mill Hill youth club days. There was an abundance of Waafs. The only drawback was that I could not get near a typewriter. This was typical of the RAF bureaucracy: having trained me, as they thought, to type and do shorthand, they placed me in a slot where neither skill was required. My job over at the Records Office consisted of shuffling files about. It was unexacting work with constant tea breaks and there were a great many civilians employed about the place, so that the atmosphere was that of an easy-going provincial insurance office rather than an RAF station. But – no typewriter. The months I was supposed to be devoting to building up a bank of cuttings to impress the editor of the *Yorkshire Evening Post* were dripping away like sand in an hour-glass; so far, since my call-up, I had had only one success – a short story sold to *Boy's Own* for two guineas, which Patricia, working in the orderly room, had typed up for me in her lunchtime. I could not see Mr Horniblow considering a boys' magazine yarn much of a qualification for covering the Leeds coroner's court.

Then one evening in the education hut, where I had gone to do some quiet reading, to my surprise I came across my friend Ray Hill. Ray, like me, had been in the RAF for several months by now but as one posting succeeded another we had lost touch of late. He was studying a sheaf of leaflets in search of some congenial part-time educational course for which he could volunteer with a view to escaping the tiresome routine tasks of an airman's life such as guard duty and billet orderly roster. The reunion was a serendipitous one for me. In the course of his researches Ray had discovered that if one volunteered to teach an evening class, given that one had the proper qualifications, one was entitled to a payment of one shilling a week per head up to a maximum of fourteen shillings weekly out of the station educational fund.

So I could solve my typewriter problem and be paid for it into the bargain. I reported to the education officer, a naïve young pilot officer, who congratulated me upon my public-spiritedness and initiative and at once set the wheels in motion. A vacant hut was commandeered and equipped with chairs and trestle tables, and the quartermaster's stores prevailed upon to produce a collection of ancient Remingtons, Coronas and Imperials, some of them such early models that you had to lift the carriage to see what you had just typed. Notices were posted on all the bulletin boards, announcing enrolment night for an evening typewriting course under the tutelage of AC2 Waterhouse, K.S.

The trouble was that not a soul turned up. Gloucester was a socially active camp and there were a hundred better ways of whiling away an evening than on self-education − the popular view, when I tried some direct recruiting, was that if the RAF wanted its personnel to acquire particular skills it could teach them in its own time. Fortunately the education officer did not turn up either, and so he was not yet to know that my scheme was a frost.

I think the idea of a phantom typing class was Ray's. It was beautifully simple. I should just take fourteen names and numbers at random off the various duty rosters dotted about the camp and enter them in my official attendance log, placing a tick against each name each week to qualify me for my fourteen shillings. Perhaps from time to time I should mark the odd name down as absent, to lend authenticity.

It was a brilliant plan but very probably a court martial offence. After my brush with authority at Wythall I had grown wily in the ways of the RAF, and I knew that sooner or later, and certainly before any money changed hands, my typing class would have to be produced in the flesh. I therefore modified Ray's brainwave. The fourteen names in my attendance log would be those of trusted friends and collaborators, in on the fraud. When the education officer wished to inspect my typists − he would have to give me notice, for the appointed evening for the mythical class would be a movable feast, changed week by week − I would round them up and sit them behind my battery of typewriters to clatter away as best they could until his arrival. For this service they would be paid sixpence each per week, or half my fourteen shillings between them. Sixpence would buy a Naafi supper. I had no difficulty in raising my phantom army.

The stunt worked perfectly. The typing class was scheduled to start the following week. On the Monday evening after supper I sat alone in the hut assigned to me where, having found the most serviceable (or least unserviceable) of my obsolescent collection of typewriters, I was composing an article aimed at the *Daily Herald*'s new youth page, on advice for new conscripts ("It's not a bad life really, so long as you keep your nose clean . . .") when, as half expected, the education officer walked in.

I snapped to attention and explained that so many men had been detailed for other duties that evening that I had had to change the class to Tuesday. The following night I had my full team on parade, for all that, owing to some mutiny in the ranks, I had had to field two or three substitutes on the promise of Eccles cakes all round in the Naafi later. The education officer duly put in his appearance. Since some of my class of imposters were coal heavers and boilermen who could barely write their own names, let alone type them, I had been rather concerned that he might want to see them in action. I sought to anticipate this by calling them smartly to attention as he entered the hut, knowing that while the rather dim PO would at once order "At ease -- stand easy", he would be at a loss how to frame any order that would cause them to sit down again and resume their typewriting activities. So it proved: they remained standing until, after wandering ineffectively up and down the hut for a while, and with a languid "Carry on, airman", he was gone. I never saw him again, for he was soon afterwards demobbed, and no successor ever materialised.

So while I continued to live in spasmodic fear of six months in the glasshouse (I already had my Conscript Prison Hell exposé sketched out in my mind for the *Sunday Pictorial*), my phantom typing class was a huge and profitable success, and my primary aim of having a machine to work on was accomplished with the bonus of a private hut to work in. Furthermore, not only was my *Daily Herald* youth page article accepted – two more guineas – but it was also reproduced in the *Air Reserve Gazette* (another half guinea, for I had remembered the *Writers' and Artists' Year Book* advice to offer First British Serial Rights Only).

I sent the *Daily Herald* cutting to Con Gordon and he wrote back:

"I will certainly do my damnedest to get you an interview with the Editor when you come out of the RAF. I can't undertake anything beyond that, because I'm not going to overshout my hand, but I think there's a sporting chance of getting you taken on. I think you have got the root of the matter in you, but we have to convince the Editor of that."

Galvanised, I threw myself into a flurry of work. Turning my back on the pleasures available to a young man in his prime with two and a half guineas in his pocket, I spent night after night in an abandoned hut at the end of a stretch of tarmac leading nowhere, surrounded by a surrealistic collection of old typewriters, clacking away at articles and stories with increasing if modest success. I sold a whole series of satirical "How to" articles to the *Writer*, a short piece to *Radio Times*, another short story to one of the boys' annuals. With one of my little windfalls I had some letterheads printed: "Writer K.S. WATERHOUSE Journalist. Contributor to: *Daily Herald*, *Yorkshire Evening Post*, *London Opinion*, *Radio Times*, *The Writer* etc., etc." The letters from Con Gordon were encouraging.

Then, just as I was getting into my stride, I was posted again – to Bicester in Oxfordshire. It was tolerable enough. Bicester was a little market town of the worst sort but Oxford was quite near and I spent many Saturdays wandering the High and staring at the colleges and hoping, in my civilian clothes, to be mistaken for an undergraduate. The RAF station, a permanent one with comfortable brick barracks, was the headquarters of No. 40 Group, Maintenance Command, which had something to do with stores and supplies. I was assigned to the staff of a group captain who, upon finding that I had verbatim shorthand, got me promoted to corporal and made me his secretary. Much of the work being confidential I was given my own little office. Since I was often required to work overtime, I also had my own key to the building, so that I could come and go as I pleased. Not only that: two stripes on my arm entitled me to my own private room in the barracks, where I could work and read in peace. Once more I was set up very nicely.

I had reached that agreeable point that eventually came in every conscript's life where one made a demob chart and began to tick off the remaining days to freedom one by one, when to my utter disgust the Russians imposed a blockade on Berlin, provoking the RAF to carry out a round-the-clock airlift of goods and supplies. I knew at once that this was going to affect me and it did. Demobilisation in

Maintenance Command was suspended until the crisis was over. I was mortified.

The setback did have two positive consequences, however. With the planning of the airlift my group captain was thrown into a series of long meetings with all manner of top brass, and I was given the quite responsible task of taking down their deliberations in shorthand, separating the wheat from the chaff and preparing minutes. This gave me invaluable reporting experience. The other consequence was that while waiting for my delayed demob I got another article in print, a significant one.

Browsing through the local newspaper with its front page fatstock prices, the *Bicester Advertiser*, I had hit upon the idea of a piece for *Picture Post* about Britain's market town weeklies, to be called "The World's Greatest Newspaper" (then the slogan of the *Daily Express*). They had turned it down, but I had resubmitted it to a popular rotogravure weekly of the day called *Everybody's*, who accepted it – or rather said they would consider it after I had written it. Taking advantage of the group captain's absence at the Air Ministry I sneaked a day off and interviewed everybody on the *Advertiser* from the compositor to the editor, plus some of the paper's readers and contacts around the market square. I wrote 1,700 words and despatched my piece to *Everybody's*. After an interminable delay – "I am sorry not to let you have the Editor's decision on your article but I assure you that it got a very good recommendation from the Editorial Reading Committee" – I received a letter of acceptance. The fee was twelve guineas, the most money I had ever earned in my life; but what pleased me even more was that I knew I had written a first-rate article. Unlike my previous stuff it was proper journalism, packed with facts, anecdotes, colourful detail and good quotes. It appeared a few weeks before I was at last released from the RAF. It was to do me a world of good.

I was demobilised on a roasting August day from Kirkham in Lancashire with its cheering view of the Blackpool Tower. I rode home through the cotton towns on a slow chuffing train to Leeds Central Station. I was absurdly pleased with myself, full of the joy of freedom and bubbling with anticipation of the heady new life to come. Not for a second did it occur to me that the *Yorkshire Evening Post* might turn me down – the more especially since I had just won one of their short story competitions with a prize of four guineas. I had no plans as to what I should do with myself if I was refused a chance – the possibility simply never entered my mind. I was full of the confidence of youth and had never been happier. I·don't think I have ever been happier since.

It was a Thursday. I rang Con Gordon from a coin box at the station and arranged to call on him the next afternoon at three, after the main edition had gone to press – "to bed", as I had learned to say. I was there punctually at ten to. He took me straight up to see Mr Horniblow, the editor, who sat behind a massive desk in a book-lined room which the Fleet Street reminiscences I had been lapping up for years now would have described as "the editorial sanctum". Mr Horniblow himself, fortyish I would say, looked like an unusually bright bank manager.

He asked me the questions on which Con Gordon had already briefed me on our way upstairs – education, background, shorthand speed, experience (I rather beefed up my *Leeds Guardian* credentials and mentioned my minute-writing stint at Bicester), and why I thought he should take me on. To this, rather than "Because I might just hang myself if you don't", I replied boldly, as rehearsed, "I consider myself a good risk."

Mr Horniblow then opened the folder of cuttings with which Con Gordon had furnished him and said, like a bank manager reviewing an overdraft, "I have been reading your cuttings and while they are very well written I would have said until recently that you were a feuilletonist rather than a journalist; but now that I have read your excellent article in *Everybody's* I'm persuaded to give you the benefit of the doubt. I'll take you on three months' trial at twenty guineas a month. When would you find it convenient to start?"

"Monday," I said.

I went home and told my mother that I was going to be a reporter. I did not mention the three months' trial. "What do you have to do?" she asked. I could not give her a satisfactory reply – I had little idea myself, that was the truth of it. For the first time I felt a clutch of fear at what I was getting into. I took down my secondhand *Chambers Dictionary* and looked up "feuilletonist".

3 Even at eight in the morning the newsroom was practically invisible under a pall of smoke from cigarettes, cheroots and pipes. The room was L-shaped – along one leg of it ran the long sub-editors' table at which sat half a dozen waistcoated or cardiganned figures, alternately red-faced or sallow-complexioned, pot-bellied or concave-chested according to whether they drank Guinness for strength or milk for their ulcers; but all of them chain-smoking, all of them resembling the Press Club caricatures of newspapermen I had mooned over in my little library of Fleet Street memoirs.

The other leg was taken up by the reporters' table, together with two or three individual desks at which sat the more senior members of the staff such as Mr Mann, the municipal correspondent, who always wore a black jacket and pinstriped trousers and looked more like the Lord Mayor than the Lord Mayor himself. The table was piled so high with books and paper that occasionally a dog-eared street guide or telephone directory would slither to the floor with a crash. Half a dozen typewriters as decrepit as the ones requisitioned for my mythical typing class at Gloucester kept a possible landslide of newspaper files, spiked copy, old notebooks and reference works in check. Two or three reporters, one of them with his hat on the back of his head like the newspapermen I had seen in films, were pecking away at overnight stories for the lunch edition. A couple more sat in the bank of wooden telephone booths at the end of the room, making the regular trawling calls to the ambulance and fire stations, the police and hospitals.

I had been haunted all weekend by the problem of how I was physically to set about starting work. I had no idea where to go or whom to ask for – not the editor, presumably. I couldn't see myself sauntering upstairs past the sales counter, even if I had been allowed to, and blundering around the editorial floor until I found the newsroom. In the end I solved my difficulty by asking for Con Gordon who, rather tetchily – he was in the middle of an article, I guessed – came down and took me up into the newsroom, where he introduced me to the news editor and his deputy, two kindly men named Alan Woodward and Ken Lemmon, and then departed – Con had his own office down the corridor, which he shared with the book reviewer, obituarist and arts correspondent (all the same person).

I was alone in a roomful of journalists. Ken Lemmon, spotting a fish out of water, tried to put me at my ease by introducing me to one or two reporters, but everyone was busy and had little time for this gauche young man in the new Fifty Shilling Tailors suit. To my relief, after five minutes of indecisive hanging about, I noticed Ken murmur to Mr Woodward who looked up from his news diary, took in my situation, and called me over to say, "You'll have seen that we carry the Leeds Market fruit and vegetable prices each Monday. I'd like you to go down to the Market and give me three or four paragraphs by half past nine. You'll find Mr Gomersall on Fruit Row very helpful, and Mr Pollard the self-styled Spud King is a good friend of ours too."

I headed towards Kirkgate in high spirits. My first assignment was a walkover (I didn't realise at the time that it was meant to be), and how appropriate that I should have to write about Market fruit and veg prices! Perhaps when I introduced myself to Mr Gomersall and Mr Pollard they would say, "Ee, it's never Ernest Waterhouse's lad, is it?" (They didn't.) And what bliss to be ambling to the Market on a sunny morning, clutching not a batch of Buckton's letters but a virgin reporter's notebook. The same feeling of liberation that I had experienced on the train home from Kirkham again swamped over me. It never quite left me all the time I remained in Leeds.

I was back at the office in good time – the first occasion ever when I had not loitered in the fragrant streets of my glass-roofed indoor city – where, perched self-consciously on a broken chair in front of a vacant typewriter, I tapped out my copy, remembering to head it with a catchline for the subs and printers as required by the manuals of journalism: "markets 1 . . . waterhouse." I handed it in to Mr Woodward who, having read it without comment, shouted "Boy!" and passed it to the copy boy who came scuttling over to carry it across to the subs' table. I was given nothing else to do and so I sat at the reporters' table pretending to read that morning's *Yorkshire Post* but surreptitiously drinking in my surroundings. I was in a newspaper office. I was in heaven. The reporters' room was empty by now — everyone out on stories. I realised with a lurching heart that if news of a big clothing factory fire came through, I should be the one sent to cover it, or anyway the one sent to do the best he could with the story until a proper reporter could be located. I half wanted and half didn't want the big clothing factory fire to happen.

The morning ticked by. I heard an exasperated sub-editor complain, "Subbing this stuff is like trying to get the Book of Genesis down to two lines!" and hoped he wasn't talking about my copy. At eleven o'clock the copy boy came round with a quire of lunch editions just off the press, and I loftily accepted one, then with casually disguised eagerness riffled through the pages.

My story, my first ever news story, occupied about four inches at the bottom of the City page. Headed "Strawberries cheaper" it began, much as I had written it, "At 8d to 10d a lb, strawberries are cheaper and more plentiful at Leeds Market than they have been all season. Bilberries are 1s 3d a lb, red currants 6d a lb, black currants 1s a lb, English cherries, both white and heart, 1s a lb, gooseberries 5d a lb, cherry plums 9d a lb . . ." This was followed by apple prices, flower prices and the news that peas were cheaper at 3d a lb, while watercress was 2½d a bunch. It was not earth-shattering stuff but it was a start. I was on a newspaper. I was a reporter.

It was a few days before I had met all my colleagues, for there was never a time when they were all in the office at once. Although one or two of them liked to give the impression of being hard-boiled — I was awfully impressed when, on my second day, our crime reporter Frank, upon ringing the Mayor of Dewsbury and being told that his worship couldn't speak to him, rasped, "Why not — has he got laryngitis?" — they were a friendly and helpful bunch.

Like all newsrooms, the *Evening Post*'s housed a cross-section of newspaper types from the suburbanly sedate to the downright eccentric. Our leader writer, Percy, who only ever surfaced to pick up a political speech from the Press Association tape machine, kept a cottage piano in his office which he would play for inspiration in his ceaseless fight against the Attlee government. Our chief photographer, the Falstaffian, ash-bespattered Charlie, who was said to have been the original of the part created by Frank Pettingell in J.B. Priestley's *When We Are Married* (and later played by Priestley himself), was famous for being so drunk when photographing the Archbishop of York that he fell off his stepladder, then picking himself and his broken plate camera up leered, "Come on, yer Grace, give us one of yer big grins!" Ron, a secretive soul who brought his own little Royal portable to the office and wouldn't let anyone else use it, was a cricket fanatic who boasted a lawn made up from sods cut from all the county grounds, and whose garden gate was made up of Test wickets begged from Headingley. Stanley, the one who never took his hat off, had spent a few weeks in the London bureau of the *Chicago Herald Tribune* and spoke with an American accent.

I was not the only recruit to be taken on board that week – a former Fleet Street man named Michael joined on the same day, his brief career on the legendary *Daily Mirror* (legendary, that is, for firing people) having been abruptly brought to a halt when, in skittish mood, he submitted a story in rhyming couplets. Nor was I the youngest: an ambitious sixteen-year-old former editorial secretary called Barbara Taylor – in later life to be better known by her married name of Barbara Taylor Bradford – was being given a trial on the women's page by the chance-taking Mr Horniblow. Barbara was apt to burst into tears from time to time when bawled out for not yet knowing her job to perfection, and I became her hand-holder-in-chief. Little did she know that it was a case of the blinded-by-tears leading the blinded-by-tears.

For a supposedly non-routine job, journalism proved to have a cosily routine core. Each morning I would be sent on two or three minor stories – a chip-pan fire, a small burglary, with any luck a six-car pile-up at Bramham Crossroads, a notorious black spot – which I had to phone in straight from my notes to the copytakers, a phalanx of invisible, schoolmarmish women given to snapping, "Come on, come on!" when I floundered, thus teaching me to think more quickly on my feet. I would then get the tram back to Town -- one of the three or four office cars staffed by the van drivers would grudgingly take you out to a job, but wouldn't wait for your return – and make for Perry's café in Commercial Street, where reporters from all three of the city's dailies lounged over coffee and chocolate biscuits each morning in an atmosphere of joshing and raillerie. While at Buckton's, I had once or twice ventured into Perry's and watched this scene of cameraderie from a distant table with a pang of envy. Now I was part of it.

I would then generally be assigned some court reporting, for which with my verbatim shorthand I was a natural. From covering the juvenile court I graduated quickly to the coroner's court, the magistrates' courts, the county court, the crown court and finally Leeds Assizes, where on important cases I would work in tandem with another reporter, the pair of us putting our copy over in alternating ten-minute takes so as to squeeze the last possible drop of juice out of the story before edition time. That was invigorating – one had to stay on one's toes and edit from one's notebook as one went along.

Reporting the courts gave me good practice in using my own editorial judgment, but more importantly from my point of view it gave me access to the coveted Town Hall press room, whose frosted-glass door I had given a wistful stare on my first quick circumnavigation of the Town Hall corridors back in the white card era. The smoke-filled press room, with its cigarette-burned old table, roll-top desks, men in hats, packs of greasy playing cards and candlestick telephones, was all I could wish for – straight out of the film of Hecht and MacArthur's *The Front Page* with Lee Tracy and Adolphe Menjou, or *His Girl Friday* with Cary Grant and Rosalind Russell.

It was here, against a background of urgent shouts down the telephone of "Copy, please . . . There were gasps from the public gallery in Leeds No. 1 Court today when . . .", that I learned to play serious poker. The card school was especially lively during the Assizes "black list" – cases of, for instance, South Yorkshire miners buggering sheep equipped with wellington boots (to stop their feet slipping), which at the time were deemed unreportable even when smothered in euphemism – when I would make desperate efforts to remain solvent until a policeman popped his head round the door and announced that the court was back to the relative wholesome normality of a good meat-axe murder.

Lunchtime would find me in the Victoria Family and Commercial Hotel behind the Town Hall for a beer and a sandwich, where, if the case across the road was big enough, I might rub shoulders with, or anyway be in the same mahogany saloon bar as, the local correspondents of the *Mail*, *Mirror* and *Express* and even some of the big boys over from Manchester. Or if there was some exclusive story the *Evening Post* was shielding from the opposition, one might seek refuge behind the pink terracotta façade of the Jubilee Hotel out in the Headrow, a splendid, five-storey authentic gin palace with art nouveau windows. The last time I ventured into it the brewers had converted it into a replica of a zoo.

If there was nothing much going on in the courts after my brief lunch I would wander back to the office when, unless there was an accident or some other hard news story to follow up, I would be given a "special" to do for the next day's lunch edition – perhaps I might be trusted to do an interview with a minor visiting celebrity (I interviewed Lana Morris in the belief that she was Lana Turner), or with a particular district's oldest inhabitant who was "99 years young".

The working day finished with the final edition going to press at four – unless, that was, you were on "late stop" duty, left in charge of the Stop Press for, where the news justified it, the occasional Late Final – the "Special" that I used to be sent running out for in my stockinged feet as a child in Middleton; or unless you were covering some evening event such as a concert or a public meeting. A small gossiping band of raffishly inclined reporters did hang on anyway, whether they were on duty or not, waiting for the pubs to open. I was as often as not of their number, for at the day's end I could not bear to tear myself away from the office – it would have been like leaving a party early.

We would sprawl around the reporters' table, feet up, smoking and talking. I had never heard proper talk before. Anecdotes were told – I had read anecdotes in books but never heard anyone telling them – only jokes, and that badly. Here we had raconteurs. A favourite story was that of an Edwardian editor of the *Yorkshire Post* who wrote to a female applicant for a reporting job, "Dear Madam, So long as I am Editor of this newspaper, the frou-frou of a woman's skirts will not be heard in its corridors. Besides, there is not sufficient lavatory accommodation." Then there was the news editor who, upon hearing from a reporter on another paper that rumour had it there was a newsroom vacancy, replied, "Dear Sir, Rumour, so often a fickle jade, errs again." I lapped this kind of thing up, and was practically open-mouthed with admiration when some of my colleagues proved to be wits in their own right – as when, reading a story about how a crowd of four hundred had been led in prayer by a kneeling clergyman while an old-age pensioner leaped from a blazing third-storey window, our religious affairs correspondent remarked drily, "I'd rather have four atheists holding a blanket."

Which pub I found myself in come opening time would depend on whose company I was in. One or two sophisticated souls preferred Polly's Bar across the street, a proper American bar with subdued pink lighting and cocktail shakers, the first such establishment I had ever set foot in, and one that in an earlier existence had seemed so much out of my social stratum that I had only once ever given it the barest flicker of a stare. Here, over gin-and-Its and Americanos, one might meet long-legged mannequins and junior fashion buyers from Marshall and Snelgrove's on the next block, as well as reasonably exquisite young women with an expensive taste in drinks who looked as if they might be mannequins but were not.

I was on safer ground in Whitelock's, with its long marble-topped bar, iron tables and snug settles, and old etched mirrors advertising soup and bread for a penny and the names of breweries long gone. Betjeman was to call it the Leeds equivalent of Ye Olde Cheshire Cheese in Fleet Street. In that somewhat orthodox era, Whitelock's was regarded as the city's hotbed of bohemianism, which was why I had for so long been so curious about the place.

It certainly lived up to its reputation. It was much used by artists, or anyway shag smokers who looked like artists, by university students trailing long scarves, and by bearded men wearing corduroy jackets with Penguin books stuffed into their pockets, who I was told either worked for the BBC or had had worked commissioned by the BBC, or were hoping to have work so commissioned. So this was what writers, producers and actors looked like! But of the select number of my colleagues who favoured Whitelock's as a drinking resort, none seemed to know any of this exotic crew and so I was not yet introduced into their charmed circle.

I did, however, meet one real live, full-time poet – R.C. Scriven, or Ratz as he signed himself, a regular contributor of light verse to the paper. As well as having a considerable local talent Ratz had a national one too, for not only was he the author of a much-acclaimed, prize-winning radio play called *A Single Taper*, about someone undergoing an operation to try to save his sight, but he frequently appeared in *Punch*. A line of his describing the advent of spring, "My foot covered five daisies", had always stuck in my mind. In true bohemian style Ratz was usually penniless, and so it was my privilege to buy him a drink. Conversation, however, was difficult, for not only was he four-fifths blind, as I had deduced from *A Single Taper*, but he was almost totally deaf and utterly reliant on an erratic battery-operated hearing-aid that only seemed to work when he was being asked what he was going to have. Although I was to become quite a chum of Ratz's in various hostelries about town, our Whitelock's acquaintanceship was short-lived. At that time Whitelock's lavatories were out in the yard, next to the kitchens. One night after a prolonged bout of hospitality from admirers and sympathisers, Ratz went out to relieve himself and was found by an outraged chef urinating against the white-tiled kitchen wall. Barred for life.

But the authentic working journalists' pub was the Pack Horse, down one of the ginnels leading into Briggate, a smoky old pub much used by both the *Evening Post* and *Evening News*, and the place for good newspaper talk about scoops and stunts and circulation wars. The Pack Horse was opposite the Empire and had accumulated a gallery of signed photographs of the stars to rival the Varieties circle bar; but I never saw any of them in there, except for a novelty act known as Kardomah, whose slogan was "Fills the stage with flags", and a mind-reading turn called Maurice Fogel, who told us that he had once got off jury service on the grounds that he might know what the accused was thinking. Fogel's visit to the Empire coincided with a poltergeist story out of which all the papers were getting much mileage, concerning a couple up in Headingley who, while decorating their new house, were hampered by paint pots floating off on their own accord, stepladders crashing down the stairs and electric light bulbs detaching themselves from their sockets and smashing against the walls. One night in the Pack Horse someone suggested getting Fogel along to investigate. It was very late and no one had any clear idea what a mind-reader would have to say to a poltergeist; but the *Daily Express* had already got a team of psychic researchers in the house and our own religious affairs man had brought in a vicar to try his hand at exorcism, so the presence of Fogel could only add to the merriment.

Everyone was rather drunk – I, still very new to this game of journalism, intoxicated twice over at being allowed in on such a lark – and we all trooped across to the Empire stage door and had Fogel brought out. He was, of course, all for the stunt, especially upon being told that the national press were already camping out in the house. Taxis were called and by midnight we had a nice little seance going, with a dozen reporters, four photographers, a clergyman, three psychic researchers, the scared couple and Fogel's publicity agent standing in a circle in the attic of the Headingley haunted house. Fogel himself sat tied to a chair in the middle of the ring with a tambourine on his knees. The door was sealed and the lights put out, then the tambourine bounded across the room. Someone put it back on Fogel's knee, when it began to shake out a message – from none other than Houdini, according to one of the psychic researchers. Fogel thereupon confessed that he had himself been working the tambourine, claiming, rather inconsequentially, that here was proof that the poltergeist was a hoax. A violent argument broke out between Fogel, the psychic researchers, the vicar, Fogel's publicity man and the afflicted householders, in the course of which some of the sozzled reporters remembered they had deadlines to keep and departed.

It was all marvellous nonsense, and I was in such a state of bliss after my night's adventure that I walked all the way home. And to think that the staid old Yorkshire Conservative Newspaper Co. were paying me twenty guineas a month to live this sort of life – had they only known, and had I had the means available, I should willingly have paid twenty guineas a month to them.

To walk home, in fact, would have been no great hardship even without the spring of exhilaration in my step, for home by now was on the Headingley side of town. Twenty guineas a month was a good sum of money to be earning – to be paid by the month at all seemed to me a sign of prosperity and on top of that there was the odd five shillings for any Diary paragraph I got in the paper, plus, I discovered, seven and sixpence for amateur drama reviews. I could well afford a small flat, and accordingly I found a modest apartment in the university district by Woodhouse Moor, within walking distance of Town.

So as well as putting clerking behind me I had now said goodbye for ever to council house living. Although I had been weaned off my mother's council house by two years in the forces, it was still something of a wrench to leave Halton Moor – not the estate, which I detested, but the essentially late-Edwardian home I had been brought up in. My little flat was by no means modern but moving into it was like stepping out of a time machine upon returning from a bygone age. No more soot-encrusted kettle simmering on the hob, no more flat irons resting in the hearth, no more blacklead, no more donkey-stone. No cobbler's last (for home boot repairs), mangle, copper (for boiling clothes), wicker clothes basket, zinc watering can, wireless accumulator, earthenware milk cooler, chimney rods.

No more loaf tins in the oven, no bread cakes the size of hub caps cooling on the windowsill. I had been familiar with these objects all my life but within days I felt as if I had been passing my life in a Five Towns story by Arnold Bennett but had now stepped into a post-war novel by J.B. Priestley.

It was, as I was not yet to realise, the beginning of a general move upmarket for the Waterhouse clan. My brothers had long ago come home from the war with as little fuss as they had departed (when Kenneth got back from the Western Desert my mother, who after all had not set eyes on him for five years, asked only "Is it still raining?" before laying out his supper) and settled into their peacetime jobs – Kenneth at the Yorkshire Copperworks in enviable Hunslet, Dennis as a car repair shop storeman, Stanley as a plasterer. Now sister Stella and Dennis married (Stanley and Kenneth did not) and produced children who, thanks partly to the Butler Education Act of 1944, were to become teachers or technological whizz-kids of the property-owning kind. Whatever stray gene had produced me stayed in the family system to upgrade the Waterhouses out of the artisan class for ever. From total illiteracy to letters after one's name and a car in the garage in two generations – no mean feat of social engineering.

Of course, I went to see my mother regularly, religiously, every Sunday, when the trams criss-crossing the city were jam-packed with young men in their best suits and young women in their powder-blue or lilac "costumes" and matching little hats, on their parental pilgrimages, and when in Richard Hoggart's memorable phrase all the dustbins of Leeds were covered with a thin top coating of John West salmon tins.

I enjoyed my walks down into Town each morning and would often vary my route, a favourite one being through the university and down through the Civic Hall, to which my brand-new National Union of Journalists card bearing my Polyfoto and the word PRESS in big letters now gave me access (I had been refused entry by the commissionaire in my white card staring days), then through the Town Hall and along Park Row past all the banks with their legions of ex-College of Commerce clerks all toiling away. I congratulated myself frequently on the fact that no building in Leeds was now denied me, from the Council chamber to the humblest working men's club, from the Territorial Army barracks to the Leeds Library; I could walk the iron-railed balcony of Kirkgate Market to

198

seek out the Markets Superintendent, or the marble halls of the Yorkshire Penny Bank to keep an appointment with the manager; my press pass would take me past any stage door or into the very parlour of the Lord Mayor himself; I had access to the cocktail bars of the Queen's and Metropole hotels, and even to Albert Cowling's cavernous, subterranean Wine Lodge. The last veil of the city had at last been torn away; but more than that, I was now a part of Leeds life – I was living it rather than merely looking at it.

In short, I was thoroughly enjoying myself, and never more alive – so much so that I quite forgot I was only on three months' trial and could be pitched back into clerical serfdom on the editor's whim. What I would have done then I had no idea, but as things turned out I had nothing to worry about – not that I had been worrying in the first place. Mr Horniblow, it seemed, was too innovative and unsettling for the conservative board of the Yorkshire Conservative Newspaper Co. He departed abruptly for Fleet Street whence he had come, and was succeeded by the benign news editor, Mr Woodward. If Mr Woodward knew of the three months arrangement, he never let on. Indeed he once stopped me in the corridor and congratulated me on settling in nicely.

Towards Christmas I got notice of an unexpected four guineas a month rise. I celebrated my new affluence with a pub crawl from Polly's to Whitelock's to the Pack Horse, in the course of which I consumed fourteen bottles of Guinness. Back at the office I fell asleep in the lavatory and awoke at seven in the morning, just time enough before starting work for a canteen breakfast and my first ever barbershop shave. Another adventure.

4   While the euphoria had not worn off (nor has it since), after about a year of this idyllic existence I began to grow restless. I had realised that becoming a newspaper reporter was not the summit of my ambition. It had seemed such a difficult goal from the view of a half-educated undertaker's clerk in a council house that I had never thought beyond it.

Now I set myself two fresh targets. The first was to get to Fleet Street, perhaps via Manchester – but less because I saw myself pursuing a lifelong career on national newspapers than because I had made up my mind that I wanted to live in London.

I had already paid one brief and confused visit to the capital, on the proceeds of my twelve-guinea windfall from *Everybody's* in the last weeks of my national service, and I was completely hooked. Like Birmingham, London was still a monochrome rather than a Technicolor experience, still essentially a Victorian-cum-Edwardian metropolis (Romano's had only recently closed its doors), with only the odd stunning modernistic edifice such as Broadcasting House, the black glass *Daily Express* building, a handful of Jazz Age hotels and restaurants and Frank Pick's elegant tube stations to indicate, as some of us naïvely hoped, the shape of things to come. This was a London of Lyons Corner Houses with palm court orchestras and wandering violinists, of coffee stalls and ABC (for Aerated Bread Company) teashops and Dickensian chophouses, of flower girls and streetwalkers and costermongers, of trams along the Embankment and chunky red buses and black cabs like truncated hearses, and bomb craters.

I stayed at the Union Jack Club, the forces hostel by Waterloo Station, and sallied forth to find Soho which, confusing it with W.W. Jacobs's Limehouse, I looked for on the river with the result that I was soon hopelessly lost south-east of Tower Bridge. I didn't mind at all: the cindery smoke of London was in my nostrils and "the roar of London's traffic" as they called it on the *In Town Tonight* wireless programme was in my ears, and I was as happy as the days were long.

And long they were, for I was up at five in the morning to discover Covent Garden market, whose cloisters I wandered for hours, marvelling at the criss-crossing ballet of porters with their own height in fruit baskets balanced on their heads. In the afternoon I perched on a shelf of the Westminster Theatre to see Flora Robson in *Black Chiffon*, and in the evening on another shelf somewhere in Shaftesbury Avenue to see my first ever revue, in which Hermione Baddeley did a Restoration comedy sketch by Alan Melville where all the s's were pronounced as f's: "Come fit on the fofa and feduce me, you filly fod." I walked all the way home to the Union Jack Club trying to compose a revue sketch in my head. There was fog coming up from the river, and the mournful hoot of lighters, and out in the trolley-bus-hissing suburbs there would be dapper henpecked husbands boiling down flypapers to make arsenic, and there would be human heads in hatboxes in the left-luggage office at Victoria Station. This was the place to be, all right.

On my last morning I made the pilgrimage to Fleet Street, had half a pint of ale at Ye Olde Cheshire Cheese, the Whitelock's of the south, and went and stared at the plaque to Edgar Wallace on Ludgate Circus where he sold newspapers as a boy: "Edgar Wallace, Reporter. Born London 1875, died Hollywood 1932. Founder member of the Company of Newspaper Makers. He knew wealth and poverty yet had walked with kings and kept his bearing. Of his talents he gave lavishly to authorship – but to Fleet Street he gave his heart."

About giving my own heart to Fleet Street I was not so sure, for the second of my targets was to become a serious writer of novels and plays. I was still turning out the odd magazine feuilleton as Mr Horniblow would have called my modest successes, and I had been paid the unheard-of sum of £25 as winner of a competition in a boy's paper, the *Champion*, for, of all things, a football story. But my heart was no longer in writing just for the sake of getting published – perhaps my few daily inches in the *Evening Post* fulfilled that need. I wanted now to become a proper writer, not just a hit-or-miss churner-out of froth at a guinea a thousand words. I saw myself set up in an attic flat in Chelsea, wherever that might be, interviewing starlets for the *Daily Express* by day and working on the great British novel, or even the minor British novel, by night.

The trouble was, what to write? While I was slowly learning to write from my own observation, I had yet to write a single word from my own experience. When my mother, not all that many years ago, had brought home for me the collected plays of J.M. Barrie, I had failed to follow up my newly acquired interest in this versatile author by reading his book *When A Man's Single*. This account of his life on the *Nottinghamshire Journal* and as a freelance writing magazine pieces gave, as I too belatedly discovered, the best advice possible for the aspiring journalist: "Do not fruitlessly aspire towards international travel and the drawing rooms of the mighty in your search for a topic, but write about the small everyday events of your own existence, and these accounts will sell." Con Gordon had said much the same thing. But even had I read Barrie in time for this wise counsel to be of any use (in the event, the only thing I learned from him, and quickly unlearned, was how to write infuriatingly arch stage directions), I might have reflected that it was all very well for him, he hadn't been brought up on a flat council estate where nothing ever happened. Arnold Bennett had his Five Towns, Lawrence his Nottinghamshire pit villages, but all I had to fall back on was a dormitory suburb and a surrogate interest in Hunslet.

But then one day I picked up at Stringer's bookstall in the Market a Guild Books paperback of Dylan Thomas's *Portrait of the Artist as a Young Dog*, a collection of short stories based on his boyhood in Swansea. It was an eye-opener. Thomas came from a world as remorselessly ordinary as my own. He was a grammar school boy, from the semi-detached end of town rather than the smoky terraces; nothing desperate had ever happened to him, he hung around with a crowd of other boys and they did the things that boys do − the kind of things I had done. The stories brought my own childhood back to life and made it seem what I had never remembered it to be − exciting.

And so there was my lesson, and my model. I began to think back over my own childhood and the small change of my upbringing in Middleton, which now seemed crowded and full of incident. I remembered a fight I had stupidly got into at the Wolf Cubs. For years it had been nothing but a tiny, rather painful half-memory, but now I let myself drift back into the past and it became vivid in my mind again. I put it down on paper and for the first time, outside of newspaper reporting, something I'd written seemed to be about something. I never tried to publish the piece because although it had life it didn't have form — it was an incident rather than a story. But I knew I was on the way to something now, and I began to excavate further. These childhood episodes, the first real things I had ever written, were to surface in due course as fragments of my first novel, *There Is A Happy Land*.

At around this time I also wrote my first radio play, stimulated largely by the circumstances that every morning on my way to the office I passed the BBC Leeds studios, housed in a former Quaker meeting house in Woodhouse Lane, and I was curious to see inside them. By giving the Pack Horse and Whitelock's a miss for a few evenings and working at a newsroom typewriter when the others had all gone, I managed to produce an Ealing-type romp called *The Town That Wouldn't Vote*. I never seriously expected this to be accepted, but I did think it showed enough promise to warrant an invitation to the BBC where I might with luck be taken under the wing of a producer who would point me in the right direction. To my surprise, after a routine postcard acknowledging receipt of the script, the next thing I heard from the BBC was a contract in duplicate, requiring my signature in acceptance of "the fee mentioned above and on the terms and conditions stated". The fee mentioned above was sixty guineas, a fortune — it bought, among other luxuries, my first ever typewriter, an Imperial portable.

A few days later I was summoned to the BBC to meet my producer, Guy Stephen Deghy, a heavily built, voluble Hungarian I recognised as one of the bearded bohemians of Whitelock's. He took me straight across to the BBC local, the Fenton Arms, showed me the framed cheque for a pound from Wilfred Pickles with its accompanying instruction, "Break glass in case of emergency", bought me a half of Tetley's bitter and then got me drunk on talk. T.S. Eliot, J.B. Priestley, Tennessee Williams, Graham Greene, Evelyn Waugh, Norman Mailer, Ratz Scriven, Con Gordon, the pre-war Berlin cabaret, Blackpool, the quality of Leeds fish and chips, the London theatre, apartheid, *Passport to Pimlico*, *Citizen Kane*, the rival merits of Tetley's and Younger's beer, Hunslet Feast, the Spanish Riding School, the works of Hank Janson and Louis MacNeice's "Bagpipe Music" were among the subjects touched upon before closing time. Despite a twenty-year age gap, Guy and I hit it off from the start, and we were to become lifelong friends and collaborate on several fruitful projects.

Guy had no faults to pick with the play at all. I was rather disappointed – I had expected, in the best Hollywood tradition, to be required to go away and do hurried rewrites, working far into the night with a cigarette on my lips. He did not even trouble to mention that my play presented something of a challenge in that it had no fewer than sixty-three characters including three real-life London BBC announcers and the commentator from *British Movietone News*. Even if we could have got these celebrities up to Leeds there was not enough studio space to hold them, or indeed for more than a couple of dozen of the cast; in fact the only way my play could be put out at all was by linking up three studios, Leeds, Manchester and London. Guy invited me to the transmission and it all went so much like clockwork that I had not the slightest inkling that manipulating sixty-three characters in three separate studios was in any way out of the ordinary. It was only at the party over at the Fenton later that I had some glimmer of the technical miracle my producer had just achieved when he said casually, "That seemed to go awfully well and I should like to commission another Thursday Play from you, but do you think next time you could keep it down to about half a dozen characters at most?"

Alas, the commission never came. A few days later Guy was arrested for drinking a few minutes after hours in Whitelock's with his friend the then landlord. Fined ten shillings. In those Reithian days it was not precisely a firing offence but it was enough to put the block on his future prospects with the BBC. Guy took off for London to act, write and generally continue the bohemian life – the fact that he was down there mingling with actresses and drinking in the French Pub was a further spur to my ambition to reach my Chelsea garret.

In the meantime, I had settled in nicely at the *Yorkshire Evening Post* as the editor Mr Woodward had put it, even though I did not intend to settle there for all that much longer. It was a wonderful if, as I now recognised, temporary way of life. There was a Press Ball at the Town Hall to which, in a dinner jacket hired from Rawcliffe's where my mother had bought my School Cap, I escorted Barbara Taylor. There were functions to cover – dinner dances and banquets for this or that federation of this or that trade or calling, where I was indoctrinated into the mysteries of the fish knife, the cigar cutter and the grape scissors, and where I stylishly made my notes on the back of a menu card.

By now, by virtue of taking on the amateur theatre reviews when

205

nobody else wanted to do them, I had established myself as second-string drama critic. The senior critic, Mr Bolton, got the Grand Theatre, the Empire was the perquisite of the chief sub-editor who had a taste for music-hall, and my beat was the Theatre Royal and the City Varieties – Theatre Royal Monday first house, City Varieties second house. It could have been the other way round but Ray Hill, with whom I often shared my pair of complimentary tickets, was convinced that I had droit du seigneur over the chorus girls. Thus Monday night would often end with our hanging around the stage door to escort two peroxide blondes – any two peroxide blondes, the first pair out – to a fish and chip supper and then back to their theatrical digs in the North Street area. There our stage door Johnny dalliance would abruptly end, for in that district self-respecting chorus girls would not hang about on the doorstep for fear of being mistaken for ladies of the night, and theatrical landladies had a strict policy of No Gentlemen Callers.

As for my reviews, attempts to emulate Ivor Brown of the *Observer* were blue-pencilled as clever-clever and I quickly learned to write in the then house style of the entertainments page – that is to say, generously. The theatres were, after all, regular advertisers. My Theatre Royal review invariably praised the Court Players' *ingénue* with whom I was in love; and I usually had a good word for the consistent, i.e. always the same, performance of the leading man who never failed to get an exit round by shouting "Good night!" and slamming the door regardless of what the stage directions might have required.

My Varieties reviews were practically written for me by the proprietor, Mr Harry Joseph, who over a liberal drink in the circle bar would literally mark my card: taking my programme he would scrawl through some names and asterisk others with a running commentary on the quality of the acts – "He's no good . . . I shan't be booking this one again . . . Now these fellows are top class – they'll be back here in six weeks on their way down from Sunderland, so give them a good write-up, son . . ." While I was hardly likely to emerge as a rival to Ken Tynan with this kind of stuff I was thrilled to be almost a part of the City Varieties' backstage life, and thus by extension of the backstage life of the city itself.

By now I was becoming something of a hardened reporter. I had seen my first murderer sentenced to death, the prisoner clutching the same spiked dock from which Charlie Peace had been despatched to the scaffold, and had been repelled yet fascinated by the black cap ritual and the dreadful formula of the sentence of execution. My hands were still so shaky after I had phoned in my story that during the press room poker session later I dropped my cards. The old Press Association hand who had seen it all before said gruffly, "It takes everybody like that the first time, young 'un."

I had covered grisly accidents where the firemen were still cutting bleeding victims out of their vehicles, I had interviewed bereaved mothers, and I had been sent up in a Tiger Moth like the one that did a loop-the-loop over the Murder Woods when I was a child, to report on the snowed-up Dales. And I had got my tram scoop.

The way of my tram scoop was that Mr Mann, the municipal correspondent, was off on his annual holidays to Whitby and it fell to me to cover the Council beat in his absence. Mr Mann was perfectly happy to leave the city's municipal affairs in my whippersnapper hands: like all specialists he was always careful to take his holiday when there was nothing very much going on in his particular field, and in any case he was well aware that I knew no one in civic circles above the rank of waitress in the Town Hall basement restaurant. I was unlikely to upstage my august senior.

Little did he know. Little did I know. After a week of ineffectual meanderings around the corridors of power I was descending the stairs of the civic restaurant for a coffee one morning when I encountered the Chairman of the Transport Committee, a blunt-speaking Alderman to whom I had been briefly introduced at the bar of the Victoria Commercial Hotel. The Alderman walked with a pronounced limp and was having difficulty mounting the stairs and so it seemed only civil to help him up. He thanked me, enquired as to the whereabouts of Mr Mann, and upon learning that he was away said, "Never mind – tha'll do. Does tha want summat to write about?" Putting his arm around my shoulders the Alderman led me out to the Town Hall steps and pointed to the junction of Park Row and the Headrow, where a great log-jam of trams, eight or nine of them queuing up behind one another like lighters waiting to enter harbour, was causing total gridlock, the first of them having broken down.

"Tha sees yon trams, lad? We're getting shut of the buggers."

Sensation. Scrapping the trams was akin to scrapping Kirkgate Market or Headingley cricket ground or the Town Hall itself, and I had it first. I sprinted over to the Civic Hall and got a quote from the Alderman's Conservative opposite number, to the effect that covering fifty miles of tram track with asphalt would put a shilling on the rates. I did not bother to note his additional comment, to the effect that the Alderman was merely flying a kite – so he was, and it was to be four or five years before the trams were finally condemned, but it was still a scoop. I telephoned the story through and went about my business. I could not understand why it did not make the early editions, to give me something to crow about in the saloon bars, but then I realised they were holding it until the Final so that it would be too late for the opposition to follow it up. And there it was, all over the front page. My first real exclusive.

Mr Mann duly returned from holiday, when he was not best pleased. Nevertheless, he was gracious enough to congratulate me. Waving away my thanks he added, "Did you by any chance notice, when you interviewed the Alderman, that he walks with a bit of a limp?" I confirmed that I knew the Alderman was minus a leg.

"Correct, laddie. And do you know where he lost that leg?"

"Passchendaele?" I hazarded.

The municipal correspondent tucked his thumbs into his waistcoat pockets. "If you'd looked up the Alderman's details before writing your brilliant exclusive," he said, "you would have seen that he was run over. By a tram."

Nevertheless, my tram scoop stood me in good stead and I was given bigger and better stories to do. These I diligently clipped and filed each evening, as did every other ambitious reporter, for when you wished to change to another paper your cuttings were your passport.

And I was by now positively in the mood for change – not only because I wanted to get to Fleet Street and London but because I felt I had lived long enough in Leeds. The Alderman might have been premature about the trams but there was no doubt that the city was stirring out of its pre-war, post-Edwardian sleep. While it would be a long time yet before Leeds declared itself the Motorway City – it would be a long time yet before we even saw the first motorway – there was a civic restlessness about, a growing clamour for clearing away the old, for comprehensive development and social engineering, and the high cranes were gathering on the horizon. From what I heard of the plans for Leeds in its transition from the provincial to the regional I didn't think it was going to be my kind of place. I had been growing up in an industrial Atlantis that was about to be submerged. Time to move on.

5   Things had gone so smoothly for me so far that it came as something of a shock to realise that getting out of Leeds was not going to be the easy ride I had anticipated. Our crime man Frank came back from an interview with the *Daily Mirror* in Manchester with the report that the news editor had openly scoffed at his impressive set of cuttings, pointing out sceptically that they could be anybody's work. This was perfectly true − indeed, I had been banking on that fact in venturing to augment my own meagre collection of cuttings with stories by other hands. In those days only two staff members' names appeared above their work − Con Gordon's and the pseudonym of the plump and pompous sports editor who for reasons of his own chose to call himself Little John. Everyone else was identified simply as *Evening Post Reporter*. It was clear that if I were to stand any chance of battering down the doors of Withy Grove or Fleet Street I should somehow have to start getting my name in the paper.

But how? With the connivance of Ray Hill I hatched a plot. We had for months been planning a holiday in London, mainly with the object of discovering Chelsea, reputedly the haunt of poets, painters and artists' models with loose morals. I proposed a stunt: that we should set off and walk to London, covering the 210-mile journey in one week flat, I phoning in a daily account of our progress. It was perhaps a rash notion. While I had whiled away many an hour wandering the streets of Leeds I had no particular love of strenuous walking, and the prospect of tramping thirty miles a day was a daunting one. But it would be a lark, and if the paper agreed to go along with it they could hardly confine my daily byline to *Evening Post Reporter*.

The ruse worked. The editor was enthusiastic, and after Ray and I had had great fun plotting a route with the aid of a Bartholomew's map spread over the big dining table in Whitelock's, my opening story featured not only my name but also a photograph of the pair of us striding out from City Square at the start of our trek.

We walked briskly through the familiar streets of Hunslet and were soon on the A1, still romantically known as the Great North Road, reaching Doncaster by nightfall. So far, so good: the only countryside yet encountered was that semi-urban scrubland of allotments, rhubarb fields and potato patches, slag heaps, car dumps and sooty fields with grazing pit ponies which was the only type of greenery I could abide. We now had to find a place to sleep. "Barns and the lee of hedges will be our makeshift beds," I had rashly promised, but it was spluttering with rain and the lights of Doncaster beckoned. We ditched our resolution to emulate W.H. Davies and the knights of the open road and established a routine of finding rooms in modest pubs. In my despatches I referred to them as inns: it seemed so much more Chestertonian.

The second leg of our journey took us through the Dukeries, a seriously wooded beauty spot that seemed to stretch for hundreds of miles. From time to time motorists or lorry drivers would slow down to offer us a lift through this uncompromising forest and I for one was tempted, but any one of them could have been a potential spy for the rival *Yorkshire Evening News*, ready, for half a guinea tip-off money, to denounce our 210-mile walk as a fraud. I pined for the line of factory chimneys, like plane trees on the horizon of Picardy, that would tell us we were nearing Nottingham. Not for the first time, it came home to me that I was an acute sufferer from rural agoraphobia.

But I was getting twelve inches or so into the paper every day, each account of our small adventures being headed "From Keith Waterhouse". For some reason, perhaps because there was not usually much room in the papers for escapist stuff, the story was generating a fair amount of interest, and pressmen on our route, tipped off by the *Evening Post* news desk, would turn out to interview us and wire back pictures of us bathing our sore feet.

The original idea was to finish up in Trafalgar Square, but in the event we completed our Leeds to London marathon at Broadcasting House, where we were to be interviewed on the popular Saturday evening wireless programme *In Town Tonight*. The visit, for me, was more of an adventure than the actual broadcast − setting foot in that hallowed Bauhaus lobby was like staying at the Savoy Hotel. While the scripted interview − bafflingly, unscripted talk was completely banned at that time — was incredibly stilted ("I must say you both look pretty well. Just how long did your walk take you, Keith?"), it did me no end of good. *In Town Tonight*, in those pre-TV days, was the equivalent to one of today's prestigious chat shows, and the *Evening Post* was heavily plugged, an unheard-of boost.

I returned to the gothic turrets of the Yorkshire Conservative Newspaper Co. to something of a hero's welcome. Apparently my series had put on sales, the paper was basking in unaccustomed publicity, congratulations had filtered down from the boardroom to the editorial floor, and I was to get a ten-guinea bonus. Nor, somewhat to my dismay, did it stop there. Mr Woodward, the editor, cashing in on my little success, took it into his head to appoint me the *Evening Post* Walking Reporter. I was to be taken off the news desk diary of courts and meetings and chimney fires and given a roving commission to roam the broad acres breathing fresh country air into the smoke-ridden pages of the newspaper.

To anyone who loved the countryside it would have been a dream assignment. To me, it was a case of being hoist by my own petard. I spent the entire summer traipsing around the Dales, following all the main Yorkshire rivers from their source high in the curlew-swirling hills, along their meandering route down through the sheep-infested moorlands to the green valleys below. The scenery was breathtaking but for me never more so than when I could see wisps of smoke rising from the mill chimneys far, far below the rooftop of England. Staying in reasonably picturesque inns or, in the more remote regions, youth hostels, I always found the golden dawns heart-lifting, but the sunsets dipping behind the hills into the unseen industrial landscape beyond were depressing — it was with a sense of yearning that I would watch the last West Yorkshire single-decker pulling out of a cobbled market square, bound for Leeds, Bradford or even the comparative hustle and bustle of Ilkley. I would compensate myself by looking for a back-street fish and chip shop, its vinegar and batter scents smothering the stench of heather and evoking a Proustian remembrance of Hunslet.

I finished this season of forced labour tramping the entire length of the newly established Pennine Way ("the walkers' Great North Road", as I called it) from the Cheviots to the Peak District — possibly the only rambler ever to follow these 250 switchback miles in suede shoes. While the prose of my Walking Reporter articles tended towards the purple – "The wind that blows tin cans down the city streets is the same wind that moans tonight along the crags and heather of the Dales, howling round peak and scar, and wresting piccolo tunes from the reed patches near Kettlewell, nestling under Great Whernside's protective wings" – I was at the same time picking up some good solid feature stories, a particular success being a talking Labrador in Bishopdale that could do sums and play dominoes. All these made impressive signed cuttings to lay before editors.

Settling back in the office I found that I was now regarded as the paper's star feature writer. Con Gordon was running so many regular columns that he no longer had time to do the colour stories he had made his speciality, and so – to his relief, he said, since he had no longer anything new to say about the bank holiday weekend at Scarborough or the St Leger race meeting in Doncaster or Children's Day in Roundhay Park – I was to step into his shoes.

Since my name now automatically went on everything I wrote, pretty soon I felt in a position to start pestering Fleet Street for a job. I had heard that the mercurial Mr Horniblow was now editing a popular tabloid, the *Sunday Graphic*, and so he was the obvious first candidate. I sent off a batch of cuttings and to my astonishment received a telegram the very next day: CAN OFFER YOU THREE DAYS A WEEK AT FOUR GUINEAS DAILY – HORNIBLOW. I showed it to Con Gordon. He explained that what Horniblow was offering me, in his flamboyant way, was casual shift work. He advised me to turn it down – the newsprint shortage was still as bad as ever and these were perilous times for Fleet Street casuals whose services could be dispensed with at a second's notice. Pointing out that I had neither the experience nor the contacts to survive on that basis, Con sought to temper my disappointment with the words, "Never mind – the day is coming when you'll be earning forty pounds a week on a national." A far-fetched prediction, I thought. Left to myself, I should probably have accepted Mr Horniblow's impetuous offer, but I bowed to Con Gordon's journalistic wisdom. Anyway, it was an encouraging start.

I began methodically petitioning the London dailies, Sundays and the three evenings. They were unanimous: in the long, austere aftermath of the war when the broadsheet papers were down to six pages and the tabloids twelve, they were simply not taking staff on. One or two of them offered a ray of hope – "It is clear from your cuttings that you are destined for an early move to Fleet Street and I wish I had an opportunity to speed it – " but none of them offered work.

In desperation I even applied for a reporting vacancy in Bermuda, on the *Hamilton Star*, advertised in the *World's Press News*. I was interviewed in London but heard no more. Very many years later I met an executive on the paper who showed me the report on me that had been sent back to Hamilton: it said that while my credentials were excellent, my thick Yorkshire accent would present a social challenge in the yacht clubs and bridge circles of the islands.

As the rejection letters piled up it was beginning to look as if I ought to forget London for a while and think about Manchester, a city I had still yet to visit. Just as I was coming round to this decision I happened to meet, in Whitelock's one day, a reporter from the Manchester edition of the *News Chronicle* who had come across the Pennines on some story or other. Over a drink or two I was flattered to learn from him that the northern editor of the *News Chronicle* had been much taken by my piece on the talking dog that could do sums and play dominoes. That was interesting: I had always had a feeling that my talking dog would do me some good one day (although when in the fullness of time I joined the *Daily Mirror* as a feature writer and was instructed in my first week to go out and find an animal story, I was told upon proudly presenting the talking dog of Bishopdale, "Shit! We need circulation in the West Country. See if you can find a talking dog that does sums and plays dominoes in Cornwall").

While I had begun to think about Manchester I had not yet begun to think about the *News Chronicle* – I knew that my strength was as a descriptive writer and the *News Chronicle*, a literate as well as a Liberal newspaper, already had more excellent descriptive writers than it could find space for. But if the northern editor had expressed admiration of my stuff, it was worth a try. I wrote off at once, and received a reply to the effect that while there were no vacancies at present and there would be little point in making a special journey, when next I happened to be in Manchester I might care to call in for a chat. Naturally I was over the Pennines like a bat on my first available day off.

The northern editor was cordiality itself and very complimentary about my work. But it was the usual story of newsprint starvation and getting quarts into pint pots. However, should a vacancy occur I could regard myself as being high up on the waiting list. Meanwhile, had I thought about London?

Diplomatically, anxious not to spoil my chances but even more anxious to learn what was behind this intriguing question, I said that while as a northerner Manchester was of course my first choice, I had never entirely ruled out Fleet Street. The northern editor went on to say that he happened to know that the *News Chronicle*'s London office would shortly be looking for a feature writer. If I had no rooted objection to living in the south and cared to write to the editor, he would be only too happy to support my application.

I went out into Derby Street with a song in my heart and spent an enchanted afternoon exploring Manchester. Another vibrant, black-and-white city: I so much took to Manchester that it almost seemed a shame to have to live in London, whither I was supremely confident I was at last on my way. Perhaps I would get back up north to write the odd feature, staying at the Midland Hotel and spending an evening at the Opera House.

I wrote to the *News Chronicle* in Bouverie Street that very night and after a couple of days on tenterhooks was highly satisfied to get a reply that could not have been more encouraging in its businesslike terseness: "Dear Mr Waterhouse, I have provisionally booked 3 p.m. on Wednesday next in order to see you. Should an emergency arise I will notify you, and suggest another date. Yours faithfully, N.S. Cursley, Asst Editor."

The cinder-bespattered, steam-belching journey to London, as I was chugged past the rhubarb fields of Middleton with the still collapsed drystone wall that had earned me my white card passport to city life, was as euphoric as the train ride from Kirkham in Lancashire on the hot day of my demob, when the *Yorkshire Evening Post* was my oyster. I would live in Chelsea, when I could find it (Ray Hill and I had been unable to locate Chelsea on any tube map), or perhaps in Bloomsbury, or Fitzrovia. I would lunch at Ye Olde Cheshire Cheese and dine at a Lyons Corner House or in one of the charming little Italian restaurants I had seen in what would turn out to be Soho. I would be no stranger to the West End theatres or the Tate Gallery or the Royal Academy. I would take Sunday morning walks to Speakers' Corner.

The *News Chronicle* being owned by the Quaker Cadburys I thought I had better not arrive for my interview with Cheshire Cheese alcohol on my breath, and so I lunched abstemiously at the

Kardomah at the bottom of Fetter Lane. I walked along Fleet Street past the *Telegraph* and the *Express* and Reuter's and the Press Association to pay my tribute to Edgar Wallace on his corner of Ludgate Circus; then I crossed over and walked down Bouverie Street where great reels of newsprint were being unloaded from lorries on to the rollers of the *News of the World*'s delivery bay. A basement roar of machinery told me that the Late edition of the *Star* was coming off the presses. And a few doors away was the *Punch* office. Oh, yes, this was where I belonged.

Mr Cursley was a homely northerner somewhat in the Alan Woodward mould. I felt at ease until the moment he said, "While I remember, you must be sure to send me an account of your expenses," when I knew that something was amiss. There was no vacancy for a feature writer. Rumour, that fickle jade, had erred yet again. But Mr Cursley had heard about my work and was impressed with it − that was a good feature story about the talking dog that did sums and played dominoes − and wanted to have a look at me. When the newsprint situation improved, he would certainly agree that my cuttings entitled me to consideration. But when that day would come he found it impossible to say.

I had shaken hands and was back out in Bouverie Street with the newsprint reels circling above my head before I realised what had happened to me, or rather what had not. I had been so certain, so cocksure, that in immediate retrospect the interview seemed almost an affront. Not since my rejection by Cockburn High School had I encountered such a setback. In shock, I blundered up into Fleet Street, past El Vino's that I had read so much about, past the Cock Tavern, past the Wig and Pen Club, all without a glance. Presently I found myself on Waterloo Bridge where, leaning against the parapet, I broke down in such shuddering sobs of rage, frustration and disappointment that passers-by stared at me.

All, in these few stinging moments, seemed lost. How was I to know then that within months I should be established in Fleet Street, that within three years I should be more familiar with New York, Washington, Moscow and Leningrad than I now was with London, that within four I should be turning down the post of the *News Chronicle*'s chief reporter, that within five I should be publishing my first novel, and that within ten I should see my name in lights on Shaftesbury Avenue and on the cinema posters of Leicester Square?

A sauntering policeman had his eye on me, perhaps discerning a possible candidate for the Thames. I pulled myself together. After all, I was only just turned twenty-two – there would be other times, other opportunities. I dried my tears and strode out to the Strand, then skirted Trafalgar Square and walked up the Haymarket. It was winter and getting dark already and all the lights were lit and there on Piccadilly Circus, along with Wrigley's Spearmint and Gordon's Gin and Schweppes was the Bovril sign all spelled out in electric light bulbs – an exact replica of the one I had first seen in Town on the way to the Mickey Mouse show at St James's Hospital, and with the same man in his little room behind flicking his light switch on and off. Home again.

STREETS AHEAD

LIFE AFTER CITY LIGHTS

Keith Waterhouse (*standing*) and his writing partner Willis Hall, *c.* 1960

ONE

St Martin's Lane

The Salisbury Tavern, its extravagantly embellished brick façade a riot of gilded cherubs, Prince of Wales feathers, coats of arms, swags and vine leaves, all thickly plastered on like a Victorian tart's make-up, stands in St Martin's Lane across the alley from what was then the New but is now the Albery Theatre.

It was, and remains, a perfectly preserved turn-of-the-century gin palace, all bevelled mirrors, brass rails, burnished copper tables, stamped-plush banquettes and bronzed nymphs supporting elaborately floral electroliers, with a winding, cast-iron-balustraded staircase down which one half expects to slink the tightly bodiced, full-bustled figure of one of the British music hall's many answers to Diamond Lil. Done up to the nines now, it has seen worse days, but in those shabbier times it had seen better ones, and it was a comfortably raffish place.

With the Duke of York's and the Coliseum just down the street and Wyndham's at the other end of St Martin's Court, it was not surprisingly a theatrical pub, although it made no concessions in this direction in the way of framed signed photographs of the stars, its only nod to its own reputation being a few frayed theatre posters on the narrow staircase, as steep as a ship's ladder, leading down to the lavatories. But it was much used by actors.

Other pubs, and there are still a good half-dozen within this little stretch of the theatre district, had their attractions for the profession – this one would cash cheques, that one would put drinks on the slate, another would send a freshly drawn pint across to one's dressing room in the interval. But it was in their particular corner of the Salisbury, below the staircase and opposite the snug where they could exchange badinage across the horseshoe bar with working friends who had just popped in for a fortifying sip before the cry of 'Beginners, please!', that these sometimes recognisable, more

225

often vaguely half-recognisable, faces were mostly to be seen – and heard, as for the benefit of hangers-on they regurgitated their oft-told theatrical chestnuts – 'If you think I'm drunk, madam, wait till you see the Duke of Buckingham!'

While the Salisbury may have been held in sentimental regard by some of its regulars, for a solid core of them their reason for giving it preference over rival pubs was as pragmatic as the reasons others had for giving its rivals preference over the Salisbury. As well as being much used by actors, it was much used by actors' agents, or anyway by two or three of them, a couple of whom had shoebox offices around the corner in the Charing Cross Road, and at least one of whom did not have an office at all, preferring to reserve whatever funds might have gone in overheads against the need to make quick getaways in taxis when his little stable of talent became too clamorous for money earned and owed.

It was customary for this little coterie of agents to pay out their clients – or in the case of the itinerant black sheep, come up with fresh excuses for not paying out his clients – at the bar of the Salisbury. Since a good part of their income at that time came from small, hand-to-mouth film producers whose cheques could not always be relied upon, the pay-out was as often as not in cash. The arrangement suited the actors: old debts – to one another, to Joe, the Salisbury's accommodating landlord, to the agents themselves (for 'subbing' on one's expectations of a day or two's filming was common) – could be paid off, while for those not working new debts could be incurred.

By the time I first began to use the Salisbury occasionally in the early fifties, it had begun to evolve into the acting fraternity's equivalent of that rialto for musicians, Archer Street – with the additional benefit of a roof. It was a market-place, a casting clearing-house. While – with some notable exceptions such as the output of Sir Carol Reed, Basil Dearden, Betty Box – the British film industry could lay little claim to being anywhere near its creative peak, in production terms it had rarely been busier. The studios at Elstree, Pinewood, Merton Park, were churning out 'quota quickies' by the dozen – third-rate second features that got a screening only because cinemas were obliged by Act of Parliament to show a certain percentage of British films. Many of them provided work for London-based American actors such as Bonar Colleano in the pathetic hope that with one of the characters chewing gum and

226

uttering wisecracks filched from transatlantic cross-talk routines, the product would thus somehow appeal to United States audiences. Certainly the stream of quota quickies appealed to the hungry actors and extras of the burgeoning Salisbury Tavern repertory company, who would drop in to pool their knowledge of who was in pre-production at this or that studio – 'nothing in it for me, old darling, but they're casting hunchbacks.'

With the coming of commercial television in 1955, this output was augmented, and eventually replaced, by a steady supply of equally unmemorable TV episodes, mostly of the cops and robbers variety, where blonde victims tended to live in smart St John's Wood apartment blocks with cocktail bars in the basement ('Leaving the Green Cockatoo Club that fateful evening, vivacious Yvette, as the Sheffield-born former typist now styled herself, was never seen alive again') and detectives were given to pacing the Embankment moodily. There were parts in plenty, including economical scene-bridging voice-overs, for the Salisbury Players.

When, by the mid-fifties, what the papers were already calling 'the new wave' of regional actors and actresses with regional accents and regional swagger began to drift south in response to a demand for vigorous new talent from the as yet not so vigorous new television companies, it was only natural that they too should make for the Salisbury – as natural as that backpacking Australians headed for the pubs of Earl's Court. The Salisbury, they had heard on the weekly rep grapevine, was where 'it was all going on'. It was in the Salisbury that they would get the buzz.

Actually, had they but known – and some of them did, or they would not have been so cocky – they had brought the buzz with them, like a virus; and what was 'all going on' was going on back home among the council estates and pit villages and redbrick universities and polytechnics they had come from. In short; there had been a revolution – although quietly, and without anyone really noticing that it had started until it had taken hold, like something craftily set in motion by Mao Tse-Tung. The 1944 Butler Education Act, establishing the right to a secondary education for all, had produced an upstart generation which instead of becoming factory fodder had come up through the grammar schools and the redbricks and the drama schools and the art colleges and was now ready to take the world on. 'The Butler Act', Richard Hoggart was to write, 'was a magnificent document, second only in vision to the National Health

227

Service.' Or as Somerset Maugham phrased it about the Butler Act's fifties alumni, 'They are scum.'

Scum or whatever the old guard chose to call them (Noël Coward chose to call them 'a lavatorial, cracking bore'), here they came, ready or not. By every train from King's Cross and Euston and Paddington, it seemed, actors, writers, artists, musicians, were pouring into London. The artists brought images the south-east had only read about, the writers wrote about the working class and the lower middle classes as if D. H. Lawrence hadn't been a one-off after all, the musicians made sounds that had previously only been heard in laundries, and the actors no longer spoke in anyone-for-tennis accents.

Their hour had come, that was what it came down to. It was not only a few years' extra education, of course, but the whole post-war social upheaval which as Ned Sherrin, who had a hand in it, wrote, 'had produced a generation which found its voice in the mid-fifties, with spokesmen who were beginning to shout from the rooftops of the Royal Court Theatre, the universities and the television studios.' Another factor, or more likely just a chicken and egg variation of the same phenomenon, was what Edward Heath, railing against Ned's programme *That Was The Week That Was* as a guest of the *Punch* Table at which I was present, was to call 'the death of deference'.

The attitude of the young towards their elders and betters would be spelled out in a 1963 memo by the bedridden Harold Macmillan in which he mused upon his possible successor and other issues: 'It is thinking about themselves that is really the curse of the younger generation – they appear to have no other subject which interests them at all, and all their books, poems, dramas and all the rest of it are almost entirely confined to this curious introspective attitude towards life, the result no doubt of two wars and the dying faith.' Jimmy Porter saw the situation from a somewhat different perspective, as did Colin MacInnes who was to put it in his novel *Absolute Beginners*, which came out at the same time as my own *Billy Liar*: 'As for the boys and girls, the dear young absolute beginners, I sometimes feel that if they only knew this fact, the very simple fact, namely how powerful they really are, then they could rise up overnight and enslave the old taxpayers . . .'

At any rate, here came 'the scum'. For those born on what had up to then been regarded as the wrong side of the tracks, the world was their oyster washed down with champagne. And in one respect at least, *Time* magazine did have it right in its summary of this limbering-up period for what it would elephantinely call the Swinging Sixties: life was a party.

It was a party that began, as often as not, in the Salisbury Tavern. From being a mere actors' hangout it became, as the fireball energy of that time took hold, and the seekers after gold continued to pour into London, a kind of railway terminus of all the talents. Within the course of a few successive evenings, drifting into the Salisbury on the way back from or on the way to somewhere else – the Salisbury was always an arrival or departure point, a rendezvous or promenade rather than somewhere to linger away the night – one might, with the right shoulders, rub them against those of figures as disparate as Allen Ginsberg and Frankie Howerd, William Saroyan and Tommy Cooper, Colin Wilson and Brendan Behan, the as yet unknown Joe Orton and unknown friend, John Braine and Tony Hancock, Frank Norman and John Neville, Peter O'Toole and Jeffrey Bernard, Alun Owen, Sean Kenny, Peter Finch, Christopher Logue, Lionel Bart, Stanley Baker, Bill Naughton, Donald Baverstock . . . and most of the cast of *Z-Cars*. Had Donald Albery, running the New Theatre next door, been persuaded to swallow his squeamish aversion to the 'bears and squirrels' sequence in *Look Back in Anger* and brought the play to the West End as expected, we should also have had John Osborne and the rest of the Royal Court crew.

While the Salisbury continued to be a job centre and pay station for a goodly assortment of actors, old, middle-aged and young, it was never what could be termed work-orientated like some mechanics' institute. The evenings were merry, and they became merrier and even madder with this new influx from what were still called the provinces but which are now the regions. The newcomers, arriving from what was sexually timid territory – it would still be three or four years, after all, before Stan Barstow's Ingrid in *A Kind of Loving* made the daring leap that later gave her cause to agonise that 'something that should have happened hasn't happened' – were enthralled to find London taking an altogether more relaxed view of such goings-on. The Salisbury, in all this, was something of a sexual swop-shop – literally so on one occasion, for it was in its discreet back room that a certain impresario, knowing that one of the rising young stars of stage and screen was interested in his wife, agreed to exchange her for a new motor cycle – specifying that it must be 1500 cc. Many Salisbury regulars were possible candidates when a film editor who was divorcing his wife was asked whom he intended to name – his reply, however, was *Spotlight*, the brick-thick actors' directory. I myself, one crowded evening, was accosted by an actress I knew but slightly in these terms: 'Do you know, darling, you're the only man at our end of the bar I haven't been to bed with?' Taking her hand, I pledged fervently never to spoil this unique and precious relationship.

But it was not all play either. It is not too fanciful to say that the Salisbury, on its good evenings, was a menagerie of the performing arts. Writers met directors and designers, directors met new actors, actors met writers . . . It was what is now called networking. There were other centres in plenty, and there would soon be more, where these creative people met and drank and gossiped, but this was one of the few places where talent at every level was to be found, where you might, for example, find a visiting American screen luminary discussing Beckett with a stage carpenter. If the history of *Time* magazine's Swinging Sixties were ever to be written with any degree of accuracy, when it would have to be faced that just as sexual intercourse began in 1963, so the sixties themselves began in 1956, and that what came about when the decade actually did reach the calendar was but the flowering of what had been planted and watered in the fifties, then the Salisbury would be more than a footnote.

It's the done thing nowadays for some writers of that vintage to deny that there was any such phenomenon as a 'movement', that it was all got up by the papers. But you only had to spend an hour in this red-plush melting-pot to see a 'movement' forming before your very eyes. There were several routes into it: from the BBC, from RADA, from Joan Littlewood's Stratford East, from the film studios, from Soho, from St Martin's School of Art, from the workshop theatres of the north and Wales, from the new commercial television stations, from the universities, whether ivy-clad, redbrick or white tile, from HM prisons even. Strangely – or perhaps not so strangely, given that it always was a deeply conservative community – Fleet Street was a little-used gateway into this stimulating company; but that is the one I took.

TWO

Fleet Street

1 By 1951, Festival of Britain year, I was becoming restless. After two years in the smoke-wreathed reporters' room of the *Yorkshire Evening Post* I was irredeemably typecast as the one with the way with words who could be relied upon to find a funny angle on the cat show at the Corn Exchange or the Whitsun Walk or the annual visitation of the Breton onion sellers; but there were only so many funny angles to the Whitsun Walk and I had found them both.

In my free moments, I had turned out a successful radio play and a few bits and pieces for magazines. I had written an unpublished (and unpublishable) volume of autobiography called *How to Live to Be 22*, a bid at clipping three years off the record set by Beverley Nichols with his precocious memoirs *Twenty-Five*. But I was not really getting anywhere. My progression was circular. Another cat show loomed, the onion sellers were on their way again, and I was beginning to feel that time was passing me by.

It was the Festival of Britain itself that gave me something of a prod. I was sent down from Leeds to cover it – in *YE Post* terms, where a day trip to Scarborough needed the sanction of the Editor himself, the equivalent of a foreign assignment. Indeed, it had all the excitement of an excursion abroad. Having established myself at the Hotel Russell in Russell Square – the first time I had ever stayed in a proper hotel, and were you supposed to tip the commissionaire as you went in? – I made my way, with the aid of a pocket *A–Z*, to No. 117 Fleet Street, the *YEP*'s London office, to pick up my Festival credentials.

My welcome was muted: the London staff doubtless felt, rightly enough, that they could have adequately covered the event themselves without the help of this young northern upstart. I couldn't blame them but I didn't mind: I was in Fleet Street, if only for a week.

As well as covering the ceremonial opening by King George VI I was supposed to roam the South Bank site picking up stories with a Yorkshire angle. This was easy enough: all I had to do was approach one of the gangs of workmen who were slogging away in the mud in declining hopes of getting the Festival ready on time, and call out 'Anyone here from Yorkshire?' – a lowly variation on the war correspondent's legendary (or mythological) cry of 'Anybody here been raped and speaks English?'

An agreeable though not too comfortable Press Club had been set up across the Hungerford Bridge in Northumberland Avenue – a colonial outpost of the Festival with pin-legged plywood chairs, boomerang-shaped coffee tables, tripod standard lamps and zig-zag wire hat-stands with little coloured balls on stalks, like overgrown cocktail cherries, for the coat hooks. Daily, I would find a place among these rickety baubles to write up my notes ('A feature of the Battersea Park Pleasure Gardens, whose official opening date has again been delayed, will be the Dancing Dolls of Castleford . . .') before wandering over to the fragile-looking bar in the hope of making valuable journalistic contacts.

These were plentiful enough – had I any ambition to join, say, the *Hull Daily Mail*, the *Leicester Mercury* or the *Melbourne Herald* (the *Melbourne Herald* had a fleeting appeal, as a matter of fact). Fleet Street colour writers assigned to the Festival obviously preferred to bolt back to their home patch. But after a day or two I did fall in with an attractive young reporter from the *Evening Standard* Londoner's Diary. I managed to get into her good books by giving her a tip-off about an Old Etonian who was working as a builder's labourer (had he been a Yorkshire-born Old Etonian, I should have kept him to myself) and after that we swopped notes daily. I confessed my burning desire to get to Fleet Street and she promised to take me to the Two Brewers in Shoe Lane and introduce me to some important-sounding *Evening Standard* types. I had never thought of the *Standard* in my daydream list of Fleet Street possibilities but I thought of it now. I had two years' evening paper experience and I could cover the Olympia Cat Show in my sleep. The job was as good as mine.

On the eve of the official opening of the Festival I thought it would be a good idea to go along to St Paul's Cathedral, where the royal service of dedication would be taking place, and, so to speak, get my card marked. The *Evening Standard* girl tagged along in the hope of picking up a paragraph. I had every hope that our recce would be followed by a lunchtime drink at the Two Brewers down Ludgate Hill.

We were met by an obliging virger (as my knowledgeable Londoner's Diary friend had already briefed me was the St Paul's spelling of verger). He was happy, once I had established that he did not come from Yorkshire and had no Yorkshire connections, to run through the order of service and VIP seating list.

'And where', I asked, producing my notebook, 'will the Lord Mayor and Lady Mayoress of Leeds be sitting?'

The virger consulted his groundplan. 'In the north transept.'

'And which is the north transept?'

'Over there.' He pointed. Out of the corner of my eye I saw the *Evening Standard* girl, evidently a seasoned churchgoer, breathing up her nostrils in impatience at my ignorance. I didn't care. It was my biggest story yet, guaranteed the front-page lead turning on to page two, and I had to get it right.

I had been told not to forget that we ran a Doncaster edition. 'And where will the Mayor of Doncaster be sitting?'

'In the south transept.'

'And where is that?'

'Opposite the north transept.' The *Standard* girl rolled her eyes.

Apart from the odd visit to York Minster I was a stranger to cathedrals, whose elaborate appointments were in confusing contrast to the penny-plain fixtures and fittings of the nonconformist chapels and tabernacles I had attended in my youth. I was determined to be able to identify every square inch of St Paul's when the time came to describe who was sitting or standing where.

I plodded on. The trumpeters of the Royal Military School of Music would be up there in the West Gallery. That row of pews where the Lord Mayor of London would sit was called the choir. The table on which he would place his ceremonial pearl sword was just called a table. And so on. The virger was patience itself. Not so the *Evening Standard* lady who by now was openly tut-tutting and grimacing.

'And what is this area ahead of us called?'

It was too much for her. 'It's the nave, you fool!' With which she turned on her heel and swept out – through, as I by now happened

235

to know, the West Door. That afternoon in the Festival Press Club she cut me dead. So much for my contact.

But whatever they thought back in Leeds about my two-column report the next morning, after I had battled my way through the crowds to No. 171 Fleet Street and dictated the spelling of v-i-r-g-e-r to a disbelieving copytaker, no one could fault its accuracy or grasp of detail: 'The Royal procession moved slowly down the red carpeted centre aisle to the two red and gilt thrones and the 24 gilt chairs brought from Guildhall to the east end of the dome . . . Mayors and civic dignitaries of 600 British towns occupied the north and south transepts. Many Yorkshiremen were present . . .'

Later, traipsing after the royal party as they toured the Festival site, I got too near in my eagerness to overhear some quotable nugget and oafishly trod on Princess Margaret's foot. As a detective led me back to where I belonged in the rear ranks of the press pack, I fleetingly caught the scornful, pitying eye of my former Fleet Street link.

Like most journalists assigned to tramping the South Bank, I wrote my quota of 'knocking copy' about the Festival. In many ways it was a monument to British tat: escalators didn't work, elegant glass entrance halls were stuck over with scrawled notices reading 'Use other door', the corporate italic display lettering was already falling off some of the façades, and the streamlined litter bins didn't look so smart when tilting forty-five degrees with overflowing rubbish. As for the Battersea Fun Fair, that had so far failed even to open. So, to my annoyance, had most of theatreland's contribution to the Festival, including Olivier and Vivien Leigh giving *Antony and Cleopatra* and Shaw's *Caesar and Cleopatra* at the St James's, and Alec Guinness's *Hamlet* (with Ken Tynan as First Player) at the New Theatre, Hampstead. For my theatrical fare I had to make do with Beryl Reid in a confection at the St Martin's, *After the Show*, so called because it was a late-night revue following three Shaw one-acters. The fact that it didn't start until ten or thereabouts raised its tolerability level considerably – I had never been to a late-night revue before, nor even known until now that there was such a thing. It seemed the height of London sophistication.

Yet the Festival, if it did not send you away feeling that you could dance like Gene Kelly, as Arnold Wesker was to say, did lift the spirits – if the spirits were there to be lifted. For me, it was not only the architectural novelty of the Skylon and the Dome of Discovery, or the John Piper mural, or the Lion and Unicorn fashioned, perhaps unwisely, out of straw; or the boldness and the brightness and the implanted belief that with any luck we should never see chocolate-brown paint and imitation parquet linoleum again. Nor – which was of course its purpose – was it that the Festival marked, if not the end of wartime austerity, then the beginning of the end.

No, it was less tangible than that, it was something in the air, especially if there was anything of a sun when the May mornings were Scandinavian in their exuberance – or so I should have said had I yet been to Scandinavia. There was more to it than the still-pristine white and peppermint rock confections I saw shimmering before me as I walked across Hungerford Bridge; there was more to it, too, than a nation letting its hair down after six years of war. Despite Noël Coward's gloomy prediction in the *Globe Revue* that 'There are bad times just around the corner', something was going on, something had started, something had happened, or was about to happen. It was not yet as easy to discern as it would be four or five years hence in the most un-Festival-like surroundings of the Salisbury Tavern, when at certain serendipitous times you only had to cross the brass threshold of that crowded chocolate-box saloon to catch it full in the face like a Mack Sennett custard pie; but it was there all right, far off, like a distant marching band getting nearer. I was not clever enough to analyse it, to piece the symptoms and the straws in the wind together – all I knew was that whatever it was, I wanted some of it.

To be less fanciful, it could simply have been the exhilaration of being in London; but I knew enough to know that if it was, it was the exhilaration of being in London at a particular time. I was very dimly aware that it was not only the Festival's spindly furniture that was 'contemporary' – the vogue word of the period. There was a 'contemporary' feeling about.

Things were different now, that was about the size of it – or becoming so. One of my jobs on the *Yorkshire Evening Post* was to write obituaries; and it was very noticeable, as is not always the case as one decade succeeds another, that it was not only a generation but an age that was fading away. Richard Strauss, Field Marshal Smuts, Al Jolson, Sinclair Lewis, Sir Harry Lauder, André Gide, Ernest Bevin, Ivor Novello, George Bernard Shaw even – only Orwell seemed anything to do with the beginning of the fifties, and he had seen only three weeks of the new decade. Even some of today's men, and there were still giants among them, were perceptibly no longer tomorrow's men, for all that Churchill was to be Prime Minister again before the year was out. And an anomalous figure he by now cut. It was as if a clearing were being swathed for a new strain to take root and flourish. If we were not yet living in a new era, we were no longer living in an aftermath – it was no longer post-war, but pre- whatever the next few years would bring. How I would fit into all this I had no idea. But I meant to be a piece of the jigsaw.

Back on the cat show beat, I took stock of my position. Whatever was going to happen, it was clearly not going to happen in Leeds. Not yet awhile, anyway. Fond though I was of the city, I had to admit that when it came to the cultural scene it did not have a seat in the dress circle – the gallery, more like. While there was the biennial Leeds Music Festival, concerts in the Victoria Hall and a strong tradition of amateur theatre, Leeds trailed a long way behind, say, Manchester, Liverpool and Glasgow. We had a touring theatre, two variety theatres, and a weekly rep playing mainly light comedies and detective dramas of the 'But, Inspector, there's one thing I don't understand' variety, but we had no innovative theatre of our own and would not have until the establishment of the West Yorkshire Playhouse well over a decade later, when Peter O'Toole and I among others made impassioned speeches in the Town Hall ridiculing the very idea of its continuing non-existence. Poetry readings were unheard of, and local writers, if there were any, lacked the focal point they were later to be given by the late Alfred Bradley of BBC North, one of those inspired and inspiring producers, now almost an extinct breed, whose greatest satisfaction was to find and prod and promote new talent. A dozen or so years on from 1951, there might have been a case for staying on in Leeds. Just now, the case for leaving had never been stronger.

The sooner the better. Upon my return from London I was given a modest pay rise, which both pleased and dismayed me. In the Festival Press Club I had met senior colleagues from other provincial papers, men in their thirties, forties and even fifties, who seemed well content with their lot as 'special writers' and who, or so I guessed, had plainly been weaned off any Fleet Street aspirations they might have had with regular pay rises, cushy assignments and the responsibilities of marriage, mortgage and Morris Minor.

I knew the route and indeed was alarmingly some way along it already. I had got married but a few months ago, to Joan Foster, a petite, brunette assistant in a Leeds photographic studio, whom I had met at the Mill Hill Sunday Night Youth Club when we were both sixteen and with whom I had enjoyed a sporadic on-off relationship over the years. We were still absurdly young – 'my Babes in the Wood', our landlady called us – but not, in that environment, unusually so. While I have no statistical tables to hand I should be surprised if twenty-one were not, at that time and in that place, the average age for marriage, and not only because it gave couples used to doing their courting in shop doorways access to a marital bed. It was the norm. There was a good deal of peer pressure on young people to 'get yourselves wed', settle down and, brought up in crowded conditions as most of us were, get from under the parents' feet. There was also, more obscurely, a feeling of obligation to the community you came from, a need to conform: marriage was the done thing, the marriage certificate a young wife's passport to the matriarchy and the young husband's membership card of the gaffers' masonic lodge. So – by no means reluctantly, for it was an adventure too, another grown-up chevron like your first glass of beer – you got on with it.

We settled cosily in a two-room flat and contentedly played at houses, but I was acutely conscious of the direction in which the scenario could lead me. A couple more of those pay rises and I could be round at the Leeds Permanent Building Society signing a twenty-five-year deal on a semi in one of the more modest suburbs. I could see myself puffing away at a briar and churning out the cat show 'specials' until I had enough put by for a house in salubrious Roundhay, not too far from the Park. Several of my colleagues had willingly chosen the Roundhay way, they had families and cars and holidays in the Lake District and a secure future, and in a nose-pressed-to-the-window sort of way I envied them. But it was not for me. It was not that I felt myself to be above that sort of thing: the feeling was naggingly akin to the one I recurrently used to have as a child, when I would come out of the house to play only to find the street empty – but far off, from I knew not which direction, shouts and shrieks and laughter fell on the still summer air. I knew that if whatever was about to happen in those early fifties was not going to happen in Leeds, whatever was going to happen to me would surely not be happening in Roundhay.

I did not consult Joan about the Roundhay option, nor did I need to. She had hitched her wagon to my star and would happily have accompanied me to the moon had I said there was a living to be made there.

For a provincial journalist at that time, reaching for the moon seemed easier than getting to London. I had a thickening file of letters from editors, managing editors, deputy editors, news editors, features editors, none of them offering hope. They were usually regretful, some of them sharing or affecting to share my belief that I was destined for Fleet Street; but all of them discouraging. Austerity might be on its way out so far as the Festival of Britain was concerned, but not in Fleet Street where six years after the war we were still, and for the foreseeable future, in the realm of six- and eight-page papers, newsprint having to be bought with precious balance-of-payment dollars.

By now I had tried every mass-circulation national in Fleet Street, though not the so-called text titles like *The Times* and the *Telegraph*, for odd as it might seem in these more malleable days, there was then an iron curtain between the popular and the 'serious' press, with little or no border traffic between them. You might progress to, say, the *Manchester Guardian* from the *Yorkshire Post*; from the brasher *Evening Post* you would expect to aim at the *Express* or *Mail*.

I had tried, that is to say, every national paper but one. I had never applied to the *Daily Mirror*, for it had a fearsome reputation for hiring and firing and for sending its wretched reporters out on impossible 'doorstepping' assignments. Its editor, Sylvester Bolam, had lately served three months in Brixton prison for contempt of court over a front-page splash touching on the arrest of John George Haigh, the acid bath murderer. The only true tabloid of its day, with a raffish reputation (hadn't Churchill threatened to have it banned during the war?), the *Mirror* was regarded in some journalistic quarters – certainly, as I was to find, by the Editor of the *Evening Post* – as just about as low as it was possible to sink professionally short of working for the house magazine of a brothel. A difficult paper to get on, it was almost as difficult to get off – voluntarily, that is, for having a spell at the *Mirror* on one's CV was regarded by some of the more conservative Fleet Street news editors as a career stigma. But involuntary departures were reputed to be a daily occurrence. One heard bloodcurdling tales of grown men reduced to tears by the tongue-lashings of sarcastic newsroom executives, who themselves were said to live in fear of their own superiors. Applying for a reporting job on the *Mirror*, I gathered, was on a par with volunteering to give evidence to the Star Chamber. One's offer might be taken up, and then what?

But I had to move. I toyed, in my desperation, with the notion of asking the communist *Daily Worker* to take me on, rejecting it not for any ideological reason but on the grounds that with only four semi-tabloid pages the *Daily Worker* was patently in less need of staff than any other title and so it would be a waste of a stamp. I thought seriously about the Birmingham *Sunday Mercury*, reasoning that it would be a hop nearer London; but the *Sunday Mercury*, when I took the plunge, did not think seriously about me.

Weekly, I scoured the classified columns of *World's Press News*. The only jobs on offer were on country weeklies or on the trade papers. I began to flirt with the possibility of the trade papers and conjured up an agreeable fantasy of life on the *Bakers' Record* or the *Caterer and Hotelkeeper* or the *Iron and Coal Trades Review* or *Farm, Field and Fireside*. For a start, it was in their favour that they were all in or off Fleet Street, where I should mingle with proper journalists. As weekly publications, they could not possibly work their staff too hard except perhaps on press days, when there might conceivably be some last-minute panic over a change in the bread ration or a new Home Office regulation for caterers and hotelkeepers or the closing price of pig iron. Smoking my pipe, I would sit at my rolltop desk pecking out articles on the latest thing in industrial loaf tins or developments in smelting, with a break for a leisurely lunch at the Cheshire Cheese. At five I would wend my way home to a garret in Chelsea or Notting Hill and there, completely untaxed by the day's labours, work on a novel. I could live with that – the fantasy, if not the fact. It was tempting.

One week an unusually large display ad in the situations vacant columns revealed that *World's Press News* itself was looking for a bright young reporter with sub-editing experience. I had none, except for an occasional subbing shift on the *Evening Post* Saturday sports final, when after a liquid lunch at Whitelocks tavern I distinguished myself by producing the headline 'Last Minute Goal Startles Sub'. But suddenly, I had rather a fancy for joining the *WPN*, as the journalists' organ was known. The weekly produced each year, in aid of the Newspaper Press Fund, a lively volume called the *Inky Way Annual*, stuffed full of reminiscent yarns by old Fleet Street hands about the murders they had covered, the scoops they had unearthed, the interviews they had engineered. I lapped it up as I had the *Sexton Blake Annual* a few years earlier. If I were on the staff of the *WPN* – an interesting job in itself, I promised myself with rash enthusiasm – then in all likelihood I should be asked to work on the *Inky Way Annual*. At that moment, not recognising escapism when I saw it, I could imagine nothing more blissful. The sub-editing experience I could lie about: I would pick it up as I went along.

I was on the verge of drafting my application when, hanging around the Town Hall press room, I heard from a visiting fireman from Manchester who had had it from the *Mirror*'s man in Liverpool that the *Mirror*'s man in Sheffield was moving to the *Express*, a substitute was being fielded from London, and there would be a vacancy.

I got a batch of my cuttings together and wrote off at once. The news was fresh on the grapevine and I had every hope of an interview at least. Bearing in mind the *Mirror*'s reputation, indeed, an interview was the most I was hoping for.

A reply came almost by return of post, bidding me to the *Mirror* office at noon on the following Tuesday. Signed Kenneth Hord, News Editor. I had heard of Mr Hord, as indeed I had heard by now of most of the news editors, features editors and editors in Fleet Street. Each name came accompanied by its thumbnail sketch, usually wide of the mark, supplied by those who had themselves been down for interviews or by friends of friends of those who worked or had worked under them. Mr Hord was supposed to be a gimlet-eyed, thin-lipped, desiccated calculating machine, as Aneurin Bevan was to call Hugh Gaitskell. Well, he couldn't eat me. I got out my best suit for pressing.

Having paid my respects to the Edgar Wallace memorial plaque on Ludgate Circus, I was pacing up and down outside Rolls Buildings in Fetter Lane, home of the *Daily Mirror* and *Sunday Pictorial*, by a quarter to twelve. Geraldine House, as the building was called, after Lord Northcliffe's mother, was an unlovely edifice of white lavatorial tiles with the papers' titles picked out in big wooden letters of gold, like the Hovis sign. Usually likened to a wedding cake, it was more like a badly made pagoda sawn down the middle. But to me it rivalled the Taj Mahal.

I already knew that for reporters the great attraction of this curious building was that together with its rambling annexes, it boasted about half a dozen separate exits, from which they could select a line of retreat when the enemy was at the gates. With some difficulty I located the main entrance, where I presented myself at three minutes before noon, to allow the commissionaire time to escort me along what I also already knew was a long corkscrew route of steps and corridors.

The interview was to take place in a small waiting room on the editorial floor, which, so I had been intrigued to learn from fellow Fleet Street aspirants who had endured the ordeal before me, was bugged. Escorted into the windowless little chamber by the commissionaire, I at once began looking for hidden wires, and indeed had Mr Hord arrived on the scene a fraction of a second earlier he would have found me on my hands and knees inspecting the underside of the table. Not that I had any reason to suppose that the nervous coughs and throat-clearings of yet one more greenhorn down from the north would be of the smallest interest to the *Mirror*'s portly, saturnine managing editor, one Cyril Morton, who had had the hidden microphone installed – the idea was of course to record legally sensitive conversations with informants and so on – but on the other hand you never knew. Mr Morton, someone else whose reputation preceded him, was understood to take a mildly sinister interest in surveillance for its own sake, an ingredient of the Hitchcockian sense of drama which he brought to the daily round. His idea of the ideal opening paragraph for a *Mirror* news story was said to be, 'The monster came down from the mountain last night and ate another baby.' I was already in mortal fear of him. Despatching a reporter to Liverpool to interview a shipwreck survivor whose sole companion had been lost overboard shortly before the rescue, Mr Morton's briefing had been, 'Ask him if he ate his pal.' A very far cry from what my instruction from the news desk of the *Yorkshire Evening Post* would have been: 'Ask him if he has any relatives in our circulation area.'

Mr Morton's duties as managing editor were, to outsiders, vague – from what I had gathered his role seemed to be that of peripatetic troublemaker or stirrer-up at large. Reviewing my slim, fourth-hand repertoire of Morton apocrypha as I cased the claustrophobic little bugged room, I began to be sweatily apprehensive about the prospect of working under his looming shadow and to half-wish more than ever that the interview might not go my way. The half-wish was to be granted.

Fortunately, job interviews did not fall within Mr Morton's province, and the News Editor arrived unaccompanied, a slight, neat, grey-suited figure wearing the rimless spectacles which were doubtless the cause of the gimlet-eyed reputation – their lenses bordered, however, by reassuring crinkles suggesting a sense of humour. Both impressions, as it happens, were correct: I was to learn that Mr Hord was a master of the chilling memo with a trademark speciality of underplayed sarcasm ('Your expenses claim appears to be undated. Perhaps the date is included in the total'). But while it was clear at once that here was no easy taskmaster, he was kindness itself in his interrogation, and flattering about my cuttings. He asked what anyone dismissing the *Mirror* as 'a popular rag' would have regarded as some peculiar, not to say irrelevant, questions. Who were my favourite authors? Did I read *The Times*? Did I go to the theatre at all? Yes? What had I seen lately? (It had been *Stars and Strips* at the City Varieties. I substituted the touring production of *The Cocktail Party*.) Was I interested in politics? That one I was prepared for. The *Mirror*, as everyone knew, was staunchly to the left of centre – had been given the credit, or the blame, in fact, for Labour's post-war election victory. The *Evening Post*, on the other hand, was under the thumb of the Yorkshire Conservative Newspaper Co. Ltd. No Judas ever distanced himself from his masters more rapidly.

The cross-examination continued. Had I ever covered a murder? No but had there ever been what the police used to call a fatal incident at the Corn Exchange cat show, I should have been up to it. I acquitted myself well, I fancied, but I had done two or three of these interviews by now and I knew that it had not really gone my way, an impression confirmed when Mr Hord rose, shook my hand, and uttered the familiar words, 'You won't forget to submit your expenses.'

For some time after I finally left the *Yorkshire Evening Post*, the myth persisted there that having been turned down by the *Mirror*'s News Editor I promptly strolled down the corridor and got myself taken on by the Features Editor. This is not quite true. What really happened was that after assuring Mr Hord that I could find my own way out, I discovered that I could not, and after several twists and turns in those labyrinthine corridors found myself outside an open door signposted 'Features Editor'. The sole occupant of the little cubicle, who was idly reading the *Financial Times*, I knew could not be the Features Editor, for that was someone else with whom I was already vicariously acquainted. His name was R. J. Eilbeck, and his career was watched with envious interest by all who had hitherto considered themselves young meteors. Having joined the *Mirror* from the *Liverpool Echo* at some impossible age like nineteen, he had rocketed up through the sub-editorial ranks to become Features Editor while still in his early twenties. It was evident even from afar that the post was but one more rung on a ladder that went up into the clouds. Stories of his flamboyant lifestyle reached us from across the Pennines. It seemed that when he went up to visit his mother in Liverpool, he would take a suite at the Adelphi Hotel and send a chauffeured limousine to fetch her from whatever homely suburb she lived in, to dine on lobster and champagne in the French Restaurant. He had been a conspicuous consumer of caviare even in his late teens.

By his baggy cardigan, rumpled shirt, spectacles perched on the end of his nose and general air of middle-aged affability – the infallible sign of the Fleet Street No. 2 – the man sitting at Eilbeck's desk must be his deputy. So it proved – a kindly, seasoned character named Bob Balmforth. I tapped lightly on the door and waved the file of my cuttings which Mr Hord had returned to me. Would it be all right, since I chanced to be passing, if I left these examples of my work for Mr Eilbeck to glance at? Mr Balmforth cordially invited me to do so – or rather, he cordially concurred that there would be no harm in leaving them, the implication being, however, that I might just as profitably drop them down the lift shaft.

A few days later two letters from the *Daily Mirror* arrived by the same post. The first one I opened was from Kenneth Hord, News Editor: 'Dear Mr Waterhouse, I do not think you will be surprised to hear that I cannot offer you a job on the *Daily Mirror*. I think our regret will be mutual and I am certainly sorry to take this decision because I liked what I saw of you and think your cuttings praiseworthy. At the same time, through no fault of your own, you are simply not equipped to be a national newspaper reporter at present. If that continues to be your ambition perhaps you will try again when you feel you can measure up to our exacting requirements.' The other was from R. J. Eilbeck, Features Editor: 'Dear Mr Waterhouse, Thank you for letting me see your cuttings. Please do come and see me when next you are in London.'

At least he would not be asking me to remember to submit my expenses. As usual when invited to drop in 'when next you are in London', I was on the first available train, as would be expected of me, since the chances of a twenty-two-year-old provincial reporter being otherwise 'next in London' were, as every editor knew, remote. I made the by now ritual visit to the plaque of Edgar Wallace, Reporter, for luck (although on this occasion I should have preferred Edgar Wallace, Feature Writer), and again was duly pacing up and down outside Rolls Buildings fifteen minutes before the telephoned appointment I had made from King's Cross. (It had not occurred to me that Eilbeck might be away, or to save myself a possibly wasted journey by phoning from Leeds – trunk calls to London, at that time, had the exotic rarity value of Interflora bouquets to Siberia.)

R. J. Eilbeck, Jimmy as he was known to all, was a gangling six-footer with a bushy ginger moustache, horn-rimmed spectacles and a taste for pin-stripe suits and stiff white collars – all with the object, I supposed, of countering his shock of red hair by making him look older. In his place, I should have tried to look even younger. While he affected a languid, nasal drawl and lolled back in his swivel chair, making a steeple of his fingers like a country solicitor, I divined – correctly – that a nervous staccato would have been more his style and that he would sooner have been restlessly pacing the office, had there been room to do so, than sitting down.

I had been warned that he was mad: this was a common slander against Fleet Street executives and I had placed little credence on it. Now that I was enclosed in the same little cubicle with him I was not too sure. Mad would have been pitching it too strongly, but certainly he did not come across as the most stable of personalities. With his subdued nervous energy, his quickfire grasp of detail and the attention span of a mayfly, he reminded me in many ways of my first editor, Barry Horniblow, whose eccentric disposition had ruffled many a feather in the hitherto complacent corridors of the Yorkshire Conservative Newspaper Co. But Horniblow had given me a job. Maybe the portents were good.

They were. My interview ran on unorthodox lines, to say the least. After asking one or two conventional questions, Eilbeck reached out a long arm for a newspaper make-up pad on a side table and, scrawling a few words in charcoal capitals across it, pushed it across to me with the words, 'What feature story would you bring in to go with this headline?'

The headline was 'AND THEY CALL THIS SPORT!' I was in luck. Hare coursing was a popular diversion in the pit villages around Leeds, and I knew enough about it to convince Eilbeck that I had the makings of at least one *Mirror* feature in me.

He next asked me about my interests. I mumbled the standard list – books, the theatre, walking – but then, lest these seemed too mundane, I took it into my head to add wildly, 'conjuring' – this solely on the basis of having once learned a few simple tricks from an *Every Boy's Bumper Book* on the subject.

To my astonishment, and concern, Eilbeck produced a pack of cards from his desk drawer – an obsessional doodler and jangler of loose change, as well as a near-compulsive gambler, he was apparently in the habit of absently cutting the deck while trying to think up features ideas – and invited me to show him some tricks. My fingers all thumbs, I shuffled the pack and demonstrated a pretty feeble sleight-of-hand routine. Eyes gleaming behind their horn rims, and by now sitting upright, he leaned forward keenly and dissected each trick as it reached its denouement. Since it seemed a point of honour with him to spot how each clumsy bit of legerdemain worked, I wasn't sure whether to humour him or try to baffle him. My dilemma was resolved by an attempt at a spectacular cascading shuffle landing half the cards on the floor, whereupon he lost interest.

Eilbeck's last question was: 'If you were to be sent up to, let's say, Birmingham tomorrow morning, do you think you could get a feature together in time for a four o'clock deadline?' I gulped inwardly. My idea of an average feature-writing stint was a leisurely couple of days gathering the material, another day thinking about it, and a fourth writing it up. But of course I had heard of the *Mirror*'s horrifically early deadlines. Then selling around four million copies daily (it was to reach five million), and with only one printing centre, its presses were already rolling even before the late finals of the three evening papers hit the streets.

I said, bending the truth a little, that I had had a good deal of experience at phoning features in from shorthand notes. After all, cat shows, I supposed, figured as features – they certainly didn't figure as hard news. Eilbeck then treated me to what seemed to be the standard sermon – I had already heard it from Mr Hord – on how tough it was on the *Mirror*, and how different I should find it in the front line of daily tabloid journalism from (as he made it sound) the rest and recreation camp of a provincial evening. Finally he said that there was only one way to see if I was up to the job, and that was to take me on the staff on a month's trial. Horniblow had offered me three months, and I had survived, but perhaps only because he himself had been fired before my probationary time was up. Maybe before my month on the *Mirror* had expired, Eilbeck's soaring career would take him to some more exalted position and his successor, like Horniblow's, wouldn't know anything about the arrangement. I accepted.

Back in Leeds I told Joan about the *Mirror*'s offer and the pay that came with it – fifteen guineas a week, nearly twice what I was getting at the *Evening Post*. She was so impressed that I did not mention the month's trial part of the deal.

A few days before my twenty-third birthday I had a formal letter of appointment – 'Dear Sir' – from none other than Mr Cyril Morton, the Managing Editor, outlining my terms of employment – 'Generally you will be expected to conform to the rules and usages of this office, including the wearing of clothes suitable to status and function', etc. I handed in my resignation at the *Yorkshire Evening Post* and not long afterwards said goodbye to the shabby, smoky reporters' room and to my friends, not without regrets. The Editor made a curiously back-handed speech in which he said that while it came as no surprise that Keith felt it time to be moving on, some might feel surprise at his choice of paper. I think he had seen me graduating to the *Manchester Guardian*. I was presented with a wallet-cum-notebook signed by all my colleagues, which I still have, and then a select company of us repaired to Polly's Bar across the street where I drowned the awaiting terrors of Fleet Street in Guinness.

2 I finished work on the *Evening Post* on a Friday and was on the London train on the Saturday. I could have done with a week's breathing space but with less than fifty pounds in the bank I could not afford a gap between salary cheques. Joan stayed behind, packing my accumulation of books and awaiting the summons to a bijou flat in Chelsea or, at a pinch, Hampstead.

In fact, far from being able to find a flat on that first chilly day in London, I was hard put to ferret out even a temporary room. I knew that finding somewhere to live in these post-war years was difficult: I didn't know it was near impossible.

I had been told that Earl's Court was my best bet, insofar as there was a best bet. I took to the area at once and indeed have lived in it on and off ever since – but then it has always been my belief that one's arrival in the capital triggers off a metropolitan homing instinct, and that for evermore one is drawn back to that side of London where one first fetched up.

It was a mite more respectable then that it is now – where other prosperous neighbourhoods gentrified themselves, Earl's Court mutinously degentrified – but yet recognisably the raffish stewpot of nationalities it is today. Crouched over the spluttering gas rings of their garden flats, half-crazed old ladies who still called themselves 'residents' had their deaf-aids assaulted by *Housewives' Choice* played in decibels on the bulky bakelite portable radios of workmen converting the floors above into holiday flatlets or student hostels. Another lorryload of pegboard, and ten rooms became thirty rooms to make an annexe for some improbably named hotel, itself remodelled on the same lines: skips in the leafy squares were permanently piled high with old lavatories and sinks, now replaced by something worse in 'contemporary' avocado, and with space-consuming bathtubs replaced by shower units.

Earl's Court then, as now, had several populations which appeared on the teeming main thoroughfare in waves as the day wore on: grey-faced clerks, typists and shop assistants off to jam-pack the District and Piccadilly Lines *en route* for their insurance companies and shoe shops; then the mad elderly ladies, walking their infirm old pooches and prodding the fruit on the costers' stalls; then the ambling, map-consulting tourists, causing serious pavement obstruction as they piled out of their pegboard hotel annexes; then the yawning backpackers, seeking out the Big Bargain Breakfast they had heard about in Melbourne; then the touts and the pushers and the pimps and the hookers and the winos and the deranged old men directing traffic and the plain-clothes policemen improbably disguised as layabouts. In the words of the old *News of the World* slogan, all human life was there, much of it centring on the Earl's Court tube station forecourt which resembled, as it does still, some foreign piazza. The neighbourhood had a twenty-four-hour life cycle and those who managed sleep could depend upon being awakened by the 4 a.m. scream, followed by ambulance bells and sirens – as ubiquitous in Earl's Court as the cockerel's crow and the dawn chorus in the countryside. My kind of town. And it had continuity. Thirty years on, when I set a novel in this seething sub-cosmopolis, *Maggie Muggins or Spring in Earl's Court*, it was still virtually unchanged, except that the ABC Teashop, the Express Dairies and the second-hand bookshop were now gone – but then they would be, wouldn't they?

From one of those postcard-festooned showcases advertising for chambermaids, barmen and two girls to share nice studio apartment, i.e. bed-sitter, I found towards the end of the day a top-floor room in Eardley Crescent off Warwick Road on what, if Earl's Court had had a fashionable side, would have been the unfashionable side. Or rather, half a top-floor room, for I had to share it with its incumbent lodger, a young City clerk – then a common requirement. I didn't mind too much. It was temporary, I was fourteen minutes from Fleet Street, and anyway there was so much of London to see that I didn't expect ever to be in my half-room except to sleep.

I started by seeing Fleet Street. I had the whole of Sunday free and while I knew I had to find a bijou flat in Chelsea, taking my bearings in what I thought of unabashedly as the Street of Adventure (Sir Philip Gibbs' novel of that name was still on every young journalist's bookshelf) was my first priority. I ate a hearty early breakfast over the *Observer* (Ivor Brown, C. A. Lejeune & Co. – icons all) at the ABC, took the District Line to the Temple and, walking purposefully in case I was trespassing, passed through those empty, tranquil courtyards into The Street.

Old newspaper hands like to remember Fleet Street as a village. This is to downgrade it somewhat: it was more of a small industrial township, on a par with Bootle or Heckmondwike. Had the area between Ludgate Circus and Temple Bar been lined with textile mills, it would have seemed incongruous and intrusive to the lawyers pondering their briefs behind the cloisters of the Temple, that haven of peace in this busy little manufacturing town, like a cathedral close in the middle of the Heavy Woollen District. Since it was filled with noisy printing factories, and the stench was of ink and hot metal rather than dye or glue-boiling, no one gave the juxtaposition a second thought; or if they did, they looked upon it benevolently as an extension of the historic affinity between wig and pen. They might have taken a different line had the mighty Hoe and Goss presses roared all through the working day instead of by night and at the weekends.

In fact Fleet Street itself, the main artery and shopping street of this factory town, housed only two printing plants – that of the *Daily Express* in its black-glass Art Deco palace, later known as the Lubyanka, and its near-neighbour the *Daily Telegraph* in, appropriately, a more conservative neo-classical edifice of the same period – and both of them architecturally a match for, say, the Boots factory in Nottingham or the Shredded Wheat plant at Welwyn Garden City.

Most of the other printing works, or newspaper offices as they preferred to call themselves, were tucked away in the warren of narrow side streets off Fleet Street proper – the *News Chronicle* and the *Star* at 19 Bouverie Street, the *News of the World* across the street at No. 30, the *Daily Mail*, *Evening News* and *Sunday Dispatch* at Northcliffe House in Carmelite Street, the *Daily Mirror* and *Sunday Pictorial* in Fetter Lane, the *Evening Standard* in Shoe Lane. *The Times*, aloof and unneighbourly, keeping itself to itself in what was the miniature equivalent of a garden village, a kind of hot-metal Bournville, was down in Printing House Square, hard by the Embankment.

Just as the mill towns fanned out into the inner suburbs, so did Fleet Street, with the *Daily Graphic* and its numerous Sabbath sisters over in Gray's Inn Road, the *Daily Herald* and the *People* in Long Acre, the *Daily Worker* in Farringdon Road. The *Guardian*, still the *Manchester Guardian*, had not yet come south, but it shared London offices with the *Baltimore Sun* over the Fleet Street branch post office opposite Chancery Lane. Having, early on my Sunday reconnaissance, spotted the *Baltimore Sun*'s Gothic masthead picked out in gold on an upper window, I later returned and loitered in the hope that if the great H. L. Mencken happened to be visiting London, I might catch a glimpse of him crossing to the Cheshire Cheese for lunch. It seemed a fair outside bet: he was still only in his mid-seventies and while he didn't write for the *Baltimore Sun* any more I was sure they would let him use the office.

In only one regard did Fleet Street fail to match the northern mill town comparison. Hardly anyone lived there. Had the barristers and their clerks been flushed out and their chambers let to the mottle-faced throng who nightly tumbled out of the Press Club into the raw light of dawn, the district would have fulfilled the formula for the ideal city as laid down by the likes of Jane Jacobs and Alice Coleman, with their eloquent plea for the mixed-use, twenty-four-hour community against which the planners still so resolutely set their faces.

In true Mother Courage fashion, the newspapers that had settled into The Street, as it was always called, attracted camp-followers from ancillary trades – much as, centuries earlier, jobbing printers and bookbinders had set up shop to service the lawyers and friars. In my exploratory ramble through the alleys, lanes and courtyards I identified scores of little businesses, some of them in rickety lock-up workshops, others – the white-collar end of the market – in office chambers whose entrances were plastered with the brass or bakelite plates of little fleas living off the big fleas.

Here were paper merchants, office equipment firms, tinplate makers, electrotype makers, stationers, plastic stereotypers, carbon makers, advertisers' typesetters, printing ink companies, lithographic roller makers, printers' engravers, advertising contractors, booksellers, bookbinders, newspaper reps, publicity consultants, news and photo agencies, features syndicates, private wire offices, typing and duplicating bureaux, schools of journalism, commercial artists, printers' valuers, typewriter repairers, literary agents, translation bureaux – all seemingly thriving despite the presence among them, between *Picture Post* and the *Farmers' Weekly* in Shoe

Lane, of that glum body the Newsprint Rationing Committee. Then there were the London offices of scores, indeed hundreds, of local daily and weekly papers, huddled together, as if for warmth and reassurance, in cramped garrets at the top of worn linoleum-treaded staircases. The *Belfast Telegraph* rubbed shoulders with the *Western Morning News*, the *Scotsman* with the *Irish Times*, the *Kent Messenger* with the *Bristol Evening Post*, the *Glasgow Evening Citizen* with the *Liverpool Echo*. At No. 171 my old paper as of two days ago, the *Yorkshire Evening Post*, nestled between the Westminster Press Provincial Newspapers, publishers of its rival the *Yorkshire Evening News*, and the *Western Mail* and *South Wales News*.

Further up the street, the D. C. Thomson papers occupied, as they still do, three floors over what was then the Kardomah Café, their titles – the *Dundee Evening Telegraph*, the *People's Friend*, the *People's Journal*, the *Dundee Courier* and the *Sunday Post* – spelled out in vaguely *art nouveau*-ish mosaic layers between the storeys, so that the building somewhat resembled a very large Battenberg cake.

Then, as exotic as a fleet of tramp steamers lined up in the Pool of London with their cargoes of ivory and apes and peacocks, sandalwood, cedarwood and sweet white wine, there were the London bureaux of the foreign papers – the *Bantu Mirror*, the *Kimberley Diamond Fields Advertiser*, the *Johannesburg Star*, the *Times of Swaziland*, the *Malaya Tribune*, the *Chicago Tribune*, Tass, the *Melbourne Argus*, the New Zealand Press Association, the Agence France-Presse, *Al Ahram* of Cairo, the India Press Trust, the Czechoslovak News Agency, the Atlantic and Pacific Press Agency, the Hearst Newspapers of America. There was still room for a host of trade and specialist publications, including several I had once thought of joining – the *Bakers' Record*, the *Tea and Rubber Mail*, the *Dairyman*, the *Cabinet Maker*, *Poultry*, *Chemical Age*, the *Fruit Grower, Market Gardener and Glasshouse Nurseryman*, the *Leather Trades Review*, the *Hardware Trades Review*, the *Whitehall Letter*, *Labour News & Employment Advertiser*, *Gas World* (whence John Osborne, later a good friend, had preceded me to Fleet Street by four years) – which chose to congregate in this little factory town for no apparent reason other than that they must have felt at home there.

Like every other commercial neighbourhood, Fleet Street had, as it still does now that it is in other hands, its proper quota of shops and services for people working in the area – tailors, travel agents, banks, cafés, sandwich bars, fancy goods dealers, jewellers, pawnbrokers, rubber goods suppliers. There were one or two commission agents, as credit bookmakers were then called, but no betting shops, which were not yet legal – nevertheless, on big race days, the bookies would come down to take bets from queues of printers stretching so far along Carmelite Street that the police were on hand to control the traffic. Although the inkies, as they were snobbishly known to those who are now themselves known as the hacks, used to squat on the pavement like miners to chomp their sandwiches while the journalists went off to their pubs and clubs and butteries, they could even then have afforded to eat at the Savoy had they wished. While not yet earning the £1,000 or so a week that the Mickey Mouses and Charlie Chaplins of the composing rooms and press halls were to pull in with what were called their 'Spanish practices', and which were to cause Fleet Street to fall in upon itself like a house of cards, they were far in front of even the highest-paid star reporter: as far back as Northcliffe's day, a fellow press magnate had complained, 'The wages are preposterous. Some of these men have motor cycles and side cars.' No wonder that on pay nights the West End prostitutes transferred their beat from Coventry Street to Bouverie Street.

Business attracts business and several enterprises had been drawn to Fleet Street that had nothing to do with 'the print' or with selling their wares to the printing trades as such. The Lord's Day Observance Society, one imagines, had taken up residence at No. 55 to be ever on hand for reporters looking for a juicy quote on the subject of Sabbath-breaking; but why had the Young Churchman's Movement made its home in Wine Office Court? The National Union of Journalists had found its natural home at No. 154, along with the National Union of Press Telegraphists and the Printers' Medical Aid & Sanatoria Association; but why the National Union of Small Shopkeepers at No. 145? What was the London Egg Exchange doing there, or the Billiards Association and Control Council? What had prompted some medal-winning exponent of the foxtrot and the St Bernard's waltz to set up a school of ballroom dancing in Cheshire Court? I had a vision of brilliantined copy boys and stoop-shouldered, widowed correctors of the press shambling around to the tune of a tinny gramophone before heading for the Aldwych to take pot luck at the Lyceum ballroom.

There were pubs, of course – were there not pubs! Fifteen of them in the short stretch between the George at Temple Bar and the Punch Tavern on Ludgate Circus; and twice as many again lurking in the narrow thoroughfares behind. A favourite trick, which I was not to fall for, was to bet greenhorns that they could not drink a pint in every Fleet Street pub between lunchtime opening and closing time. So far I had set foot only in one of them, the venerable Cheshire Cheese, which I had yet to learn was no longer really a journalists' pub but given over to American tourists. Today, when the time came round for my mid-day pint, I ventured into the Bell Tavern, erected by Wren as a hostel for builders reconstructing St Bride's Church opposite after the Great Fire.

To my disappointment, there was no one remotely like Cassandra or Hannen Swaffer or any of the other great Fleet Street luminaries propping up the tiled bar. When I knew a little more about local customs I would realise that great Fleet Street luminaries did not usually surface on Sundays and that Ye Old Bell, like the Cheshire Cheese, was also not regarded as a journalists' pub but was only used by such of them as were avoiding other journalists, usually because they owed them money. But I did discover St Bride's across the back alley.

St Bride's, with its arresting steeple, the highest Wren ever built and which, so the noticeboard informed me, inspired the first tiered wedding cake, was, and still is, the newspaper profession's church. The dispersal of The Street to Wapping and the Isle of Dogs has strengthened rather than weakened the connection, for nowadays the only time many journalists see their friends and colleagues from other papers is at St Bride's memorial services. These are touching occasions with lusty hymns and affectionate addresses; invariably one long-retired veteran will murmur to another, 'Hardly worth going home again, is it?' Afterwards, hallowed tradition has it that the mourners repair to El Vino up the street. It must be puzzling to the City whizz-kids and Perrier-sipping members of the Japanese banking community who now patronise this famous old wine bar when, every six months or so, the swing doors burst open like those of a western saloon, and a phalanx of beefy, red-faced, middle-aged men charge in and with cries of 'It's what he would have wanted!' bellow for champagne and gin. 'What', one imagines the bemused present regulars asking one another as, after an hour

255

or so's heroic drinking, the former regulars charge out again, 'was all that about?'

But wandering up and down The Street this Sunday morning, through Middle Temple Lane and Bride Lane and Shoe Lane and Serjeant's Inn and Clifford's Inn Passage, through Wine Office Court, Cheshire Court, Red Lion Court, Hind Court, Crane Court, Three Kings Court, Hen and Chickens Court, Bolt Court, Bolt-in-Tun Court, Salisbury Court and Hood Court, and Hare Place, and Whitefriars Street and Bouverie Street and Carmelite Street, the day could not possibly be envisaged, certainly not by me, when it would all be no more. That, as a traditional centre of production, it was as transient as the still-prosperous mill towns, occurred to no one except perhaps a few managerial visionaries, and they were careful to keep their visions to themselves. I paced between the Embankment and Fetter Lane – naturally I had to go and give the *Mirror* building a good long stare – and between Ludgate Circus and the Law Courts, never suspecting for a second that I was treading the pavements of a typographical Pompeii.

While the neighbourhood was still comparatively deserted, like any small town on a Sunday, and although the smell of printers' ink and metal was at this hour as stale on the air as last night's beer (it lingers on still, like cigar smoke after a banquet), there was nevertheless a stirring, a frisson, the first buzz of that excitement that always mounted throughout the day until it came to a climax with fleets of predominantly yellow vans pulling out of Shoe Lane and Bouverie Street and Carmelite Street and Tudor Street and Fetter Lane and heading like wagon trains for the mainline stations. Men in tweed jackets with copies of the *Observer* under their arms – leader writers, would they be? Feature writers? Editors? – were passing through the handsome entrances of the *Telegraph* and the *Express*. Copytakers in shiny black suits and Fair Isle pullovers were arriving for work at Reuter's and the Press Association in their Portland stone citadel opposite. Two o'clock and the pub bells were ringing time, and with no traffic to deaden the sound the hum of machinery and the clatter of linotypes could be heard from Geraldine House as the *Daily Mirror* set up a feature page story or two before the main news started flooding in. Tomorrow – the heart lurched – maybe they would be setting a feature by me. But tomorrow was still a long way off. This was today. This was The Street – the Street of Ink, the Street of Adventure – and I was over the frontier.

256

3   Above the buzz of voices, the clatter of typewriters and telex machines and the non-stop ringing of telephones, the first distinguishable human sound I heard as I was shown into a newsroom the size of an aircraft hangar was what, remembering my Billy Bunter stories, I could only call a stentorian cry of *'What pillock subbed this?'* An awesome, if not an auspicious start.

This was the gravelly, megaphone voice – in fact barely raised – of a silver-haired, bow-tied, barrel-chested, co-respondent-shod, Mississippi gambler of a man, Jack Nener, Assistant Editor and shortly to become the next Editor of the *Daily Mirror*. In a hard-swearing Street, Nener was acknowledged as the grand master of invective and abuse. When, as Editor, he was taking part in some journalistic levee at the Midland Hotel, Manchester, he was colourfully holding forth in the lounge when an inoffensive 'civilian', as non-newspaper types were termed, approached him and asked, 'Excuse me, sir, would you mind moderating your language, as there are ladies present?' Nener, mistaking him for one of the seething mob of hacks who had more or less total control of the lounge, roared, 'Do you know who I am? I am the fucking editor of the fucking *Daily Mirror*!' 'Yes,' said the civilian mildly, 'I rather thought you might be.'

Another unfamiliar sound, as I was escorted along the length of the newsroom, was the cry of 'Messenger!' from sub-editors waving sheafs of copy paper. This was a surprise: the traditional way to summon up a copy boy, even if he were no longer a boy but had reached man's estate, was by calling 'Boy!' That was what we had shouted in the newsroom of the *Yorkshire Evening Post* – in my case, not without some self-conscious pride, like a public school sixth-former yelling for his first fag – and it was what was shouted in all the newsrooms in all the Fleet Street memoirs I had ever read.

Not on the *Daily Mirror*. It was R. J. Eilbeck, I was to learn, who was the cause of this upgrading of status. It seemed that one day when working on the sub-editors' bench Eilbeck, upon uttering the time-honoured cry of 'Boy!', had found himself confronted by a large and imposing presence who far from being an inky copy boy might have been the head waiter at the Savoy.

'I am not a boy, Mr Eilbeck,' pointed out this personage. 'I happen to be the Mayor of Poplar.'

Eilbeck was not at all put out. 'I don't care if you're the Lord Mayor of London,' he retorted. 'Get me some coffee.'

As well as being the Mayor of Poplar the messenger who was not a boy was also the house representative of NATSOPA, the National Society of Operative Printers and Assistants, one of the dozen or so trades unions whose arcane rules and 'Spanish practices' kept newspaper managements constantly on their toes. It was in this capacity that he called out his brothers to a protest meeting from which they refused to emerge until an apology had been made and their dignity restored. Without copy boys to ferry material between the editorial floor and the printers, no newspaper could function. Mr Cyril Morton, the Managing Editor, intervening, Eilbeck made his apologies to the Mayor of Poplar and work was resumed. But thereafter the copy boys were known as messengers.

This Paddington Station of a newsroom was the terminus for all the news, sports coverage, features, photographs and cartoons pouring daily into the paper, only the columnists and specialist writers occupying their own monastic cells in the editorial corridors. Features, although they were subsequently decanted to a relatively small office known as the Black Hole of Calcutta, then occupied a cluster of metal desks at the far end of the newsroom, separated from the sports department by a coven of artists and cartoonists whose drawing boards served the same function as potted-fern room dividers.

I hovered shyly on the invisible threshold of the features department. A matinée-handsome young man with a hank of butter-coloured hair, Peter Baker – destined to become one of David Frost's producers – was reading a newly published American novel that a friend had sent him from New York, *The Catcher in the Rye*. Marshall Pugh, an almost unintelligible Scot who was to make something of a reputation as a novelist in the John Buchan tradition, had set his jacket on fire through putting away a pipe that was still ignited, and was patting ineffectively at the billows of smoke wisping out of his pocket. Eve Chapman, a stunning young brunette, was holding a leisurely girl-to-girl conversation on the telephone. The agony auntie, a former cleaning lady named Mary Brown (these were pre-Proops days), was handing round slices of home-made cake. It was all unexpectedly cosy, and in marked contrast to the reporters' room of the *Evening Post* where, confronted by a scene of such indolence, Mr Lemmon the News Editor would have issued a pointed reminder that we had a paper to get out.

I was at once made welcome. Fleet Street, however hostile a face may be put on by all engaged in the perpetual game of editorial snakes and ladders, has always held out a friendly hand to the newcomer. With my gauche northern ways I should have been an outsider in any ordinary office. But nearly everyone in Fleet Street comes from somewhere other than London, and all that a thick Yorkshire accent says about its owner is that he was brought up and trained in good evening newspaper country. The incomprehensible Marshall Pugh from Dundee, who made my flat northern vowels sound as if they had taken elocution lessons, took me under his wing, Mary Brown gave me a slice of her cake, Eve Chapman lent me her coffee mug, and I felt thoroughly at home.

Rather to my relief, R. J. Eilbeck proved to have taken himself off on a week's holiday. His deputy, Bob Balmforth, did not emerge and I wondered whether to go and seek him out and re-introduce myself, but a worldly, languid feature writer with an educated voice, Douglas Howell, soon to be lost to the realm of public relations, counselled me not to go looking for trouble, in other words looking for work. I whiled away the morning chatting and reading newspapers. From time to time people from other departments, either Yorkshire-born or having served on a Yorkshire paper, drifted across to say hello to a fellow-Tyke. Still no one in features was doing any work, although Douglas Howell had made a start on his expenses. I was beginning to feel that the *Daily Mirror* was much maligned. *Peg's Paper*, I concluded, would be a tougher billet.

At around noon I was carried off by some of my new friends to Winnie's, aka No. 10, this being the pub's address in Fetter Lane. The pub's real name was the Falcon but it was known as Winnie's or No. 10 to distinguish it from another Falcon around the corner in Pemberton Row, an unnecessary precaution since that pub too was never referred to by its proper name but as the Witches', after the two refugees from Macbeth who ran it. Most Fleet Street pubs were endowed with pet names such as Auntie's, Barney's and so on, usually after their landlords; the great exception, after the *Mirror* moved two or three hundred yards up the street and ruthlessly abandoned Winnie's for a nearer local – journalists are notoriously lazy in their choice of drinking venue – was the Stab in the Back, so christened by the great *Mirror* columnist Cassandra who insisted that it was a hotbed of editorial intrigue. So ubiquitously was the pub known as the Stab, and so universally unheard of was the name on its inn sign, the White Hart, that one landlord tried to persuade the brewers to make the change of nomenclature official, like the licensing equivalent of deed poll granted to the French Pub, once known by nobody who ever set foot in Soho as the York Minster.

I took to the shabby little nicotine-stained Fetter Lane pub and its gregarious inhabitants immediately. Winnie herself, although a Freeman of the City of London (a fact that for the benefit of newcomers she could ingeniously work into any conversation, whatever the subject), was the chain-smoking, gin-sipping archetypal landlady, a kindly, corseted figure inside which a chucker-out was for ever lurking in readiness to bar anyone who overstepped the mark. Winnie was renowned for her parties, run on the lines of private bottle parties – that is, the guests paid for their own drinks – when, claiming probably imaginary Freeman's rights, she would grant herself an extension to celebrate such anniversaries as Anzac Day, St George's Day, VE Day and the like. If there were no anniversary to hand and Winnie's regulars felt a pressing need to lock the doors and drink after hours, someone would ransack the almanac and come up with the birth of King Louis XI of France or the death of Nellie Melba or the invention of the Wellington boot.

Over pints of Younger's bitter I was indoctrinated into Fleet Street pub etiquette, requiring intimate knowledge of which pubs were in bounds and which were not. Winnie's or No. 10, I was given to understand, was the *Mirror* features pub, shared with the *Sunday Pictorial* and the London staff of D. C. Thomson's. *Daily Mirror* reporters and subs used Barney Finnegan's, known to the brewery as the Red Lion, further up the street. *Daily Mirror* feature writers were also welcome in Barney's, but *Daily Mirror* reporters, for some unfathomable reason, were not welcome in Winnie's. But the Blue Anchor just around the corner from Barney's was not used by journalists at all, nor was Peele's Hotel at the Fleet Street end of Fetter Lane. In or just off Fleet Street itself, *Mirror* hacks could use the Clachan, the *Manchester Guardian* pub, but not, except by invitation, Poppins which was the *Daily Express* pub, the Cogers (*News Chronicle*), the White Swan or Mucky Duck (*News of the World*) or the Rose and Crown (*Daily Mail*), known even to its conventionally excluded non-customers as Auntie's. As for the King and Keys, that was strictly the fiefdom of the *Daily Telegraph* – a pity, since it was the liveliest public house in Fleet Street. Sir Peregrine Worsthorne has noted how odd it was that the King and Keys, the favoured watering-hole of the ultra-conservative *Telegraph*'s leader writers and diplomatic correspondents, should have been the scene of nightly carousings and unseemly brawls, while the Clachan, patronised by supposedly permissive and raffish *Manchester Guardian* types, was an oasis of calm and propriety.

Two other Fleet Street drinking establishments were recognised as permitted premises, being melting-pot houses used by The Street in general: the Cock Tavern and El Vino. One of the Cock's attractions was that the public relations man for Durex held court there, and he seemed to have a generous hospitality allowance. So far as El Vino was concerned, it was impressed upon me that this club-like institution was for very senior journalists only and that should I venture through its swing doors before I had served at least five years or acquired a reputation, whichever came the sooner, I should be made less than welcome. Naturally I resolved to inspect El Vino at the earliest opportunity.

All other Fleet Street pubs, from the George west of the Law Courts to the Old King Lud on the wrong side of Ludgate Circus, and particularly the Tipperary which was notoriously used by printers, were by self-imposed edict *non persona grata* to journalists, except when featuring in occasional heroic pub crawls. The most historic of these was yet to take place – it happened in the late autumn of my first year in Fleet Street. Ian Mackay, the *News Chronicle*'s distinguished columnist – essayist, rather, in the Chesterton mould: the last ever to write for a popular newspaper – had dropped dead on Morecambe promenade at the end of the Labour Party Conference of 1952, the final loser in a lifelong feud with his liver. He was seen off at Golders Green crematorium by his friends. Two of them were entrusted with his ashes, later to be scattered at a favourite beauty spot. They repaired to El Vino ('It's what he would have wanted'), and after drinking a few toasts to the deceased proceeded, as a mark of respect, to follow his oft-trodden footsteps along the Fleet Street pub crawl, carrying the ashes which were in a cardboard shoe box, itself contained in a paper carrier bag. It was raining heavily. As they proceeded from El Vino to the Wellington and from the Wellington to the Tipperary and from the Tipperary to the Falstaff and from the Falstaff to Ye Old Bell and from Ye Old Bell to the Punch Tavern, the bag became soggier and soggier as the cardboard box pallbearers became drunker and drunker. Reeling out of the Punch *en route* for the last pub on the pilgrimage, the *News Chronicle* man's own local the Cogers, whoever had picked up his ashes felt a certain lightness. Glancing first down at the burst carrier bag and the disintegrated shoe box, the two chief mourners then looked up Fleet Street to discover that they had been progressively scattering the remains of their celebrated friend along the gutter. Reiterating 'It's what he would have wanted', they adjourned for a final whisky.

The ground rules of pub usage as spelled out to me were to hold good: in all the years I was to remain in Fleet Street I only ever crossed the thresholds of seven out of forty-odd taverns and public houses. The bond was that they would all cash cheques – that and the fact that the chosen seven were serious hostelries, refreshingly free from pub whimsy of the 'We have arranged with the bank not to give credit – in return the bank has agreed not to serve beer' variety, or foreign currency pinned to the wall behind the bar. Globe-trotting newspapermen did not give their foreign currency to pub landlords: they cashed it.

As lunchtime approached and Winnie's began to fill up, I was introduced to some of the regulars. One of them was Cassandra, otherwise Bill Connor, the Mirror's legendary columnist and one of my heroes. It was Cassandra's practice to start his column and then repair to No. 10 for an hour, leaving it, as he said, on 'automatic pilot'. While irascibility was his trademark and he was much given to glowering over his half-moon spectacles, he was the kindliest of souls. I did wonder, though, as he gravely shook hands and looked the young newcomer up and down, whether the mischievous Cyril Morton had shown him the questionnaire I had been required to fill in when returning my signed contract. One of the questions was 'What is your ultimate ambition?', to which I had impertinently responded, with the arrogance of youth and in the belief that in his early forties Bill Connor must be pretty well over the hill by now: 'To inherit Cassandra's column'. I had to wait twenty years for it.

I was almost equally awed to shake hands with George, whose surname currently escapes me, who was bureau chief of the D. C. Thomson papers and thus, by extension, the London editor of the *Dandy* and the *Beano*. George actually knew, by name, the artists who drew Desperate Dan, Korky the Cat, Lord Snooty and His Pals and other favourite strips, and promised to bring them into Winnie's for a game of bar billiards should they ever venture down from Dundee. I was most impressed.

Less of a celebrity but just as interesting to meet was Frank Ross, my first Fleet Street conman. Frank's speciality was the Catering and Licensed Premises Hygiene League, an organisation which existed only in his head. For a trifling sum of a few guineas, pub landlords and restaurant owners were able to buy from Frank an imposing certificate confirming that their kitchens and cellars had been inspected by the Licensed Premises Hygiene League and found spotless. Those who demurred were gently reminded that it could look bad for them if neighbouring establishments had a framed certificate on their walls and they did not. Even Winnie herself, for all that she knew of Frank's reputation, had bought one of his spurious certificates and hung it behind the bar. Frank's professional connection with Fleet Street was that he sold underworld news tips and the purported eve-of-execution confessions of murderers. Frank made no secret of being a former jailbird – indeed, it was his standing offer that for the right price he was prepared to commit a crime serious enough to get him remanded to Brixton, where he would interview any criminal of his client's choice then awaiting trial.

Our little group was joined lastly by one Leslie Hubble, a pink-faced, rotund little fellow who could have passed for a rural dean, together with his equally cherubic and portly sidekick Peter, a former stipendiary magistrate of Jerusalem. This angelic-looking pair ran the *Sunday Pictorial* readers' service department, the John Noble Bureau, to use its virtuous-sounding title, on whose behalf they ran down and confronted villains and conmen whose activities were then exposed under violent headlines ('DON'T FALL FOR THIS PYRAMID SALES SMOOTHIE'). I noticed that they exchanged affable greetings with Frank Ross. It turned out that they had more than once turned over his Hygiene League racket in the pages of the *Sunday Pic*, an experience that fazed him not at all – it had in fact enhanced his business. Leslie Hubble himself told me that he was constantly being pestered by a man down in

Cornwall who sold lucky pieces of tree bark by mail order; he had already been exposed as a charlatan once but now he wanted to be exposed again, since sales were dropping off.

Cassandra went off to complete his column, Leslie and Peter to expose more sharp practices, Frank to con more mug landlords and caterers. After indoctrinating me into the games of bar billiards and shove-halfpenny, George too departed, back to the realm of Oor Wullie and the *People's Friend*. It was now well after hours. Unhurriedly finishing his last pint, 'Mac' Pugh, as he seemed to be known, announced that he supposed he had better be getting back and writing the feature he was due to deliver for the next morning's paper. I admired his nerve: in his place I should have had the copy paper in my typewriter by ten in the morning; it took me a long time to accommodate myself to the accepted code of practice that you did not start writing anything for the following day's paper until mid-afternoon at the earliest, in case anything more sensational cropped up and the story was killed.

Peter Baker and I were the last to leave the pub, I for one feeling a little woozy after three and a half hours' intake of beer. Unexpectedly, as I turned to head for the office, Baker said, 'Where shall we go now? How about tea at the Ritz?' I was mightily impressed, not so much by the proposed venue – Baker, I subsequently learned, had a taste for high living – as by his airy assumption that our time was our own. While I knew Eilbeck was on holiday, Bob Balmforth, however easy-going, could be wondering even now where Baker and the new fellow – particularly the new fellow – had got to. Baker, calling a cab, pooh-poohed my misgivings – Balmforth, he assured me, would be taking a long lunch, and besides, it was far too late in the day to be handing out assignments. It was to emerge that Baker had some kind of semi-official dispensation as regards skipping off for the afternoon. With a minimalist approach to hard or anyway routine work, he had made a niche for himself writing occasional picture captions which were usually so brilliant that nobody cared to trouble him to do anything else. His last effort in this field had been the headline 'O, come *on* all ye faithful!' on a Christmas photograph of a yawning choirboy, which had gone down so well – the greetings card market had snapped it up – that Baker felt justified in resting on his laurels for the foreseeable future.

The Ritz struck me as no more and no less imposing than the West Riding lounge of the Queens Hotel in Leeds, although the staff were less homely. Remembering that I had had no lunch, I made short work of the cucumber sandwiches. Baker, I noted, took his tea with lemon: I would have to put that on my list of southern habits to try out. Having established already, in Winnie's, that I was of a bookish disposition, he talked enthusiastically about *The Catcher in the Rye* and promised to lend me his copy. It was coming as a slow and pleasant surprise to find what a literary-inclined company I had fallen in with. While I did not expect the conversation of my colleagues to be limited to the brash tabloidese of their calling, or their interests to pin-ups and the soccer results, I did not anticipate their quoting T. S. Eliot by the yard, as Mac Pugh did, and frequently so, or reciting Stephen Leacock's 'Hoodoo McFiggin's Christmas' from memory, as could Eric Wainwright, a Canadian; nor would I have bet money that one of the leader writers, Sydney Tremaine, would prove to be a published poet, that the chief features sub, Freddie Wills, was not only a published poet but a published poet in Russian, which he spoke fluently, or that another leader writer, Alan Fairclough, would lead regular philosophical seminars at the bar of No. 10 on such questions as 'What is the average time?' or literary debates on whether Defoe, Richardson or Fielding could lay claim to being the first English novelist.

Alan, to whom I warmed as a fellow Yorkshireman, was a Bradford miner's son with a double first from Balliol. When we got to know one another a little better he told me how he very nearly might not have got to Oxford. As a schoolboy at Bradford Grammar he was sitting at the kitchen table one evening doing his homework when his father, smoking a pipe over the *Yorkshire Telegraph and Argus*, alighted upon an advertisement for the local department store and commented to his wife: 'I see there's a sale of lingerie on at Brown Muff's.' He pronounced lingerie as in lingering. Without looking up, Alan – the homework he was engaged on was French – corrected him: '*Lonhzhari*, Dad.' His father flung down the newspaper, walked out of the house and did not speak to his son again for another two years.

The day arrived when Alan had to travel to Oxford to sit the Balliol scholarship that was the only means by which he would ever be able to afford to go there. He lacked a badly needed watch to time his papers. It had always been understood that his father was going to give him a watch, either for his birthday or Christmas, but these celebrations had gone by unobserved and in paternal silence.

In view of the family atmosphere his mother had never cared to raise the question and it looked as if Alan would be going to the examination hall without any means of telling the time. With any luck there might be a clock but he could not depend on it.

He was sitting in the railway carriage contemplating his lot when he heard the clump of miners' clogs along the station platform. His father, fresh from the night shift, poked his coal-begrimed face through the open window and pushed into Alan's hands the battered hunter watch and chain which he always wore. 'Here,' he said gruffly. 'And don't break the bugger.' And clomped off again.

The effects of Winnie's beer and the Ritz's tea and cherry cake eventually directed me hurriedly to the men's room where I noisily threw up under the disapproving eye of a major-domo. Returning with glistening forehead to the lobby, I was advised by the urbane Peter Baker to take myself home. He promised to cover for me in case my absence was noticed, though how he proposed to do this he did not say. It had been an inauspicious yet promising start to my Fleet Street career.

So passed my first day on the *Daily Mirror*. I was surprised, upon arriving for work the following morning, to find R. J. Eilbeck roaming the newsroom, since he was supposed to be on holiday. The story quickly trickled down the grapevine. Eilbeck had been in the south of France, where he had spent precisely three hours. There were then in force strict exchange control regulations, limiting the amount of currency one could take out of the country to £50. Eilbeck had flown to Nice, where he had stepped into a hire car organised for him by the paper's Paris office. He drove straight to the casino where he instructed the driver to wait. Entering the gaming salon and approaching the nearest roulette wheel, he put his entire foreign allowance of £50 on seventeen, his lucky number – i.e. it had recently come up for him twice in succession at some Park Lane gambling club. If seventeen came up this time he would pick up £1,750 (naturally, he would let his stake ride) and move into the Hotel Negresco for a holiday of unparalleled luxury. If not, not.

The croupier called '*Rien ne va plus*', the wheel spun, and the ball trickled into zero. Eilbeck walked out of the casino, got into his car, drove back to the airport, and caught the next flight to London. And now, workaholic that he was, he was back in the office, jangling his change and looking at me thoughtfully.

266

4   I quickly got the hang of the place. Every morning at eleven we would be expected to cram into Eilbeck's little office for a features conference, when we either had to come up with ideas of our own or suffer ideas to be thrust upon us.

Some of Eilbeck's own offerings were bizarre to say the least, but he did get results. I had had a foretaste of his creative thinking during my initial interview when he had invited me to match his scrawled impromptu headline with a feature. This was his favourite method of floating an idea. While the assembled feature writers clustered around his desk skimming the newspapers and intermittently quoting some story that might with luck yield a feature angle, Eilbeck would be scribbling away on his pad. Cockily trumpeting his newly minted headline – 'WOULD YOU RISK A BLIND DATE HOLIDAY?' or 'CAN WOMEN BE TRUSTED WITH MONEY?' or 'CALL YOURSELF A MUM?' – he would rip off the page and thrust it into the arms of the nearest writer – 'Copy by four o'clock.'

Some of these brainstorms came off the day's news, some off the wall. About half the ideas worked, a few of them spectacularly. Following a spate of shootings, Eilbeck scrawled 'THIS GUN FOR SALE' on his pad, together with a rough sketch of a revolver. Within hours a writer was back in the office with a handgun and a dramatic piece on the ease with which (he did not mention the little help he had had from the crime staff) he had bought it in Trafalgar Square. But many of Eilbeck's madder flights of fancy had no chance of panning out at all – even I could tell that. Seasoned writers would accept the assignment without demur, repair to Winnie's for a couple of hours, and then ring in to announce that they couldn't make the idea stand up.

Mercifully, none of Eilbeck's extemporised headlines winged their way to me – at least not yet. The pitifully small paper was grossly overstaffed, with half a dozen highly experienced feature writers fighting to fill one page a day, and it was evident that my role was as standby or first reserve. Hanging around the office, where the time was passed pleasantly in chit-chat, smoking and drinking coffee, I was occasionally tossed some small task, such as a review copy of some ghosted showbiz memoirs that might be good for an 150-word anecdotal filler. One day Eilbeck dropped a re-issued volume on my desk – *To Beg I am Ashamed*, the supposed autobiography of a prostitute (which only recently has been revealed as partly the work of Graham Greene). It came complete with one of his headlines: 'IT'S STILL A BAD, DANGEROUS BOOK'. I asked him what was so bad and dangerous about it. 'I haven't read it,' the Features Editor confessed cheerfully. 'Two hundred words by four o'clock.'

Another of my little chores was to compose 'come-ons' for the readers' letters columns – invented, controversial letters that, in a slow week for correspondence, would draw a furious mailbag ('With one stray cat for every fifty people, the question is no longer whether we should have cat licences but when . . .'). I was also put to work rewriting agency and syndication material that came into the office, including, on occasion, the Sagittarius segment of the astrology column. This was for the benefit of one of the *Mirror*'s more irascible executives who was a passionate believer in the stars. It had been noticed that when Sagittarius was given a bad reading ('The fiery planet Mars appears to be putting you on a collision course with business associates . . .') he would react accordingly and his miserable 'business associates' would go through the day quaking in their shoes. My job was to doctor his entry to give his colleagues a more peaceful ride: 'Nothing is to be gained from losing your temper or sense of humour if things do not seem to go your way . . .' Some years later, when the challenging aspect of the Sun and Pluto had directed his talents to another paper, I confessed to him in El Vino one day that I had been guilty of doctoring his stars. He was in no way put out. It was serenely obvious to him that I had been planted on the *Mirror* by destiny to adjust his hitherto inaccurate astrological forecasts.

My month's trial with the *Mirror* quickly expired without my having done anything to justify my existence on the paper, but since Eilbeck didn't mention that my time was up, neither did I. I pottered on, still trying to find my feet. Occasionally opportunity would seem to knock, but it was usually a false alarm. I have told in my previous volume, *City Lights*, how Eilbeck instructed me to go out and find an animal story, and believing myself to be in luck I presented for his inspection one I had previously done for the *Yorkshire Evening Post* – a talking dog up in the Dales that could do sums and play dominoes; whereupon Eilbeck, unimpressed, said 'Shit! We need circulation in the West Country. See if you can find a talking dog that does sums and plays dominoes in Cornwall.' What I didn't relate was that he actually made me go down there and look. I seriously thought of ringing up the youth hostel in Bishopsdale where the dog lived, making a bid for it and having it crated down by rail to Penzance. What I did do was to trawl all the kennels, dogs' homes and pet shops in Cornwall, to no avail. I spent three days in the West Country and, courtesy of a letter in a local weekly, finally netted a story about an acrobatic cat that did back somersaults and could walk the tightrope on a garden clothes-line. It refused to co-operate with the photographer and the story was spiked.

One afternoon I was summoned to Eilbeck's office to find him in a state of manic excitement, bent over a make-up pad on which he had scrawled 'THE SPICE OF LIFE!' surrounded by a border of stars. This, I was told, was to be the *Mirror*'s new three-times-a-week gossip column, starting tomorrow – and I was to be in charge of it. Flattering though it was to be entrusted with this commission, there were two snags. The first was that Eilbeck, at the time heavily under the influence of Walter Winchell, Earl Wilson and suchlike night-owl columnists in the New York tabloids that were air-freighted to him weekly, wanted no item to be more than twenty-five words long, followed by three dots; on top of which the column had to 'sizzle' – a favourite Eilbeck word – with exclusive snippets about 'the people who really mattered' – to Eilbeck's mind, anyone with a title, or money to throw about in casinos and nightclubs. The other snag was that I did not have a single contact in the whole of London.

Happily the delightful Eve Chapman was deputed to hold my hand in this insane exercise. The bad news was that Eve, who went home nightly to her parents in Croydon, had never set foot in a nightclub or casino in her life. We were reduced to raiding the society pages of the glossy magazines and ploughing through *Who's Who* in hopes of finding some titled personage with an unusual hobby which could be fleshed out to the maximum twenty-five words with a phone call to the butler. On one desperate occasion, with the thrice-weekly deadline looming yet again, we fell to working our way along

Millionaires' Row in Kensington, Eve on the left-hand side of the street, I on the right-hand side, questioning maids and chauffeurs about the foibles of their rich employers. This enterprise came to a stop after one of the embassies called the police. The Spice of Life column itself came to a stop after our supply of eminent people's interesting pastimes petered out.

Once again I had perilously little to do, and like an idle soldier purposefully carrying an ammunition box round the camp to make himself look busy, I would furiously attack the nearest newspaper with scissors whenever the shadow of the Managing Editor loomed. But the Spice of Life interlude apart, I was thoroughly enjoying this honeymoon period. The mornings passed quickly over gossip, coffee and papers, followed by long lunchtimes in Winnie's, alternately a debating chamber and games parlour. In the afternoons, if I had nothing to occupy me, Peter Baker would sometimes take me to the Press Club in Salisbury Court, a sanctum of leather armchairs and dark panelling and Spy cartoons, and exactly my idea of what a club should be, including the mahogany bar where the arts correspondent of the *Daily Telegraph* had once hurled the cash register at some leader writer or other in an altercation over the merits of Matisse. To the disappointment of a starry-eyed rookie still keeping a keen lookout for the big names of Fleet Street, the Press Club was usually pretty empty in the afternoons, save for a few old codgers snoozing in the best gentleman's club tradition, or playing poker in the card room. As a poker fanatic, this was Baker's sole reason for using the place. Although the afternoon game was a friendly affair with sweety-money stakes I was reluctant to join in until I learned that the card table had been presented to the club by Edgar Wallace, when not even the knowledge that I was sitting in the very chair from which he had lost hundreds of pounds could deter me from taking a hand. But I never allowed myself to be drawn into the serious poker sessions which were played in the early hours when all the papers had been put to bed. Baker never talked about his poker but from others in the school I learned that he had once won enough to buy a much-needed new fridge for the kitchen of his marital home. The old fridge carted away for scrap, his wife was stocking the new model with food when two vanmen arrived to take it away again. Baker had lost the fridge in another poker game.

In the evenings I would usually stroll to the West End, the only other part of London with which I could claim a passing acquaintanceship. I would eat sometimes at Lyons Corner House, sometimes in the cheap little Greek and Italian restaurants between Leicester Square and Shaftesbury Avenue. Rarely would I venture across the Avenue into Soho proper, where I had a morbid fear of being inveigled into a near-beer club and relieved of all my money. With two or three hours' worth of Winnie's bitter still sloshing about in my stomach I made little use of the Soho pubs. Occasionally I would take in a theatre, where cheap gallery seats always seemed available however popular the production – *Call Me Madam*, *The Deep Blue Sea*, Gielgud's *Much Ado*, and a dreadful English musical called *Bet Your Life*. Otherwise I was content enough to mooch around, sometimes walking all the way back to Earl's Court with a spring in my step, still intoxicated by the excitement of living in London and working in Fleet Street.

Saturdays and on my days off – Sunday, for a dogsbody like me, was usually a working day – I went flat-hunting, endeavouring to incorporate my search with inquisitive visits to places I had heard about or read about in Sherlock Holmes stories: Hampstead, Limehouse, Wimbledon, Regents Park, Maida Vale, Pall Mall. Eventually, in these accommodation-starved times, I managed to find two rooms on the first floor of a terrace house in Forest Hill, SE23. It was not a bijou apartment in Chelsea but it would serve to be going on with. It was four guineas a week, furnished – unfurnished flats, consequent upon some well-meaning Attlee legislation to protect tenants, were then available only to those who knew someone who knew someone or could afford a large bribe; but I persuaded the landlord to remove his sticks of furniture to the attic, leaving a token chair as evidence of the flat's furnished status, and Joan brought down our own bits and pieces from Leeds. We settled in. Forest Hill was not my idea of London – a few tram lines, street markets and ABC tea shops would have livened it up – and I missed Earl's Court. But one plus was that the landlord had a television set, the first I had ever seen except in shop windows, and he would sometimes invite us downstairs to watch *The Grove Family* or *What's My Line*?

Joan had shifted her life to London, separating herself from friends and family – two hundred miles was a much longer distance then than now – with no idea how tenuous was my hold on Fleet Street. Boats burned now, I had only to put one foot wrong – a libel, a bungled feature – and I could be writing home to borrow next week's rent while supplicating for a job on the *Wolverhampton Star* or the *Kidderminster Shuttle*. On the bright side, it was turning out that my misgivings about the *Mirror* being a hiring-and-firing paper were proving to be groundless. It was a hiring paper, certainly – all manner of recruits passed through the department while I was there – but I never heard of anyone being fired except for fiddling their expenses: fiddling them, that is, beyond the recognised norm. The ranting Jack Nener had a reputation for sacking at least one reporter and one sub-editor a week, but they were always quietly reinstated the next day.

Despite the continuing thinness of the paper there were ultimately more feature writers than there were chairs and desks to accommodate them, many of them strange bedfellows for the *Daily Mirror*. Some of the unlikeliest newcomers came from influential families and it was rumoured that Cecil Harmsworth King, the patrician new chairman, had had a hand in finding them homes in the *Mirror* sanctuary; it was not, however, beyond the eccentricity of Jimmy Eilbeck himself to have taken them on board in the hope of turning up a new Godfrey Winn, his abiding ambition.

One of these strange recruits, surfacing from who knew where, was Giles Romilly, a nephew of Winston Churchill and brother of the late Esmond Romilly, celebrated for instigating a public school revolution which would later inspire Lindsay Anderson to produce his film *If*. A sociable enough fellow and always one to propose an adjournment to Winnie's earlier than anyone else, Giles nevertheless seemed embarrassed to be working for the *Daily Mirror* and when ringing someone up for a quote or piece of information was at pains never to mention the paper's dread name: instead he would always introduce himself in the same diffident if somewhat misleading manner: 'Ah, yes, my name's Romilly, and I'm writing an article for the newspaper of *the times*, as it were . . .' James Cameron drifted about the place with a puzzled air for a month or two, but no one, including himself, seemed to know what he was doing there. Two others who seemed almost equally bemused were one of the Mitchison girls, Valerie, and Shirley Caitlin, the future Shirley Williams, who, in the absence of anything more constructive to do with her time, very kindly used to read my short stories and advise me where to send them. One day Eilbeck, drifting by and finding her idle, suggested, 'Nothing to do, Shirley? Go down to the bottom of Fetter Lane, stand outside the underground Gents' in the middle of the road and ask ten men for a penny. See what they say.' Shirley left shortly afterwards for the less hazardous world of politics.

One new arrival with a proper job was Gerald Kaufman, taken on as a research assistant to Richard Crossman who had begun to write a political column for the paper (I believe it was effectively written by Gerald, as Crossman's pensions White Paper was effectively written by Alan Fairclough, who said that had it been a company prospectus its author would have found himself in the dock at the Old Bailey). Gerald was given a little cubbyhole off the newsroom where I became a frequent caller to chinwag for hours on the events of the day, mainly the latest film releases of which Gerald was, and is, an addict.

Another was Douglas Warth, an argumentative, self-consciously Bohemian character who affected sandals, bare feet and a beard; on the credit side he was the only one among us who had already established a reputation as a tabloid journalist before his arrival. Warth had run a lively column on the *Sunday Pictorial* called Odd Man Out, so named because in it, as in life, he took the contrary line to whatever was the popular or accepted view on the topics of the day. Having quarrelled with the *Sunday Pic* as he quarrelled with everyone supposed to be set in authority over him, Warth went to the newly-started commercial TV station in Birmingham, ATV, where he conducted a spectacularly acerbic live programme called *Paper Talk*, directed – his first show – by Ned Sherrin, recently down from Oxford. It was an aggressively successful attempt to introduce the techniques of tabloid journalism to television and years before its time – the lesson learned by the young Sherrin, to be intravenously passed on to me and other contributors to *That Was The Week That Was* in the fullness of time, being that 'it is much better for your programme to be mentioned on the front pages than in the television columns'.

But with Ned's departure for the BBC there was another quarrel and Douglas Warth found himself doing TV commercials; then he dabbled in the film business, then he joined the *Daily Herald*, then he had one quarrel too many and found himself unemployed and, seemingly, unemployable. On his uppers, and one day bumping into his old editor outside the Gay Hussar, Douglas pleaded with him for a job, any job. As his office car whisked him away, the editor promised to see what he could do. A day or two later Warth received a letter: 'Dear Douglas, It was a delight to see you the other day and it will be a pleasure to offer you your old job back. I note that when you left the *Sunday Pictorial* it was to join ATV, and when you left ATV it was to advertise Zam-buk, and after advertising Zam-buk you worked in Wardour Street for a period and then you joined the *Daily Herald*. May I suggest you take the same leisurely route back?' Despite this cruel joke it was to the Mirror Group's credit that Douglas Warth was taken on again and he reigned as resident troublemaker before walking out once again, this time into oblivion.

There were several other seasoned professionals among those who came and went, although that did not necessarily mean that they did the most work, or indeed any at all. One experienced feature writer found himself with leisure enough to run a wholesale confectionery business on the side. Another was the full-time secretary of a waiters' club in Soho. A third spent so much of the working day in the pubs and clubs that returning to the office late one afternoon to write a feature, he applied his hands to the typewriter keys with such force that firemen had to be fetched to cut them free. It was this same writer who, when later hired as a film critic by another paper, replied to complaints by a film company that he had slept all the way through a preview which he had then reviewed adversely: 'Sleep is a form of criticism.'

A fourth, the late Eric Wainwright, had been a brilliant feature writer in his day but his talents for one reason or another had been allowed to run to seed. These days he pottered into the office in the morning, got a chit signed advancing him a fiver on his expenses, drifted off to Winnie's for a while, and in due course went home. Regarded as something of an office mascot – he had had an eventful war, and these things still counted – Wainwright was tolerated by a succession of features editors. When the time came for him to retire he was given a dinner at the Ritz. While the *Mirror* party was enjoying pre-prandial drinks in the corridor outside the private room, the Queen Mother and her entourage came by on the way to a dinner engagement of their own. From having encountered him at royal command performances, she recognised among our party the *Mirror*'s film critic, Arthur Thirkell, affectionately know as Upper Thirkell, and perhaps imagining vaguely that the awkwardly bowing dinner-jacketed group had been waiting to watch her go by for some reason, she paused for a gracious word. Thirkell, who happened to be talking to Wainwright, thought he had better present him, explaining that this was his retirement party. 'Ah, yes,' beamed the Queen Mother, shaking the bemused Wainwright's hand. 'We shall miss your articles.' No one cared to point out that he had not written a line for over twelve years.

A later arrival on the features scene was the delightful Peter Senn, another eccentric who was straight out of the pages of Anthony Powell, improbably appointed the *Mirror*'s arts correspondent. While he had some difficulty in getting his stories about the latest exhibition into the paper, Peter really did know his stuff and he had built up an impressive private collection of modern pictures. He had led an extremely colourful life and one day, after showing me his paintings, he swept round a hand to accommodate the four walls of his sitting room and confided, 'You know, *mon cher*' – everyone was '*mon cher*' to Peter Senn – 'I'm thinking very seriously about selling all these and commissioning the Royal School of Needlework to make a tapestry of one's life.' 'Like the Bayeux Tapestry?' I enquired, straight-faced. 'Exactly, *mon cher*. Of course, this is a small room and so they could only pick out the highlights.'

With such diverting friends, my early Fleet Street days glided pleasantly by. Gradually I began to get stuff into the paper, although nothing, as that austere Wykehamist, the new chairman, Cecil King, would have put it had he known of my existence, to set the Thames on fire. Eilbeck began to chuck the occasional headline at me – 'DEATH RATTLE OF AN ENGLISH VILLAGE', 'CAN WE AFFORD THE CIVIL SERVANTS' HOLIDAY?', 'TWO PRISONERS IN A WEDDING RING' – and I must have delivered the goods adequately enough since the feature crafted to the headline usually appeared – as well it might have done, for the page to accommodate it would have been designed and made up long before I phoned through my story. I learned to loathe the laconic male copytakers to whom I had to dictate my pieces. Not only did they never laugh at the funny bits, not only did they ruin punchlines with 'Just a sec, change of paper', but after a couple of paragraphs they would enquire yawningly, 'Is there much more of this, old boy?' After that kind of put-down the stuff seemed such dross that I would sooner have crawled along the main drain with my poor little feature clutched in a cleft stick than feed it to the copytakers.

I was not to make my mark on the paper until torrential floods hit the East Coast, when every available journalist on the paper, including even poor little Mary Brown, the agony aunt, who had never covered a news story in her life, was hurtled into the fray. I was despatched to Felixstowe. In those relatively unsophisticated days in news-gathering there was no one co-ordinating the story into one coherent whole – it was up to the sub-editors' table to spot the most graphic account and splash it on the front page. Mine was the one that was to be picked – I had stumbled across a street junction where twenty-eight people including eight children had drowned. With a notebook full of harrowing interviews the story would write itself – all I needed was a telephone that wasn't waterlogged. I found one by wading through three feet of water to a house standing on relatively high ground, and filed my story from the hall standing only ankle-deep in oozing mud.

By the time I had gathered some follow-up material it was too late to get back to London. I dozed at the railway station but was awake in good time for the newspaper train. Impatient with the wholesaler leisurely sorting out the parcels of newsprint, I cut the string on the *Daily Mirror* parcel myself. 'TERROR AT DEATH JUNCTION: From Keith Waterhouse, Felixstowe, Monday.'

In the morning I went straight to the office, where, squelching along the corridor to the newsroom, I encountered Kenneth Hord, the News Editor. He congratulated me tersely – 'Good story', I think, were his only words, but they were enough: Mr Hord's 'Through no fault of your own, you are simply not equipped to be a national newspaper reporter at present' had been rankling all these months. My ears brushing the walls of the corridor, I squelched on, only to be called back. 'By the way, Waterhouse' – I was too junior to possess a first name – 'when you've dried out I should like a memo from you explaining how you came to miss the first edition.'

I was not to dry out: R. J. Eilbeck had had one of his ideas. Among the host of human stories coming out of the floods was one about a pair of newlyweds in Canvey Island, the bride only sixteen, who had spent their wedding night in a schoolroom with other refugees. Eilbeck's instructions to me were to get down to Canvey Island with all speed, find the couple and bring them back to a dream honeymoon on the *Mirror* in the bridal suite of a Park Lane hotel.

He had, of course, already written the headlines. What I didn't know until I reached Canvey Island was that he had also written the newsvendor's bills. Stepping out of my hire car, the first thing I saw was a *Daily Mirror* placard: 'CANVEY COUPLE'S PARK LANE HONEYMOON'. I had yet even to set eyes on the lucky honeymooners.

I located the child bride easily enough at her schoolroom rest centre. Not surprisingly, she was entirely in favour of a luxurious week in London, all expenses paid, but I would have to ask her husband – and he had decided, in the circumstances, that he might as well get back to work and earn some much-needed money. He was a bus conductor. I made my way to the bus station and sought out the senior inspector. A romantic soul, he agreed readily enough to take the young bridegroom's bus out of service as soon as he had completed his route. Time was getting on. I urged him to requisition a double-decker, press-gang a relief conductor, and catch up with the potential honeymooner. This needed more persuasion but on the promise of getting his own and the company's name in the paper, the inspector finally obliged, and the commandeered bus careered through Canvey Island like a fire engine until we caught up with our man.

I got the lucky pair to Park Lane just in time to make the first edition. A *Mirror* photographer was waiting for us, together with a keeper from a private zoo carrying a large cage in which reposed a boa constrictor. It was the photographer's plan to tie the snake in a lover's knot around the honeymoon couple's necks. Why he thought this appropriate I did not bother to ask: I had long ago ceased enquiring into the seething minds of smudgers, as they are known in the trade. In the event, both honeymooners and boa constrictor demurred and he had to make do with a tasteful study of them in bed instead.

The flood saga marked a turning point in my feature-writing career. Eilbeck started to give me big full-page features I could get my teeth into – 'COME OUT OF HIDING, FATHER THOMAS, AND DO RIGHT BY THIS WOMAN' was one startling headline he threw at me. Executives on the paper who had never noticed my existence began to nod to me in corridors. Mercifully they did not include the sinister Cyril Morton with whom I never exchanged a word in all the time he remained on the *Mirror*; but they did include the Editor, Sylvester Bolam, who stopped me in the newsroom and said I seemed to be finding my feet. I had seen Mr Bolam several times without ever realising he was the Editor – I had thought he was a very senior accountant. A dapper figure in a double-breasted suit with a trim moustache and neat spectacles, he looked far removed from the *Mirror*'s sensational headlines – but he was not. Bolam, an economics graduate from Durham University, had made a philosophy out of the uses of sensationalism. He spelled it out in a front-page manifesto:

The Mirror is a sensational newspaper. We make no apology for that. We believe in the sensational presentation of news and views, especially important news and views, as a necessary and valuable public service in these days of mass readership and democratic responsibility.

Sensationalism does not mean distorting the truth. It means the vivid and dramatic presentation of events so as to give them a forceful impact on the mind of the reader. It means big headlines, vigorous writing, simplification into familiar everyday language, and the wide use of illustration by cartoon and photograph . . .

Every great problem facing us – the world economic crisis, diminishing food supplies, the population puzzle, the Iron Curtain and a host of others – will only be understood by the ordinary man busy with his daily tasks if he is hit hard and hit often with the facts . . .

Bolam's words, reprinted in Hugh Cudlipp's *Publish and Be Damned*, made a deep impression upon me. I was beginning to understand the *Daily Mirror*.

It was Mr Bolam, I learned, who instigated my first foreign assignment, Jimmy Eilbeck's words on the subject being, 'The Editor has specially asked for you on this one, so don't fuck it up.' The impression I got was that had it been left to Eilbeck he would not have entrusted me with the story. The assignment was to take myself off to the tiny Danish island of Bornholm in the Baltic, where Polish refugees were crossing daily from the port of Gdansk on pedalos. That seemed straightforward enough, but Eilbeck being Eilbeck, there was more. 'You might as well spend a day or two in Copenhagen on your way back and pick up a feature there,' he said. By way of briefing he scrawled a headline on his make-up pad: 'WONDERFUL COPENHAGEN'.

It was not only my first foreign assignment but the first time I had ever been out of the country, indeed the first time I had ever been in an aeroplane, not counting a couple of perilous trips in a Tiger Moth to cover the annual snowing-up of the Yorkshire Dales. I was more excited by the experience than by the story, my first big news feature. Indeed, beyond a hazy memory of the genial Governor of the island pouring aquavit down my throat during a convivial lunch, I have no recollection of pulling the story together at all, although I suppose I must have done it to Eilbeck's satisfaction since when I arrived back in Copenhagen my first ever congratulatory 'herogram' awaited me. What I do remember is savouring the smell of wood smoke and the tang of cold beer and the taste of soused herrings as I sat in the tiny town square with my new friends from the local *Tidende*, and thinking that if this was abroad I wanted a great deal more of it.

One half of my mission accomplished, I rejoined the chugging ferry boat across to Copenhagen where I was to spend a day and a half dredging up something to fit Eilbeck's preposterous headline, 'WONDERFUL COPENHAGEN', which he had plucked from a song sung by Danny Kaye. My brief seemed so wide as to be completely without horizons, and I was at a loss to know how to begin. I need not have worried. A call to the *Mirror*'s stringer who worked on *Politiken*, and before long I was joined at my outdoor café table by half that newspaper's features staff, all of whom seemed to be beautiful ash-blondes. Between them they prattled enough 'Wonderful Copenhagen' froth to fill a notebook, and for the rest of the evening I was able to relax, sip beer, watch the yellow trams go by and become half mesmerised by the dancing neon signs – Piccadilly Circus with funny accents. Although I was hauled off to the Tivoli pleasure gardens, which put Battersea in the shade right enough, I would just as soon have stayed looking at the trams. How exotically foreign they looked, these two-carriage single-deckers plastered with advertisements for Carlsberg and Skol and Marlboro Lites and brands I had never heard of. The only blot literally on the horizon was a rooftop sign for Guinness – a reminder of home I did not want. The foreign bug had bitten me so deeply that there skimmed through my mind the notion of learning Danish and coming over to join the bevy of blonde beauties on *Politiken*. Eilbeck could not have thought of a better headline: Copenhagen really was wonderful. But I expect I should have thought exactly the same about Oslo.

I was so ignorant about the ins and outs of foreign travel that I had no idea I was allowed to take my unused currency home with me, so that upon checking out of the Kong Frederik Hotel the next day I caused something of a stir among an eager throng of lift attendants, bell-boys and commissionaires by distributing kroner by the fistful as if it were Maundy money. Only when I found I had not enough cash left to pay the taxi to the airport – I had to augment the fare with English pound notes – did it cross my mind that I might have got my currency regulations a little confused. Never mind: I would learn; and with any luck I should find myself from now on dropping in on foreign parts as often for the *Daily Mirror* as I had until recently been accustomed to dropping in on Wharfedale villages for the *Yorkshire Evening Post*.

Not quite; but often enough to refuel my wanderlust. My next sortie abroad, I believe, was by way of a perk for services rendered – a 'press facility' trip, or free jaunt, to Venice for some European film premiere or other. Since I was not the film critic, and Eilbeck had failed to come up with the Venetian equivalent of his 'WONDERFUL COPENHAGEN', there was nothing whatever for me to do on this outing except follow the examples of my colleagues and get progressively more drunk from the moment the aeroplane left the ground. Thus the magic of Venice was consistently out of focus; yet the blurred snapshots remained vivid enough in my mind to hook me on that shimmering lagoon for the rest of my life. Oddly enough, whenever I go back there my first reaction is not the indrawn breath of wonder as the motor launch brings that first spray-drenched Canaletto panorama into view but the chill of dismay as I contemplate what they might have done to it – what, indeed, they would have done to it had Venice stood on the Leeds and Liverpool Canal instead of where it does. On my last evening, still not completely convinced that one could take foreign money home with one despite the assurances of my much-travelled friends, I bought a toy vendor's entire stock of little clockwork men on the Piazza San Marco and, inspired by a *New Yorker* cartoon, gave them their freedom and allowed them to march like lemmings into the Grand Canal.

After that frivolity, my next foreign task was a serious one, and an impressively long way to go: to Jordan, for the coronation of King Hussein of the Hashemite Kingdom. Here again, the assignment was straightforward enough – after all, if I had not yet covered a coronation (the young Queen Elizabeth's was still a month away), I had acquitted myself well on the Royal Thanksgiving Service for the Festival of Britain, and no doubt I should find a Muslim equivalent of the helpful St Paul's Cathedral virger to mark my card.

I reckoned, of course, without Jimmy Eilbeck and his make-up pad. Looking up from one of the American tabloids on which he was hooked, the *National Enquirer* or some such, he scrawled not across one page but across two, and in bigger lettering than usual, 'THE TRIAL OF JESUS CHRIST'.

I stared at the headline. 'Good yarn,' I thought I had better say – Eilbeck did not like what he called a negative reaction – and waited for elucidation. It seemed – the authority was Eilbeck's scandal sheet – that a group of American Hebraic scholars were travelling to the Jewish half of Jerusalem (then a divided city) with the object of staging a new trial for Jesus Christ at which, given that this time he would be properly represented, with reputable witnesses for the defence and a proper jury, the verdict would hopefully be an acquittal.

It was, as I had said, a good yarn – if there was a grain of truth in it. At least it would give me a trip to Israel. But while vague on Middle Eastern politics I was aware, even if Eilbeck wasn't – he did not over-burden himself with detail – that to get there from Jordan it would be better, as the Irish joke has it, to start from somewhere else. To begin with, I would not be allowed into Jordan with an Israeli visa in my passport, nor vice versa: I should have to acquire a second passport. Then, as a word with the foreign desk confirmed, it was easier to get into the sealed port of Vladivostok than to cross through the Mandelbaum Gate from the Jordanian sector of Jerusalem into the Israeli sector. I should have to fly from Amman to the Lebanon, get a boat across to Cyprus, fly from Nicosia to Tel Aviv, and then get myself by whatever means across to Jerusalem. All this was a totally new world to me, and somewhat of a change from working out the Leeds to Ilkley bus timetables. But I was not going to bother my features editor with these details – or, more importantly, with telling him the extra cost of all this shuttling around the Mediterranean. Even to a seasoned traveller with both a Danish and an Italian stamp in his passport – or, as of later that afternoon, in one of his passports – it was the expedition of a lifetime. Twenty-four hours later, in my new lightweight suit from Altman's tropical outfitters on Cambridge Circus, and with the New Testament among my file of background clippings, I was on my way.

Amman, hot and noisy and smelling of roast kid and Turkish coffee, put me in mind of what a one-horse Wild West township must have looked like in the transition from Gold Rush to Sinclair Lewis's Main Street. As was becoming usual with my widening acquaintanceship with foreign cities – three of them to date – I was entranced by the captivating unfamiliarity of it all. Inexperienced traveller though I was, I could see that Jordan's capital would never figure in anyone's list of the world's top ten places to visit, but that did not worry me a bit; nor has it ever when I have been to even more unprepossessing spots, with the possible exception of Wellington, New Zealand, where I found the North Island so boring and Sussex-like that I took the ferry to the South Island, and found that so boring and Surrey-like that I took the next ferry back again. Usually, so long as the place I fetch up in is palpably different from the place I left behind, I am well content.

Checking in at the Philadelphia Hotel, whose whirring overhead fans and tiled floors and bell-boys in their kaftans and red fezzes made it agreeably like a location for Humphrey Bogart's *Casablanca*, I was naïvely surprised to find the long, cool bar full of journalists, including some grizzled foreign correspondents of the 'old hand' persuasion. Apart from my opposite numbers on the *Yorkshire Evening News* I had never been on a story where I had had to work against the opposition, but here they were in force, and all of them looking unnervingly as if they knew something I didn't know. The old hands, though, were kindness itself and briefed me on the coronation arrangements. Eilbeck had told me to get an interview with King Hussein as a curtain-raiser for the big day, and I had been fretting over how to go about getting it fixed up. To my relief, he turned out to be giving a press conference at one of his four royal palaces. All I had to do was sharpen my pencil and be sure to turn up at the right palace. The fact that my 'interview' was in the presence of thirty or forty other hacks did not inhibit me from peppering my story with 'The King told me' and '. . . confided King Hussein'.

On my way to the Cable and Wireless office to file my story (and that was another thrill: composing for the first time in cablese, mugged up from old Western Union chestnuts culled from my well-thumbed library of Fleet Street reminiscences: 'GAME UNWORTH CANDLE, UPSTICK JOB', and the foreign editor's query 'HOW OLD NEHRU QUERY' to which the reply was 'OLD NEHRU FINE, HOW YOU QUERY') I bumped into one of the sun-baked old hands who had picked up a cable for me. Obviously he had read it before it had gone into its envelope, for he gave me a quizzical look as he handed it over. But however long he may have been in the game he could not have made much of it. It read simply and starkly: 'KILL JESUS CHRIST – EILBECK'. What this meant was that the Trial of Christ story had fallen through – no great surprise. I should sooner, however, have found that out for myself. Deprived of my circuitous trip to the Israeli side of Jerusalem, I took a cab to the Jordanian side by way of consolation. I found myself chillingly unmoved by the treasure-laden Church of the Holy Sepulchre but thoroughly at home in the warren of little crook-backed lanes which reminded me of Leeds Kirkgate Market crossed – for my architectural comparisons were now becoming cosmopolitan – with the alleys of Venice.

The coronation itself evoked little interest in the Western press, particularly since we were not permitted to be present at the Muslim ceremony, and I devoted the rest of a pleasantly restful stay to propping up the bar of the Philadelphia listening avidly to my journalistic elders and betters telling their tall stories.

Back in London, I was feeling no end of a foreign correspondent until buttonholed by Eilbeck, who asked: 'Did you bring anything back?' What he meant was that having spent an expensive week in distant latitudes getting one single story, and my other story having come to nothing, no doubt I had busied myself looking around for something else worth writing about. Green as I still was, the thought had not for a second occurred to me: certainly, upon returning from the Dales after interviewing, say, a talking dog that played dominoes, I had never been asked if I had found a singing cat into the bargain. And so when R. J. Eilbeck asked if I had brought anything back I misunderstood him.

'Oh, just some cigarettes and a camel saddle,' I said. As Eilbeck smiled thinly and went about his business, I belatedly realised what he had meant – not that it would have done me any good. I glumly reflected that it would be a long time before I was sent on a foreign assignment again.

5   Meanwhile, interesting things were happening at the *Daily Mirror*, the principal of which was the return of Hugh Cudlipp to the fold after a couple of years in exile at the *Sunday Express*. I had heard of Hugh Cudlipp, and not only because among legions of managing editors he had once sent his regrets that he was unable to offer me a job. Everyone in journalism, and a good many out of it, had heard of Hugh Cudlipp. The word legend is lightly tossed around in Fleet Street but Cudlipp's career truly was legendary. The youngest of three brothers, all of whom became national newspaper editors, he had started his career on the *Penarth News*, Glamorgan, at fourteen, becoming Features Editor of the *Sunday Chronicle* at nineteen, Features Editor of the *Daily Mirror* at twenty-two, and Editor of the *Sunday Pictorial* at twenty-four – a record that left even the youthful Jimmy Eilbeck looking like one of yesterday's men.

After some difference of opinion with the then Chairman, the brilliant but boozy Harry Guy Bartholomew, Cudlipp had banished himself to the *Sunday Express*. But now Bartholomew himself was deposed, Cecil Harmsworth King was running the show, and he had brought Cudlipp back as Editorial Director both of the *Daily Mirror* and the *Sunday Pictorial*.

There were other changes, either roughly coincidental with or consequent upon the Cudlipp arrival. Sylvester Bolam retired in ill-health and was replaced as Editor by the tetchy Jack Nener. Eilbeck, who was rumoured to have wanted the job himself, became Assistant Editor, but impatience rendering him prone to extreme fits of temperament he was in due course despatched across the river to the ramshackle warehouse building in Stamford Street where a curious offshoot of the *Mirror* empire known as *Reveille* was produced, with instructions to convert one of his outlandish ideas into reality – a woman's weekly newspaper to be called *Woman's Sunday Mirror*. Where all this left me I had yet to see.

Cudlipp's presence was immediately felt – and seen. Usually wearing an electric-blue suit, he would appear in the newsroom some time after lunch, head thrust challengingly forward like that of an enquiring tortoise, teeth clamped on an outsize cigar, as he dissected and improved upon news and features pages alike, in a normally amused voice that seemed to be forced down his nostrils without becoming nasal in the process. It was a striking performance and soon the more impressionable souls among the executives were copying the Cudlipp suit and the Cudlipp stance and the Cudlipp manner of speech – in at least one case with such diligence that when an upwardly aspiring sub-editor tried to talk forcefully down his nose, gobs of snottle appeared on his upper lip.

Marshall Pugh was particularly taken by the re-emergence of Hugh Cudlipp. Cudlipp was known to own a boat, a Channel-hopping cruiser. This, in Pugh's eyes, made him an outdoor man. Mac Pugh himself was an outdoor man, much preoccupied with rucksacks and dubbined boots, who on occasional – too occasional for his liking – Saturdays managed to get a tramping or rock-climbing feature into the paper under the rugged pseudonym of Grant Scrymgeour. With an outdoor man at the helm, so Pugh hoped, a regular Grant Scrymgeour column, a page even, was a distinct possibility.

These hopes were put to the test at a welcome-back lunch for Cudlipp held by the features department at some now defunct Soho restaurant. I remember it mainly for a kindness shown to me by the gruff Jack Nener, next to whom, rather to my surprise since I was still very low down on the totem pole, I found myself sitting. Considering that I was supposed by now to be a seasoned journalist, I was still in many ways remarkably gauche – a word which, had I then been required to pronounce it, I would have made to sound like something reminiscent of a Spanish American cowboy. So when the waiter came round towards the end of the meal to take liqueur orders, I asked in my confusion for a Drambuie, the only drink in that class I could think of. Jack Nener growled in my ear, 'You don't want that, you silly bugger. Tell him to get you a fucking brandy.' I was very grateful to my etiquette adviser.

But what should have stuck more prominently in my mind, since it was to have important repercussions, was Hugh Cudlipp's opening sentence as he rose to speak. 'Gentlemen,' he decisively announced (Nener having arranged the lunch, there were no ladies present), 'there are too many bloody tent pegs in this paper.' Marshall Pugh's face fell, and the hopes of Grant Scrymgeour were dashed.

In direct consequence of this edict, Mac Pugh decided that his destiny perhaps lay elsewhere than with the Cudlipp-led *Mirror*, and he left to embark on a successful freelance career. Meanwhile a replacement for the excitable R. J. Eilbeck had been brought in by Cudlipp – Eilbeck's equivalent in lankiness but his opposite in temperament, the equable Mike Randall from the Kelmsley newspapers, a future editor of the *News Chronicle* and of the *Daily Mail* (and to whom, when the latter absorbed the former and Randall asked her what she thought of the merger, Lady Violet Bonham-Carter, a *News Chronicle* trustee, said, 'Ah, Mr Randall, to absorb! The quality of the very best blotting paper!'). With Mac Pugh's departure, Mike Randall called me in and told me that I was to be his successor as senior feature writer, although I was to keep it to myself in case of bad feeling among the others, all of whom were senior to me. With my salary doubled, I was prepared to carry the secret to the grave.

I was given a small office – the same cubicle, as it happened, from which R. J. Eilbeck had once thrown off his manic, scribbled headlines – which I shared with Michael King, the diplomatic correspondent, who on such an egalatarian paper overcame the double disadvantage of an Eton education and being the Chairman's son with pleasant imperturbability.

Without anything being said on either side, I reached an arrangement with the easy-going Mike Randall. So long as I was reasonably on tap to write the big feature from time to time, or to fill a hole in the paper in an emergency, I was to be left pretty well to my own devices – no more distracting dashes to Wolverhampton or Sheffield to try to match a feature to a headline by 4 p.m. Michael King was out most of the time – the diplomatic correspondent's day started with the Foreign Office press conference in the morning, followed by bar billiards at Winnie's until closing time ('Should anyone want me, say I've been called to No. 10,' he would tell the news desk secretary ambiguously), followed by tea in St James's clubs with mysterious contacts – and so I had our little office pretty well to myself. I started a novel.

In practice, most of the work that came my way emanated from the fertile mind of Hugh Cudlipp. While Jack Nener remained technically Editor, that was exactly what he was – technically Editor, looking after the engine room and giving the crew their orders while Cudlipp, with a wave of his cigar, took the wheel as mood or inspiration decided.

From time to time I would be called up from my little cubbyhole to join him for the 'elevenses' – a glass of wine or something stronger – that would embark me upon some journalistic spree. I was despatched down a Welsh coal mine as a focal point for examining a fuel crisis. I was sent aboard a banana boat in Liverpool Docks to investigate 'the screwiest strike of all time' – a demarcation dispute over whether the screwholes in a piece of aluminium-covered wood should be bored by metal workers or carpenters – 'and meanwhile the bananas are still on the trees.' From such trenchant pieces evolved a whole series of what Cudlipp called signed leaders – strong, critical front-page stuff which while highly self-opinionated nevertheless reflected the *Mirror*'s preoccupations of the day. Attacking 'the prigs, prudes and preachers of stuffiness', I asked, 'How Long Must the Day of Rest Remain the Day of Rust?' I exposed the Queen's circle of friends and advisers as 'the same old men in new beards' and suggested that the Royals were losing themselves in 'a wilderness of whiskers'. When there was no particular target to attack, there was always the *Mirror*'s mantra: 'We are too damn smug. Too damn stuffy. Too damn snobbish.' It was all rollicking, if over-alliterative, good fun and a shot in the arm both for me and the *Daily Mirror*.

One small pleasure of these personalised editorials, which I had to sub-edit into the paper myself, was that they got me down into the hallowed case-room, the clanking heart of any newspaper in those hot-metal days. There, with the linotype machines shuttling away like looms and, in their inky aprons, the stonehands – the men who made up the pages – casting off damp galley proofs before their slabs of type were locked into their formes to be impressed into the papier mâché flongs, like flattened-out egg-boxes or condemned asbestos tiles, which in turn impressed the metal plates from which the newspaper was actually printed, I really did feel myself in a factory town, and I always thrilled to the strident bell that was the signal for the presses to start rolling – the equivalent of a woollen mill hooter.

On my first day down on the stone, as the smooth bench on which the slugs of type were assembled into columns and then pages was called, although it was no longer made of stone but of steel, I came close to becoming what I suppose would have gone into the records as an industrial accident. Very near to edition time, I could see from the page proof that the printer had pulled for me that my piece was four lines over length. I could also see the very four-line paragraph that would lift straight out to make it fit. Not wishing to trouble anyone, for in these last vital minutes the case-room was seething with activity, I reached out to remove the four superfluous slugs from the bank of type on the stone before me. Before my fingers could reach them, a heavy metal rule – literally a rod of iron – came smashing down on to the stone, missing my hand by millimetres. A fraction of an inch nearer and I should have been staring down at a bloody pulp. As much silence as could be mustered amid the clamour of machinery fell over the case-room. All work stopped. 'Never touch metal again, lad,' warned the hitherto amiable printer, laying down his heavy ruler like a schoolmaster putting aside his cane. It was a lesson in Fleet Street demarcation that made the Liverpool docks dispute seem like a friendly tussle. Had I been less star-struck I could have extrapolated out of the incident the end of hot-metal newspaper production. Romantically, I reflected only that printers, compositors and their ilk were proud craftsmen. They were, but their pride came before a fall engineered by kindred but lesser trades who were paid more than they were for gumming labels on parcels or tying string.

My signed leaders also got me on some interesting foreign assignments. One such, at the height of the Cyprus troubles, was to fly out to Nicosia, interview the Governor, Sir John Harding, and the troublesome Greek leader Archbishop Makarios, and propose across pages one and two 'CYPRUS: STOP THIS BLOODSHED NOW'. My visit coincided with a fresh outburst of the bloodshed I had been condemning, with the result that I had to spend the next month filing day-to-day news stories from Cyprus. This, in newspaper terms, was more than enough to endorse me as something of an expert on Cypriot affairs, so that over the next year or so, whenever trouble flared in the area, I was whisked back to Nicosia to set myself up as some species of foreign correspondent and swop yarns with cronies at the bar of the Ledra Palace Hotel.

I coped with this well enough, blotting my copy-book only once, and that was one night when my friend Denis Pitts of the *Daily*

Herald wanted to go over to Famagusta for some reason, and I agreed to cover for him. That evening there was a particularly nasty shooting of some British soldiers in Ledra Street – 'Murder Mile' as we had dubbed it – and in accordance with my promise I cabled a dramatic despatch to the *Herald* in Pitts's name. Unfortunately, in all the excitement, I quite forgot to file a report to my own paper. Thus, in the early hours, I was awakened with the cable that every foreign correspondent dreads: 'BADLY BEATEN HERALD – WHY YOU UNSEND QUERY'. Oddly enough, this shameful lapse seemed to raise rather than lower my stock among my colleagues.

After the Cyprus interlude I felt emboldened enough to start venturing into El Vino from time to time. While my occasional half-apologetic entrance attracted hostile stares from the mottle-faced, port-tippling elders of the place, I could reasonably depend on a friendly face or two.

El Vino, or El Vino's as it is often known, has changed little over the years except in that it is now more accommodating to women, and its waitresses wear pert uniforms like the old Lyons tea-shop nippies. The long front bar looks like a small Dublin pub, the back room like a Woking tea shop. It has a generally mahogany air and is agreeably smoky.

At the time I started using it, El Vino was dominated by crime reporters, who congregated in a scrum by the door, about half a dozen of them, knocking back large Scotches at the Victorian-looking cash desk which is an extension of the bar. They were all big, burly men in thick navy-blue overcoats which they seemed to wear all through summer. They looked like policemen, which, indeed, several of them had been before switching from gamekeeper to poacher. Certainly, when they were entertaining a detective-sergeant or two, which they did frequently, it was impossible to tell one from the other. Outsiders were not welcome in their company. If one went in very early, just after opening time, the one or two crime reporters already in residence might deign to greet one and stand, or more likely be stood, a drink or two; but as soon as reinforcements arrived in the way of the heavy mob from the *News of the World*, the *Star*, and the *Daily Herald*, they would close ranks.

One could listen, though. The crime reporters' talk was exclusively about crime – they allowed of no other topic – and the crime was usually murder; if not murder, then a felony serious enough to warrant a sentence of twenty years or more. They spoke in police-cockney jargon – murderers were topped, villains had their collars felt, suspects whose names they didn't want to reveal in public were known as Chummy. The crime reporters remembered all the classic murders, or claimed to: Buck Ruxton, Major Armstrong, Thompson and Bywaters, Stoner and Rattenbury. If they could not quite recall the Brides in the Bath and Doctor Crippen, they knew old-timers who could.

The crime reporters were then Fleet Street's kings of the castle. Their star waned with the abolition of hanging, which coincided with the rise and rise of the rival popular attraction of television. Thereafter the showbiz writers became the stars. But the crime reporters, reminiscing and ruminating about torsos in trunks and severed heads in hat-boxes, did not cease to block the doorway of El Vino.

El Vino is probably the only Fleet Street institution truly missed by journalists decanted to Canary Wharf and such outposts. It was a clearing-house for gossip – it was impossible to spend half an hour in the place without picking up a rumour or two – and a useful job centre for those who were thinking of making a move from one paper to another. It was also a most useful depository of current affairs. There is now nowhere where a literary editor may pick the brains of an opera critic, or an opera critic those of a political correspondent. Or where, come to that, one may expect to be enthralled by the clue of the single matchstick that brought John Robinson to justice in the case of the Charing Cross trunk murder.

To anyone at all Fleet Street-struck, El Vino was a siren sort of place and the Press Club even more so, and I had probably begun to spend far too much time in both – though much less in the Press Club than some I could have named, who, after a late-night subbing shift when they were entitled to a cab home, had been known to drop in for a packet of cigarettes and perhaps one very quick Scotch, and keep the taxi ticking away until three in the morning. What their wives had to say was not known, for wives were never seen in Fleet Street. Many of them must have been resigned to what were known as 'Petts Wood marriages' – so called after the large number of newspaper widows who lived out in this Kent suburb, recommended in Fleet Street for the all-night

291

train service it afforded sub-editors and reporters coming off late duty, thus giving them a round-the-clock, heaven-sent excuse for one more for the road.

The Petts Wood marriage could work exceedingly well. It was an often surprisingly amicable arrangement by which the wife, getting on with her own life, never expected to see her husband sober, or during waking hours at all, except at weekends, when for forty-eight hours the five-day roisterer would throw himself into a reverse Jekyll and Hyde transformation, meekly doing the gardening, putting up shelves and playing with the children.

There were many legends about Petts Wood marriages, perhaps the most oft-told, in its many versions, being the one about the well-oiled sub-editor who threw up in a mini-cab on his way home from the Press Club. Ejected by the enraged driver on a deserted country road, the only thing for it was to stagger on until he came to a telephone box and ring his wife to come to the rescue. The wife, aroused from slumber, flung a raincoat over her nightdress, got the car out of the garage and drove off to pick up her drunken husband, who climbed into the passenger seat and himself promptly fell asleep. No sooner had the wife set course for home than she felt what is always known in these stories – there are many of them on the same theme – as 'a call of nature'. Pulling up, she disappeared behind a convenient hedge. The husband, awaking with a start, found himself sitting in his own car, which in his befuddlement he imagined he must have been driving home from the Press Club when overtaken by tiredness. He slipped over into the driving seat and continued his journey. As his tail-lights disappeared over the black horizon, his wife, wearing nothing but her raincoat and nightdress (longer versions have her by now wearing only the nightdress, and a Baby Doll nightdress at that), re-emerged from behind the hedge . . .

I was never in the Petts Wood class myself but I was something of an absentee husband, as were perhaps the great majority of true newspapermen with ink in their veins. To go home before the first editions were 'up' – distributed throughout the editorial floor – was like leaving a party before anyone else had arrived. It was noticeable, too, that most of those who did go home punctually, who treated the job like a nine-to-five sinecure, were themselves nine-to-five people who missed the whole glorious, utterly pointless point of what newspapers were all about and would have been just as much in their element working for the post office.

Accordingly, and taking into account my by now quite frequent jaunts to foreign parts, I was seeing much less of my wife than in my evening paper days when I was in the habit of getting home by four or five. But we did manage some species of social life. We had by this time moved from unsalubrious Forest Hill to an Edwardian mansion block in Stamford Brook on the District Line (literally so: it was next door to the tube station, and in the best tradition of Ealing Studios four stops up the line, the pictures on the wall shook when the trains went by). This was courtesy of Mac Pugh, who had bequeathed the flat to us upon vacating Stamford Brook for the enviable King's Road. The Pughs had become family friends, as had the Bakers, Douglas Warth, who always came alone because he had acquired a mistress whom the wives refused to entertain, and the Guy Deghys, Guy being my Hungarian friend, the former BBC North radio producer who had returned to London and to acting, and who now enhanced his raffish reputation by taking a third wife, a beautiful Australian actress called Mari. With two beard-wearers among us we considered ourselves a Bohemian crowd, much given to sitting around on one another's floors, drinking beer or cider, eating paella and talking about books. We all read avidly and acted as a circulating library among ourselves – Orwell, Graham Greene, Henry Green, Angus Wilson, Gwyn Thomas, Dylan Thomas, Peter de Vries were among those passed around and their merits argued over. We went occasionally to see art-house films, most of which in retrospect seem to have been *The Wages of Fear* or *Bicycle Thieves*, and argued over them too, in small Spanish restaurants with chequered tablecloths and candles in wine bottles.

This all so matched my Chelsea-garret fantasies of London and was in such contrast to the brashness of the *Mirror* that I began to wonder in which world I really belonged, or whether I belonged in both. It was to be a long time before the question would be resolved – the answer being that it never would be. However long I have stayed away from newspapers – and it has never been for any great stretch – I have never lost that twitching of the nostrils and quickening of the pulse that afflicts all newspaper people when something is happening, however far away they may be from the story and however long ago they last clutched a reporter's notebook. Old fire-horses put out to grass, it is said, would prick up their ears, crash the gate and gallop off to the scene of the conflagration when they heard the distant ringing of fire-bells.

But life on the *Mirror*, if it could never become a routine, was becoming a habit, and I was growing restless. People came and went all the time, and that was unsettling in itself. Various writers departed, to join other papers, to go into public relations, to try their arm in television, one to start up his own newspaper in Wales, one to write popular histories, one to travel the world. Most enviably, Peter Baker was posted to Paris – a plum job marred only by his discovery, upon arrival, that the bureau chief of the day had a tendency to hog the newspapers to himself so that his new deputy had no idea what was going on. Frustrated, Baker complained to London to such strenuous effect that Jack Nener himself flew over to Paris to sort out the difficulty. Asked to explain in his own words what the trouble was, it dawned upon Baker that in terms of *One-Upmanship* (another new book we had avidly passed around) he had made a great tactical error when he heard himself bleating, 'He won't let me read the papers!' Nener delivered the Solomon judgment, 'Then for Christ's sake order two fucking sets!', and returned to London. Baker himself shortly afterwards departed for the *Daily Express*.

R. J. Eilbeck, too, severed his connection with the Mirror group – the story was that he had resigned in a pet after having been refused the company Rolls-Royce to which he felt entitled after the successful launch of his *Woman's Sunday Mirror*. He now embarked on his last and maddest venture – a late-night or early-morning newspaper called the *Mayfair Moon*, to be distributed exclusively in the nightclubs of the period such as Ziggy's and the Pigalle, which would consist entirely of high-life gossip and would cost ten shillings a copy. The *Mayfair Moon* lasted, I believe, two issues. Eilbeck, his capital gone but his head still swimming with ideas, took to hanging around Winnie's and cashing cheques, drawn up on white nightclub forms usually only seen by a head waiter's torchlight, for pathetically small sums. Most of the feature writers of Eilbeck's vintage would have been in possession of one of his nightclub cheques by way of a souvenir – no one ever tried to cash one – by the time he took himself out to Stratford East and died under a tube train. He was still only twenty-nine.

Someone I had never met on the *Mirror*, nor had any particular wish to meet, was the Chairman, Cecil Harmsworth King, a patrician and remote personage, both figuratively and physically, since he towered above everyone else in the building. In some effort, apparently, to unbend a little and get to know some of his staff, he had given a series of Christmas parties in his office at which, however, he spoke to nobody except his most senior executives. In the case of the features department this was not altogether surprising, since to a writer we turned up more or less drunk, having been celebrating at a lesser altitude earlier. King's expression as someone tapped out his pipe in a valuable Chinese vase distinctly said, 'Never again!' Some years later I was to see exactly the same look on the face of the Duke of Edinburgh when, as a softener to prepare them for a big increase in the Civil List, hordes of journalists were invited to roam Buckingham Palace swigging the royal whisky.

Thus I was very surprised one afternoon to be told that Cecil King wished to see me. I went up to the top floor in puzzlement rather than trepidation – he was too elevated to fire anyone under the rank of editorial director (in the event, the editorial director was to fire him, but that is another story), and in a fallow period I had written nothing against which he might be expected to have taken exception. I was ushered into his enormous panelled office with its Adam fireplace and real coal fire (the coal was brought up in the executive lift), where he sat writing at what looked like, and indeed probably was, the most valuable piece of furniture between the Inns of Court and St Paul's Cathedral. I stood before his desk thinking of all the film characters I had seen – Alec Guinness, Mervyn Johns, Charles Laughton – standing meekly in front of imposing desks while their employers signed letters, ignoring their presence. It seemed a petty affectation for such a giant of Fleet Street as Cecil Harmsworth King, Northcliffe's nephew, but perhaps he really did want to catch the afternoon post.

Presently he looked up, and without preamble, or inviting me to sit down, asked abruptly, 'Do you read *Reveille*? What do you make of it?' *Reveille*, which he pronounced to rhyme with jelly, was, or had been in its heyday, a hugely successful downmarket paper, originally aimed at the armed forces, full of cartoons, pin-ups, news snippets and bizarre headlines such as 'SHARPENS HIS RAZOR BLADES ON PYRAMIDS' – the latter-day equivalent, in fact, of Uncle Northcliffe's *Answers*. I had no idea why King had asked me the question – perhaps he wanted me to go and work on the wretched paper. I stammered some clever-clever answer to the effect that if *Reveille* had not existed it would not be necessary to invent it. Not a whisper of a smile crossed his face. He continued: 'And what do you make of the *Daily Sketch*?' – the *Mirror*'s pale imitator of the day, recently converted from the *Daily Graphic*, and branded by Hugh Cudlipp as 'The only carbon copy that costs more than the original'. I could not match that but, the Editor of the *Daily Sketch* having recently called me in to offer me a post I did not want at less than the *Mirror* were paying me, I did feel moved to offer a spirited summary of that paper's failings. King took me through most of the titles in Fleet Street, and at the conclusion of my interrogation, the responses to which I had decided had better rely for their effect on brevity rather than wit, leaned forward like an assize court judge about to sum up, and indeed did sum up. 'Ten years from now,' pronounced Cecil King, 'there will be three national dailies left in Fleet Street – *The Times*, the *Daily Mail* and the *Daily Mirror*.' Forty years later, Rupert Murdoch was making exactly the same prediction, but with the *Sun* substituting for the *Mirror*. When Cecil Harmsworth King died, his prophecy long expired, his obituary appeared in more national newspapers than had existed when he had originally made it.

That was the end of the interview. 'Well, I just wanted to look at you,' said King, and returned to his paper-signing, leaving me to find my own way out of the office. There had been no handshakes. It was mystifying. Back in my own little cubicle, I asked Cecil King's son Michael, who was drinking tea and reading the *Evening Standard* while waiting for Winnie's to open, what it could all have been about. Michael confided, but mysteriously: 'He's always on the lookout for high-fliers. He must have his eye on you.'

It was the first and last time I ever spoke to Cecil King, so perhaps I had failed my high-flying aptitude test. Or perhaps I had passed it. I would never know.

I continued, however, to fulfil my role as the *Mirror*'s bright spark, on hand for either the bread or the circuses with which Hugh Cudlipp, with his unerring instinct, alternately filled the paper. Cudlipp had a penchant for enlivening the paper with lighthearted stunts after a bout of editorial seriousness, whereby an important series on, say, the state of the health service would be followed by a nationwide search for Britain's Most Glamorous Granny or by a Beautiful Barmaids' Ball, held at the Lyceum, when many of the beautiful barmaids were wretchedly sick from unaccustomed champagne. One week I would be ghosting articles on the state of the Soviet Union by Harold Wilson, the next I was off on a tour of half a dozen European holiday resorts where I was supposed to disguise myself as a waiter, a gondolier, a beach attendant and so on and report on the English Abroad as they sampled the new package holidays.

One serious contribution of mine was a series on what was then called the colour bar. This was immediately followed by a wonderful Cudlipp circus, the *Daily Mirror* Dog Show – a Cruft's for the common people, held at Battersea Park but a bone's throw from the Battersea Dogs' Home, at which all the prizes went to mongrels and pooches of one kind or another – the Dog with the Waggliest Tail, the Spottiest Dog, and so on. It fell to me to write that one up too.

My story started, 'It was the spottiest, dottiest, doggiest day of the year at the *Daily Mirror* Pet Dog Parade on Saturday. Forty-two thousand people and 500 dogs thronged London's Festival Gardens and – by Dog! they had fun . . .'

It was not quite like that. The 42,000 spectators and 500 dogs of indeterminate breed were augmented by two or three bands, a clutch of celebrities – Abbott and Costello, Ted Ray, some now forgotten Rank starlets and television personalities, and an American singer in the heart-throb mould who was appearing at the Palladium, Guy Mitchell; plus a horde of gate-crashing teenagers waving autograph books. There was also a large contingent of blind people, with their guide dogs, and they happened to be promenading around the parade ring at the moment when Guy Mitchell's managers or minders chose to release their idol into the multitude. Spotting him across the arena, an onslaught of screaming teenagers and yelling women fans, including many dog owners whose pets escaped their control in the excitement, stampeded across the parade ring in the path of the blind guests and their guide dogs, a good number of which also became separated from their owners. A marching band, scheduled to parade in the arena to herald the arrival of the VIPs, did not pause to revise its instructions but marched straight into the mêlée. The park epicentre was by now reduced to a seething mob of autograph hunters, celebrities, loose dogs, blind people and bandsmen beating down stray mongrels with their drumsticks and trombones. Cecil Harmsworth King, observing the chaos from a deckchair, was heard to comment: 'I've seen crowds panicking in West Africa and this crowd is panicking.' He then departed the scene by fast motor boat. It was left to Jack Nener to identify the source of the trouble. Elbowing his way through the crowds

297

and shaking off the dogs snapping at his ankles, he made his way unerringly towards the guest star and seized him by the arm. Since he spoke in a grating undertone, only the nearest two or three hundred people could have heard him request of Guy Mitchell: 'Would you do us all a great favour and fuck off?'

Order was restored. 'The people got mixed up with the dogs, and the dogs got mixed up with the stars,' I wrote, truthfully enough. 'The Parade had moments of sheer, delicious pandemonium . . .'

6   Not all my assignments were thrust upon me – I was by now, as we reached the mid-fifties and I could count myself a reasonably seasoned journalist, in a position to suggest my own. I had long been looking for some excuse to get to the United States. The desire to see America had been implanted in me at an early age not by American films but by an advertisement for a caramelised chocolate confection called Turtles in the pages of the American comic supplements which arrived in this country as freight-ship ballast and which were sold for a penny a dozen at Stringer's second-hand bookstall in Leeds market. In the sugar-starved times I was living through – the war was on, and all sweets were rationed – I craved these Turtles. They came, as the illustration showed, in a box of twelve turtle-shaped 'candies' – the exotic transatlantic word only made the craving worse – and if by some happy chance a box had fallen into my hands from an American food parcel, I should have devoured them at a sitting. Curiously enough, when the opportunity did finally arise and I espied a pyramid of Turtles in the window of a Madison Avenue chocolate store, I merely gave them a stare of interested recognition and moved on, my sweet tooth not being what it was. Those caramel Turtles are still on the market but I have yet to taste one to this day.

My opportunity was to come on the day a benevolent government announced a slight relaxation in the strict exchange control regulations which had inspired Jimmy Eilbeck to place his notorious £50 losing gamble on the roulette wheel in Nice. The allowance was now increased to £100, which meant that for the first time since the outbreak of war it would be just about possible for ordinary British citizens – or those not blessed with generous American relatives – to visit the United States. I shot off a memo asking if I could take £100 of the *Mirror*'s money – 280 dollars – across the Atlantic to see how far it could get me. Within hours I was standing in a consul's office before the Stars and Stripes in the American Embassy, swearing with right hand upraised that I would do nothing to overthrow the United States Government. I was on a BOAC flight that night – no sense in giving them time to change their minds – and twenty-four hours after I had put in my memo, was crossing the tarmac of Idlewild Airport.

The New York I found was still much the same city as depicted by Damon Runyon, whose ashes had been scattered over Times Square from a light aircraft only a few years earlier; still recognisably O. Henry's 'Baghdad on the Subway'; still infrastructurally a Victorian city effortlessly accommodating half a century of the new.

The Third Avenue El, the elevated railroad, boarded from antiquated little whistle-stop stations up steep flights of fretwork-canopied stairs, still rattled from one end of Manhattan to the other, shaking the bones of the tumbledown conglomeration of bars, delis, coffee shops, barbershops, cigar stores, lunch rooms, juice counters, drugstores, news stands, surgical goods stores, liquor stores, fleapits and flophouses that huddled beneath its rivet-studded steel arches. If the trolleys – the streetcars, the trams – no longer criss-crossed Manhattan, there was an impression of their having only but recently given up the ghost; and the last double-decker buses, with open stairs as in some sepia picture postcard of London Town, still trundled doggedly along Fifth Avenue. The hissing clouds of vapour rising from the manhole covers on the subway-rumbling street intersections were a reminder that notwithstanding the chrome-tipped Chrysler Building this was still a steam-age city; as was the dwindling fleet of ancient steam ferry boats bobbing in the wake of liners edging along the Hudson River. Burly Irish-American bartenders manned Seventh Avenue saloons owned by, or fronted by, famous pugilists and baseball players; fire engines built like red-painted, elongated Centurion tanks zig-zagged in and out of the lines of Cadillacs and Pontiacs nudging their way down Broadway; and the Yellow Cab drivers still spoke in the accents of Brooklyn and the Bronx. The 20th Century Limited still left for Chicago daily at 6 p.m.; Delmonico's, the Stork Club, Copacabana, and Count Basie's Lounge still flourished, if one could only find them; New Yorkers met under famous clocks at the Biltmore and the Waldorf Astoria; and there, under their bronze marquees, were still the Schubert, the Morosco and the Belasco theatres, and Loew's Ziegfeld, and the Bijou.

All this and Lindy's too, aka Runyon's Mindy's, still serving the best cheesecake on Broadway, while puffs of smoke billowed from a giant pair of lips on the Camel hoarding high above Times Square, and a moving belt of white electric light bulbs over the Times Building spelled out the latest news, just like its replica over the Majestic cinema in City Square, Leeds, all those years ago now. If you listened you could hear, a block away, Gene Krupa performing a riff at the dais that ran the length of the open-to-the-street bar of the Café Metropole. The smell of Danish pastry and roasted chestnuts hung sweetly on the air, the afternoon was alive with sirens; rag trade porters pushing racks of dresses and coats up from the garment district made their own pedestrianised gridlock on the corner of Seventh Avenue and 42nd Street; and all the men going about their business wore jaunty hats like Humphrey Bogart, and all the women looked like Myrna Loy; and it was like stepping through the silver screen from the one-and-nines into a black and white celluloid Babylon.

The filmic image was augmented by the class of hotel the *Mirror*'s New York bureau had found for me. Bearing in mind that I was on a stringent budget they had played the game my way and put me in a fourteen-storey rat-trap just off Times Square, a building so thin that its bloodshot neon sign had to hang vertically down the length of the fire escape. Paying in advance – two dollars a night, I think (the Plaza itself was only fifteen dollars for a single room at the time) – I ran the gauntlet of a small lobby gathering of loafers and near-down-and-outs, each, it seemed, with his own personal spittoon, towards the elevator, as I was only too readily prepared to call the lift in my eagerness to embrace all things American. I was surprised to find that the establishment ran to a lift attendant – probably no one else could be trusted to work the antiquated machinery. As we creaked up to the twelfth floor, however, he proved to have a supplementary vocation: 'Hey, I'm a masseur, you know what a masseur is? I do massage, I come along to your room, any kind of massage you need, two dollars up . . .' Declining the offer, I let myself through a narrow, flaking door into a narrow, shabby room – both of them proportionate to the narrow hotel itself. Through the slats of the crooked Venetian blinds I looked down on a battery of flashing neon. Lying in bed, if I put up the blinds, I would be able to see the faulty green sign BUDGET HOTEL on the building opposite spluttering and flickering the whole night long. I was so far into the opening paragraph of a story in *Black Mask* magazine that I half expected, or anyway half hoped for, the sound of gunshots ricocheting around the stone corridor outside my room.

The *Mirror*'s New York bureau, to my great satisfaction, was on the thirty-somethingth floor of the *Daily News* building on 42nd Street. Two minutes to savour this experience and I was whisked off to Costello's Bar and Grill around the corner, the headquarters hangout for most of the English and Australian journalists based or passing through New York.

While Costello's was everything one could wish for in a traditional American bar and grill, with original Thurbers on the walls, behatted businessmen and cigar store owners slurping their chowder in curtained booths, and waiters built like trucks yelling for pastrami on rye and hold the dill pickle, I was anxious to be out and about and exploring the pavements of New York. Although I had been kindly promised a rubbernecking tour of the Empire State Building and such places, that wasn't what I had come for: I wanted to mooch about and stare at ordinary buildings – department stores, drugstores, post offices, railway stations – exactly as I had done when wandering the streets of Leeds as a child. I wanted to see Fire Engine Company No. 23 and the 30th Police Precinct station house and Public School No. 67. Or any other number. At five in the evening in Costello's it was not easy. Five in the evening Eastern Seaboard time is ten at night London time, and barring someone blowing up the United Nations building or a film star stabbing her lover, the working day was over for my new friends. It was to be another three or four rounds, and another stack of Fleet Street anecdotes and famous headlines and classic cablegrams (American edition) to add to my repertoire before I was allowed to stand my own corner and thus effect my release.

Somewhat woozily, I made my way along the sidewalk to where 43rd Street came to an abrupt end, culminating in a large building. Puzzled, because I had been given to understand that these arrow-straight thoroughfares ran uninterrupted from the East River to the Hudson, I passed through the modest enough doors that were in my path, and through which purposeful streams of people seemed to be heading, to find myself in Grand Central Station, than which there is no more sobering sight. 'Cathedral-like' is the expression most used about this mighty space with its vaulted ceiling illuminated by the electric stars of the constellations, and with shafts of late sunlight spearing down from the high windows on to the hunched

302

backs of the scurrying pygmies crossing the huge grand concourse or thronging around the central information desk with its gilded clock, or passing through gilded gateways or queueing at the gilded grilles of the gilded ticket booths – everything was gilded, or marble, or polished granite, or engraved glass, and all in what Americans call the Beaux Arts manner.

And not a train in sight. It was all a long way from King's Cross, although not such a giant leap from the Art Deco booking hall of Leeds City Station, now a car park. It was in search of the trains – I wanted to see an American train, preferably on Track 29 like in the song – that I stumbled across the celebrated Oyster Bar on the lower concourse, with its tiled and vaulted ceiling giving it the appearance, in the cathedral-like atmosphere filtering down from above, of an exceptionally large and busy crypt. On my budget I could not of course afford to eat there, or so I thought – I didn't then realise that in New York oysters and clams were ordinary office workers' fare, as they used to be in London before an Edwardian blight gave them the rarity value of their own pearls – but I resolved that I should, one of these days. And so I have, on every visit to New York since.

Coming out of Grand Central into 44th Street – oh, and there was the Hotel Algonquin, but with too many brown-uniformed major-domos, porters and bell-boys on the door to risk a peek inside in the hope of spotting the famous Round Table – I headed back towards Times Square, resolved to devote the remainder of the long day to walking the length of Broadway, whether up or down I knew not, until I reached the tip of Manhattan. Which I did, and after some three hours' ambling found myself at the Battery, gazing out at the Statue of Liberty. And so, as I should have known had the song been written in time, it was down: the Bronx is up and the Battery's down.

On the way, recognising it from photographs in old volumes of the *Strand* magazine, I stared at the Flat Iron building, the world's first skyscraper; and City Hall which I mistook for New York University and New York University which I mistook for City Hall; and Wall Street; and Woolworth's. From the frequent intersections I had picture postcard glimpses of the great set-pieces like the Empire State and the Chrysler Building, but really I was more interested in the little street-furniture vignettes from the Talk of the Town pages in the *New Yorker*, now miraculously three-dimensional – fire hydrants, mail boxes, phone booths, traffic signs, barbers' poles, the iron railings of the subway stations. The big bronze doors of the savings banks, chased with coats of arms and portcullises and mythical figures, fascinated me too. Bronze seemed to be the colour of New York: bronze for the fixtures and fittings in Grand Central Station, bronze for the theatre marquees and the canopies of the motion-picture theatres, as they wished to call their cinemas, bronze, and embossed with the American eagle at that, for the mail chutes and elevator gates in the lobbies of office buildings (a discovery: these were public territory, as were the lobbies of hotels, where bronze fought it out with palms. I now wished I had ventured into the Algonquin after all). A rich, bronze-age town, then. But next to the marble halls were tumbledown shacks selling cut-price haberdashery lines, and next to the banks were dull brick walk-up doss houses with street-front fire escapes (the dossers did not yet sleep in the bank doorways). Every few blocks there was a parking lot looking like a bomb site, and every few blocks more the rubble of a building coming down, and every few blocks again the girders of a building going up. Remarkable that such a well-established city should still have something of the feel of a frontier town, or of having recently survived a serious earthquake.

I had never heard of jet-lag and I did not get to bed till dawn, but although I had seen so much, all of it on foot, I had seen so little. Where was the Village – indeed, what was the Village? Where was the Bronx? Brooklyn? Central Park? Radio City? Rockefeller Centre? And why wasn't Madison Square Garden in Madison Square? Never mind: their time would come.

My journalistic object was to place as much dust as possible between New York and myself before my hundred pounds' worth of dollars ran out. My Costello's Bar advisers reckoned that living modestly and travelling by bus I should just about be able to make it to Miami Beach and back, a 3,000-mile round trip through nine states. That suited me. Accordingly, after a couple of hours' sleep, I set off with a Greyhound ticket thirty-nine inches long entitling me to stop off where I pleased, and that evening filed my first story, datelined Mrs Johnson's boarding house, Atlantic City.

And then on, entranced, to Richmond, Virginia, Newport News, Raleigh, Charleston, Savannah, Jacksonville and all points south, subsisting on hamburgers – a totally new experience, yet a familiar one from the burger-guzzling Wimpy character in the Popeye cartoon strip in the *Sunday Pic* – and root beer which again I had never tasted, and never particularly wish to taste again, but which I had seen Spanky Macfarland, Alfalfa Seltzer and Buckwheat Thomas swig often enough in the Our Gang two-reelers, and so it had to be tried. The small southern towns with their ante-bellum mansions, white clapboard houses and film-lot Main Streets were like *Gone with the Wind* crossed with *Andy Hardy Goes to College*. We had left New York City an integrated bus: below Richmond the blacks who boarded went to the back seats as a matter of course. From North Carolina on there were separate bus station diners and separate lavatories for blacks and whites, and when it came time to sleep as we drove down through the neon-torn darkness of Florida, there were thirty-cent rented pillows for the whites, wooden armrests for the blacks. I wrote it all down, as rivetted by American apartheid as by the prominently displayed company rule requiring all firearms to be handed to the driver, and all unaware that I was scribbling a tiny advance footnote to the Little Rock riots that were already festering.

I missed so much. I managed to spend a few hours around Miami Beach without ever registering its boulevards of pink and lime-green Art Deco confections like a pre-war garden city of Regals, Regents and Paramounts – perhaps because I was at the Picturedrome end of town. I was by now down to my last hundred dollars – the exact sum, as it happens, which on my next visit to Miami I mistakenly tipped a cab driver in the belief that I was handing him a dollar bill – and it was time to be heading back. I chose a route through Augusta, Georgia, and Washington, DC, where I stopped over. Washington had the distinction of being the only city, apart from Hull, that I had ever descended upon without taking to it at once. Too planned, and too over-planted with obelisks and domes – where were the alleys (I had yet to see Georgetown)? No doubt all manner of intriguing things were happening up on Capitol Hill and in the fashionable restaurants I had read about in the pages of *Washington Confidential*, but the excitement did not transmit itself to the streets. The capital was a provincial town that made other provincial towns seem like capitals.

But I had seen America, or a tiny fraction of one side of it, and from here on I would find some excuse for at least one visit annually – a charging of the batteries so necessary that to this day I get serious withdrawal symptoms if I have not walked down Fifth Avenue in longer than six months. I recommend the Greyhound or its equivalents as a means of exploring America – for years, criss-crossing the country from New Orleans to the Grand Canyon, from Boston to Santa Fe, stopping at glitzy terminals, rundown ghetto bus stations waiting for a riot, and chalked signs on telegraph poles on long dusty roads out of the crop-spraying plane scene from *North by Northwest*, I travelled in no other way.

After living on hamburgers it was only a few days more before I was living on caviare. There had been something of a thaw in the Cold War, with the result that Western journalists, if not actively encouraged, were at least not for the present being discouraged from exploring the Soviet Union – on strictly prescribed routes, naturally. My novel 'meet the people' approach to my brief American tour, forsaking the usual journalist's perks of four-star hotels, first-class travel and three-rosette restaurants for rooming houses, rattling buses and greasy spoons (I had not had much option) had appealed to Hugh Cudlipp, and he now wanted me to go and do the same thing in the USSR. I could not see myself staying in the Soviet equivalent of Seaview – it would not have been fitted up with the requisite hidden microphones – but I was all for seeing how ordinary Russians lived, and even keener to give the usually obligatory tour of the ball bearing plant a miss.

Although I had developed, in my limited travels, a weakness for any place that not only had a different language from ours but a different alphabet – it seemed that much further away – I rapidly became disillusioned with Moscow as the euphoria of first impressions wore off. Like Washington, it was stiflingly, monolithically planned, with the hand of the blueprint bureaucrat everywhere and the Lenin-Stalin mausoleum like an air-raid shelter. I missed the advertisement hoardings and billboards that could have disfigured Red Square to its advantage; the few neon signs, in that iron-railing lettering, were mainly bleak messages such as 'Keep your money in the savings bank' and 'Don't let your house catch fire'.

The Intourist guides at that time – the press had specially selected ones – were very reluctant to let one off the hook, and I had the greatest difficulty in getting to the ordinary streets which I knew must lie behind the big blockbuster set-pieces and the depressingly wide boulevards which with the absence of traffic were more like airport runways than city thoroughfares. Vera, my interpreter, could not comprehend my interest in the humdrum. Although she could lay on showcase flats for me she wouldn't let me knock on the doors of a row of shanty-town shacks I had stumbled across. Wagging a reproving finger, she would say, 'You know, we have a saying, an uninvited guest is worse than a Tartar.' Vera had a good many of these sayings. She was smugly delighted when, insisting on lingering in a street market, I got myself into trouble by taking a photograph of a small boy playing on a barrow. Immediately we were surrounded by an angry crowd who evidently thought – I suppose I was obviously a Western journalist – I was going to publish the pictures as concocted proof that Moscow children had to work. Not even Vera could persuade them otherwise. The situation was getting seriously ugly when the police arrived and Vera spirited me away – 'You know, we have a saying, one should not go looking for trouble.' After that I suffered myself to be led meekly around the Kremlin where despite my determination not to be won over by museum jewels I was quite taken by such artifacts as the thrones belonging to Peter the Great and Ivan the Terrible. All those fairy-tale names: I expected to find the original oven where Hansel and Gretel were almost cooked. The whole Kremlin, incidentally, smelled of mothballs.

Vera was only about nineteen and while a product of the system through and through and completely incurious about the West, she was otherwise lively and attractive, and rather good company when she had had a few vodkas. But either because she was not used to dealing with journalists or because she had a saying, curiosity killed the cat, it was near impossible to persuade her to go into the detail for which I craved. This was infuriatingly frustrating when, for example, I wanted an exact translation of the television programme listings in the paper so that I could get some idea of what Moscow was watching on its five-inch screens. Vera would start promisingly enough: 'First is the news, and then there is a farming programme, it is called *Agriculture Now*, then there is a programme of some interest only to women.' 'Yes? And?' 'It is for women.' 'Read out the programme, Vera.' 'There is nothing – just details.'

It was the same out on the road with other interpreters. In Kiev I wanted to see a petty-criminal court in action. My guide, who would rather I had spent the morning at the palace of culture, was disapproving. 'What's this case, Alex?' 'It is of no importance – just a drunk.' 'But what's he saying to the judge?' 'Nothing. He is only making his excuse.'

Despite such obduracy, and by the judicious use of veiled threats to report my guides' non-cooperation back to a non-existent head of foreign press affairs in Moscow, I somehow managed, in the course of a tour that took in Kiev, Odessa, Yalta, Tbilisi, Tashkent and finally Alma Ata on the Silk Road from China to Central Asia, to gatecrash a Soviet wedding and a christening – or rather, the civil registration equivalent of a christening – though not a funeral; I spent a day in a TV station where they were putting together a documentary called *Oxy-acetylene Welders of the Ukraine*; I visited a fashion show and a hairdressing salon and spent an evening at a dance hall with some English-speaking Teddy boys who taught me the current Top of the Pops, 'Evenings on the Outskirts of Moscow'. And all under the portrait of Lenin.

At that time no one was writing that kind of minutiae about life in the Soviet Union, and I closed my notebooks well pleased. Feeling no end of a world traveller, I finished up in Leningrad *en route* for the train to Helsinki, where after six weeks of bureaucratic obstruction I ungallantly decided to exact my revenge on the whole system by making a scene in the last Soviet hotel restaurant I was ever to set foot in, where I was kept waiting the usual hour for sight of the menu. I told my interpreter to get the manager. He thought this unwise. I insisted. Eventually a managerial-looking personage came and listened to my torrent of abuse as translated by my interpreter, no doubt in a much-watered-down version. A click of the fingers and menus were produced, but nothing then happened. Looking around the vast room, I saw that all the waiters had vanished. My guide gave me a 'Told you so!' look. Another half-hour passed. At last the swing doors to the kitchen burst open and out marched a deputation of waiters and kitchen hands, led by the chef who was menacingly, if only ceremoniously, brandishing a cleaver.

Through the interpreter, the chef made a long, formal speech, the gist of which was: 'The joint kitchen and dining room committees regret that a distinguished guest should have had cause to complain. This is due to faults in our internal organisation which will be rectified. The joint kitchen and dining room committees have considered and passed unanimously a motion of self-criticism.' With a bow, he then led his troupe back into the kitchen, from which they never emerged. An hour later, unfed, I was on my way to Helsinki.

So much for that adventure. Geographically I had covered tremendous distances in recent times. Professionally I had done myself no end of good, and there were prospects of further trips to pretty well anywhere I cared to go. But more than ever I was feeling that I wasn't going anywhere in particular.

THREE

Shaftesbury Avenue

1   And so it was all very well, but the fifties were hurtling by and I did not seem to be a part of them.

These were no longer straws in the wind that were blowing past my cubbyhole window on the third floor of Geraldine House, they were hayricks sucked up into a *Wizard of Oz*-strength tornado. The brash, newsy Victor Gollancz ads in what we would soon be calling 'the posh Sundays' after Jimmy Porter were headlining Amis and Colin Wilson. Every second novel seemed to be about a lower-middle-class scholarship boy, stories about factory lads by Alan Sillitoe and Sid Chaplin were appearing in the puny successors to *Penguin New Writing*, and the *Daily Sketch* editor's son, Thom Gunn, was being hailed as a poet and a key member of a mysterious movement called the Movement. Joan Littlewood was in place at Stratford East and Ken Tynan on the *Observer*, and we had had our first taste of Brecht with *The Threepenny Opera*, set in Soho. And we had waited for Godot.

Rehearsing John Mortimer's *Lunch Hour* in 1960, Emlyn Williams remarked to the author, 'Well, you just got into the New Wave as the tube doors were closing!' In the mid-fifties the tube was waiting at the station, the doors wide open and the driver having a smoke. But I was loitering on the platform.

For one who had already acquired a reputation for workaholicism (in Fleet Street terms, a workaholic is anyone who writes when he doesn't have to) I seemed, at the age of twenty-seven, to have achieved depressingly little. True, to my pitifully thin extramural portfolio I had by now added a book, a history of the Café Royal, written in collaboration with Guy Deghy. I shared with Guy a love, though in my case vicarious, for the cafés of Central Europe such as the Café New York in Budapest and the Café Central in Vienna; the Café Royal in its prime, when Oscar Wilde, Frank Harris,

Augustus John and other glitterati sipped their aperitifs under the caryatids of the mirror-reflected Domino Room, was the kind of place I should have liked to have found still flourishing when I arrived in London, and the more we began to evoke the place the more I pined for it. Being able to research in snatched hours in the British Museum Round Reading Room – the inner sanctum of London, as I regarded it, more club-like than any club – was consolation.

Never having contracted to write a book before, and being used to the inflexibility of newspaper deadlines, I took the contract delivery date very seriously and harried Guy into working far into the night to get it finished on time. It attracted excellent reviews and a good deal of media attention which, in my customary ignorance, I accepted as its due, including a Home Service radio programme produced by Guy in which we bagged Sir Max Beerbohm, John Betjeman, Sir Compton Mackenzie, Malcolm Muggeridge and Sir John Rothenstein among others. It was an exhilarating interlude and another first in my life, but having discovered in myself an obsessional regard for research for its own sake – I spent four days chasing through dusty old directories to establish the population of Glasshouse Street, accounting for eight lines in the book – I was not inclined to repeat the experience, although Guy went on to write equally successful histories of Romano's and the National Sporting Club.

One discovery I did not need to make about myself, furthermore – I already knew – was that I was fundamentally an idler: indeed I still am. All my life I have swung between industry and indolence, between bouts of furious, non-stop activity and utter lethargy; and it is probably to get back more quickly into the womb-like torpor of the latter state that I whip myself into the former. Both of these extremes can take many days to burn, or fizzle, themselves out: I can work two or three weeks non-stop except for minimal sleep, but then this furious period will be followed by a week or ten days of zombie-like ennui so total that not only do telephone calls and letters go unanswered but a pen dropped on the floor will lie there for days before I can stir myself to pick it up, while the accumulation of uncleared detritus on my desk – a cup and saucer, a glass, a crumpled napkin, a crust of toast from breakfast hours ago – will take on the glassy, elusive permanence of a still life. I tell myself that this is a process of recharging the batteries, but at heart I know the reverse is the truth and that I have a drifter's need to run my batteries down. When friends profess to marvel at the quantity of my output – it is not as great as all that – I think of the small inner voice that is telling me for heaven's sake to get off my back and get some work done – the real inspiration. It has always been fortunate for me that northern tin-roof tabernacle guilt at being unoccupied – mistaken for the work ethic – has continued, as a last resort, to drive me back to my typewriter.

All of which went to explain why the novel I had started was not getting finished. There was no other reason: I knew where it was going, I was pleased with it, I hadn't left it at a sticky patch, I was enjoying writing it – in fact only to think about writing a bit more of it induced a contented glow of anticipation. Too contented, perhaps: the contentment that should rightly arise from having done a thing satisfactorily, rather than from having it still to do but knowing that once I got round to it, I would do it well. I reminded myself sometimes of the penniless procrastinator who got a much-needed commission from the *Reader's Digest* – generous payers. He put it off and put it off until he finally got an ultimatum from the commissioning editor – either deliver the article right away or forget it. He replied by telegram: 'Commencing article as soon as I have cleaned my tennis shoes.'

Fortunately for me, after two or three not so much false starts as aborted starts – some of them legitimate, such as a welcome diversion when Hugh Cudlipp despatched me to the south of France for two weeks to compose a furious pamphlet on the sickly state of Britain's propaganda services abroad – the electricians and maintenance engineers of Fleet Street decided to go on strike in support of a demand for a £2 18s 6d a week pay increase. That was on 26 March 1955, and they were to remain out until 21 April. Journalists were instructed by their union to turn up for work, otherwise they would not have been paid, but of course there was no work to do. We occupied ourselves in various ways. Some spent their mornings in the pubs and their afternoons in the Press Club or the Wig and Pen Club opposite the Law Courts. Others applied themselves to the monumental task of getting their expenses claims up to date. One or two enterprising souls, Peter Baker among them, produced their own daily mini-newspaper, *London Cry*, which not only provided an excellent racing service but carried the exclusive story of Churchill's resignation as Prime Minister. Resisting the temptations of the Wig and Pen, of which I had just become a life member, I set to and banged out the first draft of my novel.

Called, at this stage, *The Summer of Uncle Mad*, it was a story about the adventure of childhood, different from other childhood sagas in the penny plainness of its setting – a council housing estate in the north. Autobiographical, of course, provided I had poetic licence to kill off my entire family before the story began, and to have the girl next door murdered during the course of it. But the background was authentic, as was the colloquial narrative of the ten-year-old protagonist, who in the telling of the tale was something of a north-country Huckleberry Finn. I have little recollection of actually writing or rewriting the story, only of the state of excitement, akin to that experienced when visiting a mistress, in which I would hurry back to my typewriter. Jerome K. Jerome wrote in an introduction to the umpteenth edition of *Three Men in a Boat* that he could hardly recall having written it – 'I remember only feeling very young and absurdly pleased with myself.' *There Is a Happy Land*, as I had by now decided to call my novel, was not to be my *Three Men in a Boat*, but I knew exactly how he felt. Whatever had been holding me back, I had at last nosedived through the barrier and could start calling myself a novelist.

Not that I was yet a published one, but with my customary self-confidence, or rather chronic lack of self-doubt, I had no qualms at all but that it was only a matter of signing the contract, correcting the proofs and approving the dust jacket.

Reluctantly I sent the manuscript to Hutchinson's who had published the Café Royal book – reluctantly because I had had an extraordinarily high-handed letter from Katherine Webb, the formidable Joint Managing Editor of Hutchinson's: 'Dear Keith Waterhouse, I was rather surprised to learn from one of the trade papers that you have written a novel which you have recently delivered to your Agent and even more surprised that you did not mention the fact at our Cocktail Party last Monday week. Although we have, strictly speaking, no option on this novel I should have thought that you would have given us the first refusal of it . . . In case you do not know, this is the usual procedure in the publishing world and I shall therefore be glad to have an opportunity of considering the novel . . .'

My then newly acquired agent, incidentally, was Paul Scott, who as the future author of the *Raj Quartet* knew a thing or two about fiction. He didn't think my novel belonged in the Hutchinson list of that time at all, but on the grounds that the old battleaxe probably wanted first refusal only in order to exercise that refusal and teach me a lesson in publishing manners, he thought we might as well keep the peace by letting her see it. To the surprise of neither of us it came back almost by return, together with an adverse reader's report (authors are not usually privy to the opinions of their publisher's readers) to the effect that while it was quite well done for what it was, it did not amount to much.

Paul then sent it to what all along was his first choice of publisher, Michael Joseph, where it had the good fortune to be read by the literary journalist and critic Walter Allen, a fervent advocate of the working-class novel. Walter gave it the thumbs-up, Michael Joseph gave me an advance of £75 ('payable half on signature and half on publication') and a breathless world, or anyway a breathless author, awaited publication day.

There Is a Happy Land was gratifyingly – though to me, in my green complacency, not surprisingly – well received. 'Keith Waterhouse proves himself the best reporter on the wilder shores of childhood since Dylan Thomas' – *Evening Standard*. 'Vivid, accurate, perceptive . . . how brilliantly – and how honestly – the author makes his original effect' – *Observer*. 'Remarkable for the deep and unwavering insight it gives into child behaviour' – *The Times*. And sheafs more on the same lines, which I lapped up as my due. I have occasionally wondered, later in life when not everything I did was a cue for universal acclaim, how I should have taken it had the book been badly received. I have no idea. I was simply not equipped for failure.

What did surprise me was the fall-out effect consequent upon having produced a successful first novel. Letters poured in – from agents, inviting me to be their client; from secretarial agencies, wanting to type my manuscripts; from literary editors, wanting me to review novels; from book dealers, after I had begun to do so (Walter Allen got me on the fiction roster of the *New Statesman*), offering to buy my review copies at one-third of the cover price; from publishers, wanting a quote for the blurbs of other people's first novels; from magazine editors, offering to commission short stories (I wrote a very good one, 'The Yorkshire Woollen Bank Forgeries', for *The Queen*, but was too lazy to follow it up with more – stupid of me, since it was reprinted many times and has appeared in half a dozen anthologies); from university literary societies, asking for a talk in exchange for 'reasonable expenses'; from public relations consultants, inviting my participation in 'projects' – 'Your name has been passed on to me as a possible writer of a booklet we have in mind for a bedding manufacturer . . .'

Meanwhile *There Is a Happy Land* was going into a second and a third edition and subsequently into Penguin. Kevin Billington adapted it for radio with my friend Alfred Bradley as producer, and the nameless protagonist played by a boy called Davey Jones who was to find more lasting fame as one of the Monkees. I adapted it myself for Granada Television, when it was directed by James Brabazon who shot his film in all my old childhood haunts and cast most of the children from my old school. The novel, which I would have been quite prepared to notch up as a modest *succès d'estime*, simply went on and on. Even I was impressed. But even I could not have guessed that it was to become, in due course, my secret bestseller – for while, because of its strong local vernacular, it has never been translated or published anywhere but in Britain, it has never been out of print in one edition or another in nearly forty years. This is largely in consequence, I imagine, of its being a set book for schools. I regularly get sheafs of questionnaires from whole classes of children: 'Why you write this book? Why you not give boy name? Why it sad?' The only question I have had trouble answering was, 'I liked this book a bit, but it not as good as some of the other books I have read, why is this?'

So this was the writing life, then, and I took to it. It was in the unlikely setting of Pietro Annigoni's villa in Florence that I decided, on impulse, to leave the staff of the *Daily Mirror* and chance my arm at writing full time, subsidising my novels-in-progress with freelance journalism. I had been sent to interview the painter because the *Mirror* had bought newspaper publication rights in his controversial portrait of the Duke of Edinburgh, and it was my task to get some controversial quotes. I was, naturally enough, enraptured by Florence. Annigoni had painted a Renaissance-style mural of his city around the walls of his turreted studio, so while awaiting him I was torn between feasting my eyes upon this or staring out of the windows at the breathtaking views over the red-tiled rooftops and domes of the living city. I knew, as bells rang out across Florence and the smell of expresso coffee filtered up from below, that my days of going to a newspaper office every day were numbered. It was a curious, there-and-then decision, arrived at by lop-sided logic. Instead of thinking, 'It is because I am in Fleet Street that I am able to come to places like this,' I thought, 'If I did not have to go to Fleet Street every day I could come here whenever I pleased.' I knew very well that most probably it would not work out that way at all, but there was no question of weighing pros and cons – I knew that come what may, this was what I meant to do.

Somewhere I had read that Montaigne had written, 'All permanent decisions are made in a temporary frame of mind.' I had taken this very much to heart, although perhaps not in the spirit in which it was intended to be taken. The gazelle-like leap into the future was the way I had always propelled myself. All my permanent decisions had been made in a temporary frame of mind, the kind of frame of mind that a cat must be in when it closes its eyes, puts down its head and hurls itself across a busy road.

Informed as I was only by ignorance, the challenge seemed a heady one. By this time I had a small child, Penny, and another one, Sarah, on the way. In an effort to domesticise my life – another permanent decision made in a temporary frame of mind, or in this case absence of mind – I had recently moved my family to a rented 'executive bungalow' on the fringe of Harlow New Town. This was a futuristic glass box with a walled courtyard which if perched on a hilltop in southern Italy would have excited the envy of visiting friends; perched on a feeder road for the A11 it excited only their puzzlement. It was one of a row of about half a dozen built for Harlow's managerial classes who preferred, however, to live in converted barns or old rectories in the surrounding villages; hence, at a time when the housing shortage was still acute, these architectural showplaces were going begging at around £6 a week. I had rather taken to Harlow upon arriving there on some assignment or other on a refreshingly cold but brilliantly sunny morning, when I had found in the town centre, or chosen to find, a passing resemblance to Helsinki. There was a decent local paper, the *Harlow Citizen*, very community-orientated, which I browsed through over half a pint in a not-bad pub in the main square; immediately the temporary-minded, permanent decision was made. I would become a Harlow citizen, throw myself into its civic affairs, and my expanding family would breathe clean air and ride ponies. I went home and told Joan, and she called Pickford's for an estimate.

If it was an insane place for any busy journalist to be shuttling to

317

and from, it was an even more inconvenient base for a freelance to whom time – an hour each way, minimum – was money. But then the whole freelance idea, had I but given myself a chance to think about it, was fraught with question marks. The essence of freelancing is to have a network of contacts, and although by now I was on drinking terms with a fair number of journalists from other papers, they were on my own career level and in no position to hand out jobs. The one or two papers that had expressed an interest in my services were not in the market for casual labour – the newsprint shortage again. I was giving up a reasonable income in a steady job and the chance to do what I loved doing most – travel. On the credit side, if the *New Statesman* continued to give me reviewing work I could look forward to twelve guineas every three weeks, which meant I could pay the rent for two weeks out of four with twelve shillings left over for groceries. The only heartening thing was that nobody warned me against the risk. My friends seemed to go along with my instinct that it was time to be moving on. But they didn't have to pay the bills.

It was Hugh Cudlipp who rescued me from the hole I was very probably digging for myself. Like everyone else, he did not try to dissuade me from leaving the paper. He recognised that I had got just about as far as it was possible for me to go on the *Mirror* without starting to go round in circles, or without belatedly beginning to climb the executive ladder, whose slippery rungs held no attractions for me at all. Cudlipp called me in, poured me a stiff one and made what at that time was an extraordinary proposition: that the Mirror group would pay me – give me – a retainer of £1,000 a year to have first call on my freelance services, on condition that I did not write for other popular newspapers. Naturally I accepted with alacrity – £1,000 a year, £20 a week, the rent plus £14 a week left over, was the equivalent of about ten times as much today, and if not enough to raise a family on was certainly enough to keep them from going barefoot.

With this unprecedented boost, I launched upon my freelance career with enthusiasm. My freelance career, however, did not respond to me with equal zest. Barred from the popular papers and knowing no one on the daunting text broadsheets, I made a pitch for the magazines and got one or two commissions. My friend Denis Pitts, whose memorable Cyprus despatch for the *Daily Herald* I had cabled to the exclusion of my own, found himself editing the Hulton pocket magazine *Lilliput*, and he gave me one or two pieces

318

to write. Another friend, Max Caulfield, was revamping the old *John Bull* magazine, founded by the swindler Horatio Bottomley, a forerunner of Robert Maxwell, and he found me some work too. The *Daily Mirror* also threw the odd series my way.

I was quickly finding, however, the drawbacks to being a self-employed journalist rather than a staff man, which in sum were that every commission was a two-stage affair – first of all I had to go out and get the story, and then I had to go home or to some desk or other and write it. This was all very well when someone was paying for my time, but when they were paying not for the time expended but simply for the end product, it seemed a waste of my resources. It must have been then that I acquired the taste for what in the newspaper world are known as 'think pieces' – pieces that are written off the top of one's head with the minimum of research, certainly no research that involves going out of the house and travelling long distances. Unfortunately, no think pieces were forthcoming – no one seemed much interested in what I thought.

As always, salvation was at hand. Through my friend Guy Deghy, I had come across a publisher called Jim Reynolds who was running the firm of Frederick Muller – he was a fan of our book on the Café Royal, which he said he would have liked to have published. The proposition Jim Reynolds brought to us, over a drink at El Vino, was as far removed both from the Café Royal or anything else Guy or I had ever done as I could imagine, and to this day I do not know why he settled on us. There was at the time a vogue for 'funny little books', the long aftermath, I suppose, of *1066 and All That*. Reynolds had published an American example of the genre called *The Unfair Sex*, a tongue-in-cheek attack on men and all their works. What he wanted was the masculine equivalent with women as the victim. This was when one could do such a thing without risk of the publishing house being burned down.

Jim wanted the book in six weeks, to get it into his Christmas list. We wrote *How to Avoid Matrimony*, by Herald Froy – we took the name from a fireplace firm in Hammersmith – in two weeks, evenings and weekends only, with the aid of many bottles of Spanish plonk. Although pushing the male chauvinist joke to its extremities (it would nowadays be banned by public librarians), it was very well received, serialised by the *Evening News* and printed in several foreign languages. We wrote a successor, *How to Survive Matrimony*, which equally brought home a fair slice of bacon. There were to be five Herald Froy titles in all, together with a Herald Froy column for a spell in the *Evening News*, before we decided that the well was running dry. None of them took longer than a fortnight to write, and while they ran their little course our families did not lack for new shoes.

On a more elevated level, and using a different pseudonym plucked from who knows where, Lee Gibb, we produced two other 'funny little books' – *The Joneses and How to Keep Up with Them*, and a sequel, *The Higher Jones*. These were quite acutely observed extensions of the U and non-U or who's in-who's out games of the time, and were great fun to write. The sociologically accurate premise was that in the fifties the upwardly mobile Joneses – the family the aspiring Robinsons next door were trying to keep up with as the consumer society began to come of age – threw traditional class snobbery to the winds and became a social class in themselves. The books pinpointed the characteristics – their *Homes and Gardens* home and garden, their Sunday colour-supp car or Jonesmobile, their Montessori-bred children or Jonesbrats, and their *Jones Literary Supplement* checklist of books, plays, films and exhibitions requiring of them no more than three months' running supply of knowledge of the arts – by which the Joneses became enviably identifiable as the life and Jones of the party. 'Fine, fierce satire,' wrote Betjeman in the *Telegraph*, and the critic of the decidedly un-Joneslike *Reynolds News*, a Sunday newspaper of the time owned by the Co-op, called it 'a book that makes the U-game sound like the feeble death-rattle of the old world.'

The fifties come home to roost, indeed. Our Jones game became quite a cult for a while and in consequence we were invited on to the BBC *Tonight* programme, hosted by Cliff Michelmore, to be mock-interviewed in our assumed capacities of Jones and Robinson – I cannot recall which of us was which, but it was fun. What I do recall is that the young associate producer of *Tonight*, and the producer of our particular segment, was Ned Sherrin – our first, brief encounter, and neither of us with an inkling that here was the start of an association that was still to be flourishing over three and a half decades later.

Around this time I was also diversifying into, or rather dabbling in, other television appearances in current affairs programmes with such titles as *Meet the Press* and *Press Conference*, where the likes of the young Christopher Chataway and Brian Inglis would sit around in a semi-circle earnestly questioning semi-important people in the news, or more usually not in the news at all but available for comment. I can't remember who recruited me into this developing branch of journalism but I did not shine at it.

Indeed, whatever career I might have had in that direction petered out altogether after I had done a solo interview for Associated Television, live, with one Father Potter of Peckham, a colourful cleric ministering to the poor of South London, on what was then known as the 'God slot' – an off-peak five minutes on a Sunday evening. (When, in the course of some researches into the television industry for one of the *Daily Mirror*'s political pamphlets, I had had call to reproach Lew Grade, as he still was, for the lack of cultural content on his TV network channel, he cited in his defence this particular little programme and an equally off-peak and obscure ten-minute spot called *Members' Mail*, in which MPs rambled on about their letters from constituents. To my objection that these were hardly examples of culture, Lew's response was, 'Well, they sure as hell aren't entertainment!')

The set-up for the interview was that Father Potter was to be discovered poring over some religious text in a studio mock-up of his study, whereupon I would knock at the door, he would bid me enter, and I would sit down and on some now forgotten pretext start to ask probing questions about his calling.

The rehearsal went smoothly, we trooped in and out of make-up, small-talk was made, we took up our positions, the director signalled the off, and I rapped on the door and strode confidently on to the set – only to trip up over a tangle of cables snaking around the floor and project myself headlong towards Father Potter's desk with an exclamation of 'Jesus Christ!' Like the seasoned broadcaster he was, the priest took it in his stride. Waving me to my seat he said in a chuckling sort of voice, 'Come along in, my son – you're not the first visitor to trip over my welcome mat! But you know, there's a lesson for us all there, isn't there . . .' While I slumped winded and speechless, he then trotted off a neat sermon worthy of *Beyond the Fringe*, had it only then been thought of, which took us effortlessly to the end of our allotted span. As, still unnerved, I thanked him and walked off the set, I again tripped over the cables and went sprawling through the door; but by this time we were mercifully off the air.

I would have banished this episode out of my mind but for my recollection of the programme's producer, Michael Redington, who I understood was congratulated upon its brilliant success. Michael, an affable, ebullient character not many years my senior, had been an actor, mainly in rep and in the kind of parts associated with tennis racquets and french windows; and in the fullness of time he was to become a highly successful theatrical impresario. Following my disastrous debut in religious broadcasting I did not – hardly surprisingly – set eyes on him again for close on thirty years, after he had triumphantly staged *84 Charing Cross Road* and was negotiating with my agent to put on my play about the Pooters, *Mr and Mrs Nobody*, with Judi Dench and Michael Williams. Judi wanted Trevor Nunn to direct, but the wait for his services was interminable and we were afraid of losing our two stars in the interim. I suggested another former ATV producer of those far-off days, to whose subsequent BBC *Tonight* programme I had brought rather less chaos than I had visited upon Michael – Ned Sherrin. Thus Michael, Ned and I formed a tripartite partnership that was to produce four successful West End plays. But all that was in the future.

Back in print journalism, one lucrative commission that came my way was a regular weekly column for the *Sunday Pictorial* – the *Sunday Mirror* as it now is. It was dreadful. It was one of those columns that still survive in regional dailies under titles like 'The Way I See It', subheaded, as likely as not, 'The Column That Pulls No Punches'. Mercifully my column did not have a title, otherwise it conformed to the formula – about half a dozen paragraphs, summarising this or that example of local bureaucracy or bumbledom gleaned from a week's skimming of the regional press, and ending with a supposedly pithy comment such as 'Come off it, Councillor' or 'It won't wash, Your Worship'. After about a year of addressing myself to the 'Barmy Burghers of Basingstoke' or 'The Stuffed Shirts of Solihull' I voluntarily relinquished the column – a week or so, I hazarded, before it would have voluntarily relinquished me. I knew I had a column in me, but this wasn't it. That too was still far ahead.

In any case, I had gone freelance not really to advance my career in journalism but for two reasons – to give myself the time and space to write another novel, and – perhaps the stronger attraction – to become self-employed. Perhaps because my father had been his own master I had always wanted 'to work for myself', as it was put in the north, or not to have a job to go to, as I put it privately to myself. It was the hedonistic aspect of being self-employed that was the appeal – not having to get up in the morning if I didn't want to, being able to take myself off for a walk if I felt like it, or to the pictures, or along Charing Cross Road to potter in and out of the second-hand bookshops, or to waste time in Fleet Street. I have a montage memory of my first year as a freelance when I did all these things save the staying in bed part, which had no appeal; the fact that apart from Hugh Cudlipp's £1,000 I had no means of support at this time and could least afford to fritter my working life away made the freedom to do so all the more intoxicating. I was a regular truant, both from work I did not particularly want to do and work which I particularly did. Effectively this was a double work-avoidance scheme. Not working at all kept me from doing the work I didn't want to do; doing the work I didn't want to do kept me from doing the work I did want to do, which was to write my next novel.

Or did I, and was it? Writing a second novel when the first has been a success can be a daunting exercise. Everyone knows that everyone has a first novel in them – the fact that they manifestly don't lends the belief no less credence – but how many have a second novel in them? And, given that critics seem to take a somewhat masochistic or cannibalistic delight in eating their own words, what if the second doesn't fulfil the first one's promise? A first novel is an indulgence, and it is indulged; a second tells the world that you are re-entering the ring as a serious contender, and that you are prepared, if it comes to it, to take a hammering.

A strong case for dithering, then. But I got down to it at last and wrote down the title I had thought of – *The Young Man's Magnificat* – on the first page of the shiny little memorandum book I had bought for the purpose of making notes. This was another work-avoidance technique – I have never been one for making notes, although I have always been one for possessing notebooks. Opening the *Magnificat* notebook and scribbling a few words in it allowed another month to elapse. After the usual procrastination – only being able to write on yellow foolscap, not being able to write with a used ribbon – I finally rolled a sheet of paper into the typewriter and got cracking. Pretty soon I had ten thousand words. They were as pretentious as the title itself – the supposed freewheeling inner thoughts of a north-country adolescent, they came over simply as mawkish adolescent ramblings in a narrative, if it could be called a narrative, that had neither

323

form nor shape. Mercifully, having got into the habit of carrying the manuscript about with me in a manilla folder so that I could work on it at odd moments, I left it in a taxi taking me from Fleet Street to Liverpool Street Station after a long day among 'contacts', and I never saw it again.

I went back to square one, this time slashing away at my hero's affectations as one hacks lichen off a tree. Somehow a first draft got completed. The spadework done – and I may say that for sheer labour it compares with digging a large trench in the back garden – I found that the old indolence had melted away entirely. I discovered, and heaven knew where it came from, a new and mounting excitement. Far from having to tempt myself to my desk with sky-blue rice paper or whatever, I could have written on old sugar bags if need be. I packed my family off on holiday, locked the doors and jumped in at the deep end. During this period I did not answer the telephone or the doorbell, shave, wash very much, or eat more than sandwiches. After three weeks, a novel by this time called *Saturday Night at the Roxy*, concerning an estate agent's clerk called Norman Fisher who has vague ambitions of becoming a writer, had transformed itself into a novel called *Billy Liar* about an undertaker's clerk named Billy Fisher who is a compulsive liar and daydreamer. I finished at 4 a.m. on a Sunday. I woke up at seven the following evening and by half past seven I was extremely drunk.

2 The Salisbury Tavern, to whose interestingly mixed company I had been introduced by some of my more raffish Fleet Street friends who consorted with theatricals, and where I could now count myself a semi-habitué, was around this time dominated by a noisy group of provincial actors appearing at the New Theatre across the alley, in a play about a squad of British soldiers nervously patrolling the Malayan jungle while the Japs advanced upon Singapore.

Their number included Peter O'Toole, Robert Shaw, Ronald Fraser and Bryan Pringle, all with growing reputations in the theatre but with their reputations at the bar of the Salisbury already well established. I don't think the term 'hellraisers' had yet been coined, but it would soon need to be, when it would be applied in particular to the young Peter O'Toole. Not even the hard-drinking Robert Shaw, not even Ronald Fraser with his cry of 'More Fraserwaters!' – quadruple vodkas – could match the O'Toole appetite for alcohol. One evening, after a leisurely survey of the afternoon drinking clubs and a few last quick ones at the Salisbury, he had lurched across to the New Theatre a minute before curtain-up to find his understudy, Michael Caine, dressed and waiting to go on. 'No you fucking don't, Michael!' roared O'Toole. He was changed within seconds, and pausing only to throw up violently out of the upstage window of the set, which the audience thought was part of the action, gave a flawless performance.

The play was *The Long and the Short and the Tall* by my old youth club friend Willis Hall, himself no stranger to the Salisbury – it was surprising that we had never met there. In fact I had not set eyes on Willis ever since, as conscripted servicemen, we had bumped into one another on York Station when he was on his way home from Catterick on embarkation leave, having been posted to Malaya. Like me, Willis had dabbled in journalism before his call-up. Arriving in Singapore, he looked around for something in the same line to relieve the tedium of barrack-room life and found himself writing children's plays for Radio Malaya – somewhat of a challenge, given that his young Chinese audience had an English vocabulary of around fifty words.

Back in civilian life, he used this experience to get a toehold in the BBC and was soon a busy Jack-of-all-work in radio, writing documentary features, plays and children's scripts, then landing a contract for a series of trail-blazing television plays. One of his radio plays, the north-country comedy *Poet and Pheasant*, translated first into television and then into provincial rep, and now a stage career beckoned. His play *The Disciplines of War*, presented by the Oxford Theatre Group, was one of the hits of the Edinburgh Festival. Under another title, *Boys It's All Hell*, it was equally successful in its professional premiere by the Nottingham Rep. The impresario Oscar Lewenstein, a fragile, beaky individual who looked more like a district auditor than a producer, and as if he had not the energy to turn the pages of a script, let alone read one and pass judgment upon it, was nonetheless one of the driving forces, perhaps the driving force, in the theatre of that period, and the man who as general manager of the Royal Court put George Devine in place to run the epoch-making English Stage Company. He heard about Willis's war play, went up to Nottingham to see it, and was impressed.

Oscar took an option on the play and asked George Devine if he would care to have it at the Court. Lindsay Anderson, whose stage directing experience was so far limited to one Sunday night performance, was asked if he would like to direct it. Albert Finney, who had worked in one of Willis's radio plays, was cast in the leading part of Bamforth, the bolshie cockney. The play was given yet another new title, *The Long and the Short and the Tall*. Just before rehearsals were about to begin, Finney fell ill with peritonitis. Oscar Lewenstein had just been down with John Osborne to the Bristol Old Vic to see Peter O'Toole as Jimmy Porter: the part went to him. The rest had already become theatrical history.

It was odd that after losing touch for twelve years, Willis and I should emerge blinking into the limelight at almost exactly the same time, both of us with works drawing on our own experience, he as a squaddy in Malaya, I as an undertaker's clerk in Leeds. Like *The*

326

Long and the Short, hailed as 'the best anti-war play since *Journey's End*', *Billy Liar* was an instant success; in fact in the climate of the time it was among the handful of books that attracted a buzz even before they were on the shelves. John Braine, himself still basking in the fame of *Room at the Top*, wrote an extraordinarily generous letter to my publisher at Michael Joseph, Roland Gant: '*There Is a Happy Land* was not only the best novel of 1957 but of the whole decade. It was better than *Room at the Top*; and don't think I enjoy saying this. I wished I'd written Keith Waterhouse's first novel; and now, even more so, I wish I'd written his second. This also I don't enjoy saying . . .' This was published as a full-page advertisement in the trade papers a couple of weeks before publication, and it gave the novel a tremendous boost – as John, with whom I was to become a fellow-member of the northern mafia as our branch of the new wave was dubbed, never tired of reminding me; it was his delusion, finally, that he had more or less discovered me and nurtured me to success.

The reviews were all I could have wished for. 'A sad, savage, sick, funny book,' said John Bowen in the *Sunday Times*. 'A brilliantly funny book, rich in absurdities and beautifully edged writing' – *TLS*. These and more went to embellish the dust jacket of the American edition, published only two or three months later, when it was equally well received. 'One of the year's most entertaining characters' – *Time* magazine. I did like 'An English Salinger has burst upon the scene', but as that was from the *Los Angeles Mirror News*, not noted for its literary clout, I preferred the *Boston Globe*'s 'A masterpiece of youth, imagination and laughter'.

Billy Liar was published within days of Colin MacInnes's exuberant youth-cult novel *Absolute Beginners*, and so they were frequently and glowingly coupled in reviews. (Indeed, I reviewed *Absolute Beginners* myself in the *New Statesman*: '. . . one of the few authors I have come across who has any idea what these hurrying years are all about. His hero looks around with awe and says: "My lord, one thing is certain, and that's that they'll make musicals one day about the glamour-studded 1950s."' Ah, well: they made *Expresso Bongo*.)

Some media attempt was made – with difficulty, since neither of us was drawing much of a sober breath at that point – to bracket MacInnes and me as 'youth generation' spokesmen, and I suppose that made *Billy Liar* newsy for a while; at any rate it was soon into a second and third edition, the paperback rights went to Penguin, various foreign rights were sold, and an option on the film rights was snapped up for £1,000 by the producer Sidney Cole, whose TV series *Robin Hood and the Four Just Men* had given much employment to the regulars of the Salisbury (later I bought them back, but that becomes another story). Like *There Is a Happy Land* before it, *Billy Liar* was destined, or doomed, to become a school textbook, when plodding pamphlets of 'study aids' and 'passnotes' were written about it, learnedly explaining the text – 'Shags like a rattlesnake – sexually promiscuous.' It was all very exciting, very confusing – and at times strangely anti-climactic: for the first time in my adult life, when on odd mornings there would be no mail, no reviews, no calls from the BBC, I would feel like a child who has opened all its Christmas presents and doesn't know what to do next – an occasional, self-indulgently depressive state which has persisted throughout a life that insists on regular treats. It was, I suppose, an echo back to teenage days when I was banging my articles off to magazines and thereafter awaiting the postman's knock which as often as not was not forthcoming. Even a rejection slip would have been welcome, some days.

Where it was all different this second time around was that it was clear from the start that nothing would ever be the same again. Nor was it. *Billy Liar* had not been out a fortnight when I had a call out of the blue from Willis Hall, who had somehow tracked me down to the *Daily Mirror* office where I was hanging around for some reason. Naturally I was delighted to hear from him and began burbling away as one does to an old friend after a twelve-year interregnum; but Willis typically had no time to waste on preliminary chit-chat: 'Listen, this is business, luv. *Billy Liar* – fantastic. Have you sold the film rights?'

'Yes.'

'Shit.'

I heard the expletive repeated in the background – by, I was to learn, the writer Wolf Mankowitz, who was in partnership with Oscar Lewenstein in his production company.

'Never mind, luv. I still think it would make a marvellous play. How do you feel about collaborating on it?'

The last time I had collaborated with Willis was on some sketches for a youth club concert when we were around sixteen. We had got on well then and I saw no reason why we should not get on well now. I said, 'Yes, fine', and we arranged to meet for lunch the

328

following day, when now we did indulge in reminiscent small-talk and take an extended stroll down Back Memory Lane. We did not talk much about the play.

At just turning thirty, I had yet to emerge from that euphoric, almost hypnotic state of innocence where no task seemed too daunting or too difficult. Willis, I was quickly to learn, had the same blessed approach to work, although in his case he would have called this benediction or dispensation by some more brass-tacks, pragmatic name such as professionalism. At any rate, we wasted not a second in discussing the problems of converting an 190-page novel in a couple of dozen scenes into a seventy-page play in one composite set (nowadays we would probably have had a more fluid, cinematic set and eliminated many of the technical problems I for one did not even notice we were confronting). I don't think we spent more than two or three weeks on the script, and even that not full time, for we both had other things to do. We worked mainly in Willis's ground-floor flat in Ebury Street – rather enviable 'rooms', I thought, of the kind occupied by amateur sleuths in detective stories, complete with a Mrs Hudson in attendance. Willis was then something of a first-nighter and much of our salty northern dialogue was written while he changed into dinner jacket and frilled shirt and tied his black tie. The working pattern we established was as it was to remain over the years – we would take it in turns to sit at the typewriter while the other paced the room, with every line of dialogue being rehearsed aloud before it was committed to paper. If it achieved nothing else, the method guaranteed that our speeches could be spoken with ease – not always the case with even the most seasoned of writers, as any actor can testify.

The play finished, the manuscript was despatched to Scripts Ltd in Dover Street, a tirelessly industrious battery of young ladies whose electric typewriters churned out every rehearsal script and every shooting script of every hit, flop and potboiler of those prolific years. Willis and I spent a long time – more time than we had spent on the curtain line – deciding in what colour we should have our rehearsal scripts bound. We decided on a deep blue. We have always paid superstitious attention to the colours of our scripts and deep blue remains a favourite. Pale green, we were to discover, is the colour of failure – but that is another script and another story. I was childishly excited to take delivery of my bound copies of *Billy Liar* the play – as excited as I had been to unpack my half-dozen author's copies of *Billy Liar* the novel. The tactile experience of first handling a properly presented, properly bound A5 script is the first link in the daisy-chain of absurd delights of working in the theatre -- delights which even the keenest disappointments can never eliminate.

Even I did not imagine that getting the play written was all there was to it, and that it would now be a smooth run to the opening night. In fact it could hardly have been smoother. No one even wanted to change the title (when the play that had been born of the novel gave birth to the musical *Billy*, there was an impresario's assistant who wanted to retitle it *The Wonderful Imagination of Billy the Liar*).

Oscar Lewenstein had already expressed keen interest in the play and was prepared to raise the impressive sum of £6,000 to put it on. Albert Finney, having missed out on *The Long and the Short*, was the first and obvious choice for Billy. While he hummed and hawed – I believe it was around the time he was being tested by David Lean for *Lawrence of Arabia* – there was some talk of Tommy Steele playing the part. Perhaps fortunately for all concerned, Tommy elected to do his Tony Lumpkin at the Old Vic, Albert turned down Lawrence, and we were in business. Lindsay Anderson read the play and agreed to direct. Everything was going so much like clockwork that it was really not the ideal production to cut my theatrical teeth on, lulled as I was into believing that it would always be like this. In fact I learned much later that Lindsay had not agreed with all that much alacrity after all, being much preoccupied at the time with David Storey's *This Sporting Life*, which he wanted to film. At least no one involved could complain that they were not spoiled for choice.

Beyond nodding my head sagely from time to time, I took little part in the casting process. Apart from Mona Washbourne, whom I had seen in *Morning's at Seven*, and who was to play Billy's long-suffering mother, I knew none of the names put forward, although I did recognise George A. Cooper, Billy's father, and Ann Beach, the orange-sucking Barbara, from their *Spotlight* photographs. I do recall contributing a particularly vigorous nod when somebody cautiously pointed out that at the age of eighty-two Ethel Griffies, the grandmother, might be something of a risk should the play enjoy the long run we were hoping for. In fact Ethel, whose first appearance on the West End stage was in the year 1901, left the cast of *Billy Liar* of her own volition after thirteen months, to play Dr Elizabeth Wooley in *Write Me a Murder* at the Belasco Theatre, New York. She was last heard of playing Billy's grandmother again off Broadway in her eighty-eighth year. A fine performance had improved with age – she had, she said, 'grown into it.'

I do not remember attending very many rehearsals after the first reading. We would not, I think, have been welcome. Lindsay, the son of a major-general, could be something of a martinet, and while he may have been a middle-class rebel and in favour of making waves, he did not care for them being made in his own direction. He had Willis in particular, and me by extension, down as irreverent troublemakers. While he had directed *The Long and the Short* impeccably, Lindsay was not, as Oscar Lewenstein was to record in a masterpiece of understatement, 'one of the lads'. Anxious to give his cast the bearing of real soldiers, Lindsay started rehearsal one morning by parading them in uniform outside the Royal Court Theatre, sloping arms, and marching them around Sloane Square. They had done less than a quarter-circuit when Private Peter O'Toole right-wheeled the squad into the nearest pub. While Lindsay Anderson formed close relationships with many actors, O'Toole was not among them. Nor, alas, in contrast to his connection with David Storey whose entire stage oeuvre he directed, did he show any marked enthusiasm for working with Willis and me again.

He did, however, as part of his preparation for *Billy Liar*, insist upon travelling north and inspecting the kind of suburban semi that Billy would have lived in. In vain did we try to persuade him that there were identical semis in Ruislip. Lindsay questioned us keenly on precisely which Leeds suburb he would have been raised in, regarding it as obstreperous quibbling when we pointed out that he was not supposed to have come from Leeds at all but from one of the small West Riding woollen towns some miles distant. Eventually we found him the very semi-detached, Dunroamin-type residence that would have been home to Billy, whereupon to the bemusement of neighbours he spent a considerable time walking up and down outside it, head cocked, like a prospective buyer. Finally Lindsay was positioned by the front gate with his outstretched hands forming the imaginary frame of a film camera, when the door of Dunroamin was flung open and an angry-looking householder, who could have been cast as Billy's father on the spot without benefit of auditions, barked: 'What are you on, then?'

'Oh, it's quite all right,' called Lindsay blithely. 'Just looking at a few locations.'

'Then bloody don't!' And the door slammed.

At least Lindsay's researches into suburban life were not as painstaking as those for one of the most recent revivals of *Billy Liar*, a National Theatre touring production which culminated in a season at the Cottesloe. Here, so that the Fisher family and their visitors could get the 'feel' of a suburban semi, an actual fully furnished Barratt house in East Finchley was placed at their disposal. Thus when Mum went out of the living room to make tea, she would walk into an actual kitchen and make actual tea at an actual stove; and when Gran said she was going upstairs for a lie-down she could actually do so, in any one of three bedrooms. Whether the cast ever made use of this facility I did not care to ask, so I never learned whether the great success of the revival was because of or in spite of this enterprising touch of realism.

Billy Liar was to premiere at the Brighton Theatre Royal, play for a week and then come into the West End. I did not know that a week is a perilously short time in the theatre when it comes to ironing out any kinks that might be revealed in a play once it is set before the public. Therefore it was merrily enough that I drove Willis and Albert Finney down to Brighton in the new little Austin A30 I had bought on the strength of giving up my regular employment with the *Mirror*. I had never been to Brighton before and we got lost – no easy task on that well-worn road – with the result that we deposited Albert at the theatre fractionally late for the technical rehearsal. This did not endear us to Lindsay, who liked to run a well-disciplined ship.

Things were not to get better when Willis and I returned for the dress rehearsal after a much-needed drink. As Oscar Lewenstein guardedly puts it in his memoirs: 'There was an unfortunate dress rehearsal, in the middle of which Willis and Keith, who had probably drunk too much, had a quarrel with Lindsay (with whom they were not temperamentally in harmony in any case). This quarrel at such a time had repercussions later on, which I think were unfortunate for us all . . .'

Certainly Willis and I had been celebrating, and in retrospect we should have addressed such remarks to Lindsay as we had to make down in the stalls, where he was sitting, rather than from the dress circle, where we were standing. But our point was valid. When Billy opened the cupboard in which he keeps his guilty store of purloined calendars, it was to reveal, for the first time and without consultation with the authors, a cascade of toy boats, spinning tops and other children's playthings. There was no justification in the text for this innovation and it brought to a head a difference of interpretation we had had with Lindsay from the start – that he was trying to tip Billy's immaturity into infantilism, a quality which did not suit the character at all and which certainly would not have suited the personality of Albert Finney had he chosen to go along with it. But Lindsay, airily referring us back to what he called 'the underlying text' – by now he seemed to have forgotten that I had written the original novel – would not listen. 'Watch and learn!' he barked, and we retired to the Royal Albion Hotel.

The 'unfortunate repercussions' were that after buying back the film option I had already rashly disposed of, we now sold the rights to Jo Janni for John Schlesinger to direct, instead of to Oscar Lewenstein and Tony Richardson for Woodfall Films, with Lindsay directing. We did this, according to Oscar, 'because they did not want Lindsay to direct the film.' That is nonsense. While Lindsay had yet to make a feature film he had a formidable reputation as a film-maker and despite our differences we would have been foolish to turn him down. But John Schlesinger had a reputation too; and Jo Janni made the more attractive offer, which was a three-picture deal with Stan Barstow's *A Kind of Loving* to be the first. Lindsay however did not draw the short straw: he was to make his feature debut with *This Sporting Life*. And Oscar was to co-produce *Tom Jones*. So in this highly productive period, there were no losers.

For the present, though, our concern was with Billy's theatre potential rather than any future he might have in pictures. The play opened uneasily. Out-of-town audiences seeing a first-ever performance are self-consciously aware that they are sitting there in judgment. Like a jury, therefore, they like to see the evidence properly marshalled – in other words, they want to know what they are getting. The difficulty with *Billy* was, as Milton Schulman was to put it in the *Evening Standard*, that it had 'the outward veneer of a riotous farce and the inner heart of a significant comedy'. In the first half of this opening night, it seemed that half the audience went along with the riotous farce reading while the other half either accepted the significant comedy interpretation or they did not know what to make of the piece at all. In other words the reception was patchy.

The second half was even stickier. There were intermittent mutterings and murmurings, and as the curtain came down there

333

was some booing from the gallery. It was the first time I had ever heard the sound, except in Technicolor biogs of Broadway vaudeville acts, and I wasn't at all sure what to make of it: was it exhilaratingly frightening – or frighteningly exhilarating? What had the galleryites taken exception to? The northern setting (remember we were in Brighton), the way Billy treated his grandmother, his engagement equivalent of bigamy, the raw teenage dialogue – what? The house manager put us right. It was the epithet 'bloody', with which Billy's father punctuates practically every sentence. The gallery – and for that matter the stalls and dress circle, but they did not boo – took a strong line on swear words. But we were not to worry: the *Evening Argus* would love it. (They did, too: next day's headline was 'Billy Liar Takes a Bold Stride to Success'.)

Thirty years on, when my play *Jeffrey Bernard Is Unwell* likewise made its debut at the same theatre, Peter O'Toole's first word was 'shit' and his second was 'fuck'. Both brought the house down. Changing times? Changing tastes? The language in *Jeffrey Bernard Is Unwell* has never been the subject of serious complaint – only the protagonist's prodigious alcoholic input ever raised a murmur. But Billy's father's now-innocuous 'bloody' was to dog us.

To the West End. Every play enjoying the benefit of momentum gathers with it, like moss, its own mythology, eventually accepted even by some of those who were most closely involved. One version of *Billy Liar*'s success is that it was a hit from the start; another, that it was mauled by the critics but was saved by an excerpt shown on television. The truth, as so often, was somewhere in between.

The play did get what I would learn to call 'mixed reviews', but they were not as mixed as some I have collected since without lasting damage. *The Times* could 'remember no stage study of a fantast more direct or more complete than we are given in *Billy Liar*.' Eric Keown of *Punch*, who confessed that his heart had sunk at curtain-up in the belief that 'a sitting room in a north country industrial town spells rugged social realism with an unwanted baby, at least yellow and probably black', found himself 'within five minutes adding to the gale of laughter whipped up by a first act as unexpected as it was funny.' Harold Hobson, having written in the *Sunday Times* that the play 'is very funny and its implications are deep', was moved by the slowness of the box office to go back and review it all over again. Kenneth Tynan, on the other hand, thought the play skirted 'the broader implications' and didn't examine the causes of the hero's weakness. Other critics had other reservations, but they were at least universal in their praise for Albert Finney – 'the new Olivier'.

The real trouble, though, was that we were in the wrong theatre. Given the uneven critical reception that, with hindsight, it was almost certain to get – as Lindsay Anderson shrewdly commented years later, 'The wrong things were expected of it: London "intellectuals" were apt to turn up their noses at Northern comedy, while the highbrow critics tried but found it difficult to situate the play in the current movement of dissidence' – the safest harbour for *Billy Liar* would have been in a medium-sized house on Shaftesbury Avenue or thereabouts with plenty of passing trade. But by one of those domino effects by which theatrical fortunes are made or lost, there were no fewer than a dozen productions seeking West End homes that month; we were well behind in the queue and we either had to continue touring in the hope of the right theatre falling vacant, or take what we could get.

It happened that a Cambridge Footlights revue, devised by John Bird in what was then called 'the modern manner', had caught the attention of William Donaldson who wanted to develop it for the West End. Called *Here Is the News*, with material by Ionesco, N. F. Simpson, Peter Cook and John Bird himself, and a cast which included Cleo Laine, Lance Percival and Sheila Hancock, plus an ingenious set by Sean Kenny, the revue set out on tour and baffled Coventry with its mix of political satire and surrealism, not to mention its unusual method, several years before *Monty Python*, of bringing sketches to an end with a firing squad appearing from nowhere and shooting the participants. But John Bird went down with jaundice, Eleanor Fazan took over as director, but by then the money had run out and the opening night at the Cambridge Theatre was cancelled. Willie Donaldson and Eleanor Fazan went on to console themselves by bringing *Beyond the Fringe* to London, while *Billy Liar* got the Cambridge, a barn of a theatre for a straight play, with 1,255 seats to fill and situated on the as then grimly unreconstituted Seven Dials well away from the bright lights.

With his meagre capitalisation almost gone, Oscar Lewenstein had little money with which to nurse the play along, and after two weeks of indifferent business in such a huge theatre, with acres of empty seats casting a gloom over the sparse audiences we were relying on for 'word of mouth', it was beginning to look as if the management, in the person of Tom Arnold who disliked the show and everything about it, might give us notice to clear out if any likelier prospect turned up. Then things began to happen our way.

Harold Hobson gave us his second boost, which while not sending the business rocketing at least improved it to the point at which we were reaching the 'break' figure beyond which we could not be ejected. Then, six weeks after our opening, the film of *Saturday Night and Sunday Morning* was released, with more massive 'star is born' publicity for Albert Finney – all of it mentioning his 'West End hit', *Billy Liar*. Finally, we got our forty-five-minute slot on television. The BBC then regularly went in for showing live excerpts, usually a whole act, from West End shows – it was relatively cheap for them and, so impresarios hoped, it brought business to the theatre. Sometimes in fact it had the reverse effect and kept customers away – it depended on the type of play. With a comedy crammed with surefire laughs, we felt on reasonably safe ground.

The immediate result of the television extract was that, inevitably, 'the BBC switchboard was jammed with calls', to quote the next day's papers – a repeat of the Brighton galleryites' reaction. The fact that it takes fewer than a dozen calls to jam the BBC switchboard did not diminish the scale of the hullabaloo. A Sheffield councillor counted the bloodies – there were fifteen – and condemned the play as 'shocking'. Readers of countless local newspapers, including 'Disgusted Sailorman' of Aberdeen, wrote to ask 'why oh why' we had to have this bad language, and what were the churches doing about it? Vicars responded by denouncing the play from the pulpit. In headline terms, *Billy Liar* became 'That Blue Pencil Play'.

A further and more gratifying result was that not only the BBC switchboard but the box office telephones were jammed. Advance bookings soared. Willis and I took to strolling over to the theatre in the afternoons to see the ticket queues winding around the block. For the first time, we could be sure of an extended run, and the House Full signs became a fixture in the foyer.

This was clearly and simply because large numbers of viewers had enjoyed what they had seen on television and wanted to see more. As Lindsay Anderson was to put it: 'It took television to bypass the snobbery of the critics, and to tell the enormous potential audience that this was a play they would enjoy – and recognise.' How much the 'That Blue Pencil Play' controversy brought to the box office it would be impossible to quantify, but it could not be denied that it played its part. The truth was, though, that through a combination of Finney's star quality, our own flavour-of-the-month news potential, those bloody bloodies, and the fact that it was very much a play of its time, our 'lounge comedy', as one critic dubbed it, had by now become a powerful publicity generator. It was one of those plays, like *Jeffrey Bernard Is Unwell* three decades later, that for one reason or another was never out of the papers. Soon there was a regular procession of visiting celebrities through Albert Finney's dressing room. Princess Margaret came. So did Noël Coward who, as he records in his diaries, loathed the play and everything about it – exquisitely polite at the time, he later penned a famously bad-tempered attack on the whole kitchen-sink theatre, as the press label had it. One night, to the egalitarian Lindsay's delight and the management's horror, a bunch of Teddy boys invaded the theatre. There was no need for alarm – they had come to see the play.

Albert Finney played the part for nine months before being released by Oscar Lewenstein to do John Osborne's *Luther*, producer Oscar Lewenstein. Tom Courtenay took over. It was fascinating to contrast their performances – Albert's extrovert 'I am a star!' Billy, Tom's introvert 'I wish I were a star' Billy. Both interpretations were equally correct, for locked in Billy Fisher's tangled psyche are both characters, star and nonentity, battling it out. The audiences kept flocking in. *Billy Liar* was to run for 582 performances. After the five hundredth, the production's enterprising press officer worked out that Billy had told 40,500 lies so far during the run, and his father had uttered the infamous B-word 100,000 times.

The West End run was followed by a major, seemingly interminable tour (you could then tour for nigh on a year without playing the same date twice), then countless rep productions, then more tours and summer seasons – 'the stars of *Coronation Street* in *Billy Liar*.' There were foreign productions without number, including Turkish (*Yalanci Bili*) and Polish (*Klamer Billy*). Hugh Leonard adapted the play for Ireland – *Liam Liar*, in which our hero is trying to escape from Cork to Dublin. The film, the television series, the American TV sitcom and the Drury Lane musical were still to come when somewhere along the way, critics whose initial verdict had been harsh or lukewarm began to modify their views, if not to rewrite history completely like the *Soviet Cyclopedia*. Tynan, who had found

337

the play 'a ramshackle piece of purely whimsical entertainment', was a year later writing, 'What with Harold Pinter, Keith Waterhouse and Willis Hall on the sidelines, I think it safe to predict that satire, irony, gallows-humour and other mutations of the comic spirit will be the guiding force of our theatre in the coming years.'

3   The advance on the dramatisation of *Billy Liar* having been
    £50 apiece, I had vaguely supposed that if the play took off
    at all and royalty cheques began to come in, they would be
of around the same order. In fact Willis and I were pretty soon being
pigeonholed in the gossip columns as '£500-a-week writers'. While
this sum, divided by two and deducting the agent's commission,
would these days amount to no more than the average wage, it
was then worth about £4,500 a week in present-day terms. This was
soon being hugely augmented by the other work that was flowing
our way, in films, television and the theatre.

For a while I dabbled at being rich – hand-made boots from
Lobb's, gold Omega watch, Calibri lighter, pricey casuals, mink in
the adjoining wardrobe, hire cars everywhere, outrageously priced
£6-a-head dinners at the White Elephant and Parkes' in Beauchamp
Place. Except for a daily bottle of champagne, for which I have
retained the taste, such excesses soon palled, though not before I had
acquired a Victorian three-storey family house in Vicarage Gardens,
Kensington, plus a designer-decorated flat overlooking the sea in
Brighton, and Willis and I had taken a lease on a suite of offices at
171 New Bond Street, over the salon of the up-and-rising hairdresser
Vidal Sassoon who, threading his way through the patient tiers of
actresses sitting it out on the stairs while they waited their turn for
the scissors, would often come up for a cup of coffee.

It was in New Bond Street, a couple of doors from Asprey's,
arriving each morning in chauffeured splendour, that Willis Hall and
I wrote our next play, *Celebration*, a slice-of-life double bill about a
northern extended family arranging, in the first half, a working-class
wedding reception and in the second half returning from a funeral.
Incongruous though these Mayfair surroundings were for such an
exercise, Willis and I wrote *Celebration* effortlessly, the characters

and dialogue fairly gushing out from the spring of our joint family backgrounds. It remains, out of all the work we have done together, our favourite play.

The wedding half of the bill was originally commissioned for radio by our friend Alfred Bradley of the BBC in Leeds, as a vehicle for some of the young actors he was sponsoring up there. Nottingham Playhouse encouraged us to write the funeral half to go with it, when it was taken up by Oscar Lewenstein who brought it to the Duchess Theatre, thus giving the likes of Michael Williams, Robert Lang, James Cossins, Jeremy Kemp and Thelma Barlow (doing a preliminary sketch of her *Coronation Street* Mavis) their first taste of the West End. The reviews were warm to the point of ecstatic ('Achingly funny' – Levin), and for a while we had two West End plays running simultaneously, giving us the excuse to throw a lavish party at the White Elephant for the cast of *Celebration* to meet the cast of *Billy Liar*. The White Elephant, a luxurious club in Curzon Street, was then the London equivalent of Sardi's, and one of our haunts – almost a second office. It was there one evening that we witnessed a blazing row between Rachel Roberts and her husband Rex Harrison. It was just after Harrison had filmed *Dr Dolittle*, and evidently the argument was about their respective star ratings, for in one of those lulls which always occur in restaurants when two diners are quarrelling, Miss Roberts was heard to snap, 'At least I've never played opposite a fucking giraffe!'

Celebration played to good houses, but an ensemble play featuring sixteen unknowns could not expect to do the same kind of business we were doing at the Cambridge with a starry name in lights, and after a respectable run the time came for our talented company to disperse. That was not the end of *Celebration* by a long chalk: it continued to be played in rep for years, it was done several times on radio and on television, and with its cast of what French's acting editions call 8m, 8f, it remains a favourite with amateurs to this day. Rank's, belatedly climbing aboard the northern wave bandwagon, bought the film rights for a tidy sum and we wrote the screenplay: predictably, they got cold feet and shelved it. John Wells and Cari Davies improbably toyed with the notion of turning *Celebration* into an opera. And just as half the actors I know have played Billy Liar at some distant point in their careers, so I keep meeting actors and actresses who can quote whole slabs from *Celebration*. Freddie Jones, who played the part of the bride's Uncle Arthur on television a good twenty-five years ago, can recite word-perfect to this day his advice to the groom upon reaching the honeymoon destination: 'Where do you say you're going then – Scarborough? Well, listen here. When you get there, go into that little café with the corrugated iron roof. That one on the cliff top and just say Arthur Broadbent sent you. See what they say. And if I don't get chance to speak to you tomorrow, here's a pound note to take with you.'

Uncle Arthur, originally played by Morgan Sheppard, was every audience's favourite character – the epitome of all raffish, slightly black-sheep uncles. In act two of *Celebration*, 'The Funeral', the audience would always gasp with dismay upon learning that it was Uncle Arthur whom the family were mourning. It would have been tempting to let such a strong character live on and kill off one of the others but our instinct was right – Uncle Arthur, even in his absence, continues to dominate the play. Our vivid impressions of him are augmented by his own best friend, Sergeant-Major Tommy Lodge, memorably played by Robert Lang, who arrives late and drunk. Thirty-odd years on, Willis and I have to be restrained from reciting, on appropriate occasions, and on some inappropriate ones, Tommy Lodge's swaying explanation of why he has arrived unaccompanied by his motor transport officer, Captain Yates, whom he had taken the liberty of inviting to the funeral: 'He was going to come. Only he had the great misfortune to fall down the lavatory steps of the Market Tavern. He's not hurt, missus, no, but it shook him. He picks himself up and of course, he's fallen in this disinfectant. I had to leave him there.'

Uncle Arthur and Tommy Lodge remain our favourite characters. We did once toy with the idea of resuscitating them to see what happens when these two old friends – who of course never meet on the stage – get together. Wisely, no doubt, we resisted the urge.

I have only the haziest memory of our actually writing *Celebration*, with the two of us acting out chunks of it in that New Bond Street office as we rescued characters from a Hunslet that was vanishing as the terraces came tumbling down. I do recall that there was a good deal of laughter. More than *Billy Liar*, I think, *Celebration* set the seal on our long collaboration, for after exhuming so much shared experience and observation we were thereafter able to speak in shorthand.

Although I was going to an office every day, I have no impression of it being work. In fact, considering that we were by now being tagged 'the prolific pair' in newspaper interviews, it is only with the greatest difficulty than I can recall us doing any work at all. At the urging of accountants we had turned ourselves into not one but two limited companies – Waterhall Productions Ltd and Hunslet Productions Ltd; while individually we became respectively Willis Hall Productions Ltd and Keith Waterhouse Ltd – but the bakelite plate on the door proclaiming this new status did little to induce gravitas. The most impressive aspect of being directors of our own little mini-conglomerate was that according to our articles of association we were entitled to operate tramways. It was a greater temptation, some mornings, than the immediate prospect of writing scripts.

We did evolve a daily routine of a kind, even if it was not always, or for weeks at a stretch sometimes, a working routine. The day would begin at nine with a car from Miles and Miles, the show business hire car firm, picking us up and depositing us at 171 New Bond Street. In the first flush of executivism, our secretary had a secretary, a delightful young thing who emblazoned herself upon our corporate memory by one day filing a cheque for £35,000 under Receipts Miscellaneous, where it remained for several weeks. The secretary's secretary fetched us coffee, and we would then review the excesses of the night before.

We were both at the time fairly hard drinkers, and while we were by no means in the hellraiser class there was as often as not a shared adventure to recollect. One celebrated occasion was when I had been instructed by Joan to buy a Christmas tree. One festive drink that day had led to another, and we were still propping up the bar of the Salisbury Tavern by the time Covent Garden closed. I had no option but to negotiate for the Salisbury's own six-foot Christmas tree – lights, baubles, fairy and all. The deal clinched, Willis and I decided to take the tree to the Embassy nightclub for a drink, and with difficulty got it into a taxi. The doorman at the Embassy, a man of some humour, refused it admittance on the grounds that it was not wearing a tie. We therefore bought the cab driver's tie for some absurd sum, draped it around the topmost branches in a Windsor knot and, having signed the tree in, took it downstairs, trailing electric flex and shedding artificial snow and glitter powder, and plied it with champagne. The Embassy was one of those clubs where one may enjoy the undivided attention of a hostess for a consideration. Tiring of the tree's company by now, we introduced it to a hostess and went over to join friends, remembering, however, to send it across a drink from time to time. It was a somewhat dishevelled Christmas tree that I finally got home to Vicarage Gardens, but my children declared it was the best one they had ever seen.

Our next serious task was to find some way of evading or avoiding the morning's work. Nearly all writers have a large repertoire of excuses for putting off writing, but when one is working, or rather not working, in tandem, it is not so easy, since it takes more ingenuity to fool one's partner than to fool oneself. Luckily we were able to find a way.

Early in our partnership Willis and I discovered that we had a mutual passion for board games, card games and jigsaw puzzles. Whole hours could drift by while we searched for an elusive piece of sky or Cornish fishing boat; mornings would pass on an interminable two-deck card game called Lapin. Ostensibly, of course, we were thinking – dreaming up plots, inventing situations and characters, solving script problems. If that were so, I have no recollection of either of us jumping up from the Monopoly board with a cry of 'Eureka!'

The game was the thing, and our desks were piled high with imports from Hamley's – Scrabble, Cluedo, chess, a complex battle game known as L'Attaque involving opposing armies, and an even more complex one called Tri-Tactics where there were so many platoons, battalions and divisions, cruisers, battleships and destroyers, fighters, bombers and anti-aircraft batteries, that a war of cardboard enemies could rage on for weeks. Some of our board games were not all that much fun with two players, even though we invented a Maxwell-type variation of Monopoly whereby we formed ourselves into a huge corporation and finished up owning everything on the board between us; and so on occasion we would take a cab to the George, the BBC pub just around the corner from Broadcasting House, and more or less press-gang any stray couple of actors we found having a morning drink there into coming back to the office with us and playing Scrabble or Cluedo. As for Lapin, we finally got so hooked on this, for it was a gambling game, that with the tax inspector now beginning to catch up with our large earnings we faced the prospect of bankruptcy unless we buckled down and got some work done. Passers-by in the street below must have been surprised when it began snowing playing-cards one fine morning –

we could not trust ourselves to dispose of the cards in the wastepaper basket, for one or other of us would have compulsively fished them out again.

Another of our work-avoidance schemes was an elaborate practical joke – the Frankenstein-like creation of an invented writer, one Vernon Laxton, whom we set out to get recognised and talked about even though he had never written a word. Or rather, he had written exactly one page – of an excruciating sub-Christopher Fry verse drama called *Arise All Ye Pheonixes* (sic), based on the life of the patron saint of cobblers, St Crispin. Copies of this page were despatched to all the theatrical impresarios in London, with a covering letter apologising for it having been omitted from the script Vernon claimed to have already sent for their consideration. This yielded a concerned correspondence from producers anxious to point out that they had never received Mr Laxton's play, could not take responsibility for unsolicited manuscripts, and in any case were not in the market for verse drama.

Vernon then turned his attention to selected fellow-writers, not so much offering to adapt their work for the musical stage as declaring his unilateral intention of doing so. This brought in an entertaining crop of indignant letters. Arnold Wesker, to whom Vernon, in offering commiseration on his last play having come off ('Perhaps it was the religious title?'), had proposed a musical of 'your comedy *Roots*', replied testily that if he were considering a musical of *Roots* he would write the lyrics himself, and that furthermore it was *I'm Talking about Jerusalem*, not *How about Jerusalem*. Ted Willis, for his part, replied more amiably that if anyone was to dramatise *Dixon of Dock Green* ('not Nixon, as you have written'), it would be himself. Vernon responded, 'Very well, then, my dear Mr Willis, it will just have to be PC 49 of radio fame', and then turned his attention to a Councillor Melling of Sheffield, congratulating him on his courageous remarks against the outrageous and disgusting *Billy the Liar*.

With the connivance of Ned Sherrin and David Frost we got Vernon Laxton a screen credit on *That Was The Week That Was*. Paragraphs about him began to infiltrate the trade papers – he was hoping that Lindsay Anderson would be directing *Arise All Ye Pheonixes*, he was working on a musical of the life of St Crispin, and so on and so on. The culmination, for us, was after we had written to our respective agents informing them that Vernon Laxton proposed

344

to call upon them with his son Norman to play the three-hour taped score of his new musical with Norman accompanying on the electric guitar – 'trusting you have socket availability for 13-amp plug.' Both wrote hastily back to claim other appointments. A few days later we had lunch with our two agents. Unprompted, my agent asked Willis's, 'Have you ever come across a writer called Vernon Laxton?' 'Yes,' said Willis's agent. 'Have nothing to do with him – he's a terrible nuisance.' Someone finally leaked our monster's true identity to the press, he found himself exposed in the *News of the World*, and that was the end of Vernon Laxton.

The morning rounded off with twenty minutes or so at the *Evening Standard* word game, we would then, unless we had more pressing business such as finding all the straight-edged bits of a 400-piece jigsaw or completing an exhausting round of Lapin, take ourselves off to lunch. Unless, that is, we were belatedly motivated by guilt, fear of the Inland Revenue or, as a last resort, inspiration, to settle down and do some work, when the secretary's secretary would be sent out for sandwiches.

Lunch was usually at an exclusive little dining club in Albemarle Street in which we had bought a partnership – or rather we had been sold a partnership, which is not necessarily quite the same thing. It was a place much used by film people, and so we could convince ourselves that we were networking. The club went in for fancy cooking, but taking advantage of our proprietorial *droit de seigneur* we would toss the menu aside and instruct the chef to make us plate-sized Yorkshire puddings with rabbit gravy, as served up for Sunday dinner back in Leeds. He was a good chef and they were just like our mothers used to make, although now washed down with claret instead of Tizer. These epicurean feasts went on until one lunchtime when the ever-discreet maître d' murmured in our ears that if the chef was obliged to make just one more Yorkshire pudding it was his intention to come out of the kitchen and 'pan' us – a technical expression of the culinary world meaning to assault somebody with a frying pan. We transferred our affections to the Caprice, the maître d' moved on to run an industrial canteen on a trading estate in Crawley which he no doubt regarded as upmarket from serving plate-sized Yorkshire puddings, and without our custom the club foundered and passed into other hands.

After lunch we might possibly go on to a club of the non-exclusive, non-dining sort, or indeed to two or three, making a crawl of it.

There were then, when public houses were required to shut down for a couple of hours at three o'clock sharp, no fewer than 472 registered clubs in central London, of which a great many were afternoon drinking clubs. We were members of a good dozen of these establishments – that is to say, either we had signed a grubby banker's order form which, unless we ever got round to cancelling it, would continue to disgorge a guinea a year to some improbable-sounding company long after the club registered in its name had been closed down by the police; or we had been made honorary or life members in recognition of our services to the till. We were also occasional or one-off visitors to very many more, where if membership formalities were insisted upon – they usually weren't – there would always be some acquaintance to sign us in.

Although these places were spread all over the West End and as far afield as Fulham, and an afternoon spent trooping from one to another could involve half a dozen cab rides, they were essentially the same club, with the same peripatetic clientele, drawn from a central pool – the Salisbury Tavern was the main casting agency – of resting actors, hacks, artists, 'models', petty entrepreneurs, and the flotsam and jetsam of Soho – no more than a couple of hundred or so all told. The club was either down the steps in a basement or up a narrow flight of stairs on the first floor – ground-floor premises, where too much could be seen from the street, were hardly ever favoured as a venue.

The club would consist of a simple room just big enough to accommodate, typically, no more than twenty-five people – not that it any longer held out hopes of ever seeing as many. Its furniture and fittings would comprise a few odd chairs and wobbly tables picked up at fire sales, a scuffed, linoleum-topped bar, and a fruit machine maintained and emptied periodically by beefy men in double-breasted suits of whom the club owner always seemed to be in awe. The staff would consist of the owner or someone purporting to be the owner, and a drop-out student, colonial backpacker or out-of-work actress who had been working behind the bar on a temporary basis for so long now that the oldest member was a new arrival by comparison.

Another fixture would be a chain-smoking, gin-swigging lady in her forties or fifties with a blonde beehive hairdo, perched on a rickety stool at the end of the bar, whose birthday we would be celebrating that day. It was always her birthday, but she was not always the same person – although she might just as well have been. The birthday girl, as she would insist upon calling herself, was but one of a number of stock characters – the compulsive gambler poring over his racing sheet, the near-alcoholic trying to pace his drinks, the jack-the-lad looking for an easy lay, the easy lay looking for a mug punter, the estranged husband drowning his sorrows, the depressive poet going rapidly to seed – who if one had put them into a television play would have guaranteed its rejection by return of post. But they would occasionally produce a line of dialogue to which Willis and I would be joyous eavesdroppers. Once, the estranged husband figure was bemoaning his lot to the bar in general: 'I don't know what it's all about any more, I really don't. You buy your wife her own car, you give her an account at Harrods, you let her have her own private dressmaker – and then she goes and takes up parachute-jumping.' While Willis tried valiantly to conceal his mirth I could not resist asking, in the drinking club vernacular, 'Had it away with the instructor, did she?' Estranged husband nodded glumly, then brought us both within his warm embrace. 'Not for nothing are you two gentlemen the perceptive writers I know you to be.' We left hurriedly.

But although handy scraps of dialogue and usable characters did sometimes come our way – these supposedly wasted afternoons were to give us our long-running TV drama series *Budgie*, after all – we did not loaf around the clubs in any spirit of research. Recharging the batteries may have come into it but we would have recharged them somewhere else had we not simply liked the atmosphere – an atmosphere that, with drinking at four in the afternoon resurfacing to respectable ground level for the first time since the 1914–18 war, has by now all but vanished. Seedy, smoky, scruffy, smelly, some of those clubs we found ourselves in would have been unendurably depressing had we been condemned to drift out our lives in them, as so many of the regulars were, prisoners of their own lethargy. As visitors from the outer space of New Bond Street, who if the cash ran short had only to lift a telephone for the secretary's secretary to arrive with emergency supplies, we were in a position to find them amusingly, anthropologically tolerable.

The services of the secretary's secretary as money-runner were indeed quite often required, for during this clubbing period we developed a passion for fruit machines – no doubt an extension of the board games syndrome. The secretary's secretary's duty was to

347

take a petty cash cheque to the bank and obtain a large bag of silver sixpences, then take a cab to the nominated club where she would nervously thrust the loot into our hands, gape around in astonished apprehension at what she imagined to be a den of vice and iniquity, and flee back to the safe haven of New Bond Street. One day we arranged to take delivery of twenty pounds' sworth of sixpences at the Down Under Club off Sloane Square, run by the Australian actor Kenneth J. Warren, for it boasted the very latest of the electronic, bleeping, buzzing gaming machines the size and style of pintables that were still such a novelty, and we were determined to have the jackpot. Unfortunately it turned out to be out of order and so we were left with a heavy consignment of sixpences on our hands. It happened that the Down Under featured a particularly noxious juke box on which members were for ever playing a tune called 'Amazing Grace', a great favourite at the time, though not with either of us. Rather than drag our burden of sixpences about with us we fed them all into the juke box, thus programming it to play 'Amazing Grace' eight hundred times in succession without pause, and then left. I believe that may have been one honorary membership that was not renewed.

Like everyone else in this wandering tribe of afternoon nomads, we had our favourite, which is to say our least unfavourite, clubs. The afternoon drinking clubs, I had found, had an affinity with Fleet Street pubs in that potential customers adopted them or avoided them for the most arcane reasons. This one had too many steps, that one was quite handy for the next port of call, this one would always cash a cheque, that one wouldn't, this one had a surly barman, that one always made one feel welcome. Not to mention, of course, that this one had barred one for life. Then, obscurely, there were those clubbable folk who after the manner of small field animals would not move outside their territory. We knew members of the Tree Trunk Club in Albemarle Street who would willingly cross Piccadilly to the Georgian Club in Bury Street, but would not venture further afield to the Tatty Bogle in Kingly Street; while there were members of the Tatty Bogle who would plunge happily into the depths of any Soho club one cared to mention, but who would twitch nervously at the suggestion of a quick one at the Buckstone Club in Sussex Street or the Steering Wheel in Shepherd Market. I once knew an actor who was visited by his mother from the sleepy hollow in the West Country where he had been raised and she still lived. For want of something better to do with her he took her on his regular little round of drinking clubs. Though all of them were enjoying, or enduring, a quiet afternoon – par for the course – she was enthralled. 'Son,' she enthused as he escorted her to her train, 'you have shown me a side of life I did not know existed.' Little did she fathom that the side of life she had seen was as tame and parochial as her own.

Soho's most famous club was, and is, the Colony Room in Dean Street, universally known as Muriel's after the black-clad, chain-smoking crone who then ran it. Neither Willis nor I used to go much to Muriel's, since it was policy to charge the last bottle of champagne to whomever she thought could best afford it, regardless of who had ordered or consumed it, and if either or both of us happened to be on the premises, that usually meant Willis or me. For my taste, Muriel, with her throaty cry of 'Come on, cunty, you're not buying enough champagne!', was one of those legends who are better encountered in the oft-told anecdote rather than in the flesh.

We did call quite often at Soho's next most celebrated drinking club, the Kismet, although quite what there was to celebrate about the place I never learned. Known as the Iron Lung, the Kismet stood opposite the Arts Club in Great Newport Street – decidedly not on the afternoon circuit – and was reached down a deep, narrow stairway leading into a dimly illuminated cellar still reeking of curry from its previous existence as a condemned Indian restaurant. Its dank interior extended under the pavement where, it was said, a loose paving stone served as the emergency exit.

The Kismet was mainly the resort of out-of-work actors, alcoholics and tiresome Soho 'characters' such as Maltese Mary and No-Knickers Joyce who were later to infest Jeffrey Bernard's Low Life column in the *Spectator* – Jeff himself was naturally a member, or anyway a regular (not necessarily the same thing). At one end of the bar customarily sat a former graduate of the Rank Charm School, once quite a household name, quietly drinking herself to death; at the other, hunched in what he used to call the prompt corner, the actor John Bay, later to marry Elaine Stritch and live in the Savoy, observed the tawdry passing show with laconic amusement. One day a new member, not yet inured to the stench of vindaloo and drains, wrinkled up his nose and enquired, 'What's that smell?' Without looking up from his *Evening Standard* John Bay replied, 'Failure.'

A fixture in the Iron Lung, having been barred from everywhere else in the West End, was a heavily built, gravel-voiced B-picture actor named Dennis Shaw, who was to loom large in my play *Jeffrey Bernard Is Unwell*, where he is described as 'the face that closed a thousand cinemas: twenty stone and encrusted in warts – imagine a toad wearing a dinner jacket and that was Dennis Shaw.' Shaw, now long dead but still widely impersonated by all the actors who ever played British officers to his Gestapo colonels or detective-sergeants to his Mayfair crooks, was a thoroughly obnoxious type, insufferably rude even when he was borrowing money. It was not only from every pub and club within a six-mile radius of Charing Cross that Shaw was barred, but from cafés and restaurants too. He was a former habitué of an old-fashioned little restaurant just around the corner from the Kismet where one night he ordered duck *à l'orange*. When the dish arrived it was not to his satisfaction (few dishes were). The following dialogue ensued:

'Waiter, what are these hard green objects?'

'They are peas, Mr Shaw – *petit pois*.'

'These are not peas, you prat! They are the pellets you shot the fucking duck with.'

'Mr Shaw! I have been a waiter in this establishment for twenty-five years and never before have I been spoken to in such a fashion!'

'I am not surprised you are still a waiter in the same place after twenty-five years, when you serve used ammunition as a vegetable!'

That agreeable character actor John Le Mesurier was an unlikely regular at the Kismet – unlikely because the few minor celebrities who occasionally wandered into the place had to run a gauntlet of supplicants and freeloaders. Gentle soul that he was, Le Mesurier had a soft spot for Dennis Shaw, whose roguery amused him. Shaw was to reward his kindness – in his own fashion. On tour in Australia, Le Mesurier suffered a heart attack and was taken to hospital. This being reported in the English papers, he was touched to receive a phone call from Dennis Shaw wishing him well. Shaw being Shaw, however, he was unlikely to be calling at his own expense. Thanking him very kindly for his solicitation, the actor asked where he was speaking from. Shaw's reply, boomed from one hemisphere to the other, was not conducive to a quick recovery: 'Your flat, old man. Afraid I had to knock the door down a bit to get in.'

Dennis Shaw's *persona non grata* status meant that if he were ever to have an enjoyable evening out in the West End, for he was a gregarious man as well as an impecunious one, he had to attach himself, like a twenty-stone barnacle, to anyone foolhardy enough to take him about and assume responsibility for his behaviour. Leaving the Kismet one afternoon at the same moment as Dennis – or Den-Den as he liked those he counted as his friends to call him – I saw no harm in allowing him to take my arm, the better to propel his bulk up the stairs. A tactical error. Several hours later he was still clutching my arm and we finished up eating supper in the Stork Club. Another foolish mistake on my part – or perhaps not so foolish, for in the fullness of time the ensuing incident was to form the basis of one of the funniest scenes in *Jeffrey Bernard Is Unwell*, adapted to feature my protagonist. I ordered a bottle of champagne, Dennis Shaw a bottle of gin. We ate the meal and finished the bottles and the place began to empty. The bill was presented but since I had been paying all evening I pointedly refrained from picking it up. So did Den-Den. After a while the waiters started stacking chairs on the tables, then the cleaners trooped in and began vacuuming the floor, but still we sat there with the bill untouched and unread on the table. Presently the head waiter came over and even in the cold grey light of dawn I could see his face turn white as he caught sight of Den-Den.

'Good morning, Mr Shaw,' said the head waiter guardedly.

'So you remember me?' rasped Shaw.

'Indeed I do, Mr Shaw.'

'Tell this gentleman where we last met.'

'At the Pigalle, Mr Shaw, when I was head waiter there.'

'Under what circumstances did we become acquainted?'

'You refused to pay your bill, Mr Shaw.'

'Tell this gentleman what your response was to that.'

'I called the police, Mr Shaw.'

Den-Den thumped the table and roared in a voice that could be heard out in Piccadilly Circus, 'Call the bastards again!'

My last visit to the old Iron Lung before it closed down, or was closed down, was on the occasion of the farcical annual general meeting which it was solemnly required to hold by law. The Chairman was drunk and the representative of the wine committee sent his apologies by virtue of being in Wormwood Scrubs. The proceedings having been gabbled through and the obligatory question, 'Any other business?', being put, the former

351

Rank starlet perched at the end of the bar said in her gin-pickled voice that she would like to ask about the tidy sum shown in the accounts as having been set aside for the decorating fund. This was quite obviously some exercise in creative book-keeping and she was the only one to take it seriously. Pointing to the nicotine-stained plasterboard ceiling, in which numbers of stars and crescents had been fretsawed back in its regime as an Indian restaurant, the Rank Charm School product slurred, 'If we have all this money available for decorating, couldn't the ceiling he painted sky blue with billowing clouds, and pretty fairy lights twinkling out of all those cut-out stars?' The Chairman's reply was terse: 'Fuck off. There being no other business, I declare this meeting closed.'

From the Kismet we might go on to the Billiards and Snooker Association in Great Windmill Street, the Snooker Centre as it was known, the haunt of taxi drivers and musicians all trying their level best to look Runyonesque. My snooker was not up to much but they did the best bacon sandwich in London, and it sat well on the lunchtime Yorkshire pudding. Pub opening time having been reached by now, when the afternoon drinking clubs were deserted by their members with the speed of rats leaving sinking ships, we would then move on to the Salisbury for an hour – but not before we had called in at the Lamb and Flag, one of London's tiniest pubs up an alley off Garrick Street, much used by actors to fortify themselves before memorial services at St Paul's, Covent Garden, the actors' church. Here we would engage in a silly practical joke with one of the barmen who, although by no means half-witted – that would have been cruel – never seemed to suspect that he was having his leg pulled. The dialogue would be on these lines:

'Good evening. Could we have two pints of bitter and three hundred and fourteen pork pies, please.'

'What was that again, sir?'

'Two pints of bitter.'

'Right.'

'And three hundred and fourteen pork pies.'

'I'm sorry,' the waiter would then respond in all seriousness, 'I don't think we've got that many pork pies, in fact I'm sure we haven't.'

'In that case, two large gins and tonic and seventy-nine, no, better make that eighty-three, Scotch eggs.'

'No Scotch eggs left, I'm afraid.'

'Then we'll just have two small brandies and a panatella.'

The last laugh was on us. One evening we ordered two bottles of Guinness and a hundred and twelve ham sandwiches, forty-seven of them with mustard. Instead of taking his cue and protesting that he didn't have that many sandwiches, the waiter said, 'Just a minute, gentlemen' and vanished. We sipped our Guinnesses, wondering what was going on. After a few moments the guvnor appeared with a tray piled high with an enormous pyramid of sandwiches. Completely straightfaced, as if it were the most everyday thing in the world, he called out across the crowded bar, 'Who ordered the hundred and twelve ham sandwiches?'

While having to admit that our bluff had been called, we tried one last throw. 'Are forty-seven of them with mustard?'

'Forty-seven with mustard, sixty-five without.' It transpired, subsequently, that the sandwiches had been cut for some club or other that was meeting in an upper room. It was a wonderfully deadpan performance: there was nothing for it but to pay for the sandwiches without demur and carry them off on their tray to the Salisbury, where we distributed them among the throng of actors, extras and stuntmen with cries of 'Victuals for the poor! Victuals for the poor!'

From the Salisbury, we might drift on to the actors', writers' and directors' club Gerry's, then in Shaftesbury Avenue, nowadays continuing to thrive at the bottom of Dean Street. At that time it was still run by its founder, Gerry himself – Gerald Campion, the comically irascible actor best known for his Billy Bunter in the TV series. Gerry's had only two rules, both of them unwritten. The first was that everyone was equal, from star to stand-in. Thus the likes of Peter Finch, Stanley Baker, Ian Hendry, Jack Klugman merged seamlessly into a company of bit players and character actors, while an aspiring scriptwriter might find himself chatting to William Saroyan (who would sit at the bar writing peeved letters on Savoy Hotel notepaper to the critics who had spurned his play) or Jack Trevor Story, who one night asked me in all seriousness if I happened to know the address of the British Union of Fascists, as he wanted to send for their prospectus.

The other rule was that no one was allowed to mention Bunter, a topic on which Gerry was for some reason morbidly sensitive – to do so meant instant expulsion. Gerry's was a positive cut above the dives on the drinking club circuit – while open at lunchtime, when it was the resort of theatrical agents, it was primarily a supper club where those who had given of their all in the theatres of Shaftesbury Avenue could relax after the show. Pleasantly scruffy, it had a relaxed and congenial air and I whiled away many an evening there. Often Joan would come down and we would sit round the big corner table with a large company of friends, gossiping, playing nonsensical games and making up limericks.

One night the actor-writer John Junkin and I, both Laurel and Hardy buffs, were discussing the art of custard pie comedy, and whether the ritual customarily followed by the recipient – pause, long-suffering smile, left hand brought slowly up to left eye to wipe away cream with a mannered flinging gesture, ditto with right hand to right eye – would instinctively be observed by anyone at the receiving end of a custard pie assault happening in real life. We decided to put it to the test. Arming ourselves with a coconut cream pie each, we positioned ourselves at the foot of the staircase, pledged to splosh them in the face of the first person to come down the stairs, regardless of who it might be. It happened to be that seasoned character actor John Blythe, who had just put in a hard day playing the matinée and evening performance of *The Sound of Music* at the Palace Theatre. Our aim was impeccable and he got the cream pies squarely in the face, one in each eye. John's reaction was magnificent. He did a splendid slow burn worthy of any Keystone Cops two-reeler, then went meticulously through the classic routine. Had we been filming, only that one take would have been necessary. The spontaneous applause for this sporting performance brought Gerry out of the kitchen. Taking in the source of the disturbance, the exhausted actor standing at the bottom of the stairs with cream dripping down his face, he pointed melodramatically at John Blythe and squeaked, 'You're barred!'

From Gerry's it was usual to go on to the Pickwick Club close by Leicester Square, a top-class restaurant and bar which was, I suppose, the Groucho of its day. Certainly it was the first place in London to cater specifically for what by now were being called sixties people, or, more nauseatingly, the Beautiful People – that heady mélange of new-wave actors, writers, directors, composers, impresarios, designers, photographers, painters, and pop stars, most of them with provincial accents, whose fifteen minutes of fame had arrived – a market astutely spotted by Desmond Cavanagh who ran the club. Cavanagh, with his innate sense of ambience, was

354

probably also the first restaurateur to relax the rigid dress rules that then prevailed – Carnaby Street rather than Jermyn Street was the fashion arbiter here, and it was more or less compulsory not to wear a tie.

The Pickwick, while it lasted, was the most star-studded establishment in the West End – there were nights when the crowded room with its black leather chairs and gleaming chrome resembled the celebrated parties that Harold Wilson, when he became Prime Minister, was to give at No. 10 for the famous, the talented, the powerful and the beautiful. It was here that table-hopping was brought to a fine art – if anyone remained at the same table and in the same company for more than fifteen minutes, Cavanagh regarded the evening as a dud. He positively encouraged 'happenings' – rows, scenes, encounters between enemies whom he deliberately placed next to one another – anything, including the Kray Brothers, to make the place buzz. Certainly he raised no objection when Frank Norman, observing his friend Jeffrey Bernard asleep over his dinner one evening, advanced upon him with a sauceboat . . . Bernard still has the dry-cleaning bill: 'To removing tartare sauce from top pocket.'

The last port of call would be Peter Cook's Establishment Club in Greek Street – unless, that is, the party was to continue until dawn in Sean Kenny's huge studio-cum-flat up in the rafters, where the affable designer kept open house. Still only in their very early twenties, Peter Cook and his partner Nicholas Luard had made a roaring success of the Establishment, which was packed nightly – it was one of those places to which belonging carried enormous social clout, with non-members pestering members to take them down there, just to say they'd been. There was drinking and there was dancing – the Twist, that curious gyration where the otherwise stationary occupants of the dance floor looked as if they were manipulating invisible hula-hoops, had London in its grip – often to the music of Dudley Moore and his friends. But what everyone was waiting for was the uncensored midnight cabaret (the Lord Chamberlain's blue pencil did not extend to clubs) with John Bird, John Fortune and Peter Cook himself, to which Willis and I contributed occasional sketches – a taster for *That Was The Week That Was*.

The Establishment's most celebrated, or anyway most notorious, act was of course the scatalogical Lenny Bruce, the world's most banned stand-up comedian and a formidable lateral thinker. One evening after the show I fell into a conversation with Lenny which developed into a fierce difference of opinion about something or other – I forget what. Lenny Bruce culminated the argument by scrawling on the wall, 'Keith Waterhouse is a prat – Lenny Bruce' – except that he used a characteristically much stronger word than prat. With consummate 2 a.m. wit I scribbled in retaliation, 'Lenny Bruce is another – Keith Waterhouse.' When next I went into the Establishment my contribution had been scrubbed out, but Lenny's remained. I asked Nicholas Luard, who chanced to be passing, why this was so. He replied solemnly, 'This is satire. Yours was graffiti.' And so to bed.

4   We had taken the New Bond Street offices on the fag-end of a lease, and upon its expiry after a year or so we moved to No. 32 Shaftesbury Avenue, an altogether more suitable address for us. It was in one of those grimy Edwardian blocks that I remembered so well from my Leeds days, the office equivalent of mansion flats, packed with seedy private detective agencies, marriage bureaux, moneylenders, bucket-shop travel agents and suchlike fly-by-night enterprises. We were on the top floor, reached by a wheezing lift manned by two ruffianly porters, and we overlooked the Lyric and Apollo Theatres.

Newspaper interviewers, borrowing from one another, always called our office the Word Factory, and indeed it was, for although money was still pouring in from all directions for various productions of *Billy Liar* around the world, we were by now inclined to settle down and do some work. Not that we really had much option, for attractive commissions, projects we really wanted to get our teeth into, were being presented to us daily. For the next twenty years or so, we were never to have fewer than four assignments on the go at any one time – always a screenplay, always a play or musical, always a television series, always a commission to write weekly for this or that TV series.

Our next theatrical enterprise after *Billy Liar* and *Celebration* was something new for both of us, a revue. For no discernible reason, since our only experience in that medium had been the youth club productions we used to stage in Leeds in our adolescence, we were asked by the veteran revue team Peter Myers and Ronald Cass to contribute to their new show *The Lord Chamberlain Regrets*, probably the last of its genre to reach the West End stage after *Beyond the Fringe* had broken the mould of the familiar 'intimate revue' with its knowing references to Binkie and Noël. Our sketch

357

'The Daily News', played by Millicent Martin and Joan Sims, about two women at a bus-stop conversing in what the newspapers imagine to be natural speech ('Because we sent our son Walter, seven, to school in a spaceman hat, his headmaster, a man new to the district, has banned him from lessons; yet other children wear equally outlandish garments') was the hit of the evening. In consequence, we were asked by a man we knew but slightly, a wine merchant turned theatrical producer called Andrew Broughton who was married to our French translator, Lucienne Hill, if we would write a full-blown revue of our own.

At first we were dismissive. *Beyond the Fringe* really had seen off the old-style revue – as witness the fate of *The Lord Chamberlain Regrets*, whose run was very short. But then, in our meanderings around the Soho clubs, we began to think about it and talk about it. If we did do a revue, it would be different from all that had gone before, including the Cook-Bennett-Miller-Moore exercise that was still packing them in at the Fortune Theatre. There would be no 'in' jokes, no name-dropping, no topical quips, and above all nothing centring on Shaftesbury Avenue and the world of cosmopolitan theatres, nightclubs and fashionable restaurants. It would be about ordinary, regional people living in the provinces. Instead of revue artistes we would employ straight actors who would portray their characters naturalistically rather than 'sending them up' with exaggerated accents and gormless George Formby mannerisms. The show, in short, would be not about the world of revue but the world we all actually inhabited. It would be called *England Our England*.

We got to work, writing songs and sketches daily. We thought about a director. Here again, we did not want a conventional revue director but someone schooled in drama. We found him in R. D. Smith – Reggie Smith, as he was universally known, a notable BBC radio producer, friend of Auden and Louis MacNeice, husband of Olivia Manning and the original of the memorable Guy Pringle in the Balkan Trilogy. Reggie was a big, shambling, disorganised fellow with the pockets of his shapeless sports jacket stuffed full of Penguin books, holes in his pullover, shirt hanging out of his corduroy trousers and his glasses always perched on his head. He did not own a suit and once when he went for an interview with the British Council to beg funds for some obscure production touring the Middle East, he had to borrow one; it was three sizes too small and he could not understand why he did not make an impression. Reggie was a brilliant drama producer but in too little control of his own talents and perhaps too fond of visiting the George around the corner from the BBC, where he was renowned for casting plays at the very last minute from among anyone who happened to be around and who needed the work.

Firmly vetoing the unemployed and the unemployable from Reggie's list, we drew up a solid, impressive cast for *England Our England*, including Billie Whitelaw, Alison Leggatt, Roy Kinnear and Murray Melvin. Dudley Moore was to write the music, and our choreographer would be Gillian Lynne. We had both fallen under the spell of L. S. Lowry (his painting *The Playground* hung on our office wall) and Alan Tagg designed for us a striking Lowryesque set that was a considerable distance from the conventional revue setting of drapes and dazzle.

The thing took shape. We had sketches about the language of trade union officials, the Churches' opposition to unconventional tombstones, the prejudices of lay magistrates ('Grossly unfair' – *Punch*), the bizarre mail-order advertisements in the Saturday newspapers; songs about the Sunday closing laws, life in a new town, the conformity of council housing estates. We even essayed a mini-ballet for Gillian to get her teeth into – 'The Tree', about a council decision to chop down a cherry tree and replace it with a concrete lamp post. 'The Daily News' sketch was given another outing. Revue audiences reared on Herbert Farjeon and Alan Melville might not like what we had to offer, but at least they couldn't complain that it wasn't different.

Rehearsals began – rather too slowly for our liking. Reggie, while wildly enthusiastic about our ideas and talking in his Hampstead left-wing way about 'the first proletarian revue' (which it wasn't – the Unity Theatre had done that long ago), was less sound when he had to be weaned from theory to practice. Rehearsing twenty-four sketches, songs and monologues and getting them into a practical running order, allowing for costume changes and so on, requires an organised mind and discipline, and these were not Reggie's chief qualities. Furthermore we were rehearsing on the stage of the Phoenix Theatre, which was perilously close to the Salisbury Tavern, where Reggie would repair for lunch. Often we would drop in to the theatre in the early afternoon to find the cast assembled and looking impatiently at their watches, and no Reggie – he would have fallen among chums (he had chums in every pub in London) and would be regaling them with his tales of Dylan Thomas, or be in full flow in one of his rants against the faceless men of the BBC. For anyone to arrive late for rehearsal – and Reggie would sometimes keep his cast waiting a good hour – is a very serious matter indeed, and we did not wonder that Billie and the others, who could see how much work there was to do, were chafing at the bit somewhat.

It was becoming clear that while we had cast an excellent company, we had seriously miscast our director. Things came to a head when Reggie rolled back from lunch one afternoon with six Irish labourers he had picked up in the working men's pub he had adopted after we had hinted that he might be finding the Salisbury something of a distraction. He had been enthusing to the Irishmen about our 'revolutionary' concept for a revue, and had invited them back so that they could see at first hand what we were driving at, and so that he for his own part could judge what 'ordinary people' made of our material. Actors hate rehearsing in front of strangers and it was hardly surprising that as the six Irish labourers plonked themselves in the front row of the stalls and lit their Woodbines, our cast formed an orderly queue at the pay-phone to ring their agents.

We had about a week to go before our short pre-West End tour opened in Cambridge. Reggie had to go, that was clear. Who, at a moment's notice, would step in as his replacement? To our relief, John Dexter agreed to take the show on as a personal favour. Dexter, immortalised in theatre lore as the man who said to Arnold Wesker during the rehearsals for *Chips with Everything*, 'Arnold, if you don't shut up I'll direct this play as you wrote it', was a director of outstanding visual talent and iron discipline, and he soon had the piece licked into shape, taking it up to the last dress rehearsal and then disappearing to Tunisia on holiday. Even with the order he had imposed on the show, things were still pretty chaotic. Roy Kinnear, dressed as John Bull for a mock-patriotic song finale, could never find the time to get his knee-length boots on properly and from the beginning to the end of the run would hobble on with his right boot half on, half off, flapping like a seal's flipper. Dudley Moore, with many other commitments, worked so close to his deadline that he was still lying on his stomach in the centre aisle, writing out the band parts, even as the invited audience for the dress rehearsal began to stream into the theatre.

Our West End theatre was the Shaftesbury, then called the Princes. For a revue, an aircraft hangar would have been more suitable. The show called for audiences of around four to five hundred – the Princes seated fourteen hundred. But Andrew Broughton carried little clout as an impresario and it was all we could get. 'Revue that cries out for smaller theatre' was one review headline with which we fervently agreed.

About half the show worked. Owing to the switch-over of directors and the usual out-of-town plague of laryngitis and sprained ankles, the cast were hard pressed and replacing material that wasn't quite up to the mark had to be low on our list of priorities – at times like this, getting the lighting right takes precedence over rewriting the lines. But there were a couple of sketches in there – 'Which Way to the Tomb?' and 'Nostalgia', both performed by Roy Kinnear and Murray Melvin – that were destined to become revue classics: they have been done hundreds of times since. And 'The Daily News' proved to be worth its second outing.

It was back to mixed reviews again. A few critics missed the whole idea of the show completely, chastising us for not having written what we never set out to write ('Revue, like it or not, is a form with its own very special requirements,' advised *The Times*). Harold Hobson got the point: '. . . the first revue I have seen which is centred firmly in the provincial life of Britain. Binkie Beaumont and Mr Macmillan, the twin fixations of our fashionable writers, are not even mentioned.' Richard Ingrams in the magazine *Time and Tide* equally saw what we were getting at: '*England Our England* is satirical in the best sense of the word in that it cocks a critical eye at a whole society and not just a lot of well-known figures or a few hackneyed television personalities . . . The actual satirical point is always subordinated to the human situation, a fact which explains why some critics have dismissed the revue as a misguided attempt at intellectual music hall.'

Alas, *Time and Tide* did not put bums on seats, and playing in a barn at the top end of Shaftesbury Avenue did little for our chances. *England Our England* was not destined for a long run. To our regret, although understandably, Reggie Smith never came to see the show. He became quite embittered about his sacking and talked wildly of taking out a writ, although against whom and to what purpose he never explained. To the end of his days he would chunter on darkly about what he saw as a capitalist plot to usurp him – he had some idea, completely a figment of his imagination, that an influential backer of the show had wanted him removed because of his pinkish politics. He was a dear man, and we were glad that we all remained good friends, although if he had thought it out properly he must have seen that it could only have been Willis and I who had got him fired.

Someone who did come to see the show was Ned Sherrin, last encountered on the BBC's *Tonight* programme, who turned up for no other reason than that he saw everything, as he still does. The first consequence of his visit was that he promptly put the 'Nostalgia' sketch on his programme on some thin pretext or other. The second consequence was to be rather more long-term.

One of the delightful bonuses of this writing business, a kind of commercial serendipity, is the ripple effect, as of a stone thrown into a pond, whereby one thing so often leads to another. A sketch for *The Lord Chamberlain Regrets* led to *England Our England*; *England Our England* led to an invitation from Ned Sherrin to contribute to the pilot of a TV show he was cobbling together called, tentatively, *That Was The Week That Was*.

I believe we trotted out 'The Daily News' again to do further service. At any rate, Ned's pilot got a greenish light, and we were summoned to Lime Grove, that cluster of more or less condemned terrace houses knocked together that was the home of some of the BBC's best output (interesting how the more ramshackle the premises, the more stimulating the product), to lunch with Ned, the young newcomer David Frost, and the BBC heavies Grace Wyndham Goldie, Donald Baverstock and Alasdair Milne, and kick the thing around. Mrs Wyndham Goldie, who had the demeanour of a magistrate about to impose a stiff sentence for shoplifting, talked a good deal about German cabaret. Donald Baverstock talked about *Picture Post*. David Frost talked about his pension insurance, advising Willis and me, ten years his senior, that it was never too early to start. Ned Sherrin told his theatrical stories. As Willis and I left the table we casually agreed to contribute to the show whenever we got an idea. In the event, we wrote for every single edition of TW3 from the first to the last, saving only the special Kennedy Assassination tribute programme – usually for Roy Kinnear and Millicent Martin, although we did once bag the services of Dame Sybil Thorndike.

Our opening sketch, touching on a news story about private

soldiers now being allowed to stand for Parliament, had Roy Kinnear as a squaddie doing a party political broadcast ('Turning to Home Affairs, on the vexed question of taxation and allowances, our Shadow Chancellor officers' cook Maloney will iron out the many anomalies in our economy – why, for example, should a technical sergeant get more than a cook sergeant?'). Ned Sherrin records in his autobiography *A Small Thing Like an Earthquake* how Roy's agent called his client the following morning to reassure him: 'Don't worry – it was horrible, and they have a contract; but I have talked to people in very high places at Broadcasting House and I am assured it cannot last three weeks.' Roy remained to do our postscript sketch for the show. ('Well, it was satire, wasn't it? Mucky jokes. Obscenity – it's all the go nowadays. By law, you see. You're allowed to do it. You can say bum, you can say po, you can say anything.') What went on in between is oft-told history.

Willis and I tended to write our TW3 sketch at the last minute on Friday morning, when the BBC would send round a taxi to whisk it over to Lime Grove for the cast to learn and rehearse for the following evening. Sometimes, if inspiration faltered, we would hear the cab meter remorselessly ticking away in the street below even as we wrestled with the final lines. The fashion at the time for sketches without black-out punchlines was put down to the influence of *Beyond the Fringe*; I am inclined to think it was often more to do with the impatient presence of a cab at the door. We must have contributed significantly to the BBC's famously astronomical taxi bill. As well as our £70 a week fee, we added further to the Corporation's expenses with a bill for £5,000 out-of-court damages from the writer C. P. Snow who, in a series of mock, not to say mocking, letters from Dylan Thomas to his wife Pamela Hansford Johnson, we had likened to an icicle. Perhaps the most famous TW3 sketch, though, was the fly buttons one. Because it was performed by Roy Kinnear and Millicent Martin, we were persistently credited with it, to as much embarrassment on our part as was generated by Roy having his fly buttons open. But it wasn't ours; it was, as we never ceased to point out, Steven Vinaver's.

After *That Was The Week* had rocketed to its inevitable demise, rather in the manner of a flying bomb, we continued to write for Ned on its sprawling successor, the three-nights-a-week *Not So Much A Programme, More A Way Of Life*; and after that, the confusingly titled *BBC3*, which Ned rightly wanted to call *It's All*

Been Done Before to pre-empt jaded critics, and on which Ken Tynan famously used the word 'fuck', which most certainly had not been done before. In all, our work with Ned totalled 145 sketches and monologues.

Even after four years of these late-night shows, or rather because of them, the pebble kept on rippling. Ned went on from the BBC to do other things, but we stayed to write for twenty-two episodes of the BBC2 *Late Show*, which was somewhat in the Sherrin mould. On *Not So Much A Programme*, we had written often for Roy Hudd who had made his mark on the show: now we wrote for the *Illustrated Weekly Hudd* and, later, the *Roy Hudd Show*. Then there were twenty-six segments of *The Frost Report*, followed by *Frost over England*, followed by *Frost on Sunday*, followed by *The Frost Programme*, where as well as producing sketches we turned our hands to gag-writing, with such well-remembered quips (by David, anyway) as 'Here are the results of today's Sheepdog Trials: all the sheepdogs were found not guilty', and 'See a pin and pick it up, all the day you'll have a pin'.

The Word Factory acquired such a reputation for turning out, as distinct from churning out, four-minute sketches to suit all performers that we seriously thought of investing in a small delivery van bearing the legend 'Scripts Written While You Wait, No Job Too Big Or Too Small, Reliability Our Motto, Let Us Quote You, Money Returned If Not Satisfied'. It would have saved on taxis.

Over the years we wrote regularly for Millie Martin's *Mainly Millicent* series, *The Lance Percival Show*, *On the Braden Beat*, Dora Bryan's *According to Dora*, *The Diana Rigg Show*, *The Dick Emery Show*, and various odd spots long forgotten. All spinning out of a single revue sketch.

We even had a brush with the demented world of advertising, when we were invited by the agents Mather and Crowther to script an egg commercial, to be directed by Joan Littlewood. The new-wave directors were then not too proud to do commercials when work was thin on the ground or they needed the money – Lindsay Anderson, for example, did Ewbank carpet sweepers and Iron Jelloids; John Schlesinger did Stork margarine and Enos fruit salts; while Joseph Losey did Ryvita and Horlicks.

And Joan Littlewood did eggs, in a mini-series of domestic soaps called 'Sheila and Eggs', featuring Avis Bunnage, George Sewell and Gaye Brown, produced by Anthony Shaffer. The invitation was irresistible. Our contribution, which we thought quite avant-garde, was to have George Sewell coming down the stairs to the kitchen where Avis Bunnage was frying breakfast, and moaning, 'Eggs! Eggs! Eggs! If I'm not sick of fried eggs!' Avis's reply was to be, 'You don't have to have fried eggs every morning – I could do you an omelette.' The Egg Marketing Board were not over-impressed by our soft-sell approach, and what we thought of as a potentially mould-breaking commercial was shelved.

Nor were we ever to work with Joan Littlewood. Someone who thought our respective talents would make an interesting mesh arranged a lunch, at a time when Joan could have brought an East End pub concert into the West End had she felt so inclined. We talked around one another warily and respectfully. Various kites were flown. But Joan could see that we were words-on-paper merchants, who preferred the lines spoken on stage to have been mostly written down first. Joan, of course, was of the opposite persuasion, a passionate believer in extemporising, which suited her form of theatre, and her choice of actor, very well. So we were not destined to work together. But it would have been nice to have made that egg commercial.

Eggs apart, the Word Factory's many illustrious customers were well satisfied and the work kept pouring in. 'They make their points better than they know,' wrote someone in the *Sunday Telegraph* – a beautifully patronising testimonial which we thought of having engraved on our letterheads.

Meanwhile we had two more plays on the stocks – a northern comedy called *All Things Bright and Beautiful* at the Phoenix and, opening less than a week later, our double bill *Squat Betty and The Sponge Room* filling a production gap at the Royal Court. *All Things*, about a slum family being rehoused in a soulless high-rise against their wishes (this was when tower blocks were still being hailed as 'vertical terraces'), whose pitch for some element of colour in their lives involves acquiring a huge wooden lectern in the form of an eagle from a derelict church, brought the megaphone-voiced Peggie Mount roaring back into the West End; later it was televised with Thora Hird and a very young John Hurt. We smiled ruefully when some of the critics carped that such an uncouth family would have no eye for beauty: the play was based on a true-life incident – a Yorkshire demolition gang labourer who somehow smuggled home a Montague Burton's mahogany shop counter which he kept propped up on the stairs, to the great inconvenience of his family, because he admired its meticulously carpentered dovetail joints.

Squat Betty and The Sponge Room was a new departure for us: a pair of middle-class playlets, the first about a suicide-prone *ménage-à-trois* in a remote mountainside hostel, the second about harassed lovers meeting in the National History Museum where they are offered the loan of a much-needed room by a kleptomaniac attendant in exchange for smuggling out stuffed birds; the cast of both being Robert Stephens, Jill Bennett and George Cole. These too were televised after their brief run – the early sixties were something of a golden age for dramatists, in that just about every play that reached the West End, and even some that didn't, was more or less guaranteed a profitable tour and a star-studded TV production. *Squat Betty and The Sponge Room* then played a season at the East End Theater off Broadway. Not bad for a couple of one-acters originally intended as no more than curtain-raisers.

Actually, our long-term intention did have something more to it. We had been getting increasingly dissatisfied with being typecast as northern writers – Yorkshire writers, Midlands writers, Black Country writers, Staffordshire writers, even Lancashire writers, as we were dubbed by southern-based critics unsure of their north-of-Watford geography – and we were anxious to broaden our base. Those whose business it is to write about writers love to put labels on them like the zinc tags pushed into hothouse plant-pots. We were part of the so-called Northern Wave which was part of the so-called New Wave – the north's chapter, if you believed all you read, of the equally so-called Angry Young Men movement. From time to time we were wheeled out with the likes of Stan Barstow, Sid Chaplin, David Storey, Barry Hines, Bill Naughton and John Braine to take part in round-table discussions in the radio and TV studios of Manchester, Liverpool and Leeds. The producers were usually, I think, disappointed: never was any group less angry. We were all, indeed, deeply content that northern writing had at last come into its own, and we would sit around in hotel lounges ordering large drinks and discussing royalties.

J. B. Priestley, hearing of our existence, instructed his agent to 'mix me up a few of these new writers I've been hearing about', and accordingly some of us trooped round to his rooms in Albany to be given dry sherry and told, 'Angry young men, are yer? I were angry before any of yer were born.' Only the larger-than-life John

Braine played the part for all it was worth, basing his John Blunt act on the Old Grumbler himself, though suitably adjusted for his own preposterous, born-again right-wing opinions. Kingsley Amis has told the definitive version of how after some TV appearance together, John was ranting on at the socialist tub-thumper Lord Soper about what a wonderful open society was the United States, to which Soper retorted mildly, 'All right if you're not black.' The John Braine response was, 'But I'm not black, you stupid bugger!' My own cherished Braine story is of when Jack Clayton was filming his *Room at the Top* and he was asked down to the studio to meet Sir Donald Wolfit, Laurence Harvey, Simone Signoret and the rest of the cast. Invited to say a few words in between shots, John mounted a chair and bellowed, 'Ladies and gentlemen, you are all figments of my imagination!'

Willis Hall and I were always happy to see our fellow-northerners – even John Braine, within reason – but we did not want to go on writing about the north for the rest of our careers, particularly since we no longer lived there and young regional writers were coming up who knew far more about the current scene than we did in our Shaftesbury Avenue watchtower. *Squat Betty and The Sponge Room* was a modest first effort at getting away from our kitchen-sink image.

Our real breakthrough came with a telephone ringing in the middle of Epping Forest. I was driving through it one day on my way to Cambridge where we had something playing, when I had to stop to answer a call of nature, as a Fleet Street raconteur would put it. As I was about to get back into the car I heard the shrill and altogether unexpected sound of a telephone bell. It came, as I saw, from a wayside phone box on the other side of the road. What the need was for a phone box in the depths of Epping Forest I have never figured out to this day, but, curious, I crossed the road to answer its persistent ringing. Just as I tugged open the phone box door, it stopped. I picked up the receiver but the line was dead. I gave the caller a minute to ring back, but nothing else happened. My little adventure over, I drove on.

I reported the incident to Willis who was as intrigued as I was. For some days, over numerous games of Scrabble, we kicked possibilities around. Spies? Criminals? Mundane business contacts (this was before car phones and mobiles)? Lovers? Just a simple wrong number? The last possibility we immediately buried. We were, of course, looking for a drama plot, probably for a television play: we had promised one, I believe, to Sydney Newman, the pioneering producer who had commissioned the first TV plays of Harold Pinter, Alun Owen and Angus Wilson, and was now responsible for BBC drama. (It was to the colourful Newman, I am reminded, that his fellow-Canadian, the director Ted Kotcheff, when taunted by his friend and mentor – it was that kind of a relationship – 'Don't forget I dragged you up from the gutter!' jeered back, 'From the gutter to you, Sydney – this is up?').

A mystery, we thought at first: we had long had a hankering to write a mystery play. But Scrabble gave way to chess and chess to L'Attaque and L'Attaque to Tri-Tactics, and not a glimmering of a mystery play was forthcoming. Not our scene. Lovers, then. The ringing telephone was pivotal to a lovers' tryst; they were both married, or anyway one of them was married, and it was the only way they dared communicate to arrange their meetings.

Somehow – we were by now on Monopoly – the phone box shifted from the middle of Epping Forest to outside a pub in South Kensington, the local for a smart block of flats which is home to a young couple, one of whom, the wife, unknown to her husband, is in the habit of lending out the flat to a friend of hers who is having an affair with a married man who believes, wrongly, that she is a married woman . . . We brought in the unfortunate experience of a friend of ours whose wife, when she discovered that he was being unfaithful, cut off the sleeves of all his suits. Somehow we had the makings of a play – a stage comedy rather than a TV mystery. All we had to do now was put the board games away and write it.

We called the play, at first, *The Story So Far*, since that is exactly what it was. In most comedies with a sex theme, the extra-marital affair never actually takes off. In ours, it has not only taken off before the house lights go down but it is on a collision course from the very beginning. All actions have consequences and what we had written was an exercise in consequences, which the audience can see all too clearly will continue to ricochet long after the curtain has fallen.

For all that he had already produced four plays of ours, we did not take it to Oscar Lewenstein, feeling that it would not be up his street. In this we were right. He was to write bleakly that following *All Things Bright and Beautiful*, 'Keith and Willis wrote some successful plays for the West End – I was not involved but I do not think it's sour grapes that makes me think they were not a patch on their early north country plays.' Here he was mistaken, at least so far as this new offering was concerned. Like *Billy Liar*, our non-north-country piece was far more than comedy passing itself off as farce, or farce passing itself off as comedy. A little-noticed phenomenon of the Swinging Sixties, to use the ghastly phrase coined by *Time* magazine, was that people wildly unsuited for promiscuity were nevertheless grimly promiscuous, not because they were seized with uncontrollable lust but because they didn't want to miss out, they wanted to be invited to the party. Since it takes two to tango, this was as applicable to women as to men. This was the theme of our play – probably the first stage comedy to recognise, in the character of the flat-borrowing Valerie, the sixties sexual suffragette.

We took it to Peter Bridge, an energetic, ebullient if overweight commercial producer who had the theatre in his blood, having been in management since his very early twenties, with a string of successes, near-successes and non-successes in the ensuing two decades. A restless soul who would roam the West End theatre scene and its fringes until the last neon sign had gone out in Shaftesbury Avenue, and then go home to read scripts, Peter tackled our new play at three in the morning – a dangerous time to read a comedy. But he loved it, and was on the phone sickeningly early the next morning to say that he had already sent it to Ian Carmichael, with whom he had been discussing working if the right play turned up.

What he did not add was that, never being one to do things by halves, he had also sent Ian half a dozen other scripts by the same messenger, inviting him to take his pick. But even had we known that we were being lined up in a kind of theatrical identity parade, there was nothing to worry about. Ian reports in his own memoirs that the play made him sit bolt upright from the very first page. He rang Patrick Cargill, to whom Peter Bridge had already sent a copy – presumably also among a mixed batch – and got his confirmation that he too thought the play 'hysterical' and would love to take the other male part. Ian then records, characteristically, 'I then rang Peter and said, *"The Story So Far*, my dear old bean, is the first play I have ever read in my life on which I have never wanted a second opinion. I'm wildly enthusiastic."'

There was only one slight hitch, which was that Peter Bridge was hell-bent on changing the title. Had we looked him up in *Who's Who in the Theatre*, we might have had some premonition of what turned

369

out to be a bizarre idiosyncrasy of his: 'Entered management 1948 when he presented a tour of *Set To Partners*, which was subsequently produced at the Embassy Theatre under the new title of *Rain Before Seven* . . .' It emerged that Peter was a compulsive and almost superstitious changer of titles, sparing only revivals of the classics. His case against *The Story So Far*, his rationale, was 'What sort of a title is that? No, got to be changed, got to be changed.' Ian Carmichael argued, Willis argued, I argued, our agents argued. Our producer adamantly refused to sign a contract containing the offending words *The Story So Far*.

Finally, just to get the show on the road, we gave him an alternative title – *Say Who You Are*. It came from the instructions then printed in telephone directories and apparently aimed at imbeciles: 'When you lift up the receiver, do not just say hello but say who you are.' As a title it would have some significance – but only to those who had both already seen the play and read the telephone directory. But as Willis put it, 'So long as the bugger doesn't want Ian Carmichael to change his name, we could be in business.'

We were. Ian Carmichael and Patrick Cargill were signed. Opposite them were Jan Holden as Ian's wife Sarah Lord and, originally, Lana Morris as Patrick's mistress Valerie. I was somewhat diffident about meeting Miss Morris, since the last time our paths had crossed was back in my *Yorkshire Evening Post* days when I had somehow managed to interview her for an hour in the sustained belief that she was Lana Turner. It was with mixed feelings of regret and relief, then, that I heard that Lana Morris had been taken ill and would have to be replaced, as she most effectively was by Dilys Laye.

Since the play is very strong on women's role in the sex war we wanted if possible a woman director who understood comedy. We were lucky enough to find one in the Chicago-born Shirley Butler, an extremely attractive former Dior mannequin who had made a reputation for herself directing James Saunders' *Next Time I'll Sing to You* and *A Scent of Flowers*. The West End would have heard a good deal more of her after *Say Who You Are* had she not died prematurely. Our designer was the highly experienced 'Jay' Hutchinson Scott – experienced he needed to be, for he had to cram into a single set for us the Lords' top-floor Kensington living room, a section of the hall and staircase, a working lift, the front of the pub next door and the all-important GPO telephone box. The set worked, the lift worked, the telephone box worked and the play worked. Apart from fussing about with the ending, I don't think we needed to alter a line.

We opened at the Yvonne Arnaud Theatre, Guildford, where despite the fears of the *Farnham Herald* that 'Keith Waterhouse and Willis Hall would appear to have forgotten their origins', we played to packed houses. Fortunately for our reputation – for the *Farnham Herald* also went on to say, 'Even more regrettably they have shut out the poignant shadows which filled the mean little Yorkshire backwater of their childhood' – the play was immediately condemned by the Rector of Holy Trinity, Guildford, as 'squalid rubbish which makes a joke of adultery and desertion'.

Say Who You Are stayed out on tour for an unusually long time – two months – while Peter Bridge, with unflinching nerve, turned down one West End theatre after another until he had secured the one he was angling for, Her Majesty's in the Haymarket. He had promised Ian Carmichael, who had had a big success there with *The Tunnel of Love*, that he would get it for him if he could. Besides, Her Majesty's had a seating capacity of 1,280, making it one of the four biggest straight theatres in the West End.

We were, as *Variety* reported, 'a runaway hit', with universally ecstatic reviews. Metro Goldwyn Mayer bought the film rights the day after we opened – or as *Variety* preferred to put it, 'MGM Acquires "Say", London Legit Hit' – for a sum so dizzying that Peter Bridge's fraction of it, added to the takings from capacity houses during our nine weeks out of town, put his production in profit within a fortnight.

The play filled Her Majesty's for fifteen months, closing then only because of Ian Carmichael's commitments. With Nicholas Parsons and Prunella Scales, it crossed town to the Vaudeville Theatre for a respectable run before going out on a prolonged post-West End tour. Needless to say, the film never happened, but there were innumerable foreign productions, including 'Say', to quote *Variety* again, being 'skedded for Broadway bow next fall'. By the time *Say Who You Are* had run its course, I think we could safely say, no doubt to the chagrin of the *Farnham Herald*, that we had put our cloth-cap image behind us.

371

5   While we had had several productions off Broadway –
    some further off than others – *Help Stamp Out Marriage*
    in 1966 was to be our Broadway debut. *Help Stamp Out
Marriage* was yet another title for *Say Who You Are*, which our
American producer said was the only element of the play he didn't
understand. That made three of us.

We established ourselves, with wives, at the Algonquin, the first
time I had ever set foot in this renowned hotel, and indeed only
the second time I had set foot in New York. I took to the place
at once. While the legendary round table of Dorothy Parker fame
was something of a disappointment, in that it turned out to be simply
a corner table in the restaurant area – I suppose I had been expecting
something of Arthurian proportions – the lobby seethed with life.

American hotel lobbies, used much as the French use their
boulevard cafés, have always fascinated me, and none so much as
that of the Algonquin, presided over at one end of the room by the
owner's wife – she who had memorably introduced William Faulkner
and John Steinbeck to one another in the lift with the words, 'Do you
boys know each other?' – and at the other, the cigar-stand end, by
Hamlet the cat, who twice or three times during the evening would
take a dignified stroll around the lobby and nip selected patrons in
the ankle.

As a cat lover, I was pleased to find that there were almost as many
stories about Hamlet, a stately black and white animal of advancing
years with the mien of a family retainer, as about the Vicious Circle
or Thanatopsis Literary and Inside Straight Club, the Saturday night
poker school, often confused with the Algonquin round table, over
whose sessions in a second-floor suite presented by the management
the *New Yorker* was born. Checking in one day, a guest is supposed
to have seen, or thought himself to have seen, a mouse in his room.

Having called the front desk and received managerial assurances that the matter would be dealt with at once, he sat on his bed and waited for someone to arrive and conduct him to another, mouse-free room. There was a knock at the door. Picking up his suitcase, he opened it, to receive the bell captain who thrust the cat Hamlet into his arms.

The handsome 1920s lobby, with its sombrely ticking grandfather clock, delicate Japanese lamp shades, comfortable sofas and mahogany cocktail tables equipped with strident bell-pushes to which the hurrying waiters, all of them built like Brooklyn truck drivers, paid not the slightest attention, was always thronged with English actors, writers and directors. It would have reminded me of the Garrick Club, were I yet a member.

One morning I was standing with Donald Pleasence waiting for the lift, which was always notoriously long in coming, when we were joined by a middle-aged lady. After pressing the bell in resigned mock-exasperation, she turned to us and said, 'My husband always used to say he wrote most of his stories while waiting for the elevator at the Algonquin.' As she got out at the third floor Pleasence said, 'Do you know who that was?' I shook my head. 'It was Mrs James Thurber.' I was suitably impressed and filed the remark away to regale my friends with – until Donald added: 'She repeats that story to everyone she shares the lift with. I've been here six weeks and I've heard it a dozen times.'

The Algonquin staff, from the doorman to the under-manager, were models of urbanity. As I was collecting my key one day a self-important American bustled in and said to the desk clerk, a man of practised superciliousness who could have been played by Edward Everett Horton, 'When a Mr So-and-so arrives, send him to me in the Oak Room. You can't mistake him – he's very Briddish.' The hotel, as I said, was packed with British people, most of them with famous faces. The desk clerk remained unfazed. 'Oh yes?' he drawled. 'Got Lord Harlech's nose, has he?' Very many years later, when the third and last of my children, Bob, was grown up and studying at New York State University in Buffalo, I invited him down to the Algonquin where I was staying for a few days. When I reserved his room this same desk clerk apologised for its smallness. 'But all your rooms are small,' I pointed out – as indeed they are, notoriously so. 'This one is unusually small,' said the desk clerk guardedly, which meant it was the size of a broom cupboard.

Since I did not have to sleep in it I was unconcerned. I retorted that as my son was a student, he was very fortunate not to be sleeping on a bench in Central Park. The desk clerk beamed. 'That's the spirit, Mr Waterhouse. In future years your son will be able to say, "I may be rich and famous now, but I can remember the days when I had to rough it at the Algonquin."'

I was to rough it at the Algonquin two or three times a year for another three decades, giving it up only when the hotel changed hands, and the tiny panelled Blue Bar, whose regulars would draw visiting firemen into their nightly seminars on the arts, politics and the universe (usually presided over by a white-haired professorial figure who had been a well-known broadcaster until, signing off one night in his cups, he had said 'Good night and fuck you, America', and who now happily announced train departures at Grand Central) was brutally turned into offices.

Having made ourselves thoroughly at home in this delightfully eccentric institution, my collaborator and I strolled down West 44th Street to the Booth Theater where we would be playing, to meet our all-English cast – Francis Matthews, Roddy Maude-Roxby, Ann Bell and Valerie French – and our director. This was none other than the legendary George Abbott – Mister Abbott as he was known to all who worked with him – then in his seventy-ninth year. Ours was to be his 107th Broadway show, his previous credits including *Damn Yankees*, *Pajama Game*, *Wonderful Town* and *Call Me Madam*.

Our producers, the Theater Guild, were equally distinguished, having staged the original productions of *Mourning Becomes Electra*, *Come Back Little Sheba*, *Philadelphia Story*, *Oklahoma*, *Carousel* and *The Unsinkable Molly Brown* among many others, and having been responsible for introducing the works of Shaw, Molnar, Terence Rattigan and Christopher Fry to American theatregoers. In such company, how could we go wrong? We had yet to learn that in the theatre, one can go wrong in any company.

The Theater Guild's producer for our play was the gangling, highly civilised product of a famous American theatrical family, Philip Langner, among whose distinctions were that he was the producer of the Rod Steiger film *The Pawnbroker*, and of *Judgment at Nuremburg*, also that he was responsible for my first hangover on American soil. This was consequent upon his introducing me to the vodka martini, straight up with a twist of lemon, for which lethal concoction I instantly acquired a taste, and have been downing regularly from that day to this. Philip poured his generous measures from a chilled proprietary bottle of ready-mixed vodka martini, a preparation I did not know existed – I believe it still does not on this side of the water – and he told me an interesting story about its invention. A branch of his substantially well-off family was in the habit of throwing lavish theatrical cocktail parties at which martinis were always served. The hostess began to observe that for several days after each party her butler was as stiff as one of her martinis, and indeed while serving dinner one evening was so drunk that he fell into the lobster bisque. She had him watched and discovered that following her parties it was her butler's practice to collect the dregs from all the dozens of martini glasses littering the place, pour them into bottles, and store the bottles in his pantry fridge, taking copious nips from them daily until the supply ran out. Nobody but he had known until that moment of discovery that it was possible to bottle and preserve an already mixed martini. The hostess fired the butler, marketed the product, and made a fortune.

Rehearsing on Broadway was a blissful experience in the mild East Coast fall, rather like being inside one of P. G. Wodehouse's New York novels such as *Jill the Reckless*. After breakfast we would chat to one or two fellow-exiles in the Algonquin lobby, tickle the cat's ear, get bitten in the ankle and hobble down to the Booth where we were rehearsing on the stage. There we would loll away the morning before going across to Sardi's for lunch. The afternoon was passed in the same agreeable way. As we never ceased to remind ourselves, it beat working for a living.

Mister Abbott was a lean, grizzled, ramrod-straight figure, who would have been sent for by Central Casting had they been looking for someone to play an archetypal theatre director. He was courteous but authoritarian, with the autocratic air of one who knows he is monarch of all he surveys – in his case, Broadway. It did not need much writer's intuition to tell us that unless we had a brilliant idea for a piece of business, our director was not in the market for comments or suggestions.

Mister Abbott directed from a seat in the stalls. Arriving promptly at ten each morning, he wasted little time in chit-chat, and less on interpreting the characters. Having got the play efficiently blocked and all the actors' moves worked out in a remarkably short period, his method was to run it through scene by scene over and over again, colouring in and making adjustments as he saw fit.

376

Like Hitchcock, whom we were later to work with, he used his actors like chess pieces, playing out a game which he had already planned to its completion in his mind. If he would not take interference from us, he certainly wouldn't take it from his players. One afternoon towards the end of rehearsal, we could see that Francis Matthews was unhappy about one of his moves in a scene which Mister Abbott had been running through several times over. Finally, with the scene set to our director's satisfaction, Francis came downstage and asked, 'Mister Abbott, since neither my mistress nor I smokes in this scene, I wonder if you could explain why I am carrying this ashtray from the mantelpiece to the coffee table?'

Mister Abbott favoured him with a wintry yet benign smile. 'Why, Mr Matthews, because I'm asking you to.'

Motivation explained, the near-octogenarian, a keen ballroom dancer, excused himself to go off for his tango lessons.

In the privacy of the Blue Bar, Willis and I confessed to one another our growing unease about Mister Abbott's direction. While the slickness of his production could not be faulted technically, it lacked a certain zip. We reminded ourselves that this was the man who had won the Pulitzer Prize for *Fiorello!*, that among the 107 Broadway productions with which he had been involved, he had directed no fewer than eighty-five, including scores of hits such as the wildly successful *A Tree Grows in Brooklyn* which he had both adapted and staged. The man must know what he was doing, and if his direction was not as vigorous as it might be, we had to remember his great age. We were not to know that Mister Abbott had yet to live so long that the significance of that figure 107 would no longer be that it was the number of his Broadway productions, but his age; and that when on his 105th birthday his protégé Hal Prince, calling to congratulate him, found him sitting up in bed writing and asked what he was doing, Mister Abbott's reply would be, 'Revising *Damn Yankees*.' The revamped show was still playing on Broadway when he died two years later – which is more than could be said for *Help Stamp Out Marriage*.

We previewed satisfactorily, in one of those charming, autumn-tinged barn theatres out in Connecticut that are such a pleasurable feature of the East Coast drama scene. Previews back at the Booth went equally well. The show's publicist had been at work, defacing the pavements of New York with white-painted male and female footprints leading to the Booth Theater. The advance was encouraging. I was dubious about the 'How To Make A Pay Station Call, London Style' advice which someone had inserted into our playbill programme ('1. Find a thrup'ny bit') but hoped it would not make our audiences feel that they were in for a culture shock.

The first night was warmly received, with its full quota of applause – Mister Abbott, with his vast experience, had not missed one laugh. We got a standing ovation. As we trooped through Schubert Alley for the first-night party, the veteran Sardi's doorman Tony Fratino greeted us with, 'Great show, boys!' We should have been less heartened by his enthusiasm had we known that Mr Fratino had only ever seen two plays in his entire life, *Where's Charlie?* and *The Subject Was Roses*, for which he had been given free tickets. What was even more heartening, however, was the comment of the only man at the party still wearing his hat, which, since it was his trademark, he understandably did not check in at the cloakroom. He too thought it was a great show. Coming from Walter Winchell, this was praise indeed.

You win some, you lose some. Dozens of English dramatists, particularly English comedy dramatists, have written of the Sardi's experience. It is always the same scenario. The party is packed with theatricals, backers, friends, socialites, celebs, columnists, hangers-on, gate-crashers, all prattling away about everything but the show – they are waiting for the reviews to tell them what to think. The champagne flows. You go out to the lavatory or to make a phone call. You are away three minutes at most. You return to a near-empty room, with the producers, the company and a few loyal friends being the only ones remaining. The champagne supply has been cut off. First editions of the *New York Times*, the ink still wet and smudgy, litter the tables. The reviews have been unfavourable.

Unfavourable but not totally disastrous. *Help Stamp Out Marriage* enjoyed a shortish run – it was not yet like today when a thumbs-down from the *New York Times* means that the show closes Saturday or even tonight. The afternoon papers were a little better, and Mr Winchell reported in his column that 'the Britcoms had a hitcom'. I found this immensely cheering, since I had always been given to understand that a few lines from Walter Winchell could make or break a show. Alas, the days of the old-style Broadway column were numbered, and the ageing Winchell was no longer an influential voice. Indeed, his once-famous syndicated column, now appearing in a cannibalised conglomeration of defunct newspapers called the *World Journal Tribune*, had only a few months to run before his contract was terminated and the paper folded. Like the Winchell column, *Help Stamp Out Marriage* staggered on for a while and then came off – yet one more English comedy that could not survive the choppy journey across the Atlantic. It fared rather better with some of the American stock companies, and of course under its previous name of *Say Who You Are* it continued to play in various parts of the world. It is occasionally revived to this day – particularly in Italy where the play's theme has a strong appeal – and only a few years ago Derek Nimno took it on a successful tour of the Far East. You lose some, you win some.

We were not downhearted. The business we were in is a game of snakes and ladders, and however disconcerting it may be to find oneself slithering down after so many heady climbs, there is always another shake of the dice. And we were, as they say, bankable. We continued to be bombarded with projects.

Not all of these, obviously, came to fruition – indeed only a fraction of them were destined to do so. As in the film industry, the product that the public sees in the theatre is only the tip of an iceberg that has otherwise sunk without trace – a great wealth of ideas that were before their time or after their sell-by date, of vehicles that nobody wanted to drive, of enterprises that ran out of speed or out of money or both, of crackpot productions that were mercifully aborted before they were given a chance to bankrupt their backers, of projects that simply foundered through inertia or inability to get to grips with some fatal flaw, of brilliant concepts whose gloss wore off like the gold paint on a made-in-Taiwan Christmas tree bauble.

Several examples stand out. Itching to make a musical some day, we began work on, and shortly afterwards abandoned, a commissioned adaptation of Priestley's *When We Are Married*. We were wise to ditch it: every line of dialogue excised to make room for a lyric would have been an act of theatrical vandalism. Then we were encouraged by Oscar Lewenstein to write an original musical about the suffragette movement – an interesting theme, but after a few games of Scrabble and a few rounds of the clubs, that too was shelved. The idea we had come up with, of a completely fictitious group of factory suffragettes, implicitly examining why the movement was almost exclusively a middle-class one, was more up Joan Littlewood's street than ours.

An American judge with theatrical aspirations who had some rights on one of the several plays about the Barretts of Wimpole Street, I forget which, approached us about doing a musical of that. At our first and last script conference the judge gave us his suggestion for a key lyric: 'So Barrett gets back from his club and he goes up to the daughter's bedroom and finds she's been seeing this guy Browning against her father's wishes, so he drags her out of bed and beats the shit out of her. Now how would you say we should encompass that in song?'

Perversely, the musical we were most qualified to write we turned down. Mister Abbott's friend and associate, the distinguished director-producer Harold Prince (his credits start with most of the Sondheims and continue with *Cabaret*), expressed an interest in making a musical of the ubiquitous *Billy Liar*. We met and talked about it – on our part, I am afraid, rather listlessly. The truth was that so far as Billy was concerned, that old enemy of promise ennui had set in. I had already written the novel and the pair of us had already written the play; by the time the possibility of a musical was raised we had also written the screenplay and the long-running TV series. Four bites of the cherry seemed enough, and we let it go.

Fortunately so: for when Don Black as lyricist and John Barry as composer eventually began to dream of making an English musical of *Billy Liar*, those fellow-craftsmen Dick Clement and Ian La Fresnais (*The Likely Lads* and a string of other successes) were able to bring completely fresh minds to our by now somewhat jaded hero. *Billy*, at the Drury Lane Theatre, was hailed as the brightest British musical for years, and it made a superstar of Michael Crawford.

All very satisfactory: but we had yet to write a musical ourselves. Another opportunity presented itself a few days after the death of Charlie Chaplin, when the producer of *Billy*, the late Peter de Witt, called us to the Connaught Hotel where at vast expense he had installed the distinguished choreographer-director Jerome Robbins of *West Side Story* fame, to discuss with us the possibilities to be found in a musical of Chaplin's life.

Overnight, Willis and I had hurriedly skimmed through biographies of Chaplin, but, busy that day with our own separate activities, we had had no chance at all to discuss the project before meeting Mr Robbins over dinner at the Connaught. When we got down to the nitty-gritty, which any observer would have noted we were all reluctant to do, it was clear that we were all three prowling around the subject in ever-increasing circles. From Willis's private signals to me, and mine to him, we gleaned from one another that from our cramming we had come independently to the joint conclusion that we detested Charlie Chaplin and everything about him. This conclusion being tactfully transmitted to Jerome Robbins, he seemed relieved, ordered us all a large brandy and returned to New York the following morning.

Our most enjoyable stab at a musical around this time, even though it too came to nothing so far as we were concerned, was when the affable Philip Langner and the Theater Guild brought Willis Hall and me together with E. Y. (Yip) Harburg and Jule Styne to adapt Arnold Bennett's *Buried Alive*. Harburg had given us *Brigadoon* and *The Wizard of Oz*. Styne had *Funny Girl* still playing on Broadway, with a revival of *Gypsy* in the offing. Their joint song credits would have run the length of Tin Pan Alley. We were in distinguished company.

We would have worked with Yip Harburg and Jule Styne for the sake of working with them even if the vehicle had been a creaky one, but it was in fact a first-rate story. We were both Arnold Bennett fans and *Buried Alive* – which Bennett himself adapted with Edward Knoblock as a stage play called *The Great Adventure* – was what its author would have called 'done up to the knocker'. It concerns a celebrated artist, Priam Farrl, who is mistaken for his own valet, Henry Leek, who has just died. Jaded by fame and notoriety, Farrl allows Leek to be buried in Westminster Abbey in his name, then takes himself off to Putney where Leek, through a matrimonial agency, has been about to pursue one Alice, the homely widow of a small builder. Famous Farrl, now known as Leek, marries ordinary Alice and leads a contented life until he is recognised by a Bond Street art dealer, which takes us up to the Act One curtain.

Setting back in at the by now cosily familiar Algonquin, we met our collaborators. Jule (pronounced Jooly) Styne was a small, florid, excitable personality who rarely finished a sentence before going on to the next one, which he didn't finish either (his long-time collaborators Betty Comden and Adolph Green defined his rapid-fire verbal shorthand as 'Stynes (or Styne-ese), n, language circa middle 20th century, spoken and understood by only one man'); he was a through-and-through showbiz character with Broadway in his bones. Yip Harburg, by contrast, looked like an Ivy League lecturer in English lit.; bookish and tweedy, he observed the world with amused detachment.

Jule and Yip were fond of reminiscing to their two young English writers about their origins. Jule had been born in Bethnal Green, of Ukrainian immigrant parents who, confusingly, kept a Welsh dairy. When he was three, he was taken to the music hall to see Harry Lauder. The child Jule, or Julius as he then was, astonished everyone by leaping up on stage and, encouraged by the Scottish entertainer, singing a song. Lauder suggested to the Stynes that they buy him a piano. They couldn't afford one but they did arrange for him to have piano lessons. The family moved to the United States where Jule continued his studies at the Chicago College of Music. The story finishes, or rather begins, with his forming his own band and playing in Mob joints for the likes of Capone and Dillinger.

As for Yip, he had reluctantly been something in the electrical appliance trade, in which he had made enough money to support himself in his proper vocation as a poet. Wiped out in the 1929 Wall Street crash, he was advised by his friend Ira Gershwin to try his hand at lyric-writing. Yip thought this over and said he had an idea for a song about the Depression. Gershwin was horrified. 'That's the last thing people want to sing about!' he warned the young poet. 'Give them something to cheer them up, like "It's A Hap-Hap-Happy Day".' Disregarding his advice, E. Y. Harburg gave them 'Brother Can You Spare a Dime' and restored his fortunes.

We were assigned an office in the Theater Guild building on West 53rd Street, where we established a pleasant routine. Each morning we would amble along Fifth Avenue from the Algonquin and write a few pages, then repair for lunch. I had developed a passion for New York delicatessens and got into the habit of popping over to the Stage Deli on Seventh Avenue, where all the sandwiches with their accompanying dill pickles are named after the personalities of the day – for instance, a pastrami on rye would be a Frank Sinatra. I often wondered what they would do about it if one of their sandwiches was arrested on a rape charge or took an overdose; the answer seemed to be that they reprinted the menu with a substitute name.

After lunch, Yip and Jule would come along and read our pages, then gathering us around a battered upright piano in true Tin Pan Alley fashion, would play and sing the latest songs they were working on. Then, after one of Philip's mouth-numbing vodka martinis, we would all troop across to one of the theatres where we were holding almost daily auditions for the part of Alice, who had to be a homebody without being dumpy, down to earth without being unsexy, and placid without being dull, or as Jule was wont to explain it, 'She's gotta be – she can't be – she has to be – she mustn't be – but at the same time she's gotta have . . . ' A tall order.

Jule always made his mind up within seconds as to whether the latest candidate should be shortlisted; then, anxiously consulting his watch, he would as likely as not vanish. It emerged that he was a keen and almost compulsive gambler, and that the Belmont Park and Aqueduct racetracks frequently beckoned. The casting session over, I would usually stroll along Seventh or Eighth Avenue with Yip, who like me was fond of walking, our perambulations culminating as often as not with a glass of beer in an Irish bar. Yip was a great one for literary and philosophical conversations, and gathering that I was interested in politics revealed himself to be something of a socialist – a dangerous thing to be at that time, or indeed at any time.

Jule and Yip were proving to be a mismatched pair so far as their personalities were concerned. In private conversation, neither one ever made any reference to the other. It was easy to see, without anything being said, that Yip regarded Jule as brash and vulgar, while Jule regarded Yip as an intellectual pinko. One day there was an unpleasant scene when Jule played a tune that Yip had found difficulty in fitting lyrics to – exasperated by the song, he described it as cheap barrel-organ music. Flushing slightly, Jule laughed apologetically and explained that he found it difficult to work to words that were not proper song lyrics but a 'pome'. These jibes were addressed not to one another but to us, as if to mediators. It was painful and embarrassing to observe the composer of 'Don't Rain on My Parade' falling out with the lyricist of 'Somewhere over the Rainbow' in this childish way.

Willis and I tended to remain neutral in such spats and squabbles, but in one instance we had to intervene with our lyric writer and composer. They had completed, and were very pleased with, a scene-setting ensemble number called 'Putney on the Thames'. It was a lively song with jaunty lyrics, but we had to explain to Yip that there was no such place as Putney on the Thames – there was Putney, and that was that. Yip demurred. He had consulted a London map. Putney was on the Thames, was it not? There was

Henley-on-Thames, and there was Kingston-upon-Thames, so what was wrong with Putney-on-Thames – or, for the sake of scansion, Putney on the Thames? Well, because it was simply never called that. It was like talking about Hampstead on the Heath or New York on the Hudson. But Yip would not be budged, and Jule, who knew a good tune when he had written it, supported him to the hilt. Brought in as arbitrator, Philip Langner came down on the side of the songwriters, arguing that anyway most New Yorkers wouldn't know whether Putney was on the Thames or the Danube. Thus our efforts to persuade the author of 'April in Paris' that he would be badly advised to add 'Putney on the Thames' to his repertoire failed.

These were highly enjoyable weeks, with, courtesy of the Guild, theatre tickets on tap (Jule Styne escorted us proprietorially to Barbra Streisand's dressing room, where ignoring us totally she entered into a harangue about the brass section being too loud, to such lengths that Jule obviously regretted having set foot in the theatre) and the whole of New York to explore. Having by now located Greenwich Village, I used to while away my Sunday mornings in its cafés, poring over the arm-numbing Sunday *New York Times* which in contrast to our own still-skimpy papers devoured, so an ecologically inclined student working as a barman informed me, 227 acres of woodpulp forest per issue. A voluntary insomniac in this city of the night, I would hang around the theatre-district bars until the small hours, returning to the Algonquin only to watch old George Raft movies on one of the seven milkily wobbling and cross-eyed TV channels. I marvelled that New York had thirty-nine radio stations and that I could get up at five in the morning if I chose – as I sometimes did – and go down to Times Square for breakfast.

This Gotham idyll was to be rudely interrupted. Before coming out to New York we had contracted to do some play-doctoring on the Leslie Bricusse musical *Pickwick*, starring Harry Secombe with Roy Castle as Sam Weller, which the excitable impresario David Merrick was bringing to the United States. The original book had been written by Wolf Mankowitz (with a little help from Charles Dickens), but the show needed some work for an American audience and since Wolf was otherwise engaged we took this not very demanding chore on. We had written several new scenes and touched up others and waved the show off to its prolonged West Coast tour prior to its New York opening; engrossed in *The Darling of the Day*, as *Buried Alive* had now been retitled, we had almost forgotten our contractual obligation to be on call for the production when we had a telephone message from Mr Merrick's very English secretary. *Pickwick* had just opened in San Francisco and one or two scenes still needed fixing. Could we fly out there at once?

This was awkward. We had reached a point in our own musical where we needed continual consultation with Jule and Yip. It would be inconvenient to leave New York at this stage. On the other hand we did have a contract with Mr Merrick and we knew that this colourful producer was used to getting his own way. It was David Merrick who, when the press panned one of his shows, scoured the telephone directory for people with identical names to the half-dozen top critics such as Walter Kerr and Clive Barnes, and paid them handsomely to endorse the rave quotes of his own devising with which he then plastered the theatre and the show business pages. When Anthony Newley steadfastly refused to remove a song from the New York production of *Stop the World, I Want to Get Off* to which Mr Merrick had taken exception, the resourceful producer resolved the impasse by creeping into the orchestra pit shortly before curtain-up and impounding all the band parts.

Diplomacy was needed. We told the English secretary with the English-rose voice that while we were only too happy to fly to San Francisco, this would be an inopportune moment because of our commitments in New York. But we would gladly telephone Peter Coe, the *Pickwick* director, talk over his problem, do whatever rewrites were needed and telex them to him, then after he had put them into the show travel to San Francisco to see how the new work looked.

She said she would transmit the message and we turned back to our own preoccupations. After an afternoon's auditions, for the unending search for an Alice continued, we returned to the Algonquin to find a message from David Merrick's English rose asking us to ring her urgently.

We did so. It appeared that Mr Merrick had dictated a telegram to her but Western Union had refused to accept it in its present form. Could she read it?

By all means. The English rose cleared her throat, and in her Harrods crystal glass department accent read: 'Gentlemen, if you do not get up off your arses instantly and proceed at once to San

Francisco, I will sue you for every fucking penny you possess. Cordially yours, David Merrick.'

We proceeded to San Francisco, by the night flight.

One look at the Golden Gate Bridge with its harp-string cables shimmering out of the mist and I knew that this was a my-kind-of-town kind of town, its proportions human, its cable cars clanging up the hilly streets an invitation to explore. Checking in at the St Francis Hotel on Union Square we stepped across to the handsome Curran Theater and did what work there was to be done. There was little enough of it, considering that we were picking up 1 per cent of the gross box office for our pains: our main task in San Francisco was to get a few more laughs into the Dingley Dell Christmas sequence, and the blessed Harry Secombe had already achieved that by tottering on wearing ice skates and, after explaining that he was about to do some figure skating, moving gingerly forward on both feet for a couple of steps and declaring, 'Eleven!'

Three thousand miles seemed a long way to come to laugh at somebody else's joke but, our mission accomplished, I bought a guidebook and proceeded to plan a couple of days' intensive exploration of the Bay city before our return to New York. Its rows of three- and four-storey wooden-frame houses like tall pastel-painted marzipan cottages completely bowled me over, as did the panelled old-fashioned bars and grills – the Tadich Grill, Sam's Grill, the Hayes Street Grill, Jack's Grill, John's Bar and Grill – that are still such a feature of San Francisco life. But much as I have subsequently tramped up and down those forty hills, some of them so steep that the local joke has it that when you're tired you just lean on them, on this occasion I was to be afforded the merest tantalising glimpse; for on our second day there, just as I was setting off to pay a lunchtime pilgrimage to John's Bar and Grill, in Dashiell Hammett's *Maltese Falcon* the favourite haunt of his private dick Sam Spade who is to foggy San Francisco what Sherlock Holmes is to foggy London, an excited Jule Styne came on the phone.

He had just seen a singer on one of the talk shows who was absolutely right for the part of the elusive Alice. 'Boys, there's no doubt about – she's – and she's got that certain – I think we oughta . . .' What emerged after some minutes of these fractured burblings was that the lady in question, whose name escapes me at this distance in time, was playing cabaret in Las Vegas. Jule was flying out there at once. Could we join him tonight at the Desert Inn?

Much as I was reluctant to leave enchanting San Francisco, I had no objection to a side trip to Las Vegas. After watching the *Pickwick* company assimilate the bits and pieces we had written for them into their matinée performance, we took the next shuttle flight out there. I have a confused, car-chase-sequence memory of a Yellow Cab hurtling us through the darkness of the desert to the dazzling neon strip and decanting us with a screech of brakes on a palm-fringed hotel forecourt; another confused memory, of hundreds of fruit machines clanking away like factory lathes in the film *Modern Times*, as we checked in and left our bags with the bell captain.

We hurried through to the cabaret where our putative perfect Alice was well into her first set. Jule was already there. As we joined him he snapped without preamble, 'Not right – she's too – and she can't . . .' He was correct. She was a good ten years too young and about as homely as Eartha Kitt. Jule was obviously anxious to be off, but etiquette forbade him to leave since she had been informed that he was in the audience. He fiddled impatiently with his glass as she sang his own 'Diamonds Are a Girl's Best Friend' in his honour, and then after applauding perfunctorily was out of the room like a bat and heading for the nearest roulette table. The girl was so manifestly wrong for the part that even if Jule could not be proved to have dragged us out to Las Vegas with the sole purpose of playing the gaming tables, the fact that there would be gaming tables next door to the cabaret must have been a factor in his decision to check her out.

We watched Jule play for a·while. He had some complicated system that had him covering half the table, so that while he was consistently raking in winning chips, it was difficult to see how much he was consistently losing. We went and lost a little money of our own on the fruit machines, had something to eat, and then ventured out to explore Las Vegas. The desert night air was cold, the dazzling Strip completely bereft of human beings except doormen and cab drivers; and one clanking hotel lobby looked very much like another. We went back. I should dearly love to have seen Las Vegas as it conducted its ordinary daily business in the velvety blackness behind the neon curtain, the Our Town community where people lived and took their children to school and to the dentist, and went to the launderette and to church and to the pizza parlour, and to the funeral parlour; but now was not the time for sociological wanderings. I promised myself to return one day but I have yet to get around to it.

Back in the Desert Inn it was evident from his pile of chips that Jule was either ahead of the game or that he had refuelled his supply. We watched – and watched – and watched. He was consistently winning, no doubt about it. It was a slowish haul, but the stack of chips was getting steadily higher. Jule was a dedicated player and did not even notice our return to the table – if, indeed, he had ever registered our departure. We continued to watch, for there is something hypnotic about a person who is remorselessly winning.

There are no public clocks in Las Vegas – a profitable policy, no doubt – and I had never bothered to adjust my watch from Eastern Seaboard Time when flying out of New York. Ploddingly working out the zone difference, I was surprised to find that it was already five in the morning. Jule had arranged to return on an early breakfast flight and we had decided that we might as well go back with him, risking the possible wrath of David Merrick should he arrive in San Francisco demanding to know where we were.

Jule was still on a winning streak and I hesitated to remind him that time was moving on. Probably, I judged, if his luck kept holding out he would forget the flight anyway and take a later one. I was wrong. One more turn of the wheel and Jule reached for one of the little baskets in which winners heaped their chips. As he shovelled them into this reverse cornucopia I estimated that he must have won in the region of a hundred thousand dollars.

I have always pictured what followed as a medium long shot in a film. Carrying his basket of chips with the bemused air of an Oliver who to his utter surprise has been granted the more that he asked for, Jule walked the length of the gaming hall towards the cashing-in grille at the far end – a considerable distance. Within three or four feet of the point at which he could have exchanged his chips for a wad of hundred-dollar bills his steps faltered. He stopped and turned, and then headed decisively for the nearest roulette table a few feet away. Five minutes later when he picked up his overnight bag I had to tip the bell captain on his behalf and when we reached the airport Willis had to pay for the cab. As the sun rose over the desert it struck me that this was the first time I had ever stayed in a hotel and never seen the inside of my room.

Owing to our being in the doldrums in the area of casting, for as well as being unable to find an Alice we were unable to find a satisfactory Priam Farrl, the Arnold Bennett musical was soon afterwards put on hold and Willis and I returned to London. By the time the Theater Guild was ready to run with the show again we were deep into some screenwriting assignment and the book passed into other hands. I believe it was tried out on the road and then flickered out. If this seems to suggest a certain lack of curiosity, it is true. It is a peculiarity of working in the theatre – film and television too – that however deeply and passionately one may have been working on a property, the moment it passes out of one's realm one's interest goes with it.

We did see Jule once more, when he came to London to sound out Laurence Harvey, who was appearing in *Camelot*, as a possible Priam. Going round to Harvey's dressing room with Jule after the show, we found him engaged in the most complicated game of patience I have ever encountered, involving five decks of cards – a work-avoidance scheme on a monumental scale which Willis and I promptly adopted, clearing a desk at No. 32 Shaftesbury Avenue for the purpose. Over dinner Jule tried to interest us in another musical that had become something of a bee in the bonnet with him – a stage version of the Powell-Pressburger film starring Moira Shearer, *Red Shoes*. Knowing nothing about ballet, we declined the invitation with thanks and directed him to the nearest casino. Very late in his long life, Jule finally got his *Red Shoes* dancing, when in financial terms it proved to be the biggest turkey in the history of the Broadway musical. It was sad that this had to be the last new show from the man who as well as two thousand songs had given us *High Button Shoes*, *Gentlemen Prefer Blondes*, *Gypsy* and *Funny Girl*.

6 So far, give or take the odd time-jump, this narrative has been more or less chronological. If it now loses something of that ordered approach it is because my own life, by the point we have now reached, had ceased to be chronological. I was living, at any rate in career terms, in layers, with my multitudinous activities – my work with Willis (itself sub-divided into categories), my journalism, my books – all flying around in my head like stacked aircraft awaiting permission to land.

Another reason why a proper date order begins to elude me is that these hurrying years of the sixties and the early seventies very much ran into each other in a kind of medley or montage of events. Sometimes, checking back on this or that milestone on my way to wherever I was going, I find that I have had it fixed in my head some five or six years out of place. Never mind: at least I know that if I am in the wrong year, I am in the right era.

Back in London in between our American travels, Willis and I had many irons stacked up in the fire, with a lot of television, film and stage work lined up. One of the many ripple effects on our particular pond was that as a result of appearing in *England Our England*, Roy Kinnear was engaged for *TW3*, and as a result of the sketches we wrote for him on that and subsequent Ned Sherrin shows we were asked by Yorkshire Television to come up with a series for him – the new station's first-ever sitcom. We devised *Inside George Webley*, the misadventures of a neurotic fat man inside whom not only a thin man but several other people are trying to get out as he struggles with his anxieties and obsessions. With Patsy Rowlands as his uncomplaining wife, the series ran successfully enough for a couple of seasons – sufficiently so, anyway, for Roy to achieve what he once touchingly confessed to me had always been his secret and

391

ultimate ambition, and that was to see his picture on the cover of *TV Times*.

Roy was a joy to write for, and we would probably be doing so still but for his tragically untimely death. Although he was an actor and not a comedian, he had the comedian's gift of drawing people to him to bask in his warmth. When my son Bob was born and I was a little late one evening in getting to Queen Charlotte's Hospital where Joan was confined, I took the precaution of taking Roy with me and wheeling him through the corridors on a mobile stretcher. The nurses and sisters were all over him and I managed to present my grapes and flowers without any bureaucratic obstruction on account of the hour.

Another series for Yorkshire was something of a spin-off from our play *All Things Bright and Beautiful* – *Queenie's Castle*, featuring the irrepressible Diana Dors, earth mother of a family of cheerful layabouts living in Quarry Hill Flats, Leeds, the enormous pebbledash Bauhaus development, now long ago demolished, that I had subjected to many a stare in my childhood exploratory wanderings. An unexpected snag in the series touched on Queenie's husband who was to have been played by Diana's real-life husband Alan Lake, as volatile a personality as she. Just as we were about to go into production our unfortunate co-star was imprisoned for causing a fracas in a public house. It was too late to recast and so we hastily wrote him out of the series, neatly accounting for the absence of a father for Queenie's grown-up brood with the explanation that he was in prison for causing a fracas in a public house. I believe we got three series out of *Queenie's Castle*.

We had constantly been nagged by various ITV companies to make a series of *Billy Liar*. We were highly resistant at first, for we didn't want Billy hanging around our necks like an adolescent albatross all our lives; but finally we succumbed to the blandishments of London Weekend, thanks to their light entertainment producer Michael Grade who had briefly represented us at our present agents, London Management. With hindsight we should have made it into a comedy drama series rather than a sitcom, but it settled into a good long run and it was an excellent vehicle for a young man fresh out of drama school – Jeff Rawle, now one of the stars of *Drop the Dead Donkey*. Meanwhile over in California, Dick Clement and Ian La Fresnais were hatching an entirely different Billy sitcom series – with our blessing of course – for the American market, starring

Steve Guttenberg and billed by CBS as 'He's a lover, a winner, a hero, a nut! If you've ever let your imagination soar, Billy's your kind of guy.' And so the *Billy Liar* industry rumbled on. From New York, a theatre company asked us how we felt about a black Billy. *Billy Ebony*, as it was to be called, has yet to happen, as has *Billy Liar on Ice*.

There were to be other sitcoms on and off but they were not really our forte, and we were constantly keeping our eyes open for a really meaty drama series to get our teeth into. The opportunity came when that resourceful and enterprising producer Verity Lambert asked if we could come up with an idea for Adam Faith.

Hanging around the drinking clubs, as we still did, we had often talked in a desultory sort of way about setting a television series in and around Soho. We had made the acquaintance of some of the minor villains in 'the naughty square mile', as the more impressionable Sunday papers still liked to call it, as well as one or two major ones including the odd psychopath. We were on chatting terms with a couple of policemen who chose to pretend that they were not policemen, and with a goodly number of ponces, club doormen, strippers, hookers and suchlike Soho riff-raff, and they all constantly refreshed our knowledge of the area and its workings. Adam Faith, we saw at once, would fit very nicely into this world as a Jack-the-lad, or better, a would-be Jack-the-lad, scraping a living in the sex shops and strip clubs of these seedy streets.

He would have to have a boss, obviously, a Mr Big who would put the fear of God in him but upon whom he would be totally reliant; and so we presented him with such a father figure in the person of Charlie Endell, a mini-tycoon of the porn circuit, loosely based on an acquaintance of ours who enjoyed such a position, having risen in the world of Soho from strip-club doorman to controller of his own little sex empire. Adam Faith would be our minnow in this murky pond.

We called the series *The Loser*, a terrible title inviting the nemesis of poor ratings, which LWT rightly scotched. So we called it *Budgie* instead, after the character's nickname, his real name being Ronald Bird. His employer, Charlie Endell, we had envisaged as a South Londoner, and a character so peripheral to our eponymous anti-hero that he was to appear in only three or four episodes of the first series. But with the casting of Iain Cuthbertson who played him as the larger-than-life laughing Glaswegian so soon to be featured in the repertoire of every TV impressionist, we saw that we had got the perfect pairing that every scriptwriter dreams of, a copper-bottomed double act who reacted to and rubbed off one another like every classic duo from Laurel and Hardy onwards. Hastily we wrote Iain into the episodes that had lacked his dominant presence (so dominant that when the series finally wound up, there was a spin-off Charlie Endell show on Scottish Television). *Budgie* was a huge success and ran and ran for season after season until we all began to think it was time to move on to other things.

Another big television hit for us was the long-running *Worzel Gummidge*. In the course of the frequent trips down Back Memory Lane in which my fellow Leodsian and I indulged, we often reminisced about the old wireless programmes of our childhood such as *Band Waggon*, *Monday Night at Seven*, *Garrison Theatre*, and the magical *Children's Hour* when we would hurry home from school to hear Uncle Mac introducing the latest adventures of Larry the Lamb in Toytown, Romany and the dog Raq among the hedgerows, and the living scarecrow Worzel Gummidge on Scatterbrook Farm. We sometimes talked about adapting the Worzel stories for television but never got around to doing anything about it until we heard, in a casual way, that Jon Pertwee was equally a fan of the rascally scarecrow and had always wanted to play the part.

He was perfect casting. We promptly acquired the television rights of the original books by Barbara Euphan Todd and the three of us got together. It proved remarkably difficult to get Worzel off the ground – Thames, for example, turned us down flat – but after several frustrating months we persuaded Southern Television to take a chance on what was to prove the most popular children's TV series since *Dr Who*, and which shared the *Dr Who* ratings secret of being a kids' programme that adults couldn't bear to miss.

We were well served in all directions. Our producer-director was James Hill, whose impressive credits included the feature films *Born Free, The Belstone Fox* and the Oscar-winning *Giuseppina*. The softly spoken but quietly assertive James, as would be expected, displayed a sure understanding of the series' half-real, half-storyland rural settings and its caricatured but not cut-out rustic characters; but more than that he could on occasion brush the programme with magic – some of the scenes he shot, particularly those touching on the eccentric Crowman's powers of creation, had a mystical quality that quite made one's back hairs bristle. The Crowman, an invention of our own who owed nothing to the original, was superbly cast in Geoffrey Bayldon of *Catweazle* fame, as was the part of Aunt Sally in the person of the incomparable Una Stubbs who made the character her own. In the Barbara Euphan Todd books Aunt Sally is a disagreeable, peripheral figure who really is a maiden aunt; we made her much younger and the object of the scarecrow's hopeless passions. Our development made the stories a saga of unrequited love, with Aunt Sally's snooty, wooden head filled with unattainable dreams of marrying a prince, Worzel's turnip heads (we gave him several – a thinking head, a singing head, a dancing head, and so on, as required) stuffed with unworkable plots to ensnare the object of his affections, and the mysterious Crowman keeping some semblance of order with his Jehovah-like threats to throw Worzel on the bonfire and chop Aunt Sally up for kindling. With this as our basic formula, we ran to fifty-two episodes plus several hour-long Christmas specials, which sold all over the world.

The series would probably be running still had not Southern Television lost its franchise in the periodic shake-up of ITV companies, when our admittedly expensive series was promptly discontinued by the incoming outfit which in the interests of 'improving standards' was required to build expensive new studios within its region and so had to cut costs. Such are the workings of television quality control.

But we had a glorious run, in the course of which we incidentally found ourselves knee-deep in a branch of show business new to us – merchandising – and literally knee-deep at that, for our offices were awash with Worzel pens, Worzel painting books, Worzel paperbacks, Worzel T-shirts, toys, puppets, posters, games, lollipops, audio-tapes, a Worzel weekly comic, all awaiting the endorsement of Waterhall Worzel Ltd (for we had had to form yet another new company, to deal with the scarecrow's finances).

Although we enjoyed playing some of the games, all this was a little too near the legitimate business world for our taste; we were far happier working on the Worzel Gummidge stage show, an altogether more satisfying spin-off. This, with music by Denis King to our own lyrics, and with the original stars, ran for two successful tours and played a packed Christmas season at the Cambridge, once the home of *Billy Liar*. I have a vivid memory of standing at the back of the stalls on our opening night at the Birmingham Repertory Theatre, when we were playing to a huge audience of obviously television-orientated children, not all of them tuned in to the ways of the theatre. The curtain went up in a cloud of dry ice. Dramatic, Genesis-type music. Worzel, the motionless scarecrow, stands attached to his post in the middle of Ten Acre Field in the classic position, arms outstretched like the Saviour on the Cross (a coincidence to which James Hill did not mind drawing ever-so-subtle attention on occasion). The Crowman in his dusty top hat and mouldering frock coat arrives on his ancient tricycle. Murmuring incantations and waving a magic twig, he brings the scarecrow to life as lightning flashes across the cycloramic backcloth sky and thunder rolls from the orchestra pit. Worzel, a straw Frankenstein's monster, staggers forward. It is an impressive moment – literally a moment, for the whole dramatic sequence took less than a minute. A twelve-year-old boy in the back row immediately in front of me turned to his father and said, yawning: 'Dad, is there much more of this?' You learn nothing if not humility in the theatre.

Which brings me back to our stage activities. They had been continuing unabated. Following *Say Who You Are* we wrote an unabashed boulevard comedy called *Who's Who*, with Joe Melia, Francis Matthews, Judy Cornwell and Josephine Tewson. Mr Matthews was once again required to carry an ashtray about but this time, under the ingenious direction of Robert Chetwyn, it was because he was wandering around in the potted-plant jungle of a Brighton hotel palm court of J. Hutchinson Scott's labyrinthine design, looking for the table he had just vacated and now finding himself hopelessly lost, as indeed was everyone else in the play at some point or other. I would not attempt to summarise the plot, for as the *Sunday Telegraph* said, it was a mathematical conundrum so confusing that it would have given even Pirandello a headache; suffice it to say that in their pursuit of dangerous liaisons, Mr Black always lies while Mr White always tells the truth, and the play – in reality two plays, both acts commencing at 5.23 p.m. on Friday the thirteenth – put their theories to the test.

If anything, *Who's Who* got even better reviews than *Say Who You Are*, our fellow-dramatist Frank Marcus (*The Killing of Sister George*) paying us the compliment of describing it as a textbook example of farce, by 'just about the most skilful craftsmen in the business'. The piece was to prove immensely popular in France, likewise in Italy. Tony Randall was going to direct it on Broadway, and while he has yet to get around to it, *Who's Who* has meanwhile had many fruitful outings in the United States. But here at the Fortune Theatre we opened at the beginning of a heat wave, which blistered on unabated all through a tarmac-bubbling July.

Heat waves are high on the twenty-five plausible reasons given to backers for the loss of their investment, the others being cold spells, fog, snow, rain, gales, rail strikes, bomb scares, Asian flu, VAT, the Depression, the Budget, lack of passing trade, absence of American tourists, new parking restrictions, higher tube fares, restaurant prices, no glitzy names, roadworks in Shaftesbury Avenue, theatre too big for show, theatre too small for show, theatre inscrutably wrong for show, box office incompetence, sudden illness of star, and critics' mafia conspiracy of bad reviews. We had a conspiracy of good reviews but we came off in short order. The only predictable element in the theatre is its unpredictability.

One afternoon in Piccadilly I bumped into Ken Tynan. He had had a long lunch and so had I. He asked – he was then Literary Manager of the National Theatre – how Willis and I would feel about adapting *Saturday Night and Sunday Morning*. I said I rather thought it had already been done. Tynan said yes, but not here: the author's work had never been done in this country. Mystified, I asked him to continue; he turned out to be talking not about Sillitoe but the great Neapolitan dramatist Eduardo de Filippo, and the play was of course – he now corrected himself – *Saturday, Sunday, Monday*.

In due course I reported this fuzzy conversation to Willis who said, 'I hope he doesn't want us to do it north country.' It proved, when the three of us met up, that such an idea had been in Tynan's mind, which was why, given that neither of us had any Italian, he must have thought of us. Fortunately for de Filippo's reputation, and for ours had we gone along with this quaint idea, he had thought about it a little more and did not need persuading that the only location for Eduardo's excitable extended Neapolitan families was Naples.

Franco Zeffirelli was to direct. Given that in one of his blacker moments I heard him muttering that it was like rehearsing an episode of *Coronation Street* (his substantial cast was led by Joan Plowright, with Olivier in a cameo role), I did fleetingly wonder how the sprawling Neapolitan opus would have fared had we set it in Oldham. With the smell of ragout wafting out from the stage during the beautifully orchestrated lunch scene, *Saturday, Sunday, Monday* was predictably a hit, transferring in due course from the National to the Queen's.

Zeffirelli was practical and proficient in the rehearsal room, but somewhat inscrutable away from it. Our first meeting with him was in his suite at the Carlton Tower Hotel, with Ken Tynan. Tynan, as we arrived, had yet to turn up. We engaged in a little small-talk, then Zeffirelli excused himself and went into the next room, presumably, as one would have thought, to make a private telephone call or go to the bathroom. Then Ken Tynan bustled in (for so languid-looking a personality, he was a great bustler, arriving for meetings with the air of an agitated Larry Grayson late for a show). 'Franco shouldn't be long,' he announced. One of us said, 'He's here already – he's next door in the bedroom.' 'No, he can't be,' said Tynan. 'I just saw him outside the hotel, crossing the street.' We talked among ourselves until Zeffirelli reappeared twenty minutes later – via the bedroom – and without a word of explanation plunged straight into his notes on our script.

Saturday, Sunday's success was followed, two or three years later, by Zeffirelli's production of our only other Eduardo adaptation, *Filumena* – ex-prostitute seeking respectability for her three grown-up sons – again starring Plowright, this time at the Lyric. It was nice to look out of the office window and see our names in lights, even if in very small lettering, as was only proper. *Filumena* was an even greater success for Eduardo, for all that Herbert Kretzmer, echoing Franco's passing *Coronation Street* misgivings, called it a pizza-flavoured soap opera – 'Neapolitan hokum'. Bernard Levin, while raving about the piece, grumbled, 'I do not care for the growing practice of engaging writers who do not know the language of the original to put foreign plays on to the English stage; how can they, working from a crib, get into the mind of the author?' Why, by being dramatists themselves. There were, as Levin pointed out, several excellent (but academic) translations of de Filippo – but they would have emptied the Lyric instead of filling it.

One more adaptation: at last we got a musical into production, and of another Arnold Bennett novel, *The Card*, the picaresque story of Denry Machin, that rising star of the Potteries identified, in the memorable last line of both story and show, 'with the great cause of cheering us all up.' The idea was brought in by our composer Tony Hatch and his lyricist wife Jackie Trent, herself a product of the Five Towns. Jim Dale starred, supported by Millicent Martin, Marti Webb, Joan Hickson and Eleanor Bron – a powerful distaff side for any show. Our producer was the stripling Cameron Mackintosh, then barely out of his teens, staging his very first original stage musical. The piece has remained, and not only for sentimental reasons, a favourite with Cameron, and twenty years after its respectable run at the Queen's Theatre he had us revive and revise it, with additional lyrics by the talented Anthony Drewe, first for the charming little Watermill Theatre at Newbury, then for the Regents Park Open Air Theatre, with Peter Duncan as the Card, Hayley Mills as the Countess of Chell, and Ian Talbot directing. The Regents Park production – the first time we had ever worked in the open air, and an invigorating experience – was blessed by an excellent summer and was followed by a national tour culminating in, for reasons which now escape me, Moscow. Both Peter Duncan and the production itself were nominated for Olivier awards.

There were other theatrical adventures – shows that went on, shows that went down, shows that have been long forgotten, shows that are suddenly remembered and resuscitated, shows that still soldier on. There were only a few regrets, mostly for productions that should have made it but didn't, or which nearly made it. We were particularly sorry to lose our adaptation of Priestley's haunting novel *Lost Empires*, about the last days of the old variety halls (and much, much more), with music by Denis King and lyrics by ourselves, a touring production commissioned by the Cambridge Theatre Company. It would have been worth working on and bringing into London. 'It may well', wrote Sheridan Morley, 'turn out to be the best theatrical treat for family audiences in the whole of London this autumn.' Alas, family audiences had another treat in store – the full-scale Granada TV serialisation of *Lost Empires* whose imminence was closer than we had imagined. We closed, I think, in Birmingham. A *Guardian* critic cannot have known he was penning our valedictory when he wrote, 'I ought to say right now that I think this show is going to be a considerable commercial success . . .'

But disappointments are part of the currency of the theatre and setbacks come and go as easily as Jule Styne's roulette chips. We were enjoying ourselves, that was the main thing. There was only one show that caused us any anguish, and which, had we not both been of the temperament that says a contract is a contract (even when it may require an unprintable telegram from David Merrick), we should have walked away from at an early stage. This was a musical based on the life of the Regency clown Grimaldi, which under the title *Joey Joey* played briefly at the Saville Theatre.

Joey was the near-lifelong preoccupation of Ron Moody, who had spent five years working on the book, music and lyrics of this star vehicle for himself, turning down lucrative television contracts and parts on Broadway, following his triumph as Fagin, to pursue his obsession. This in itself should have been a warning: actors so closely involved with material of their own finding are tricky to deal with. Another danger signal was that Ron Moody was reported as having developed an interest in 'the psychology of laughter' while studying sociology at the London School of Economics.

But it seemed a good idea at the time. Bernard Delfont persuaded us into it. Oscar Lewenstein, who had many business dealings with Delfont, quotes him as saying, in connection with his brother Lew Grade: 'You can rely absolutely on anything Lew says, but as for me you mustn't believe a word I say.' Paradoxically, Mr Delfont, as he still was, never spoke a truer word. To Ron Moody he apparently said that he was bringing us in only as play doctors, to tinker with the show as we tinkered with *Pickwick*. To us he said that we had absolute *carte blanche* to do with the book as we pleased, to start from scratch if need be, so long as we got it right.

Thus, with this recipe for inevitable confrontation, we commenced work. It was trouble from the start. Shirley Butler, our brilliant director on *Say Who You Are*, joined the project early not only to provide what is nowadays called 'input' but, at our request, to referee the tiresome squabbles between Ron and ourselves as we argued our way line by line towards the ultimate birth-pangs of his musical love-child. Eventually, after what seemed like a very long swim through a sea of glue, we bickered our way to the Palace Theatre, Manchester.

We hoped that once in rehearsal, with a demanding part to worry about, Ron would ease off. Not a bit of it. 'Why has this been changed?' 'Well, it's a better line, Ron.' 'I'm sorry, but I can't agree.' I suppose he would have called himself a perfectionist, but worrying away at the thing like a dog with a bone was not making it better. Ron's trouble, insofar as I concerned myself with the psychology of Ron as he concerned himself with the psychology of laughter, seemed to me to be that here was a man who was never going to top his own peak as the definitive Fagin – as Topol, for example, was never going to top his Fiddler – yet who gnawingly, nit-pickingly, wanted to do better. Furthermore, as he constantly reminded us, Grimaldi was almost literally his life's work. For us it was another show – not that we did not give it our best shots, but working with somebody else's obsession is difficult.

Away from the show, if one could get him away from the show, Ron was a nice enough man, engaging even; but he did test us, and our director, with his flair for the unexpected improvement. One matinée he enlivened a difficult domestic scene which we had just rewritten and were still easing in, by playing it with a plant-pot strapped to his head.

The thing was not working properly in Manchester and eventually Bernard Delfont himself came up to sort us all out. He sat patiently, not speaking, while we all chuntered our grievances. The upshot was that Shirley Butler, who was admittedly out of her depth by now, was replaced by the greatly experienced Arthur Lewis, Delfont's long-time associate. It was a pity he did not replace the writers.

For the opening night at the Saville we had supplied Ron with a whole bunch of supposedly freewheeling, off-the-cuff material for Joey Grimaldi to ad lib, as it would appear to his audience of the time, carefully written period lines to give him a breather in between his renderings of 'Typitywitchet' and 'Hot Codlins', the songs with which the great clown used to beguile his audience. These were going well enough until Ron spotted Bernard Levin in the audience. Departing from his painstakingly prepared contemporary ad libs he at once jumped a century and a half to extemporise, 'Ho! If it ain't my old friend Bernard Levin, what I was at the London School of Heconomics with . . .' Across the aisle from me, as Ron then took it into his head to descend into the audience, leaving the stage completely empty, I saw Bernard Delfont bury his head in his hands.

A letter in the *Stage* newspaper a few days later succinctly summed up both this maverick talent and our critical reception in the words: 'It will doubtless be of interest to learn that during his lifetime Joseph Grimaldi (1778–1837) never got any good press notices, either.'

Ah, well. There was always the safe, sane world of Hollywood.

7 Improbable and even incredible as it seems when I look back on the substantial body of work we were taking on, together with the time-consuming devices we employed to avoid doing it, Willis and I never ceased to continue working on our own individual enterprises. In fact, glancing at the list of children's books, sporting books, stage and television work that represents Willis's solo credits during this fertile period, I wonder that he ever managed to get to the office at all.

For myself, I continued to turn out the odd novel and keep my hand in at journalism, writing for an hour or so at home before the car arrived to deliver me to the office, and at weekends, as well as sometimes for a couple of hours at No. 32 Shaftesbury Avenue after we had finished work, or on occasion what passed for work, for the day.

My first novel after *Billy Liar* was *Jubb*, published in 1963, which caused something of a flutter because of its subject-matter. C. L. Jubb is a sexual inadequate, a pedestrian kerb-crawler who makes voyeuristic tours of the sodium-hissing streets of the new town where he is a rent collector and youth club leader, hoping to find something to slaver over through the chinks in imperfectly drawn bedroom curtains, and dreaming of his Mecca, the Reeperbahn red-light district of Hamburg, or 'the gutter of Europe', as he has seen it described.

For the background, I drew on my brief sojourn in Harlow. For the character – 'one of the slugs of the postwar English welfare state', as an American reviewer called him – I took some of my inspiration from a solicitor's clerk of my acquaintance, who did indeed somewhat resemble a slug in that his lips were always coated in a white sludge. Cyril, as I had better call him after my eponymous anti-hero, was totally sex-obsessed and talked about no

403

other subject in our occasional conversations at the bar of El Vino. He had a weakness for secretaries, but as a former grammar school boy and a snob he would entertain them only if they were educated to a proper standard and lived north of the river. When he became inflamed by a flighty office girl who lured him with promises of lust in the bath, but who lived in Peckham and had only two O-levels to her name, he hastily rewrote the rules to accommodate girls who, while otherwise disqualified, came from 'good families' – as his current passion could claim, her father having been a squadron leader.

Cyril was completely serious in these preoccupations and they were a good starting-off point when I began to dig into Jubb, thereafter mining ever deeper until I was reaching facets of his character so dark that they were quite frightening. My object was to present a sexual misfit sympathetically, so that even as one is repelled by him one understands how he came to be that way and feels for him in his odyssey through the cruel world in which such hideously alienated souls, like sexual Quasimodos, have to make their way.

I think, in fact I know, that I succeeded; and such was the verdict of most of the reviews. Irving Wardle, a fiction critic before he became a drama critic, commended in the *Observer* 'a generosity of imagination which banishes the stock image of the drab little fetishist and substitutes a desperate human being whom at one time or another we have all seen in the mirror.' Most of the others said much the same thing. Elsewhere, words like 'revolting' and 'grubby' were employed, and a now long-forgotten but then briefly flourishing newspaper called the *New Daily*, blaming what it saw as a tide of filth on 'the "satirical" magazine *Private Eye*, which not to mince words is often disgusting', observed that while there was nothing new about disgusting literature, 'what is new and alarming is that such stuff as this novel by a favourite playwright of the Royal Court and the BBC should be accepted and praised and seriously talked about'. It came as news to me that I was the pet of the Royal Court. *Jubb* headed for the bestseller lists and was banned by the Irish Censorship of Publications Board. Granada Television, having recently set up a film unit, bought the screen rights, and Donald Pleasence, who would have been perfect casting, was aching to play the part; but in the event the Granada film unit only ever made one film, and *Jubb* was not it.

Wearing my journalism hat I was writing spasmodically for various publications, but most regularly for *Punch*. When poor Mr Punch met his demise and I was asked how long I had written for the venerable journal I would say, 'Thirty years, but they've only been printing the stuff for twenty.' In fact, under various editors – Bernard Hollowood, William Davis, Alan Coren – I wrote regularly for *Punch* from the early sixties until the late eighties, eventually becoming a member of the coveted Punch Table, which entitled me not only to add my carved initials to those of a distinguished company that included James Thurber, A. P. Herbert, John Betjeman and W. M. Thackeray (Mark Twain declined to carve his, saying that two of Thackeray's initials would do for him), but also to lunch weekly at the Table for life should I so please.

I got to the Punch Table whenever I could: it was always a lively, noisy gathering with some interesting guests. Some were more interesting than others. I met S. J. Perelman twice at the Table: on the second occasion he ran through exactly the same repertoire of Mike Todd and Marx Brothers stories as he had on the first, and in the same order. On another occasion I had the privilege of becoming Princess Margaret's ashtray.

We were having pre-lunch drinks in the Editor's office, where HRH, as always, was smoking through a long holder. Her cigarette had accumulated about an inch of ash and it was very clear that rather than seek out an ashtray herself she expected one to be produced. A self-appointed minion among our number located one on the Editor's desk but could not get back through the throng surrounding the Princess to proffer it. Standing next to her, I extended my hand to receive the ashtray. Princess Margaret, without pausing in her discourse and without looking down, flicked her cigarette ash into my open palm in the confident belief that an ashtray had been located and was in position. Since she was in mid-anecdote I had no option but to stand there with a handful of hot ash and a fixed grin. I carried the scar with pride at having been of some small service.

The Punch Table, particularly in the effervescent William Davis's day, was a fountain of stunts and journalistic exploits, such as launching Alan Coren upon society disguised as an Arab sheikh, or, in honour of A. P. Herbert who once demonstrated the legality of making out a cheque upon the rump of a cow, inscribing such a cheque on such a cow and leading it up to a Fleet Street bank to be cashed.

Davis was fond of getting his writers out of the office on to cross-Channel steamers or up in balloons, and one of his wheezes was to despatch various contributors and cartoonists to various cities to record their all-too-frank impressions, and then defend their corner to the local media. Good for circulation. I went up to Manchester with Bill Tidy of Cloggies fame, who introduced me to an enchanting north country of his own invention, full of soot factories and smoke-works and sludge depositories, and pubs called the Wall-Eyed Signalman and the Lisping Cockroach. We need not have left London. Stanley Reynolds, a garrulous, cigar-chomping East Coast American who had somehow fetched up on *Punch*, drew Newcastle-upon-Tyne, where he spent as little time as possible before demolishing the city in print. Unknown to him, his arrival and departure had been monitored by a local radio journalist, so that when the time came for him to justify his attack on air, the first question was: 'Mr Reynolds, how can you condemn a city in which you have spent only one and a half hours?' 'Listen,' snarled Reynolds, 'I've condemned cities I've only flown over!'

Unfortunately, the fun days of *Punch* were numbered. During Alan Coren's reign, company marketing men – 'The Suits', as Alan despairingly called them – began to infiltrate the Table. I compared them with the Stoats and Weasels invading Toad Hall. With an unerring sense of mistiming, they began targeting a younger profile just as the fifty-five-plus age group had been identified as one of the most prosperous segments in the readership spectrum – and just after the launch of the wildly successful, youth-orientated *Viz*. Alan went. His successor David Taylor went. In protest not only at its declining standards but at the ruthless way the Suits were reducing staff like new brooms on a gutter tabloid, I not only stopped writing for *Punch* but became the first, and I believe the only, person ever to resign from the 150-year-old Punch Table. I thought I had better put this in writing and in return received an irascible phone call from Stanley Reynolds who had been appointed Acting Editor: 'So whaddya want me to do – erase your initials with Polyfilla?'

Some of us, including Bill Davis, Alan Coren and several subversives who with rent to pay were still working on the ailing magazine – by now it had only weeks to live – formed a Punch in Exile Table which met periodically in a private room at the Garrick Club, where we passed around the port as of old and hatched dark plans to make a takeover bid for *Punch* and restore it to its former self. They came to nothing, of course, and by and by the Punch in Exile Table, as is the way of these things, fizzled out.

Somehow I found the time to write a fourth novel, *The Bucket Shop*, which was well received although perhaps underestimated. It took roughly the same theme as *Say Who You Are*, of someone dabbling in promiscuity who is wildly unsuited to the life; but I wrote it in a style new to me, though no doubt influenced by my work in other fields with Willis – a sparse, cinematic narrative, cutting into and out of scenes to eliminate everything except the crucial moment, with some chapters consisting of only three or four lines of dialogue. It worked and I was pleased with it, but I cannot claim that it made much of a splash.

In fact my principal recollection of *The Bucket Shop* is of writing it, to the strains of such tunes of the times as 'Grocer Jack', 'A Whiter Shade of Pale' and 'Simon Smith and His Amazing Dancing Bear', played incessantly on a kind of tannoy contraption which reminded me of the RAF-camp radio stations I used to listen to in a variety of billets during my National Service. This was, however, no Nissen hut but a reasonably elegant residential hotel of thirties vintage, the White House in Regents Park, where I had a tiny bed-sitting room and kitchenette and worked at a little portable typewriter set on a fixed shelf which doubled as a dining table. For by now I had become unmarried.

It had been on the cards, I suppose, ever since we had come to London sixteen years earlier. Most of the Fleet Street 'Petts Wood' marriages I had known had in the long run failed to survive their transplant from north to south. My own career had undergone not one but three transitions: Fleet Street, Shaftesbury Avenue, and now the United States. Joan never stood in the way of my plans but they were plans which often, by their nature, could not include her. The camaraderie of a close working relationship can't have helped, either: professional partners who have unburdened themselves to one another over at the pub after a harrowing day don't really feel like going through it all again when they get home. Inevitably, Joan felt herself increasingly excluded from my life and after some futile efforts to resolve the situation, I moved out.

I had been spending so little time at home that the children barely noticed. I had resolved, however, to be as responsible and caring a father as I could be in the circumstances, and having decanted myself to the White House I at once established a pattern of contact that would lend continuity both to their lives and to mine. Every Wednesday evening I would take the three of them out to supper. Every Saturday I would go round and spend the day with them, if possible avoiding the forlorn haunts of divorced fathers such as the zoo and the waxworks. Every Sunday morning, come rain, shine, fog or snow, we took their little dog for a three-hour amble around Richmond Park: this was compulsory, and it was a routine that continued well into their teens. Nothing was allowed to get in the way of these arrangements. Only if I had to be abroad were they ever interrupted. What with this regime and our annual holiday together, I was seeing far more of my children, in terms of real time spent together, than when I was at home. While I would not recommend divorce as a way of life I would, if there is no other way, recommend this formula for salvaging some degree of order and security from the shipwrecked family vessel. It certainly did me good, anyway, and I don't think it did them any harm either. They are long grown up now but our Wednesday suppers continue to this day.

From the White House I moved via an apartment in Upper Wimpole Street and a stubbornly ungentrified street in Islington to my present home in Earl's Court among an unexpected cluster of cottages that once served the local farm, and only across the way from the shared room where I started my life in London. Somewhere along the way I remarried, but this was not destined to last for ever either, although we remain the very best of friends, and I was forced to the conclusion that I must be very difficult to live with. I now live contentedly alone, shuttling serenely back and forth between salubrious Earl's Court and a flat in a Georgian street in Bath.

It was while I was still at the White House that there was a significant development in my writing life. While I no longer had the cheek to accept Hugh Cudlipp's annual retainer, I still kept up my contact with the *Daily Mirror*, writing the odd series and occasional special articles. In the late sixties, prematurely as it turned out, the *Mirror* launched a pioneering colour supplement, *Mirror Magazine*, brilliantly run by Mike Molloy, a future editor and later editorial director of the *Mirror*. It lasted six months, the marketing men's ingenious explanation for its demise being that it had been found too thick to fold into four and tuck into the knee pocket of workmen's overalls, thus reducing the factory-gate sales potential. The real reason was probably that the final issue of the

408

magazine, which never got on the streets (or into workmen's overall pockets), was devoted to an explicit (for the time) Guide to Sexual Knowledge, with expert contributions on such matters as childbirth, birth control and venereal diseases. This was responsible, even dull, stuff, but for an outspoken radical newspaper the *Mirror* had a prudish collection of directors' wives.

My own contribution to the *Mirror Magazine* was a back-page feature, initially meant to run for six weeks, in which I was at liberty to ramble on – or 'sound off', in the tabloid phrase – about any topic of my choosing. Having learned a lesson from the experience of my old *Sunday Pictorial* column, I gave the barmy burghers of Birmingham a wide berth and wrote about any subject that took my fancy, not necessarily talking-points of the day. I figured, perhaps belatedly, that if it interested me, it should interest a sufficient number of my readers; considering that this was the advice I had been given down the years by various mentors in print and in person, it had taken me a long time responding to it.

When the *Mirror Magazine* was on its last legs, Hugh Cudlipp called me in, poured me a large drink, and made a hypothetical, inscrutable, and, to anyone who hadn't learned the corkscrew language of Fleet Street, baffling proposal: 'Should it be found necessary for the *Daily Mirror* to cease publication, and should we decide to publish the *Mirror Magazine* in its place on Mondays and Thursdays instead of simply on Fridays, how would you be placed for writing your column twice weekly?'

I got his drift, and a couple of weeks later began the twice-weekly column that has now been running for twenty-five years – sixteen in the *Daily Mirror* then subsequently in the *Daily Mail*. It was a success from the start, winning two of the national press awards in its first few months and continuing to pick them up at intervals through the years. Why it should have caught on I have never dared analyse. I write it as well as I can on the day that it has to be done – some days are better than others – and even when picking an obvious subject, as a columnist must from time to time, I try to avoid the obvious points and above all refrain from echoing 'what the man in the pub is saying'. It always seems to me that people who want to hear what the man in the pub is saying would be better off buying a pint than a newspaper. I have, like all columnists, several hobby-horses but I avoid indignation and in any case would never simulate it – the columnist who fakes it is palpably closing his or her eyes and thinking of the cheque. One firm rule I have is never to think about the column until the deadline looms. If possible, I arrange to go out to lunch on column-writing days: the knowledge that I have to be out of the house at 12.45 induces just the right degree of panic to start the adrenalin flowing.

The *Mirror* column was a very happy arrangement; I could go where I pleased and write what I wanted, and no one could touch a comma. Continuing my love affair with the United States, I always wrote half a dozen columns a year from America where there was always a column waiting to happen – a convention of barber-shop singers in Boston, where blazered white quartets were chanting Negro spirituals even as black-related bus riots raged all around the hotel; a New Orleans cab driver who couldn't find the Democratic Convention; the grotesque Kennedy Museum in Dallas where the assassination point on the relief map of the presidential route lit up with a flashing bang every few minutes.

After some years of these jaunts, to jump ahead somewhat, I was in San Francisco for another Democratic Convention when I had a call from Roy Hattersley, who was there as a Labour Party observer, to join him for drinks at the Top of the Mark bar in the Mark Hopkins Hotel on Nob Hill. I cannot at the moment recollect whether the nineteenth-storey bar was one of those which revolve, or whether I just had the sensation of it going round and round after I had heard what Hattersley had to tell me, which was that Robert Maxwell had bought the Mirror group. I should like to say that knowing Maxwell's reputation I was appalled; the truth is that on dramatic occasions such as this the newspaperman's instinctive reaction is one of high excitement – something happening, however dire the consequences, is always preferable to nothing happening.

It was on this occasion that I became a footnote in all the subsequent biographies of Maxwell by inventing his nickname. Roy Hattersley recalled for some reason that as an MP the old monster had traded under the name of Captain Maxwell. When it came to calling for the bill I insisted on picking it up on the grounds that 'Cap'n Bob would wish the *Daily Mirror* to entertain the Labour Party spokesman for home affairs.' Thereafter, whenever the *Daily Mirror* stood anyone in San Francisco a drink, the toast was to Cap'n Bob. The name had crossed the Atlantic within hours, and it stuck.

One of Cap'n Bob's first acts was to call in all the senior figures on the *Mirror* one by one for a chat – in other words, to tell them what he required of them. When my turn came I demurred – I didn't want Maxwell to waddle away with the impression that I was on the staff, or as nearly on the staff as made no difference; and so to underline my independence I asked to meet him away from the *Mirror* office, over lunch. 'He won't come,' said Mike Molloy, by now the Editor. 'He never goes out for lunch.' I said, 'It might amuse him', and seemingly it did, or at any rate he agreed to have lunch.

I asked one of his many secretaries to reserve a table at the Connaught, in my name but to stress who was to be my guest. On the day, I arrived at the hotel ten minutes early with a view to having a bottle of champagne on the table before Maxwell arrived, and with the further object of having a nerve-steadying quick one in advance of the ordeal. This, it proved, was to be needed; for when I came to announce my presence, there was no restaurant booking in my name.

'Try Maxwell,' I said, the sweat already glistening on my forehead.

Again the maître d' drew a blank. I said, 'Never mind, there must have been a mix-up.' (The silly girl had booked a private room at the Connaught Rooms.) 'Just give me the nicest table you have.'

'I'm sorry, sir, the restaurant is completely full.'

I thought very swiftly about the possible courses of action available to me. I could go down to the men's room and hang myself with my tie. I could simply walk out of the hotel and keep on walking, eventually being found exhausted on a park bench far from home, apparently suffering from loss of memory. I could take the coward's way out: ring Maxwell's office and say, 'Keith Waterhouse here – just confirming my lunch with Mr Maxwell tomorrow.' I thought seriously about the coward's way. Then I produced a £20 note and said to the maître d', the sweat now soaking my collar: 'Look. The man who may well be buying this hotel today is even now on his way. I must have a table.' The maître d' despatched me for another stiff drink while he saw what he could do. A few long moments later I saw a waiter ushering a pair of Americans out of the restaurant with the words, 'If it's a steak you're requiring, gentlemen, I think you'll find the grill room more to your taste.' I got my table, and my champagne. Maxwell was late. In my relief, I had drunk the whole bottle by the time he arrived.

The lunch began amicably enough. 'You are an institution!'

boomed Maxwell, having been briefed to this effect by Molloy. He quoted something from that morning's column – the only one, I believe, that he ever read all the way through or even part of the way through: Molloy told me that he found it incomprehensible. I gave him a bottle of Château Latour which he seemed to appreciate – at any rate, when I told him what he was drinking he boasted, 'Ah, yes, I have ten thousand bottles of this in my cellar!' – a remark that could have been made by Toad of Toad Hall himself.

After he had shovelled away a huge plateful of food at record speed, Cap'n Bob then delved into a folder and produced some boring-looking reports about ballot corruption in one of the trade unions, which he invited me to write about. I explained gently that the subject was more up Woodrow Wyatt's street than mine and that it wouldn't interest me. Cap'n Bob seemed genuinely perplexed. 'But you are my columnist. You work for me' – the implication being that I did as I was told. Perhaps emboldened by having drunk all my portly guest's champagne, I said, 'No, Mr Maxwell – you work for me. You produce the paper in which I write. I am like a music hall act – I am at present top of the bill at the Palladium, but if the Palladium doesn't like my act there is always the Coliseum.' The analogy appealed to Maxwell, and whenever I came across him after I had left – as I saw there and then that I should have to – he would always chuckle, getting it slightly wrong in his Mr Malaprop way (it was Maxwell who once famously said, 'Jerusalem isn't built in a day'), 'Don't forget, Keith, if you don't like it at the Haymarket you can always come back to Drury Lane.'

As soon as the word got around Fleet Street that I was set to part company with the *Mirror*'s new owner, my telephone gratifyingly never stopped ringing – I think I had an approach from every national daily except the *Financial Times*, and most of the Sundays. The bidding was won by Sir David English of the *Daily Mail* who on the day he took me to lunch at the Savoy had one of the regular columns in his paper made up as an exact replica of my *Mirror* column, so that I could see, without the matter being referred to in any way, how much at home I should feel in the pages of the *Daily Mail*. This display of what the late Nicholas Tomalin called the journalist's prerequisite of rat-like cunning won the day, and I signed up with the *Mail*.

Cap'n Bob, not a man to be thwarted, did not give up easily. Periodically he would call me up to his office to thrust a tankard of champagne into my hands and offer various inducements and blandishments. The last of these approaches was when he asked me if I belonged to the *Mirror* pension scheme. I explained that as a freelance I had my own arrangements. Sloshing out more champagne, Cap'n Bob invited me to outline my private pension plan, listening, as I did so, with the amused tolerance of a rich uncle hearing a favourite nephew's boast of having saved up four and sixpence in his piggy bank. At the end of my account he patted me confidentially on the knee and in a fog-siren purr promised: 'I could enhance that pension scheme, Keith.'

When the column began to appear in the *Daily Mail* he still refused to accept my defection and chose to treat it as a temporary aberration. He would ring my house from time to time, usually late at night, to slur, 'Tell Keith he is to come home', for all the world as if I were an errant son out on the tiles. One evening he had me traced to the theatre and dragged out of the stalls in the middle of the performance, to be propelled to the manager's office where he was waiting on the end of the phone. 'Keith, I have the new editor of the *Daily Mirror*, Mr Roy Greenslade, sitting here in my office. What have you to say to him?' I said I wished him the best of luck. 'Mr Greenslade agrees with me that you are needed here. When are you returning to the Hippodrome?' It was the last time I ever spoke to him. A rogue, a bully, a monster – but I could not help but be glad that he had enlivened, however briefly, my passing show.

But all this was another life away.

FOUR

Sunset Boulevard

1   The working life of a novelist or dramatist co-opted into screenwriting is generally around ten years or fifteen at the outside. After that one has either had enough of Hollywood or Hollywood has had enough of one. In this period the writer will have earned a great deal of money, but is unlikely to have seen more than a fraction of his or her work reach the screen.

Given that in the period when we were tapping into the golden lode of the film industry around ten screenplays were being commissioned for every one that went into production, Willis Hall and I could count ourselves fortunate that between the sixties and the seventies exactly half our big-screen output was actually produced – a dozen films reaching the cinemas out of twenty-four draft scripts in various stages of finality. Not a bad score.

Of the twelve made, some were run-of-the-mill, a couple were out-and-out stinkers, but three, all of them British – *Whistle Down the Wind*, *A Kind of Loving* and *Billy Liar* – are regarded as minor classics of the cinema (*Billy Liar* was among the hundred best films chosen by the BBC and the British Film Institute to celebrate the centenary of talkies in 1995), and one of the few American films we wrote that actually got made, the court-martial drama *Man in the Middle* with Robert Mitchum, wasn't half bad (good enough, anyway, for him to be able to persuade a reluctant Trevor Howard to accompany him to India to co-star in it).

During this time we were paid some pretty enormous sums, especially by the Hollywood studios. Although things were supposed to have tightened up considerably since film industry shareholders were rocked by P. G. Wodehouse's famous *Los Angeles Times* interview when he let the well-fed cat out of the bag – 'They paid me 2,000 dollars a week – $104,000 – and I cannot see

417

what they engaged me for . . . I feel as if I have cheated them' – the studios were still lavish in their script development budgets, which if the film didn't materialise were absorbed into overheads and charged to other productions. Willis and I were once paid four thousand dollars a week for fourteen weeks largely to sit around a pool while our director tried to iron out the snags in his filtering system and chlorine supply – problems which seemed to absorb him far more than the twist ending of the thriller we were all supposed to be wrestling with: so far as I recollect, the screenplay was never completed. At our peak we were earning, or rather getting, the then considerable sum of a hundred thousand dollars per picture. Come to think of it, it is not so inconsiderable even now.

The first film we ever wrote was an indifferent and now completely forgotten submarine drama called *The Valiant*, starring John Mills and featuring most of the cast of the Salisbury Tavern. There was only one memorable line in it, and that finished on the cutting-room floor. An Italian limpet mine stuck to his hull, timed to go off no one knows when, Captain John Mills tries to keep up morale by parading the crew on deck and giving them a pep talk. Inspecting his men, he stops by one of them at random and asks, 'And what do you do?' Replies the rating (John Meillon) smartly: 'I'm in the Navy – sah!'

So enraged were we at this excision that when the film opened at the Odeon, Leicester Square, we exacted our revenge. Inflamed by a bottle of champagne cognac, a present from our agent to celebrate Willis's impending wedding to the actress Jill Bennett, and which we had drunk in its entirety in the belief that it was vintage champagne (we had yet to get used to high living), we weaved our way along to Leicester Square and began to harangue the queue, urging them to boycott the film and take their custom to the Empire across the street. Just as we were getting into our stride we were approached by two fresh-faced young men in raglan overcoats, who – as we gathered when one of them produced his warrant card and asked politely, 'Shall we walk or would you prefer to take the van?' – proved to be policemen. We set off in double file to Bow Street with one officer in attendance each. Being arrested is a rapidly sobering experience and as we walked along I was able to explain coherently enough to my escort that while I personally had no rooted objection to spending a night in the cells (in fact I thought the experience might be interesting), Willis was getting married in the morning to a somewhat temperamental actress and it might cause him some

418

inconvenience disproportionate to the offence. Within sight of the police station, the young officers relented on condition that we got into separate taxis and went straight home. Chastened, we did just that.

Although an improvement on our naval epic, *West Eleven*, with Eric Portman, Alfred Lynch and Diana Dors, was still awarded the symbol for 'Don't waste your time' in the *Sunday Times Guide to Movies on Television*. Based on a novel by a hippie writer with the exotic name of Laura del Rivo, who accepted £1,000 for the screen rights and at once took off for South America, never to be heard of again, *West Eleven* was a confused story centring on a young man inveigled into agreeing to murder a rich aunt for a share of her money, and is at this distance memorable only for two things – first, the refusal by our producer, Danny Angel, to countenance the casting of James Mason on the grounds that he was old hat and the still-novitiate Julie Christie on the grounds that she was a B-picture actress; and secondly, the fact that although he has become a friend since, we never once set eyes on our twenty-seven-year-old director, Michael Winner, whose third production it was – in fact the film was showing in the cinemas before we even knew it had been made.

Fortunately for our reputation, Willis and I had other fish to fry. Shortly after the West End opening of *Billy Liar*, we were introduced by our then agent, Richard Gregson, to Richard Attenborough, who wanted us to read a short novel he was proposing to film – or rather, a peculiar request we thought, he wanted us on no account to read it until he had first told us the story, which he proposed to do over lunch.

The book was called *Whistle Down the Wind*, by Mary Hayley Bell, the wife of John Mills. It was a far-fetched story about three children living on a farm who discover a wanted criminal in the barn and mistake him for the second coming of Jesus Christ, this being the oath he utters when they wake him to ask who he is. Browsing through the novel later, it was easy to see why Dickie Attenborough had been loath to put it into our hands before telling us what he wanted to do with it. It was very much a middle-class, home counties, pony club sort of yarn – not our cup of tea at all. That soft-centred milieu, and the fact that the story really did take some swallowing, very much worked against it so far as we were concerned and we should undoubtedly have turned it down had we simply been asked to read it and give a yea or nay.

But Attenborough had had a brainwave. The reason he had called us in rather than any of the stable of screenwriters he had worked with before was that he wanted us to 'northernise' the story – shift the locale to a working farm in Yorkshire or Lancashire, and take the children down a few pegs on the social scale to become working-class village school kids. The idea was not so much to ride on the wave of gritty northern films then being made – *Saturday Night and Sunday Morning*, *Room at the Top*, *The Loneliness of the Long Distance Runner* – although their popularity at the box office would certainly help; it was to strip the sugar coating off the narrative and toughen it up to make the sentimental kernel of the story slither down smoothly with the roughage of craggy background and characterisation.

At that same lunch Dickie, who always had a few irons in the fire, sounded us out on our interest in Gandhi. We passed on that one (it was to win him eight Oscars) but accepted the *Whistle Down the Wind* challenge with enthusiasm, inventing several excellent parts for the Salisbury Tavern repertory company, notably an embittered vicar – a keynote character – who is more preoccupied with the slates and guttering that keep going missing from his church roof than with the spiritual questions arising from the three children's revelation in the barn. Having got the storyline as outlined by Dickie Attenborough in our heads, I don't think we ever consulted the book again – indeed, I am quite sure that I never finished reading it. As reconceived, it was a story right up our street: the words flowed, the characters invented themselves like the back-street cast of our play *Celebration* and we finished the screenplay in record time, with only minimal work needing to be done on the second and final drafts.

The film was to be directed by Guy Green, a former lighting cameraman who had directed Attenborough's previous film, *The Angry Silence*, from a screenplay by Bryan Forbes. For some reason Green had to drop out – a previous commitment come home to roost, something of the sort – and Forbes, a partner with Attenborough in the company Beaver Films which was to make the film, stepped into the breach. It was to be his directorial debut. Hayley Mills, fourteen-year-old daughter of the original author, was to play the eldest of the three children – the others were to be recruited locally. Bernard Lee was to play her father. Alan Bates would star as the Jesus figure.

Forbes could not have asked for a better film to cut his directorial teeth on. It was a blessing that we were still – just – in the black and white era, so that he could get the most out of the grainy chiaroscuro of the northern light and of silhouettes dancing along the bleak horizon. Shot in mid-winter, almost entirely on location on what the local paper meticulously identified as 'the Clitheroe side of Pendle Hill' near Burnley – a far cry from the original Sussex – with camerawork that has occasional echoes, as Bryan acknowledges, of René Clément's *Jeux Interdits*, it is yet a highly original film, with no signs of a tyro director's nerves in the crucial 'Jesus Christ!' exclamation on which the entire story stands or falls.

Forbes got some wonderfully natural performances out of the hordes of local children taking part, as well as from our professional performers, not all of whom hailed from north of the Trent. But all involved, the critics too, were at one in agreeing that the show was stolen by a diminutive five-year-old called Alan Barnes, a born actor who is now, I believe, a milkman. Alan only had to stand on his mark and say his lines and he was magic. Bryan Forbes had but one problem with him and that was in a tearful scene when he would not or could not cry. Bryan tried all the directorial tricks – pretending to be angry, telling the child to imagine his granny was dead, his kitten had been run over, his favourite teacher had fallen under a tractor, and so on. Not a teardrop. It was an outdoor scene and the light was going. Finally Bryan exclaimed in exasperation, 'Look, Alan, you're supposed to be an actor! If you can't cry, you're off the picture!' The tears rolled and the cameras rolled.

Whistle Down the Wind, according to the young critic of the *Western Press and Bristol Mirror*, one Tom Stoppard, was a triumph for 'those two currently O.K. duets, Richard Attenborough and Bryan Forbes, and Keith Waterhouse and Willis Hall.' It was a resounding success not only here but in America, despite the distributing company there premiering it in the unlikely venue of Dallas (where Jack Ruby, the man who shot Lee Harvey Oswald, who shot President Kennedy, offered to rub out the Greek chef who had given the Forbses an indifferent meal in his nightclub, the venue for the promotional lunch). *Whistle* was to prove to have a good deal of mileage in it. Waterhall Productions had a share of the producer's profit and cheques trickle in to this day – the most recent from a charming musical adaptation of our screenplay by Russell Labey and Richard Taylor, which the National Youth Music Theatre have played to great critical acclaim in such venues as the Lilian Baylis Theatre at Sadler's Wells and the Riverside Studios,

Hammersmith. Its latest reincarnation promises to be a new rock musical film version with music by Andrew Lloyd Webber and lyrics by Jim Steinman, the locale transplanted yet again – this time to a small sugar plantation eighty miles out of New Orleans.

It was time to implement what the *Daily Cinema* described as 'Producer Janni's Triple Deal with Waterhouse-Hall New Wave Writing Team'. Joseph Janni, a voluble and charming Italian, had come over to this country from Milan at the beginning of the war, just in time to be interned. He had made several films including *The Glass Mountain, A Town Like Alice* and *The Captain's Table*, and now he was about to make his most prestigious picture yet, Stan Barstow's raw tale of unhappily requited love in the industrial north, *A Kind of Loving*, improbably recommended to him by Woodrow Wyatt. Jo Janni had already held the rights to Alan Sillitoe's *Saturday Night and Sunday Morning* but had sold them to Harry Saltzman. This one he wasn't going to let go.

Stan's novel was set in Yorkshire, but with the New Wave in full cry it was impossible to climb a slagheap in that region without tripping over a camera cable, and so we decided to shift the action to Lancashire. Since, on paper at least, Willis and I were co-producers with Jo, this meant accompanying him to a variety of possible locations, touring the north-west in his purring Jaguar.

Jo was uniformly and extravagantly courteous to everyone he met and it was fascinating to see how he would captivate the most down-to-earth and dour people of Lancashire. One day he inadvertently offended a pair of mill-girls – this was when there were mills to employ them – by parking the Jag at their bus-stop in order to study a run-down dance hall that had possibilities for our film. As we sat in the car, the bus to which we had unwittingly presented an obstruction bowled past us, the driver unable to see his waiting passengers. One of the girls banged on the windscreen and yelled, 'We've missed t' bloody bus through you!' Jo, impeccable in his camelhair overcoat and Paisley scarf, leaped from the car, donning his hat only with the object of elaborately removing it. With a courtly bow he addressed the mill-girls: 'Dear ladies, a thousand apologies. You must allow me to drive you wherever you wish to go. I insist.' He threw open the nearside rear door with a flourish and assisted the bemused girls into the Jaguar. Chatting pleasantly about what a salubrious town we found ourselves in – I think it was Salford – Jo drove them not merely to the mill gates, which were opened for him unhesitatingly by an impressed commissionaire who must have taken him for a director, but to the very workpeople's entrance. Here he jumped out, opened the car door for them and escorted them across to their clocking-in lobby. Watched by a crowd of their astonished fellow-workers, he bowed, kissed their hands, and with a final word of apology, took his leave. They were his friends for life.

One lunchtime, far from the *Good Food Guide*-recommended trattorias of Manchester which would have been Jo's preference, we introduced him to the delights of fish and chips in a humble back-street chippie which had one oilcloth-covered table with a tin salt shaker and congealed vinegar bottle for those wishing to eat on the premises. Having ordered his haddock and chips, Jo then enquired of the buxom, steam-flushed proprietress, for all the world as if she were the manageress of the Caprice condescending to take his order personally, 'And do you think I might very possibly have a green salad, with no onions if you please, tossed in an oil and lemon dressing with just a little garlic?' I doubt whether the establishment had ever served any vegetable matter in its existence other than chipped potatoes and gherkins, but Jo got his salad, dressed approximately as desired. His next request, however, which was for a glass of water, did somewhat faze the proprietress who by now, like the mill-girls earlier, was his adoring slave. In a loud stage whisper she asked of Willis and me: 'What's up – has he got to take some tablets?'

John Schlesinger, noted for his TV work on *Monitor* and his award-winning film documentary *Terminus*, but a newcomer to feature films, was our director. Alan Bates was bought out of the Broadway production of *The Caretaker* for ten thousand dollars to star. A twenty-year-old unknown, June Ritchie, was cast opposite him, with Thora Hird giving one of her best ever performances as her mother. The film was one more hit for us, breaking box office records wherever it went and winning the Golden Bear award at the Berlin Film Festival. It was denounced as shocking by the usual town councillor (Leamington Spa), and, doubtless to Stan's annoyance, Godfrey Winn blandly retold the story for the benefit of readers of the *Daily Express*.

On to *Billy Liar*, whose screenplay we had by now already written. Here we came up against something of a casting quadrille. The showbiz writers assumed that the big-screen Billy would be played by Albert Finney, but the showbiz writers were wrong. Jo had originally wanted Albert for *A Kind of Loving*, not only for the star's box office potential but as a consolation prize for not offering him the film of *Billy Liar*, which he wanted to give to Anthony Newley. But it turned out that Albert did not wish to do *A Kind of Loving* and as it happened would only have considered *Billy Liar* had it been directed by Lindsay Anderson and produced by Woodfall, who had an option on his services. And neither we nor John Schlesinger, who was again to direct, were in favour of Tony Newley, who would have been wrong for that particular part. To our relief it went to Tom Courtenay. Mona Washbourne and Ethel Griffies were also to re-create their stage parts, and Wilfred Pickles was cast as the father, which he played to perfection. But Julie Christie was not, at that stage, remotely involved in the film that was to make her name.

The part of Liz, Billy's nomadic and slightly mysterious girlfriend, originally went to a now little-remembered actress known as Topsy Jane. Location filming around Leeds and Bradford actually started with Topsy Jane in the part. But suddenly, when we were two or three weeks into production, she was taken ill, with apparently no prospect of a speedy recovery. There was nothing for it: she had to be recast and her scenes reshot. Jo Janni, a shrewd talent spotter, had had his eye on Julie Christie ever since, only a few months earlier, she had made her TV debut in the science fiction serial *A for Andromeda*. I believe, indeed, that he had put her under contract. At any rate, she was immediately cast as the substitute Liz and transported north with all speed, when John Schlesinger did retakes of all the scenes between Billy and Liz that were so far in the can.

All except one. A centrepiece sequence of *Billy Liar* is the march-past of Billy's imaginary Ambrosian army, many hundreds strong, when he takes the salute from the balcony of Leeds Town Hall together with his Eva Perón-type companion Liz. This scene, which took days to complete and required the services of legions of police to block off roads, was simply too expensive to reshoot. The close-up balcony shots were eliminated but the long shots had to remain. Anyone who watches a video of *Billy Liar* on television, and freezes the frame at the point where Billy and Liz are shown on the balcony, will see that Billy's consort is not Julie Christie at all but a mystery figure who appears nowhere else in the film – Topsy Jane.

Willis and I spent a good deal of time hanging around the *Billy Liar* set, the more so after Julie Christie arrived on the scene. Like every other male involved in the production, I fell madly in love with her. Julie went on to do *Darling* and *Far from the Madding Crowd* also with John and Jo, then after a few more films repaired to Cornwall where she involved herself in various good causes of the environmental sort. Two or three years ago, in connection with one of these, I was enchanted to receive a letter from this stunning actress which began: 'Dear Keith, I don't know whether you will remember me . . .'

Billy Liar was of course a hit, with six nominations for the British Film Academy Awards. I don't think we were denounced by any clergy or councillors this time round, but a now-forgotten columnist did write peevishly, '*Billy Liar* has gone on and on. Mr Waterhouse must be making quite a little out of all this.'

There was a somewhat spooky sequel to 'all this'. The character of Liz was based very loosely on a teenage girlfriend back in my Leeds days, who had abruptly vanished after I had become engaged to Joan. I heard she had gone to Canada. Thirty-five years then elapsed. One evening I was sitting at home watching television when there was a ring at the doorbell. There on the threshold stood a middle-aged, matronly figure whom, the years rolling back, I could just recognise as 'Liz'. I invited her in and gave her a drink and asked where she had been all these years. 'Oh, round and about,' said 'Liz', quoting a line used by the fictional Liz. It turned out that she had indeed gone to Canada and then had spent a good many years drifting about Europe, teaching English. But it also turned out that she seemed to identify herself totally with the made-up Liz of *Billy Liar*, that she imagined I was Billy and she was Liz, and that inside her plump frame there was a Julie Christie trying to get out.

Why she had after all these years decided to descend upon me out of the blue she did not explain. She said she had read that I was now divorced, as she was herself, but that seemed pretty thin – her source for this information was *Who's Who*, and her only purpose in looking me up in the first place must have been to find out my address. My belief is that she had arrived at some crisis point in her life and this seemed to her a way of dealing with it. At any rate, after that strange evening, 'Liz' kept on turning up in my life. I would be giving a talk at the City University when I would recognise her sitting in the middle of the audience, like some figure in a Charles Addams cartoon. I would be signing books at a literary festival and there she would be in the queue of purchasers. I would be catching my weekend train to Brighton and there on Victoria Station she would be not so palely loitering. And then, after a few weeks of this, again she vanished, as abruptly as she had arrived. I toyed with turning my encounter with 'Liz' into a short story, but then I decided that if I delved into her motivations closely it would prove too sad to write.

Our third segment of 'Producer Janni's Triple Deal' was destined not to happen. This was to be a World War I epic called *Roses of Picardy*, very loosely based on a couple of the glut of war novels that had followed *All Quiet on the Western Front*, but relying very heavily on the propagandist music-hall songs of the period and contrasting the home front patriotic fervour with the reality of the trenches. We did quite a lot of work on this and were about to present a treatment to Columbia, who had put up the seed money, when Joan Littlewood came up with *Oh What A Lovely War*. Jo Janni tried to get the film rights but Dickie Attenborough was ahead of him. *Roses of Picardy* went on the shelf. These things happen.

They happen indeed for much of the time, and to anyone becoming addicted to the film industry they can happen for most of the time. I cannot say we were addicts but after three resounding successes, albeit not on a *Ben Hur* scale, we did have the smell of celluloid in our nostrils. It could be a tantalisingly elusive aroma.

Another non-starter at around the same time was the screen version of John Osborne's and Anthony Creighton's *Epitaph for George Dillon*, which we did for Dirk Bogarde's production company. We were pleased with it, John was pleased with it and I think Dirk Bogarde was pleased with it – at any rate we took it into a second draft before, for who knows what reason, the project quietly fizzled out. It was a pity, for Dirk Bogarde was a most agreeable and civilised producer to work with and we should have thoroughly enjoyed seeing him bringing the film to life.

In marked contrast was our next producer who as well as proving to be more or less clinically insane seemed hellbent on driving us as mad as himself. All I remember now of the police drama on which we miserably slaved for weeks was his suggestion, or rather his command, that we mark the passage of time with leaves torn off a calendar which then float away down the Thames. After a torrent of such hare-brained silent-movie ideas we downed tools in mid-script and told our agents that contract or no contract we would do no more work unless our producer kept his theories on film-making to himself. On that note we parted company, and the film was never made.

Yet other film commitments, most of them now lost in the mists of time, were never even started. Why did we spend a week cavorting up and down the Via Veneto with Joseph Losey and Gina Lollobrigida? I no longer have the slightest idea but it was fun while it lasted; we must, however, have agreed to differ for not a word ever got written. And what happened to the proposal that we make a musical film about Noah's Ark with Robert Fosse, all I can remember of which is that we were going to have the English Channel off Brighton pier bobbing with abandoned opened-out umbrellas as far as the eye could see? Some questions about those hectic, hazy days I can answer. What were we doing occupying a producer's suite at Elstree Studios, then briefly the enlightened fiefdom of Bryan Forbes? We were about to produce a soccer film of our own devising called *We Are the Champions*; unfortunately Bryan had the rug pulled from under him just as we were putting out the welcome mat for the Salisbury Tavern Players.

Some of the films we worked on were completed but not with our scripts – a very common occurrence in this curious industry where draft screenplays are handed from one writer to the next as in a game of pass the parcel. One such was Franco Zeffirelli's *Brother Sun, Sister Moon*, the life of St Francis of Assisi, on which we toiled for what seemed like for ever – long enough, anyway, to work up an original 200-page, 500-scene screenplay from a treatment by Franco himself and a couple of his associates. This entailed a stay in Franco's Roman villa, a luxurious establishment seething with unexplained wandering strangers like an exclusive private hotel, with the proprietor himself dropping in and out with various script development ideas. These ranged from the ingenious to the ingenuous – at one stage, this being at the height of the flower power movement, he toyed with the notion of updating the story to the Haight-Ashbury quarter of San Francisco. It would have been a dated film by now. On other days he extemporised scenes so brilliantly that if only we had been able to write fast enough to take them down we could have saved ourselves a good deal of work.

How much of our contribution, if anything, survived into the final shooting script I have no idea, for I never saw the film. But in his memoirs Zeffirelli notes that he must have had twenty English writers in all submitting scripts, adding airily that in the end he 'took such dialogue as we needed from the various English versions.' This is by no means unusual, especially with *auteur*-directors of the Zeffirelli calibre. But apparently the trouble was that his English writers kept seeing Francis in Protestant terms. Had I known this was a problem I could have recommended some very good Irish writers living in Dublin.

By now we had fallen into the clutches of Hollywood and were doing most of our film work for the Americans. There were, however, a couple of non-American interludes, though not lacking that surrealistic touch that is the Hollywood trademark.

The first was the directorial entry into films of Peter Coe, best known for his stage production of *Oliver!* and with whom we had worked on the American version of *Pickwick*. Coe had directed the opening production at the Mermaid, the Lionel Bart-Laurie Johnson-Bernard Miles musical *Lock Up Your Daughters*, and had now been invited to film it. Or perhaps he had invited himself. Notwithstanding, he proposed to remove the musical element from the show and fill the gap with a Restoration sub-plot which he looked to Willis and me to supply by cross-fertilising Fielding's *Rape Upon Rape*, on which the stage original had been based, with Vanbrugh's *The Relapse*. Justice Squeezum meets Lord Foppington. The film gave employment to most of the Salisbury Tavern Players and for some reason, based doubtlessly on sound economic principles, was shot mainly in Kilkenny, where I spent some enjoyable days. It was what is usually described as a 'romp' and like many filmic romps was perhaps relished more by the cast and crew than by the audience. But it was all good practice. No one who has grafted a 1696 drama on to a 1730 host body without the joins showing need ever be thrown by the outlandish demands of American producers.

The second was a curiosity for us, a film called *Dingaka* which was a courtroom drama shot entirely in South Africa, and with an all-black cast apart from its star and producer, Stanley Baker. Baker, who had had a big hit with *Zulu*, had set up *Dingaka* with the liberal South African director Jamie Uys specifically to create work for black actors, and it was on this basis that he brought the subject to us. He knew that we were both fiercely anti-apartheid and that we refused to allow our plays to be performed in South Africa except before mixed audiences, which in those dark days of the early sixties were virtually non-existent. Stanley persuaded us that it was a sight

428

more constructive to give black actors a chance that was otherwise unlikely to come their way than to sit at home boycotting Outspan oranges. And so, although not without some misgivings, we had our jabs, packed our bags, and set off on this unusual adventure.

I loathed Johannesburg on sight. Expecting to find an updated expansion of a vibrant gold-rush city such as San Francisco had become, I could see only a lacklustre commercial centre of stultifying complacency, with, thanks to the notorious pass laws and the reluctance of the white population to roam beyond its own suburban barricades, an almost total absence of street life.

Not that we ventured into Johannesburg much: we had been put into a large bungaloid hotel far away from town, and here, in between writing stints, we gloomed the days away. Our favourite pastime was watching battalions of ants carrying bits of twig about. Occasionally we would take a drive out to stare curiously at the depressing African townships, reminiscent of Leeds housing estates, with which the city was ringed. Once we were taken out to Pretoria to view the Voortrekker Monument, surely the most vulgar memorial ever constructed by man. One rainy evening we amused ourselves, though not the hotel management, by forming a provisional government of Indian waiters. We were told by the head barman, aka the Chancellor of the Exchequer in waiting, that our jest had been reported to the authorities – he had heard the manager on the telephone.

As we pottered on with our screenplay – it was a total rewrite of an existing script – we were becoming increasingly incensed at not having yet met any of the actors we were writing for. Since most of the parts had already been cast, it would have been useful, not to say a common courtesy, to be introduced. Stanley Baker not yet having arrived in the country, we took our complaint to Jamie Uys who completely agreed with us, and at considerable trouble and probably at some risk, given the rigidity with which the apartheid laws were then applied, arranged for us to meet Stanley's African co-star. For this routine social meeting the actor had to obtain – or rather, have obtained for him, since there was no way he could have got it on his own initiative – a special permit allowing him to travel into the white suburbs of Johannesburg from Soweto for purposes other than working the lawn sprinklers and trimming the hedges; notwithstanding which, the visit had to take place in the hours of daylight.

We convened, Jamie, ourselves and some of his production team, at the home of a lady involved in some way in African theatre, where drinks were served. As the moment approached for our guest of honour to arrive, someone collected up our glasses and the gin and whisky bottles and with awkwardly assumed casualness whisked them off to the kitchen – not only was no alcohol allowed to be served to a black man, but none was to be visible. I don't suppose anyone would have been any the wiser had we kept the drinks circulating and helped our co-star to a few stiff ones, but in the atmosphere of the time you never knew whom you could trust. Hitler's Germany might have been an exaggerated parallel but it did come to mind.

Our visitor was shown in (by a disapproving coloured maid who had never seen such a thing in her life) and tea was served, probably illegally. We talked a little about the film and about the cinema and theatre in general – mostly about the cinema, since our man did not get many opportunities for studying the European theatre. Although our conversation was relaxed enough, the prevailing atmosphere was tense and embarrassed. The fact was that while they all seemed of a liberal disposition, our South African colleagues were plainly ill at ease at engaging in social intercourse with a black face in a white drawing room. They had simply never had any experience of it – for experience of it was forbidden.

Willis and I were still not happy. There were three or four other black actors whom we particularly wanted to meet, and we made our wishes known, hinting that while we understood the difficulties there was always the alternative of the thrice-weekly flight back to London. The problem was resolved, or the production company imagined it to be resolved, by the imminent arrival of Stanley Baker when a big party was to be thrown in his and his English screenwriters' honour. At this, we were assured, as many of our cast as would make no difference would be present.

Mollified, we attended the party. It was big, lavish, as glitzy as any party could be in Johannesburg – and all white. Willis and I, a two-man deputation, sought out the production man responsible for the social arrangements and pronged him into a corner where we discreetly but forcibly pointed out that we had accepted our invitation on the promise of meeting our black cast. He was genuinely astonished. 'But you already have – didn't you know? The man with the torch who waved you into your car-parking space will be playing the part of so-and-so, the cloakroom girl who took your coats is one of our leading actresses, that fellow carrying round the tray of drinks is an excellent supporting player . . .'

Shortly before leaving Johannesburg, we were asked by the publicity office to do a radio interview, on the understanding that we would be talking about our film and the film industry in general, steering well clear of South African politics. Fortunately – for the radio station, anyway – the broadcast was not live. We rambled on for some time about the possibilities of the Great Trek as material for the country's answer to the Hollywood western, and the inspiration to be drawn by some Transvaal John Ford from the ring of ox wagons drawn up around the Voortrekker Monument. With lemming-like insistency, our earnest young Afrikanner questioner got to what to him was the kernel of his interview: 'And tell me, having spent some little time in our country, what impression have you formed about South Africa?'

Willis looked at me. I looked at Willis. One of us had to say something. I left it to Willis, with his concise turn of phrase. 'It wants a fucking bomb dropping on it.'

Stunned, the young man switched off his tape recorder. When Willis and I returned home it was to find letters already awaiting us from the Secretary for the Interior. I still have mine framed in my lavatory: 'I have to inform you that the Hon the Minister of the Interior has under the powers vested in him withdrawn in your case . . .' and so on and so on. What it came down to was that I would no longer be allowed into South Africa without a visa, and if I did apply for a visa it would be refused. I still don't know whether it was our provisional government of Indian waiters or Willis's blunt verdict on Dr Verwoerd's dream world that brought down the shutters, but I expect the ban has been rescinded by now. At all events, our immediate travels were to take us closer to Orange County than to the Orange Free State.

2   Going by the impressions of countless visiting firemen who had learned to loathe Los Angeles, I thought I wasn't going to like it either. The first moonscape glimpse as we came in to land, of ruler-straight boulevards arrowing into infinity, graph-paper developments of Lego houses and pocket-handkerchief swimming pools like rows of quarantine dog kennels with their attendant water bowls, freeways ribboning around the hills like dried-up river beds, and the actual Los Angeles River itself, concreted over and serving as a giant drain, looking like a freeway, was a daunting one indeed.

But despite confusing, densely printed maps like transistor radio circuit board print-outs blown up to the size of bedsheets, and street numbers stretching into their tens of thousands, I managed to establish some sort of order out of this galactic metropolis by treating it firmly from the start as a series of interlinked cities and villages: villages the size of small cities, cities the size of large villages – Hollywood, Beverly Hills, Westwood, Santa Monica, and so on – like Greater Manchester or the Yorkshire Woollen District. This was despite the rigid belief of my southern Californian friends that an evening out is not an evening out unless it starts with a forty-mile drive, so that I was regularly hurtled along the freeways to some seafood restaurant or steakhouse identical in all respects to the seafood restaurant or steakhouse across the street. When I ventured to ask if the Brown Derby I was being driven to was superior, then, to the Brown Derby fifty yards from my hotel door, I was told no, the cuisine was pretty much the same but the one we were going to was shaped like a hat.

Left to my own devices, I quickly mastered the bus system, which I seemed to share exclusively with Mexican maids and Japanese gardeners going on and off duty, and by that means explored the

433

county from downtown Los Angeles to the ocean. I also, preferably in the cool of the morning but sometimes in the baking heat of the afternoon, covered tremendous distances on foot. Having been warned that walking was regarded by the police with deep suspicion in this part of the world, I worked out an eccentric Englishman act in case of challenge, but the non-walking rule turned out to be as mythical as the one that said you got arrested for crossing the street against the lights. The only time I was challenged was when I set off one stifling Sunday with the hare-brained idea of walking the length of Sunset Boulevard to the Pacific from Hollywood, as I had once walked the length of Broadway from Times Square to the Battery. A bemused traffic cop, finding me mopping my brow under a palm tree a hundred yards from the Beverly Hills Hotel, suggested that if I didn't want sunstroke I should go into the Polo Lounge and buy myself a cooling beer and thereafter return to my own hotel in a cab. This I gratefully did.

I did do some marathon walks, though. By night I sought out the source of the searchlights that swept the Hollywood sky like the opening of a Twentieth Century-Fox black and white gangster movie, much as, thirty years earlier, I had tramped across the rhubarb fields of Leeds seeking the wartime anti-aircraft searchlights that were supposed to pinpoint enemy bombers while Spitfires engaged them in thrilling dogfights (but, alas, never did). At weekends I traipsed along the Hollywood Walk of Fame – the star-studded pavements of Hollywood Boulevard where all the heroes and heroines of all the films I had ever seen had their names inscribed in brass, including Woody Woodpecker and Snow White (but not King Kong). I located, and had a rather indifferent milkshake in, the Schwab's Drugstore on Sunset Boulevard where Lana Turner was said to have been discovered, only to learn that this had been an invention of a press agent and that she had really been discovered at the Top Hat Malt Shop across from Hollywood High School on Sunset Boulevard and Highland Avenue. Hollywood High, schoolroom to the stars (but not as chic as Beverly Hills High which has its own oil wells in the playing fields), also came in for a meaningful stare.

I did all the rubbernecking things like inspecting the concrete footprints outside Grauman's Chinese Theater, and the stunning *beaux arts* movie houses along downtown Broadway, pinpointing the exact location of 77 Sunset Strip (actually 8524 Sunset Strip), and getting as near as I could (another lunatic trek) to the 450-feet-long HOLLYWOOD sign up in the scrubland of the Hollywood Hills. I became a fixture at Hollywood's oldest and so far as I know only chophouse, Musso and Frank's ('Since 1919'), where the martinis are still as eye-watering as when Scott Fitzgerald, Hemingway and Faulkner occupied their regular booths there. And before and after lunch I would wander for hours around the eye-dazzling, Casablanca-white alleys and avenues of Hollywood, identifying street corners and clapboard houses and fire escapes and beaten-up old buildings and parking lots which I recognised, or fancied I could recognise, from the Laurel and Hardy and Mack Sennett two-reelers of my childhood.

Hollywood I liked for its tawdriness and its tackiness and its shabby glamour, and the sensation that wherever I went I was on the back lot of a film studio dedicated to churning out cheap bad movies. So closely does this town under the hot purple night sky, with its neon and its billboards the size of Cinemascope screens mounted on flagpoles and its Chandleresque haciendas and its rustling palms and lawn sprinklers and chirruping crickets, resemble the celluloid image it exists to exploit that one wonders, in a chicken and egg sort of way with the arrival of the film industry whether, the camera set out to simulate what was there already, or what was there already set out to imitate this strange new mutation of the creative arts.

Willis and I, on and off, made sojourns to the tinsel city for periods ranging from one-day, fly-in fly-out script conferences to three- or four-month stints in writers' blocks as categorised by Dorothy Parker who, when a party of tourists passed under her window on whatever studio lot she was serving time, yelled down at them, 'Let me out – I'm as sane as you are!' At one end of the *per diem* scale (the daily expenses rate negotiated by one's agent, and an important element of the contract) we stayed in the palm-fringed, poolside, prawn-cocktail-pink splendour of the Beverly Hills Hotel, and at the other in a dowdy, neon-flashing motel on the Sunset Strip just a few billboards down from the eccentric Chateau Marmont where we used to take wine with Stanley Holloway, Mona Washbourne and other members of the cast of the celluloid version of *My Fair Lady* who had established an English colony there.

My favourite hotel was the Beverly Wilshire, in that it was in the middle of that chic little city, Beverly Hills. At that time film stars did not keep themselves so much in purdah as their lesser counterparts now do, and wandering those expensive boulevards, where you could buy anything in the world so long as it was by Gucci, Hermès or Giorgio (I once asked a fellow-screenwriter where the Beverly Hills set got their groceries, and he said, 'Doggy bags'), one was so likely to come across a Doris Day or James Stewart or Lauren Bacall that, as with downtown Hollywood, one might have imagined oneself on a studio back lot – but this one for a Technicolor extravaganza directed by Busby Berkeley. Or, on occasion, not: driving along Rodeo Drive with a producer of liberal disposition one day, we spotted John Wayne crossing the road. 'Shall I run the bastard down?' asked our employer of the moment.

Our first American film, based on Howard Fast's novel *The Winston Affair*, was *Man in the Middle*, starring Robert Mitchum and released by Twentieth Century-Fox. There was a kind of script summit at the St Regis Hotel in New York involving ourselves, Mitchum, our director, Guy Hamilton, the producers, the studio boss, Richard Zanuck, who was the son of the legendary Darryl, and what I can only describe as several front-office suits. We had written a first draft and now we had to bat our corner.

Our first meeting was with Bob Mitchum who, hooded eyes further blurred with sleep, received us in his dressing room and conducted us, yawning, into his suite. This, we considered, recalling that when asked what he looked for in a script Mitchum had replied 'Days off', was going to be a walkover. Another of the laconic, laid-back actor's much quoted sayings was to the effect that he stood on his mark, said the lines and took the money. But we forgot that Mitchum had been among other things an accomplished screenwriter himself before he became a star. He turned out to know the material far better than we did, taking us through our first draft page by page, analysing the purpose of each scene and suggesting changes and improvements, not only for the enhancement of his own part but for those of his co-players, Trevor Howard, Keenan Wynn, Barry Sullivan and Sam Wanamaker. He had a particular regard for Trevor Howard, observing, 'You can never tell when the bastard is working.'

After the gruelling but exhilarating Mitchum session we then met up with Richard Zanuck, who was equally informed and helpful about the script. By now all concerned had copious and constructive notes. With Zanuck's departure for the West Coast, this did not prevent one of the front-office suits taking it upon himself to summarise our deliberations in the following terms: 'Okay, gentlemen, let's go through this again from the top, as agreed. Scenes one through eleven are fine. Scene twelve is shit. Scenes thirteen through fifteen, okay. Scene sixteen through eighteen, shit. Scene nineteen, okay. Scenes twenty through twenty-three, shit . . .' We finished the night helping Mitchum demolish a bottle of bourbon while he reminisced about his own screenwriting days and some of the 'asshole' producers he had tangled with, and crawled off to bed well after five in the morning. Duly revised, the film was shot in India and at Elstree. And it was okay.

Our next American film venture found us sitting around a lunch table with Walt Disney and a couple of other, if identical, front-office suits, discussing the screenplay of Dodie Smith's *I Capture the Castle* on which we were about to embark as a vehicle for the still not entirely grown-up Hayley Mills, then under contract to Disney. With one bottle of wine between five of us the conversation did not sparkle, and it did not help much when either Willis or I – to this day we blame one other – threw in a grovelling reference to Mickey Mouse, for Walt's face contorted into a snarl and he began to chunter on about having had that 'blanketty' mouse on his back for thirty years. I suppose, like most of us, he just wanted credit for having done something else besides. At any rate, the outburst was sufficient for all present to knock back their wine nervously. Willis and I, used to drinking on the English scale, twiddled significantly with our empty glasses. We were almost on the verge of tipping them up to our eyes like optics in the manner of the character in the Peter Arno cartoon when Walt finally got the hint and began to question his sidekicks: 'Do you have any work this afternoon, Al? You, Gus?' Receiving joshing negatives, he turned to us: 'And I guess you boys won't be writing much after lunch?' We agreed that it was unlikely – it was a Saturday, after all. Making an impetuous, you-only-live-once decision on behalf of the five of us, Walt slapped the table: 'Hell, it's the weekend – why don't we kill another half-bottle!'

The Dodie Smith story, by the time we had finished draft three – indeed, by the time we had finished draft one, for these things are not automatically improved by reworking – would have made a good Disney film, but it never happened, possibly because while it was being shuttled from one suit to another Hayley was growing too old for the character. We did, however, write one more film for her, and that was *Pretty Polly*, based on Noël Coward's short story *Pretty Polly Barlow*, shot mainly in Singapore and co-starring Trevor Howard. Coward was very nice to us in person, much less so to the production in the privacy of his *Diaries*: 'Common, unsubtle and vulgar. Trevor Howard was horrid. Guy Green [director] should have remained a cameraman.' When Coward delivered a verdict, it left little room for appeal. In fact I think we did as well by his story as it could be done by. We had already warned, somewhere along the line, that it lacked a third act – to which his crisp response was, 'It is a two-act story.' He liked the television version written by William Marchant, and should have settled for that.

So far most of our American work was conceived in Hollywood but written in London. I believe the first time we spent any great length of time on the West Coast was when we were working on Hitchcock's spy drama *Torn Curtain* – not his best film, perhaps, but one that would have ranked even lower in the oeuvre had we not been called in to improve the script and polish the dialogue. For this piece of celluloid play-doctoring we were paid huge sums by Universal – little did they know that we would almost have paid them for the privilege of working with the Master. The production was within a very few days of rolling when we arrived at the studios, so that we often found ourselves revising scenes only hours before they were to be shot, while on occasion a messenger would be waiting to rush our latest rewrites across to the *Torn Curtain* sound stage, where they would be thrust into the hands of the actors even as Hitchcock lit them for the scene. This day-to-day, hand-to-mouth aspect of the craft of screenwriting was an experience new to me, and it awakened an appetite for deadline fever that had lain dormant since my news reporting days, or anyway since I had last heard a taxi meter ticking away as Willis and I struggled to finish a sketch for TW3.

Sitting almost literally at Hitchcock's feet – for when we were not actually writing he liked us close at hand on the set, scripts at the ready in case he wanted to confer on any small point – we were treated to a crash course in film-making as we observed him at work in his trademark uniform of crumpled blue suit, white shirt and tie and highly polished black shoes, arms always hanging loosely by his sides unencumbered by paper – only very occasionally would he refer to the shooting script being meticulously monitored by his long-time assistant Peggy Robertson, for by this stage in the game the whole film existed, frame by frame, as pictures in his head.

It is widely known, at least by film buffs, that Hitchcock treated his players like chess pieces – the kings and queens and bishops and knights as much a part of his endgame as the rooks and pawns. The moves were his. He was, it has to be said, harder on the pawns than on the kings and queens. It was painful, one day, to see a wretched bit player being harangued by the distinguished director for not jumping off a bus in the proper manner. Hitchcock made him do retake after retake, cruelly tormenting him for being unable to comprehend a simple note of direction when he called himself an actor. The poor fellow was jumping off the bus in what he must have firmly believed, from his own observation, was the way that people do jump off buses; unfortunately, this did not coincide with the picture in Mr Hitchcock's mind. The director wanted the actor to emulate, to perfection, a photograph he had never seen.

Against this, while the kings and queens could expect to be spared the flicks and taunts, they too were expected to do exactly as was required of them. Our stars were Julie Andrews and Paul Newman. While Miss Andrews, with whom we got on famously, presented no problems to Mr Hitchcock, Mr Newman did, in that in his method actor's way he would persist in raising points of motivation, which Hitchcock had not the slightest interest in discussing at all. Bob Mitchum's 'Stand on your mark and say your lines' philosophy, had it not been self-effacing hokum, would have met with Hitchcock's approval. It became quickly apparent that one of our duties on the film was to keep Paul Newman out of our director's non-existent hair, spelling out the thinking behind any scene or piece of dialogue that troubled him, and if necessary inventing far-fetched explanations for the characters' behaviour. This we became quite good at.

There was one small scene, however, that continued to trouble our conscientous star, and no amount of waffle on our part could convince him that he had its proper significance within his sights. This was where, as an American scientist in East Berlin for reasons I need not go into, he has a meeting with Julie Andrews who has to place a package into his hands, for reasons I no longer remember. Newman's problem, as he agonised it to Hitchcock during the camera rehearsal, was on the lines of: 'Hitch, it seems to me I have a situation here with Julie, I have a situation with the package, I have a situation with being in East Berlin and I have a situation with the problem of our being observed. Now how should I be relating in this scene?' Hitchcock, having listened courteously, delivered his judgment in his measured, plummy accents: 'Well, Mr Newman, I'll tell you exactly what I have in mind here. Miss Andrews will come down the stairs with the package, d'you see, when you, if you'll be so good, will glance just a little to the right of camera to take in her arrival; whereupon my audience will say, "Hulloh! What's this fellow looking at?" And then I'll cut away, d'you see, and show them what you're looking at.'

I have heard no better or more concise an analysis of what film-making is all about either before or since.

There was a written part of this highly-paid seminar, besides the valuable lectures both on and off the sound stage. Willis and I had been assigned a comfortable star dressing-room bungalow, just around the corner from Hitchcock's suite of offices at Universal City Studios. Every morning when the studio limo decanted us, there would be awaiting us a big buff envelope containing Hitchcock's notes on the current day's work, dictated between looking at the rushes the previous evening and going home to Bel Air to read that day's London *Times* before his customary dinner of Dover sole, both of them flown in to him daily along with his breakfast kippers. I have kept over twenty closely-typed A4 pages of these ruminations, which one day I really should hand over to the British Film Institute archives since they comprise a concise correspondence course on writing for the cinema.

Some of them show Hitchcock's almost fanatical obsession with accuracy: 'Scene 88. We should eliminate the Floor Concierge. My information is that they do not have these in East Berlin.' Others show his sense of meticulous cinematic detail: 'Scene 127C. I would like to discuss the place where the sausage is carved . . .' On Scene 139, where we had someone describing the Julie Andrews character as beautiful, Hitchcock comments: 'Not that I wish to cast any aspersions on Miss Andrews' physiognomy, but do you think beautiful is perhaps too much, and cannot we say lovely instead?'

Above all, there are the notes that reveal the seething mind of Hitchcock at work as he jigsaws the pictures in his head into place. He takes two long paragraphs to detail how he envisages the reaction of refugees on a stolen bus as they witness the approach of the real bus that must give their game away. He wants one character to see the bus in the distance but keep it to himself . . . then someone else sees it, and someone else, until panic spreads through the bus:

'It would be rather like the play within a play in Hamlet which starts with the King and then spreads to the rest. Anyway, let's talk about this little moment . . .' There was nothing to talk about. He had already conceived the whole sequence exactly as he was to shoot it.

I treasure, of course, the note that discusses, using the third person, the scene in which Hitchcock himself makes his traditional appearance. It is interesting to see that the shot is not simply an ego trip but that it incorporates valuable background information: 'Scene 25. Should we have a brief establishing shot of the lounge of the Hotel d'Angleterre? This could be a spot for Mr Hitchcock's appearance in the film. I made a suggestion the other day that I should be seen sitting in an armchair in the lounge with a nine month old baby on my knee and I'm looking around rather impatiently for the mother to come back. This impatience could be underscored by shifting the baby from one knee to the other, and then with the free hand, surreptitiously wiping the thigh. Having this shot would enable us to show the sign announcing the presence of the convention members in the hotel. We might even show some of the delegates crowding around the elevator which, of course, would then lead us to the corridor scene on page 10 . . .'

Away from the studio, Hitchcock put himself to some trouble to be agreeable to us, inviting us back to his unostentatious home and to Dover sole suppers in the austere, club-like surroundings of Chasen's, Hollywood's answer to Sardi's in New York, and sending over his back copies of *The Times*. When we took a couple of days off to jet back to London for one of our first nights, we returned to find that Hitchcock had had all the reviews flown over, and that he had arranged a little celebration party in our honour. I did not care to linger over the question of how he would have handled it had the reviews been bad – with masterly indifference, I imagine.

Hitchcock was an entertaining companion, endlessly reminiscing about the long-lost days of Famous Players Lasky British Studios and Gainsborough Pictures, and of long-gone associates such as my Fleet Street hero Edgar Wallace. He was fond of rehearsing the opening sequences of the unwritten films that were rattling around in his head. One concerned the fisher girls of Grimsby, who evidently used to follow the fishing fleet down the coast, gutting and packing the catch for market. A particularly pretty fisher girl is engaged to be married to the first mate of a vessel who is hated by the crew. We follow her from port to port as she contentedly goes about her work, until eventually, and doubtless after we have seen Alfred Hitchcock pass camera in the guise of a straw-hatted fishmonger, we arrive at a remote quayside where the unloaded herring catch trundles along on rollers to the waiting line of fisher girls with their gutting knives. Our girl is at the head of the line as along the conveyor belt of clanking rollers bumps a flat fish-crate containing the body of her lover, packed in dry ice . . .

Working with Hitchcock was an education and a joy, and our only regret was that we could not persuade him to let us get to work on an immortally bad line uttered by Julie Andrews: 'East Berlin? But – but – that's behind the Iron Curtain!' Mindful of geographically unco-ordinated audiences in such centres of insularity as Dubuque, Mr Hitchcock steadfastly refused to modify the line, not even to the extent of getting rid of the superfluous 'but' and its hesitant dash. Hitch, as we would never have dreamed of addressing him, campaigned valiantly with the American Writers' Guild – the body that has the final say on these matters – for our names to be included in the screen credits for *Torn Curtain*. I hope it does not seem ungrateful when I reveal that we were campaigning just as vigorously to have our names kept right out of it.

There were other long sojourns in Hollywood, much to the envy of Gerry's Club friends who thought we were living the life of Riley there. In fact the pace was extremely sedate. The West Coast is an early-to-bed, early-to-rise sort of region and I could never get used to being invited to dinner for 6.30 and on my way home by 9.00. The occasional Hollywood parties I found dull. I have vague memories of discussing crime in the garment industry with Judy Garland and the difficulty of getting two-tone leather brogues with Danny Kaye. A movie would then be screened in someone's honour, coffee and cake would be served, and the room would empty.

My favourite after-work activity, as a matter of fact, was to potter along to the reading room of the Beverly Hills public library, a sensationally beautiful Art Deco building set in the Spanish-baroque City Hall complex, just across the street from the equally stylish Church of the Good Shepherd, known locally as Our Lady of the Cadillacs. This whole stunning confection of palms and pastel colours looks like the set for a college musical and in fact is as recognisable from countless movies and TV segments as the skyline of New York.

After an hour or two in this cool and calming oasis I might then take a cab along Santa Monica Boulevard to The Losers Club, then Hollywood's answer to Gerry's Club. The club took its name from a blackboard displayed in the window on which would be chalked the name of the Loser of the Week – usually an actor who had failed to land a part or a writer who had failed to sell a script, but occasionally outsiders such as television executives who had lost their jobs or politicians who had been found out. When President Kennedy was assassinated the Loser of the Week was The Losers Club. Besides being a hangout for actors, The Losers was much used by screenwriters, at whose table – or rather tables, for there were a good many of them – I was always welcome, and good company they were. While there is probably not a living soul on the West Coast who does not have an original film treatment or television pilot in his or her glove compartment, those who do it for a living are a hard-working, professional bunch with a true respect for their own craft. Unlike this country where scriptwriting is regarded even by many writers themselves, and certainly by critics, as selling out or cashing in, in Hollywood it is a proper and legitimate branch of the writer's trade – for all that every sitcom writer is secretly at work on a novel.

Spending our working days together, Willis and I tended not to see much of one another in the evenings – I would not like to suggest that Willis spent his free time in the public library – but we did sometimes get together at the weekends when we would make rubbernecking trips to such exotic resorts of Orange County and district as Knott's Berry Farm and its ghost western town or the Movieland Wax Museum. During one stay the veteran English actress Gladys Cooper, long a West Coast resident, rather adopted us, and we arranged one Saturday to take her and her sister Grace to Disneyland, which Grace had never visited.

Rather than put Gladys to the trouble of making a long detour to pick us up, we made our own way to Disneyland, but it was agreed that she would be driving us all back. The sights seen and the rides ridden and a pleasantly exhausting day having been enjoyed, we all trooped off to find, with considerable difficulty, the Cooper car. People often lose their cars in big car parks and it did not occur to either Willis or me that Gladys might be seriously shortsighted until, with us all aboard and the car moving, she asked, pressing her forehead almost up against the windscreen,

'Are we on the freeway yet?' We were still filtering out of the car park.

Navigating from the back seat – Grace wanted to sit in the front, next to her loving sister – we guided Gladys on to the Santa Ana Freeway and then relaxed. Getting off a Californian freeway except at a designated exit, one would imagine, is as difficult as disembarking from a fast-moving conveyor belt, but Gladys somehow managed it, for I woke from a light doze to hear her complaining querulously, 'This isn't the freeway, surely!' We were bumping along a dirt track leading to a farm.

Willis clambered out into the dusk, and scattering hens and sheepdogs and offering implausible explanations to the bewildered farmer's wife, guided our driver into a succession of semi-three-point turns. We never regained the freeway but, rather to our relief, rode along the parallel old road – 'the surface street', as Californians call any pre-freeway thoroughfare – until an unceasing series of bumps told us we were in trouble again. Like characters in a Mr Magoo cartoon, we were riding along the tracks of the Aitcheson, Topeka and Santa Fe Railroad. Since the railroad tracks then ran straight down the middle of Santa Monica Boulevard, it was in this fashion that Miss Gladys Cooper eventually deposited her visiting admirers at the door of The Losers Club.

Our working pattern on these assignments was pleasant. After an early morning swim we would be picked up at a civilised hour and driven by a studio car to the office or bungalow we had been allocated. There we would collect the trade papers (I never got over the childish pleasure of seeing our names announced in the *Hollywood Reporter* as having arrived to work on this or that screenplay) and walk across to the studio commissary for breakfast. There would usually be a smattering of British actors, either visiting or resident, with whom to pass the time of day, and through them we would get to know some of the American actors with whom they were working. Phil Silvers, a fervent Anglophile, became a commissary friend who would regale us daily with lengthy excerpts from *Itma*, the Tommy Handley radio show which he lapped up from old BBC recordings. And so an hour would pass painlessly by.

We would drift back to our desks and work on 'the pages', as they were always called. In Hollywood, at least if one is working in – or 'out of', as they confusingly put it – a major studio, draft scripts are not delivered whole and complete but in daily batches of however many pages one has managed to get written, I suppose so that the front office can monitor just how much highly paid work is actually getting done. If inspiration failed, we might stroll out to the back lot – another childish pleasure, wandering through false-fronted western streets and Paris boulevards, and spotting marquee names in convict suits or crinolines enjoying a Marlboro Lite outside their dressing-room bungalows. After a light lunch at the commissary we would engage in enough concentrated effort at our typewriters to produce a sufficient quota of 'the pages' for the day, perhaps eight or at the most ten – there was no point in overdoing it, for the studios distrusted prolificity, and anyway, one was being paid by the week. We would then hand over our day's output, maybe chat with the producer about how the script was progressing, and ring for a car to take us home. Hollywood has often enough been called the dream factory. It was certainly like working in one.

Reaching the end of the screenplay did not mean one had reached the end of the assignment. There would be rewrites, when 'the pages' would be mimeographed on different-coloured paper, blue or pink or yellow or green according to whether it was the first or second or third or fourth rewrite, until the script looked like a cross-section of a rainbow. This process continued either until one's stipulated time ran out or until the story was turned over to new writers. I should explain that we ourselves were on occasion the new writers involved, taking over someone else's screenplay and producing pages of varying hues until it was time for the script to be passed on again. One always knew when this moment had arrived, not from any word from the producer but by the fact that one morning the studio limo failed to arrive, one's West Coast agent was suddenly out of town, and the hotel front desk now wanted an imprint from one's credit card. At this point one packed.

If a good deal of this seems like a chronicle of wasted time, it was not wasted opportunity nor wasted experience. I always hugely enjoyed working in Hollywood and we always learned something from it, even though much of our output, this being the way of that world, was destined never to get off the drawing board. I never, unlike some writers who made the celluloid foray from time to time, had the 'take the money and run' attitude. We gave the best of what we had to give – and in return had some interesting times and met some interesting people. I cannot imagine any other walk of life where, for example, I might have found myself discussing the chariot race sequence in *Ben Hur* with Charlton Heston (scripted – it is the briefest of screen directions – essentially 'There is a chariot race'), or speculating on what might have been the future of James Dean with the director of *Rebel without a Cause*, Nicholas Ray.

Nor do I suppose our paths would have crossed with those of the Rolling Stones. This – a commission to write the screenplay of Dave Wallis's 1960s novel *Only Lovers Left Alive* – was one of our more colourful adventures.

This bizarre episode commenced with the arrival – landing would be a better word – in our office of the Stones' manager, Andrew Loog Oldham, who cannot then have been more than twenty-one years old. His first act was to grab the telephone, demand to know from whoever answered it at what position in the charts stood the Stones' new release, and in reply snarl, 'I want that fucking single at number fucking one by tomorrow morning, have you got that?' before slamming down the receiver. Since he had only just come from his own office, from which he could equally well have made the same call, I assumed the idea was to impress us.

Mick Jagger turned up a few minutes later and sprawled in a chair smoking and saying little while Oldham went through his spiel. *Only Lovers* was a near-scifi epic in which the young take control of the world after all the oldies have fallen prey to a mass suicide epidemic sparked off by international gloom (we were then of course heavily into presentiments of a nuclear holocaust). Britain rapidly reverts to its tribal origins, and the saga concerns itself with rival tribes in a power struggle, one of them in possession of Windsor Castle, and the other led, of course, by Mick Jagger. I have told it baldly and badly but the story could have made (for obviously it didn't) a memorable film in the right hands. Whether it was in the right hands was a moot point. The young Oldham and Allen Klein, who was the Stones' American minder and would soon replace Oldham as their overall manager, would be joint producers. The film would be shot at Borehamwood Studios. It would be financed by Decca, the first picture ever to be entirely underwritten by a record company. It would be the Stones' first film. It would make them £300,000. Perhaps Marianne Faithfull would be in it. ('She', put in Mick Jagger with laconic humour, 'could play the bird.') Nicholas Ray was a possible director, others being Lindsay Anderson or John Schlesinger. When could we start, given that the Stones were about to take off for Los Angeles and it would be good if we could get on a plane and spend some time with them there so that we could tailor their parts to their particular characters, as our friend Alun Owen had done for the Beatles in *A Hard Day's Night*?

A few days later we were installed in adjoining bungalows the size of private dwellings in the grounds of the Beverly Hills Hotel, where we were met by the pudgy, rather unsavoury-looking Allen Klein, who had the air of a litigation lawyer but was in fact an accountant by trade. He placed a large wad of twenty-dollar bills in our hands by way of expenses and promised to deliver the Rolling Stones in due course. Considering that we had been flown six thousand miles specifically to meet them they seemed uncommonly difficult to find. We were not even staying at the same hotel. For two or three days Willis and I hung about at the Beverly Hills, watching game shows on television and running up bills at the poolside bar. Then, at about eleven one evening, a stretch limo arrived to whisk us off to the RCA recording studios where the Stones were just getting down to work.

There were just the five of them in the studio – no minders, no roadies, no technicians, not even a teaboy. Mick was fiddling with the console, the others flopping around on tip-up seats. Mick effected an introduction of sorts by pointing at his colleagues in turn: 'Keith. Brian. Bill. Charlie . . .' We all shook hands stiffly. The atmosphere was awkward, the conversation, such as it was, stilted. The age gap did nothing to help cement a relationship: in our mid-thirties, and with our formal lightweight jackets contrasting with their ragged denim and scruffy tops – only Brian, wearing what appeared to be a fur-trimmed doeskin dressing gown that gave him the appearance of a youthful Bud Flanagan, seemed in any way exotic – we must have looked to them like a pair of middle-aged, lawn-mowing householders on the verge of retirement.

I was mightily relieved when they started twanging their guitars in preparation for running through the number they were about to record. To the best of my recollection this was 'Have You Seen Your Mother, Baby, Standing in the Shadow?', but it is difficult to say for certain, for after a few bars Mick decreed that they could not possibly continue without the services of a harmonica player of their acquaintance. Why this should be so, since one of them had been playing the harmonica perfectly well himself only a few moments earlier, I did not pretend to comprehend and did not care to ask. Studio minions were despatched to scour Los Angeles for the vital mouth organ player, with lists of various haunts and hangouts where he might be run to earth.

To fill in time the Stones began a half-hearted rehearsal of some of the stuff they would be performing in whatever concert had been lined up for them. We were treated to a private performance of 'Jumpin' Jack Flash', or anyway part of it. Tiring of this, they flopped back in their seats. Keith Richard delivered a snatch of a number entitled 'Auntie Millie's Caught Her Left Tit in the Mangle'. A joint was passed round – like Andrew Loog Oldham's telephone outburst in our office, this was probably for our benefit, but instead of relaxing our disparate company it seemed to inhibit us even more. Conversation grew even more stilted. I managed to stand between Bill Wyman and Charlie Watts in the urinals without any of us exchanging a single word.

The night wore on. Mama Cass waddled in to pay her respects. Nobody introduced us – I doubt if anybody remembered our names. A couple of naked teenagers streaked across the studio floor pursued by security men. The Stones did not even look up. The pair were cornered and led out, the guards doubtless enjoying *droit de seigneur*. One or two of the Beach Boys wandered in. Another joint was passed around. Other, no doubt famous, young figures in dark glasses began to drift into the studio and make themselves at home. Of the harmonica player there was as yet no sign, and it was by now about three in the morning. Feeling more and more out of place, Willis and I silently departed. I don't think anybody noticed.

Presumably Allen Klein made private enquiries of Mick Jagger as to what he was getting for our *per diem*, and did not receive a satisfactory answer. At all events another meeting was set up, this one in the daytime, in some film star's house up in the Hollywood Hills that had been borrowed for the purpose. Willis and I arrived at the appointed time and flipped through glossy magazines for two or three hours, when the five Rolling Stones arrived together in an excited bunch, giggling and chattering over the newly acquired garb they were wearing. They had discovered a store down on Hollywood Boulevard selling military gear and had got themselves togged up to look like German or South American generals.

Brian Jones, in particular, resembled Hitler about to address the Nuremburg Rally, minus the moustache. He had acquired a Luger pistol which he showed me proudly – of the group, Brian, while in no way forthcoming, was the one we could most easily talk to. He asked me if I thought he would have any problem getting it through customs on his return to London. I said I knew nothing about such things but I had an idea he would need a firearms certificate. In that case, said he decisively, he would smuggle the thing in.

Oh yes? How? Brian had the answer. He was taking home a box of grass seed which he had been persuaded possessed special powers to transform a troublesome lawn. He would conceal the Luger in that.

I had a vision of Brian Jones attempting to pass through customs, dressed as a Nazi stormtrooper, with a clanking wooden box under his arm, and the customs officer enquiring, 'Excuse me, sir, but could I ask what's in that box?' and Brian Jones saying, 'Only grass seed.'

I thought that as one of the two elder statesmen present I was qualified to offer him some advice. I said, 'You are one of the Rolling Stones. Do you seriously imagine that when you've told him that all there is in the box is grass seed, the customs man is going to chalk a cross on it and wave you through?'

'We'll have to hope so,' said the optimist.

I never learned whether he managed to get his Luger through customs, for I never saw him again. The deliberations and discussions we were supposed to be having with the Stones were as unproductive as before – apart from Mick, I don't believe any of them had read the book we were there to talk about. Allen Klein having tired by now of putting wads of ready money into our hands, we flew home and worked out a meticulously crafted, 150-page, 650-scene screenplay, carefully tailoring the dialogue to the varying degrees of taciturnity of our leading players. Nicholas Ray flew over to London to spend a stimulating two or three days with us kicking this first draft around, then we got to work on a second draft and finally a shooting script. The rest was silence. I imagine that when it came down to it Mick Jagger didn't want to commit himself to a feature film at that stage. I heard later that while he would run risks in the recording studios, he was nervous of taking on the movies, a medium he knew nothing about. He turned down several major films but eventually, as a solo player, agreed to star in *Performance*, with James Fox. The most tangible outcome of this pairing seemed to be that shortly after completing the film, Fox abandoned his acting career to become a born-again Christian.

Willis and I have never worked in tandem for American television, the other hemisphere of the mad world of Hollywood; but I did have a couple of adventures of my own in that direction. I wrote for

Thames Television a series for John Alderton called *The Upchat Line*, about a young opportunist who lives out of a left-luggage locker on Marylebone Station and is a kind of benevolent conman. CBS became interested in making an American version of the series and I flew out to meet the team who were doing the adaptation, since I was supposed to have script approval. They assured me that the stories, apart from being transplanted to Los Angeles, or it may have been New York, would remain virtually untouched, and could I think of someone in the Wilfrid Hyde-White mould who might play the whacky uncle?

'What whacky uncle?' I asked. 'He does not have a whacky uncle. The whole point of the series is that he is a loner who thinks on his feet.'

'Ah. In our version he has this rascal of an uncle who feeds him all his ideas.'

Given that ninety-nine out of one hundred American TV sitcoms in preparation never even reach the pilot stage, I did not expect to hear any more about this project, and nor did I.

My other brush with this peculiar medium was when I was asked to develop a series about two brothers, one black, one white, who are striving to live in middle-class, Mid-West harmony. Why they chose an English writer for this essentially American comedy I have no idea, but I embarked on a season of shuttling back and forth to Los Angeles for the countless meetings, conferences and ideas sessions that are meat and drink to the world of American television. Needless to say, this too was eventually shelved, with the firing – or 'letting go', as Americans prefer to put it – of the script development executive for not having fulfilled his ratings norm – a common cause of TV pilot cot death.

During the course of these confabs, which customarily took place around a large conference table accommodating enough executives to form the board of a large corporation, I had become aware of the constant presence of an unsmiling, unblinking young man who never spoke, but made copious notes on a yellow pad. I finally asked my West Coast agent who he was. (Agents, on these fraught occasions, stay close to their clients like lawyers sticking to first-degree murderers on the eve of indictment.)

He murmured the question to the TV exec next to him. The reply came whispering back. 'He is', I was solemnly informed, 'a trainee humour evaluator.'

FIVE

Old Compton Street

Writing partnerships, if they do not end in acrimony or with one half of the act deciding to give it all up and travel the world on his residuals, tend in the long run to peter out or potter on. Ours has been of the pottering-on variety. Collaboration, for all its diversions, is a rigorous regime, demanding regular hours and application to the task at hand. The solitary writer, for all that he has no one to tempt him into a game of Scrabble or a visit to the pub, can work when he pleases – at three in the morning if he likes – and on what subject he pleases; and if he chooses to take a few days off and go on the razzle, it is nobody's business but his own and his accountant's.

Both Willis and I were aware all along of the danger of losing this freedom, which is why we always kept our hands in on our own individual writing commitments. Gradually, over the years, with one commission after another demanding attention, we began to weary of the office treadmill. Without either of us saying anything – we never discussed anything so frivolous as long-term plans – we began to ease off, leaving the office to its own devices for days on end and finally, as the lease expired, abandoning it to the demolition gang. We were by now working on long-haul series such as *Worzel Gummidge*, so that it was easy enough for us to write separate episodes at home and liaise by telephone or over the odd lunch. With other fish to fry, the new arrangement suited us both.

The ties were to be loosened further by Willis's decision to return to his 'roots', as he put it – his roots by now having transplanted themselves from a back-to-back in Hunslet to a Jacobean mansion on Howarth Moor – and my own subsequent move to Bath. Although we talk on the telephone most days, for with such a backlog of credits Waterhall Productions is still a going business concern, we tend by now not to take on new joint work but to exploit what we

453

have already done. Our most recent joint credit, for example, looks like being a West End revival of the musical *Billy*. There is always something in the offing: a revival, a renewed interest in some old property. Occasionally some long-dead project arises from the slab like Lazarus. The partnership potters on.

Having thus relaxed our joint routine, we both of course immediately fell into strict routines of our own. The usual Waterhall phone call is around 8 a.m., by which time we have been at our respective desks for a good hour – and now that we don't have to work five days a week with one another we tend to work seven days a week independently. But these days my desk sees little of me after one o'clock, by which time I have usually departed for lunch, an institution which I have taken up as a hobby: indeed, I produced a little book on the subject, *The Theory & Practice of Lunch*, which with its companion volume, *The Theory & Practice of Travel*, accounts for my only outside interests.

With the mornings to fill and no distractions, I embarked on a string of books, plays and television assignments, as did Willis two hundred miles away. And I also had my twice-weekly newspaper column to write. I have always said that whereas some people wake up in the morning wondering 'Where am I?' I wake up asking 'Who am I?' If it is Wednesday or Sunday, I am a newspaper columnist. If any other day, I am author, dramatist or wearer of whatever hat has to be donned that day.

It was arising out of my column, which was then appearing in the *Daily Mirror*, that I wrote one of the most satisfying non-fiction books I have ever had published. I shared with the *Mirror*'s then editor, Michael Molloy, a fascination for newspaper English, particularly tabloidese. In late-night seminars at Tramp, Annabelle's and suchlike centres of learning, we often discussed the rapidly growing tendency of newspapers, broadsheet as well as tabloid, regional as well as national, to express themselves in words never heard outside Fleet Street – bid, rap, slam, blaze, vigil, romp, and so on: the subject, now I came to recall, of 'The Daily News', the very first revue sketch that Willis Hall and I had written all those years ago now. We agreed on the need for the press, or anyway that section of the press that concerned us most, to return to vigorous doorstep English, using the language of the people rather than the language of the tabloid sub-editor. One day Mike asked me if I would care to write a *Daily Mirror* style book setting out these thoughts for the benefit of new recruits and of such *Mirror* staffers as were not too irrevocably hooked on tabloidese. Most newspaper style books restrict themselves to preferred spelling of words, the use of capitals and quotation marks and so on. This one was to be about the use of English. It was an attractive proposition, particularly when in the approved Cudlipp tradition Molloy said I could go anywhere I pleased to write it. I agreed to take it on, provided I retained the copyright.

Stashing a month's back numbers of all the tabloids into a large suitcase as research material, I embarked for my favourite city, San Francisco. Here, opening my suitcase for inspection upon arrival, I met with the same puzzled reaction from customs as the Rolling Stones' Brian Jones must have encountered with his box of grass seed.

'What are these, sir?'

'They're some newspapers that I have to read through while I'm here.'

'We have newspapers of our own, sir. Why don't you try the *San Francisco Chronicle*?'

I was back with the manuscript a fortnight later, having dined well and frequently at Sam Spade's favourite bar and grill into the bargain. It was produced in a plain white cover in an edition of one thousand copies and was gratifyingly well received. Soon I heard that journalists on other newspapers were begging copies from their *Mirror* colleagues, albeit for amusement rather than enlightenment. *Daily Mirror Style*, as John Naughton was to note in the *Observer*, rapidly 'acquired something of a samizdat status in Fleet Street, with dog-eared copies changing hands for "considerations"'. Perhaps this was because, as Roy Hattersley was to put it in a review in the *Listener*, it was 'a missal as well as a manual, a testament as much as a textbook'. The *New Statesman* rated its smuggled copy 'one of this office's most valued possessions'.

The initial print-run was soon exhausted and *Mirror* recruits, for whom after all it was primarily intended, had to make do with tea-stained, cigarette-burned rejects left behind in the desk drawers of disillusioned old hacks who had taken redundancy and gone off to work as PR consultants or to open village shops. That was if they could find a copy. When I heard that my copyright manual was being illegally run off on office photocopiers, I got Molloy to persuade Mirror Books Ltd, the group's publishing arm hitherto specialising in cartoon collections and puzzle books, to bring out a bookshop edition of 10,000 copies. Mirror Books not being geared to sending out review copies – I imagine that the *Andy Capp* and *Perishers* collections are little in demand among literary editors – I turned myself into a cottage industry and personally despatched the book to persons and papers I thought might be interested. Within a few weeks we had major reviews in the *Times Literary Supplement*, the *Times Educational Supplement*, the *Listener, UK Press Gazette, The Spectator*, the *Observer*, and other journals – including even *World Medicine*, whose unprecedented recommendation was that 'it could benefit not only doctors who take refuge behind jargon, but also their frequently baffled patients'. The Cabinet Office bracketed it with Fowler's *Modern English Usage* and Partridge's *Usage and Abusage* as recommended reading for civil servants trying to write plain English.

As I wrote in the introduction to a subsequent edition: 'Thanks to this quite extraordinary reception, plus its previously acquired almost underground reputation in the taverns of Fleet Street, *Daily Mirror Style* quickly established itself as a standard textbook for journalism courses up and down the country, as well as a manual for teachers and students of English generally.' But when Cap'n Bob Maxwell bought the Mirror Group, and despite his having built his fortunes on the sale of technical publications, he showed no interest in keeping it in print. Once more it began to circulate in unauthorised samizdat editions. I didn't know whether to be flattered or incensed when on a train one day a student of journalism asked me to sign a copy hot from the photocopier. But much revised and expanded, and under the new title of *Waterhouse on Newspaper Style*, my little book eventually found a home with Viking Penguin, where it remains in print as a standard textbook, as does the companion volume I wrote for the general reader, *English Our English (and How to Sing It)*.

As when I was working more or less full time with Willis, I continued to have several irons in the fire, or to juggle several balls in the air. There was usually a television project – for example, the *Andy Capp* series for Thames with James Bolam, beautifully directed in a kind of cartoon format come to life by John Howard Davies; *Charters and Caldicott*, following the further adventures of the cricket-besotted pair from *The Lady Vanishes*, played to perfection by Michael Aldridge and Robin Bailey; *The Great Paperchase*, a film based on Anthony Delano's book about the press jamboree surrounding Scotland Yard's failure to bring the train robber Ronnie Biggs back from Rio, which was to cost the BBC £50,000 in out-of-court damages to Slipper of the Yard.

And there was always a book in the pipeline. With twenty-seven titles on the shelves so far, not counting published plays and stuff written under pseudonyms, it would be exhausting to plough through the catalogue, but one or two titles do stand out. There is my 1981 novel *Maggie Muggins*, highly praised but undervalued, which women friends have been kind enough to say gets unerringly under the skin of a young woman belonging to that period. Then there was *Our Song*, 1988, the story of an obsessional love affair, which at Ned Sherrin's instigation I turned into a play, starring Peter O'Toole.

We had of course worked with O'Toole before, in *Jeffrey Bernard Is Unwell*, and that I shall be coming to; but *Our Song* presented a problem not encountered in that runaway success. The play concerns itself with a successful advertising executive in his fifties who is so infatuated by a woman in her twenties that he throws away his ordered life for her – his job goes, his marriage crumbles, he turns to drink and is heading for certain self-destruction. For the audience to believe that such a man would embark on such a course, the girl has to be someone special – elusive, endearing, infuriating, and capable of captivating, tantalising, taunting, haunting her tormented lover without our ever wondering why he doesn't just push the spoiled brat under a bus.

We got round to casting: or rather we didn't. Ned and I arrived at the casting session with long lists of possibles, only to have them all instantly vetoed by Peter with comments like, 'No, not her, darling, she's two bubbles short of an Aero.' Arising out of our star's threat to saw our heads off if we so much as mentioned A, B, C or D, several names were eliminated even before they were put forward. Peter knew exactly whom he wanted to play opposite him. The only problem was that she did not appear to exist.

We arranged an exhausting series of auditions – exhausting, that is, for Peter O'Toole, who insisted on attending every one, and reading two or three key scenes, sometimes more, with each and every actress. This went on for days, in the course of which we must have seen a good hundred hopeful applicants for stardom, which meant that Peter acted the same batch of scenes a good hundred times, varying his performance to accommodate the personality of the actress reading opposite him. Never have I seen an actor work

457

so hard. Finally, we got our reams of CVs and photographs down to a shortlist of half a dozen, and then started the auditioning process all over again, this time in the privacy of Ned's flat where we spent an hour or so with each one in turn, with Peter coaxing and coaching from them some approximation of the elusive performance he was looking for.

The last name on our list we had been told might not be able to make it, as she had been ill with a stomach bug. We were dithering between two girls we had already seen, unhappily so because they were not quite right, when she did after all turn up, looking very pale and shaky on her feet. She had a sore throat into the bargain and so couldn't read very well. Nevertheless, we knew we had reached journey's end, and Tara FitzGerald got the part. After the ordeal of auditions the rehearsal seemed practically a walkover. Supported by Jack Watling, Lucy Fleming, Cara Konig and Donald Pickering, and with a dreamlike all-purpose set by Tim Goodchild, the play was a triumph, the only downbeat note being that towards the end of his run, already exhausted by a nightly two-and-a-quarter-hour performance when he was never off the stage, Peter was carried off to hospital with an abdominal infection. We continued, however, to play to full houses in Athens, of all places, where, completely uninhibited by his inability to speak a word of Greek, Ned directed a production which to our mutual astonishment ran for over six months.

If I thought of my life in terms of ups and downs, *Our Song* would be one of the ups. In fact, although I suppose I could trace a fairly dramatic switchback graph of success and setback, I have always seen my life as a series of plateaus, to which I have leapt or clambered like a mountain goat. Fleet Street. My first novel. *Billy Liar*, in all his phases. *Whistle Down the Wind. Budgie. Worzel Gummidge.* My last book, *City Lights*. And so on. And on occasion I have ascended to a plateau without knowing for some time that I was on one. Such was the case with *Mrs Pooter's Diary*.

In 1983, after producing half a dozen novels on contemporary themes, I had the urge to do something completely different. I was a great fan of the Grossmiths' classic of Victorian lower-middle-class suburban life, *The Diary of a Nobody*, which I still read at least once a year, and I had the idea of an affectionate pastiche in the shape of a companion volume, the diary of Charles Pooter's dear wife Carrie, covering the same period and many of the same events, but from the distaff point of view.

I had the greatest fun writing it, browsing in old department store catalogues and bound volumes of *Exchange and Mart* for inspiration, and inventing such Pooterish household necessities as Neave's Varnish Stain Remover, *Jepson's Sunday Newspaper* and that indispensable part-work *Lady Cartmell's Vade Mecum for the Bijou Household*. But I awaited publication day with trepidation, fearing the wrath of Pooter purists. I need not have worried – it was ecstatically received, to the point at which Judi Dench was prevailed upon to give daily readings from *Mrs Pooter's Diary* on *Woman's Hour*.

Here is where I began to sense that I was climbing to another plateau. In the course of an interview with *Radio Times*, Judi said that she would love to play Mrs Pooter on stage. That was good enough for me. I set to work.

But Carrie's diary, while amusing enough, is hardly the stuff of drama. I solved the problem by dovetailing it with the original Grossmith text, so that we have, so to speak, the two rival diaries fighting it out. The juxtaposition of Charles Pooter's complacent record of his humdrum life with his wife's secret and scornful asides to her own diary are what makes *Mr & Mrs Nobody*, as I called the finished confection, work as a theatrical entertainment (I have always hesitated to call it a play). With the exception of a silent maid and a non-speaking factotum, I had all the parts played by the Pooters themselves. This convention was so successful that several times I have been congratulated on the vividness of characters in the piece who do not in fact appear.

As well as being tailor-made for Judi Dench, it was equally well suited to the comic talents of her real-life husband, Michael Williams. Reunited with Michael Redington and Ned Sherrin, I was on course for my first solo venture in the theatre.

There was only one major problem that I could see: the thing was about an hour too long. While some scenes could be trimmed in rehearsal – when I discovered that Judi so much delights in ripping pages out of her script and tossing them over her shoulder that I wished we had left in a few more superfluities for her enjoyment – we had some savage cutting to do. Ned and I tackled the problem by a method which we have used to advantage ever since – what we came to call the Jackson Frères solution. A feature of life with the Pooters at The Laurels, Brickfield Terrace, Holloway, is the Jackson Frères champagne which marks every celebration. Indeed, it marked the opening performance of *Mr & Mrs Nobody*, when I had Jackson Frères labels made up and pasted over bottles of rather better vintage as first-night presents. Depicting what appears to be a pair of Victorian poisoners, the label reads: 'Jackson Frères, Importers of Fine Wines & Vintners' Sundrymen. Runner-up, Isle of Man Bottlers' Exposition Medal 1883. Lower Ground Floor, Paxley's Varnish Warehouse, 235–239 Female Penitentiary Road, N, to which all complaints should be addressed.' On this and subsequent plays, Ned and I settled down with a bottle of the Jackson Frères or its latter-day equivalent and a sharp pencil each, and ruthlessly cut. *Mr & Mrs Nobody* was what Sherlock Holmes would have called a three-bottle problem. Scene after scene was jettisoned until we thought we had got it down to the requisite two hours. On the first night of the out-of-town try-out it ran for two and a half hours. The extra time had been added by audience laughter. Such problems an author can live with.

We took up residence in the Garrick Theatre. To the strains of a string quartet up in a little minstrel gallery – an inspired touch introduced by Ned – the curtain went up on a delightfully cluttered Victorian parlour designed by Julia Trevelyan Oman, and it was soon evident that we had a hit. I don't think there was an empty seat in the house for the length of the run.

This, however, was not the end of it: the plateau was not yet reached. Encouraged or perhaps inflamed by this success, I began to think seriously about another theatrical diversion that had been lurking at the back of my mind for some time. I had a vague hankering to write something about Soho: a kind of obituary or valedictory for the sleazy old square mile as it was in its grainy black-and-white era, before the afternoon drinking clubs closed down and the pavement cafés opened, and when 'models' still outnumbered design consultants; before it was given a wash and brush-up like a northern mill being turned into a heritage centre. I had no idea how I was going to set about this – the nearest I could get to it was a bunch of Soho leftovers reminiscing on the last night of the Kismet Club before it was lost behind the plastic fascia of a fast-food joint. It didn't seem very dramatic.

The more I walked round the subject the more I came to realise that the only authority by a mile on Soho was Jeffrey Bernard, who apart from one or two ill-considered ventures into the realm of grass and trees had spent virtually all his working life there, if you could call it a working life. A one-man show based on Jeff's *Spectator* columns and other scribblings? That wasn't very dramatic either, and I couldn't arouse much enthusiasm from either Ned or Michael. One-man shows are popular with actors, who like to have a portmanteau performance they can trot out between engagements. But they are not popular with managements. Much backers' money has been lost in indulging the one-man show.

Then one night at the opera, I got it. Earlier, I had been having a few drinks with Jeff Bernard at the Groucho Club, and we had got to reminiscing about some of the less well-appointed clubs of Soho we had known in our time. This led us inevitably to Gerry's, where Jeff had once worked as a barman. We had both known in Gerry's a casting director for Granada Television named John Murphy, now dead, then not noted for his abstemiousness. One night John was slumped over his Scotch when he caught the eye of a young actor across the bar. The casting director's card-index mind whizzed round. He could not place the play but he could place, as he thought, the theatre. 'I saw you in that thing at the National the other night and you were marvellous!'

The young actor was polite, as all actors are to casting directors. 'That's very kind of you, Mr Murphy, but I've never worked at the National.'

'Then it must have been at the Prince of Wales. In that musical,' hazarded Murphy, naming the only other theatre he had set foot in recently.

'I've never been in a musical, Mr Murphy.'

'Then where the hell did I see you? Television?'

'I haven't done any television for two years, Mr Murphy. In fact, things have been so bad that I've been working full time in the Food Hall at Harrods.'

The casting director snapped his fingers in triumph. 'That's where I've seen you! On the bacon slicer! And you were bloody fantastic!'

But John Murphy's true moment of glory was the night he got locked in Gerry's Club. Emerging from the gents' after everyone had gone and the staff were occupied collecting empty glasses and switching off lights, he decided before making the long journey up the stairs to have a refreshing forty winks under a bench. Upon awakening two or three hours later, he found himself locked in. Pausing only to pour himself a large one, he called Gerry Campion at the number posted up by the telephone and explained his predicament. Gerry, mindful of his stock and who was let loose among it, screeched down the phone: 'Don't move! Don't touch anything! Don't drink anything! I'll be down in ten minutes!' And to the rescue, of Murphy and of his own peace of mind, he duly arrived.

And so, after my trip down the gutters of Memory Lane with Jeffrey Bernard at the Groucho, to the London Coliseum, where not being much of an opera buff I dozed through a performance of *Tosca*. Nudged hazily awake during a dull recitative, an image formed in my mind of the old Gerry's Club – probably some feature of the set resembled it – with John Murphy emerging from under his bench to find himself locked in. For John Murphy I substituted Jeffrey Bernard. Then – I can't remember whether this was instantaneous or something I worked out later – for Gerry's I substituted the Coach and Horses pub in Soho, much more his home from home. I would have Jeff locked in the Coach and Horses for the night. Literally coming out of the woodwork while he awaited his rescue by Norman Balon, the cantankerous landlord, would be all manner of ghosts from the past. His life, and the life of Soho in the fifties and sixties, would be encapsulated, celebrated, re-enacted, in vignettes, scenes, two-line crossovers, brooding monologues. A supporting cast of four, playing all the parts. I had what Hitchcock used to call the McGuffin – the element that makes the whole thing tick.

Having known Jeff for over thirty years, I had quite an accumulation of Jeffrey Bernard lore to start me off. I delved through the published collections of his *Spectator* columns and through sheaves of tear-sheets from the magazine itself. I ransacked my own memories of Soho and its passing show. The thing had to be slowly pieced together – a sentence from this Low Life column, a paragraph from that: it was like a cross between doing a jigsaw puzzle, assembling a mosaic and painting by numbers. Then it had to be coloured in with dialogue, asides, movement, and spliced with the running thread of his attempts to get 'old Norman' (who I decided must never appear: he is a more powerful character for being a looming offstage presence) to come down and open the pub. It turned out to be more about Jeff than about Soho, but none the worse for that.

Ned wanted to call it *Jeff Bin In?*, the catchphrase used in Michael Heath's *Private Eye* strip, The Regulars. I opted for *Jeffrey Bernard Is Unwell*, the line always used by *The Spectator* when his column fails to appear (except on one occasion when, as Jeff reminds himself in the play, the announcement read, 'Jeffrey Bernard's column does not appear this week as it is remarkably similar to that which appeared last week.') Someone wise in the ways of publicity pointed out that 'unwell' had a gloomy ring to it. So, I responded, does *Les Misérables*, then playing in five countries.

And now who was to play Jeff? We had talked to John Hurt. He was a friend of Jeff's and he knew the scene, and of course he could play it on his head. But perhaps because he was too close to it all John finally didn't want to do it. Without very much hope I sent the script to Peter O'Toole, whom I hadn't met since the seventies when we shared a platform in Leeds Town Hall in the campaign for the new West Yorkshire Playhouse. The part of Jeff is a taxing one, and I had heard anyway that Peter was busy well into the following year. But it was worth a try. Less than twenty-four hours later I came home from some meeting or other to find a memorable message on my answering machine: 'Keith, you bastard, you have screwed up my fucking life. I had this whole year all mapped out and now I have to change all my fucking plans. I hate you. Love, Peter.' I believe that when Shaw sent round a copy of *Pygmalion* to Beerbohm Tree for his consideration, Tree's reply was, 'Dear Shaw, I have it in mind to accept the part.' I liked my message better.

We cast the other parts without difficulty – Royce Mills, Sarah Berger, Annabel Leventon and Timothy Ackroyd, playing a host of poets, hacks, wives, girlfriends, thespians, policemen, waiters, jockeys, trainers, bores, publicans and sinners, etc. John Gunter designed us a faithful replica of the Coach and Horses, but with everything tilted at a crazy angle, so that when O'Toole saw it for the first time he crowed with delight: 'A pissed pub!'

Needless to say, the play was far too long – a four-bottle problem. We were to make enough cuts for a touring production of *Jeffrey Bernard Is Unwell II*. I often felt guilty about making further incisions, for Peter had arrived for the first day of rehearsal word-perfect not only in his own part but in everybody else's as well – twenty thousand words committed to his head, via a Walkman on which he had taped the entire play, and which accompanied him everywhere. Did I read somewhere that O'Toole is an undisciplined actor? But like Judi Dench, he liked nothing better than a big fat cut, and during the out-of-town tour delighted in murmuring to the rest of the cast, as they played a scene that had that day been condemned, 'This one's a corpse!'

We opened in Brighton. With the house packed to the rafters with racegoers, Soho riff-raff who had come down by the coachload, and champagne-swigging hacks who were supposed to be covering the Labour Party Conference, it was difficult to judge whether the tumultuous reception we were getting was a one-off or par for the course. It would be par for the course. As with *Mr & Mrs Nobody*, we had to take an extra half an hour out to allow for audience laughter.

We moved to Bath. There we gave a press conference in the theatre pub, now my local, the Garrick's Head. Jeff, having spent most of the previous week savouring our success in Brighton, was looking even more fragile and haggard than usual. As he trembled a vodka to his lips, a young man from one of the local weeklies, a rookie reporter on his first assignment, had a question. He pointed at Jeff. 'If I stay another forty years in journalism, will I get to look like that?' I assured him gravely that the possibility was there. I like to think that we guided that young fellow into a responsible career in insurance.

There is a legend about a butterfly at the Bath Theatre Royal, a theatre which firmly believes in ghosts. High up in the flies hangs a giant prop butterfly from some long-ago production of *Madam Butterfly*. It is said that if a real butterfly flutters down on to the stage during a performance, it will bring the production luck. It was October and our expectations of such a blessing were low. Yet flutter down a butterfly did, and the fact that earlier in the day Ned Sherrin was rumoured to have been seen coming out of the garden centre opposite the theatre carrying a jam jar containing a cabbage leaf was neither here nor there. The butterfly settled on the Coach and Horses bar counter during one of Peter's monologues. Up in the dress circle, we prayed that he would not bang down his glass and kill it. Instead, he addressed himself to the butterfly, offered it a drink and said that if it sat quietly he would tell it a story. Its duty done, the butterfly fluttered up into the flies.

Did we need good luck? Every show needs good luck. But there was something about this piece that generated its own good luck. From the start, there was an aura of excitement about it that I have never experienced before or since. We were newsworthy, that was one element: the combination of O'Toole, Bernard, Sherrin and Waterhouse seemed to my fellow-journalists to be a rich field. Anyway, we were certainly good for a quote. Interviews, profiles, opinion columns, gossip paragraphs about the show and about the four of us, either as individuals or as a group like the Marx Brothers, filled scrapbook after scrapbook in the publicity office. We were pursued by photographers, TV cameras, radio microphones. For some reason the cartoonists took us up and there were joke drawings by the dozen not only about the show itself ('I know someone who's seen it twice – Jeffrey Bernard on the opening night') but ringing topical changes on our title – 'Boris Yeltsin Is Unwell', 'John Major Is Unwell', '*Bernadette* [a flop musical] Is Unwell', 'Jeffrey Archer Is Unbelievably Bad', and so on.

We were a smash hit before we opened. The buzz was there, the box office queues forming. The reviews were raves, and it was a personal triumph for Peter O'Toole, who had not been seen in the West End lately. 'With this performance he comes home and takes command,' wrote Michael Coveney in a cherished review in the *Financial Times*. 'Waterhouse and O'Toole present one of the greatest comic creations of our day.' We broke all box office records in our first week at the Apollo Theatre, and for the first time in his life Jeff Bernard had to hire an accountant, to look after his share of the proceeds.

The publicity continued unabated. Rather to my surprise, remembering our *Billy Liar* experiences of old, no one objected to the salty language, but there were one or two attacks on the play's supposed preoccupation with alcohol. The Salvation Army newspaper, the *War Cry*, more in sorrow than in anger, ran a front-page leader headlined 'JEFFREY COULD BE BETTER'. A contributor to the *Hospital Doctor* magazine, under the headline 'ALCOHOLISM IS NO LAUGHING MATTER', called for a theatre equivalent of the Press Council to which the public could complain.

We were number one in the box office straight play ratings, and number one on the celebrity circuit. On successive evenings when I was still so intoxicated by the play's reception that I was dropping in every night, I found the little hospitality room off the stage occupied by, in turn, Placido Domingo, Rupert Murdoch, Cliff Richard and the King of Norway. The fifth evening, rather to my consternation, I bumped into Lord and Lady Callaghan. I was concerned first of all because I didn't think it was their kind of play and secondly because, since characteristically they had not signposted their visit, the hospitality room was already spoken for. I found someone from the management and told him that we had to entertain Big Jim in the interval. He regretted that every available nook and cranny was already taken and that since the bars would be jam-packed we should just have to give the Callaghans a drink out in the corridor. I said, 'I am not going to entertain a former Prime Minister and his wife out in the corridor!' After some argy-bargying the management agreed to lend me the box office booth in the foyer, where I had champagne waiting for the Callaghans. Big Jim was enchanted – he thought it was the cosiest little place he had ever seen, and offered to sell tickets to latecomers. It turned out that the visit to the Apollo was a birthday treat from Audrey Callaghan. Diffidently, I suggested that I was afraid it was perhaps not quite their cup of tea. Big Jim beamed benignly. 'Well, perhaps a superfluity of the F-word, but there we are, there we are!' I think he enjoyed his little stay in the box office more than he enjoyed the play.

The real-life Jeffrey Bernard more or less took up residence in the theatre, applying himself to the stalls bar, presided over by the archetypal barperson, Mrs Mac, who had served him many a vodka at the classic race meetings she occasionally graced with her presence. Jeff never bothered to see the play – I don't believe he ever saw it all through more than three times – but would settle down for a snooze until the interval bell. One night a situation straight out of Pirandello developed. A holiday relief manager came down and, perceiving a comatose figure slumped over a table, hissed to a commissionaire, 'Get that drunk out of here!'

Mrs Mac was most indignant. 'He can't do that – that's Jeffrey Bernard!'

The manager was scornful. 'Don't give me that! Jeffrey Bernard's up there on the bleeding stage!'

Talking more or less non-stop for two hours and never off stage, Peter O'Toole was obviously only going to do a limited run. But it was unthinkable that the show should come off. Tom Conti triumphantly took over in a very different but universally applauded interpretation which did not, however, entirely meet the approval of Jeff Bernard, who commented sourly, 'He doesn't know how to hold a glass' – a view coloured, I believe, by Tom's failure to stock vodka in his dressing room. The vodka supply, however, was restored with

the arrival, in the fullness of time, of James Bolam in the part –
our third Jeffrey Bernard, and the audiences still cheering. Nor had
we finished yet. After our long run at the Apollo, Peter O'Toole
returned for an astonishing ten-week season at the Shaftesbury,
where again he broke all theatre records, filling 1,400 seats nightly,
with the crowds having to fight their way through mobs of ticket
touts. This revival, as I suppose it should be regarded since we had
been off for a few weeks, attracted the usual rave reviews – not least
from Jeffrey Bernard himself in the *Sunday Mirror* where he then
had a column. 'What surprised me was that the theatre was packed,'
he wrote among other enthusiastic noises. It surprised me too, for at
the time of this excellent notice the play had yet to reopen. Bumping
into Jeff at the Groucho, I pointed this trifling fact out. 'Christ!' he
gasped. 'Do you mean to say I dreamt it?' He had.

And so we rolled on, winning the *Evening Standard* Comedy of
the Year Award. What was the show's secret? Peter O'Toole had
spotted it, when he agreed to take it on. It is not a play about Soho,
although Soho figures. It is not a play about drinking, although the
protagonist is required to consume a good litre of water (fortunately,
vodka is colourless) in the course of an evening in which he is off
stage for only three seconds. It is a play about friendship, about
failure, about vulnerability, about coming to terms with life. It all
rounds up to a portrait of a man, warts, vodka bottle and all. There
is no better subject.

Jeff had yet other territories to conquer. Dennis Waterman took
the show exuberantly around Australia, opening in Perth where
I flew out in time for the tripe and wine party which Ned, with
his unerring sense of occasion, had deemed was just the thing
to mark our first Australian preview. There we lolled by Alan
Bond's swimming pool as the guest of his wife, Big Red, while
government officials sought the former billionaire in connection
with his affairs. It was a surrealistic week, with Bernard somehow
mixed up inextricably with Bond. As we sat around in the café
opposite the theatre reading our first enthusiastic reviews, Big Red
burst in with cries of, 'They've got him! They've got him!' Nobody
could say we didn't have competition for the public's attention, but
we did have a great tour. Dennis followed it up with a long English
tour and finally played a brief season in Dublin, the only venue that
did not quite take us to its heart. I think it was a case of taking coals
to Newcastle. The tenor of some of the reviews seemed to be, 'Why

are you sending us this play about a witty drunk, when we've got all the witty drunks we need?'

The foreign productions began: a big tour of Scandinavia, a three-city tour in Italy when Ned and I flew out to see what Rome was making of us. It was mystifying. Although the show was playing to capacity it was received in more or less total silence. Yet the producer did not seem in the least concerned. He explained that the audience regarded it as a kind of social document, an insight into the peculiar pub life of the peculiar English. There was one big laugh only, in the middle of the second act. Meeting our Italian Jeff in his dressing room afterwards, we naturally, having no Italian, wanted to know which line the audience had found so amusing. He was apologetic. 'Oh, that was a joke of my own which I took the liberty of putting in.'

My favourite out-of-town production, however, was in Buffalo, New York State, where the play enjoyed its American premiere in four feet of snow. My son Bob was then artistic director of Buffalo's Ensemble Theatre, where naturally enough he set his face against ever producing any of his father's plays. When he heard, however, that the rival Kavinoky Theatre was proposing to put on a production of *Jeffrey Bernard* starring its own artistic director, David Lamb, Bob announced, 'If that play is coming to Buffalo, there is only one possible director.' He then called London to tell me I was barred from rehearsals.

I did, however, struggle through a blizzard to get there for the premiere, expecting to find the theatre three-quarters empty. In fact it was packed. The production was first-rate, and David Lamb's Jeff was one of the best I had seen – and by now I had seen a good many. I had thought the play might be too 'Briddish' for an American audience and a regional one at that, but they lapped it up, and the reviews were glowing. There was a first-night party nearby and after we had congratulated the cast Bob conducted me through the pelting snow to the restaurant where most of our audience were gathered. As father and son entered arm in arm, the entire room rose and applauded – the Sardi's of Buffalo. It was an eye-prickling moment. A plateau reached.

There is a melancholy passage in *Jeffrey Bernard Is Unwell* where on the occasion of one of his frequent visits to death's door, our hero's thoughts drift towards the Grim Reaper: 'Sometimes, when I wonder whether this interval on earth might be just a bit of nonsense,

I think about all those friends who've gone. Frank Norman. John Le Mesurier. Sean Lynch who ran Gerry's Club. Dennis Shaw even. And the lunchtime sessions when they were all still here was worth all the trappings of all the success stories you've ever heard. I do worry about my own wretched mortality, though. Shuffling off this mortal coil it seems as though we're in a queue that's shuffling along towards a sort of bus stop. "Who's next?" "No, sorry, chum. You were before me." Maybe the party could go on, though. Different premises and no closing time. A kind of celestial and sterilised Colony Room Club . . .'

And reading back through these pages I too think about all the friends and contemporaries or near-contemporaries who've gone now, people I've known or worked with since I gained my platform ticket to the Salisbury Tavern. John Osborne. Alun Owen. John Dexter. Reggie Smith. Tony Richardson. Lindsay Anderson. John Braine. Ken Tynan. Roy Kinnear. Jo Janni. Peter Cook . . . It is an impressive roll-call – and do I hear the tolling of a distant bell?

And then my eye catches a report in the *Daily Telegraph* about a newish writer from the north, Tim Firth: 'All the signs are that London theatregoers will take to a writer who is being heralded as a young Keith Waterhouse or Alan Bennett . . .' And for some reason I remember a line from *Camelot*, when Willis and I and Jule Styne went to see Laurence Harvey: 'Run, boy, run!'

Although I get a little winded now I have never stopped running and I don't suppose I ever will, or anyway not yet. Here comes the next lap.

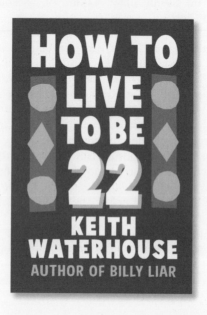

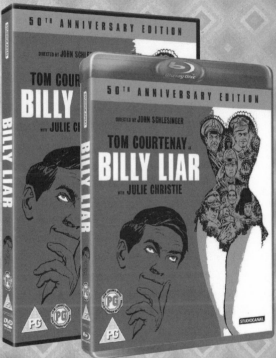